To Kirsten, Angie, and Michelle,
my beloved daughters, in whom I am well pleased

Caleb Sparks

CHANGED
into His
IMAGE

GOD'S PLAN FOR
TRANSFORMING YOUR LIFE

JIM BERG

JOURNEYFORTH

Greenville, South Carolina

Library of Congress Cataloging-in-Publication Data

Berg, Jim 1952-
    Changed into His image : God's plan for transforming your life /
Jim Berg.
        p.   cm.
    Includes bibliographical references and indexes.
    ISBN 1-57924-205-7 (pbk.)
    1. Sanctification. 2. Christian life—Biblical teaching.
I. Title
BT765.B38   1999
248.4—dc21   98-52722
                                                               CIP

Cover photographs by PhotoDisc, Inc.

All Scripture is quoted from the Authorized King James Version.

Changed into His Image: God's Plan for Transforming Your Life

Edited by Elizabeth B. Berg
Cover and design by Chris Hartzler
Page layout by Theresa Dodson and Peggy Hargis

© 1999 by BJU Press
Greenville, South Carolina 29614

JourneyForth is a division of BJU Press

Printed in the United States of America
All rights reserved

ISBN 978-1-57924-205-3

15   14   13   12   11   10   9   8

TABLE OF CONTENTS

FOREWORD

Although I have enjoyed studying about the great campaigns of the Civil War, the battle of Gettysburg remained a puzzle to me even though I had read several books about this strategic battle. Not until I sat in bleachers overlooking a thirty-by-thirty-foot map of the battle at the Gettysburg Visitor Center did the battle make sense to me. I wanted to find the map's designer, shake his hand, and give him a heartfelt thank you for helping me see the big picture.

Changed into His Image is like that large-scale map to me—only the issues at stake are far greater than any battle of the Civil War. To understand a long-ago battle is one thing, but to catch a panoramic view of what God expects and desires for my Christian life is quite another. God has given Jim an ability to *bring the whole picture together*, as you shall see as you read the book for yourself. This book is a view of the Christian life from the highest of vantage points.

Bob Jones University Press graciously allowed THE WILDS Christian camp to field-test this book in a prepublication edition for 250 summer staff and counselors. It was not unusual to hear staff members say the book was life-changing for them. I have used its message for discipling new believers, instructing newly married couples, encouraging new parents, helping parents heartbroken over wayward children, and even explaining to teenagers how to have meaningful devotions! How can one book be so comprehensive? Because it is first and foremost about knowing and loving God—the basis for everything in the Christian life.

My family and I have sat under Jim's ministry for over ten years. He is my peer, yet he is my mentor and friend. His family has a refreshing loyalty to and love for God and each other. The family mission statement you will read in the Preface is a reality for them, a fact that adds even more credibility to the message of this book. Solid theology has been made intensely practical in their lives. Although this book was written for his three daughters, Jim invites us to join them in learning how to be *Changed into His Image*. You will indeed find *God's Plan for Transforming Your Life*.

Ken Collier
Director, THE WILDS
Brevard, North Carolina

PREFACE

In August of 1996 I presented the original draft of this book to my three daughters with a personal letter that outlined my intent for its writing. I have occasionally written "letters from dad" to them about biblical truths I want to be sure they understand. I soon realized there are *many* truths I wanted them to not soon forget—truths they have heard repeatedly at home and during their formative years growing up on the campus of Bob Jones University. In order for you, the reader, to get a better grasp of the passion I feel for this project, I am, with the permission of my daughters, reproducing here a portion of the letter that accompanied their original draft of this book.

Dear Kirsten, Angie, and Michelle,

These chapters are the lengthiest "letter from dad" you have received yet, and perhaps the most important one. In December of 1993 we forged a family mission statement together that God has used to mold our direction as a family. I want to restate it here so that you can see where these chapters fit into the picture.

The Mission of Our Family
To passionately know our God,
and to love and please Him by
living together in harmony,
serving each other in humility,
growing together in godliness,
helping others with cheerfulness,

and thereby, as a family,
to provide a "living advertisement"
of Christlikeness
for others in this generation and
for our children
in the generations to come.

Ever since we together crafted this statement I have been burdened to make sure you have in your hands the information you need about the Christian life to insure that our family can indeed be a "living advertisement" of Christlikeness. This book is one means to that end. It is written in such a way that others outside our family might benefit from it, but I want you to know that it was written for you. If no one else ever reads it, I have accomplished my primary goal by placing it in your hands.

I have told you before that your mother and I will probably not be able to pass on to you any kind of earthly inheritance. If we can pass on to you a passion for God, however, we will have given you something more valuable than silver, gold, or rubies and more satisfying than anything a mortal can experience (Prov. 3:13-15). Your mother and I can honestly say that "[we] have no greater joy than to hear that [our] children walk in truth" (III John 4). Our prayer is "that our daughters may be as corner stones, polished [as for] a palace" (Ps. 144:12).

May God use all of these to draw you to a greater love and devotion to our matchless Savior, Jesus Christ. You truly are our beloved daughters in whom we are well pleased.

Love,
Dad

The two years that have gone by during the writing of this book have been two of the most spiritually refreshing of my entire life. Writing this book has forced me to clear away the chaff in my thinking about the Christian life and has driven me to consider only the fundamental issues of life with God. As I have culled through sermon notes of messages I have preached or classroom lectures I have delivered, I have been compelled to continually ask myself, "Do I consider the material I am examining essential for my daughters' pursuit of God and godliness, or is it merely peripheral? Is this idea or that thought indispensable for their walk in the Spirit, or is it only incidental? And most important, will it stir within them a thirst for God, a hunger for His Word, and a desire to represent Him well as salt in the earth?"

This book is intended to be a sort of travel brochure for them, enticing them to fellowship with God and to behold for themselves the breathtaking vistas of the glories of God in Christ Jesus. It is also to be a basic road map of Christian growth, showing them the way to that kind of relationship with God. It is an attempt to present to them in writing a biblical world-view—an ambitious project (thus the length of this book). A "concise world-view" would, indeed, be an oxymoron.

Please keep in mind that the illustrations you will encounter as you read this text have been greatly changed "to protect the guilty." Names and details have been altered so that no situation, as it is printed, represents any actual individual in my acquaintance. While I do not wish for anyone's personal identity to be exposed, I would hope that all of us would see ourselves often in the various scenarios so that biblical truth can be more readily understood and applied.

Although the primary target audience for this book is my daughters, it is also my prayer that you too will have a greater passion for our God and will be enabled by God's Spirit to have a godly impact in this darkening age that precedes the imminent return of our blessed Lord. We shall stand before Him soon! There is much to be done in us and through us before then.

ACKNOWLEDGMENTS

I would be remiss if I did not give "honour to whom honour [is due]" (Rom. 13:7). This has not been a solo project. I am indebted to Gail Yost and Dr. Guenter Salter who read my first, very rough draft and who provided needed insight in the beginning stages of the project. I owe special thanks as well to those who read the final manuscript and offered valuable critiques: Dr. Michael Barrett, Dr. Steve Hankins, Dr. Randy Leedy, Dr. Greg Mazak, and Ted Harris, M.D. Many other friends in the pastorate—too numerous to mention—have read the manuscript in its various stages and have offered valuable suggestions and enthusiastic encouragement.

Rebecca Moore, who initially edited the manuscript so that it could be field-tested in small group studies and individual counseling situations, and Elizabeth Berg, my sister-in-law and member of the editorial staff at Bob Jones University Press, worked grammatical miracles on the various drafts of the book. They have my deepest admiration and sincerest thanks for their craftsmanship and heart for this project.

My thanks go also to the entire BJU Press team that helped produce the book and to the seminary faculty of Bob Jones University, who were used of God to instill within me an unshakeable confidence in God's Word. My professors provoked me to love God for myself as I observed their passion for Him when they stood before me in the classroom. Although that was twenty-some years ago, the fire the Holy Spirit kindled in my heart through their example and instruction still remains, and I "esteem them very highly in love for their work's sake" (I Thess. 5:13).

Finally, I am deeply grateful to and for my wife, Patty. I have watched her pursue God for the past twenty-five years of our marriage. Her love for her Savior, her confidence in her God, and her thirst for His Word have been a constant delight to behold. She has contributed her *life* to this book. Her daughters have watched her live its themes. They "arise up, and call her blessed; her husband also, and he praiseth her" (Prov. 31:28).

CHAPTER ONE

UNDERSTANDING BIBLICAL CHANGE

*And be not conformed to this world: but be ye transformed by the renewing of
your mind, that ye may prove what is that good, and acceptable, and perfect,
will of God.*
Romans 12:2

Have you ever set out to help someone, not really knowing what you
were doing or how you were going to do it? Have you ever tried to tackle
some gnawing problem in your own life but didn't have a clue about how
to get started? Christopher Columbus experienced this problem when
he set out to find a westward passage to Asia. Because he had little idea
about what he was doing, someone proposed the following award in his
memory for those who emulate him.

Christopher Columbus Award

Citation: This award goes to those who, like good old Chris, when
they set out to do something, don't know where they are going; neither
do they know how to get there. When they arrive, they don't know
where they are, and when they return, they don't know where they've
been. (Source Unknown)

Tragically, many Christians set out in life with little more understanding
of what they are doing than had Mr. Columbus. While he possessed no
accurate charts to lead him to Asia, the journey that we take as believers
was very carefully mapped out for us by the Captain of our salvation.[1]

This book is about *sanctification*. "Sanctification" is the word used to
describe the Bible's teaching about how we are "sanctified" or made holy.
The Bible teaches that a person becomes a Christian by accepting Jesus
Christ as his personal substitute for the penalty of sin. Once he becomes

---

[1] Hebrews 2:10.

a child of God, God begins a process in him that changes him to become more like Christ in his attitudes, ambitions, and actions. God will use many things to accomplish this change, including temptations, trials, the local church, Christian friends, His Word, and His Spirit. Sanctification, in the sense we are discussing in this book, is progressive. A person's likeness to Christ is not something that happens all at once. It is a *process* of change that the Bible calls "growth." As we look at various aspects of the Christian life in this book, remember that whenever you see the phrases "change and grow," "becoming like Christ," or "biblical change," we are talking about the Bible doctrine of progressive sanctification.

The discussion of growth toward Christlikeness in this book will help you navigate more skillfully the sometimes treacherous waters of daily living. A sea captain who understands the basics of navigation and sailing knows how to make progress no matter what the direction of the winds or currents. In much the same way, if you understand these basics for biblical change (i.e., sanctification), you can experience growth in your life no matter what challenges confront you at the moment. Furthermore, you can effectively help others to change and grow as well.

NOT JUST ANY CHANGE WILL DO

The title of this book announces that the subject under discussion is *change*—but, for the Christian, not just any change will do. Consider the following scenarios.

A spoiled teen may stop his sulking (a desirable change), but only because his parents have acquiesced and have given him the car he wanted.

A depressed wife may become "her old cheerful self" again (a desirable change), but only because her alcoholic husband has granted her a divorce.

A college student may be getting better grades (a desirable change), but only because she has found a boyfriend whose affection has lifted her spirits so that she feels like studying again.

An embittered dockworker may stop his complaining about the foreman's decisions (a desirable change), but only because the foreman was transferred to another terminal.

As you can see, we have to be more specific about what kind of change we are talking about and how it is to be accomplished. A mere relief of the symptoms of despair, anger, fear, and so forth does not necessarily mean the real problem has been solved—as is apparent from the situations above.

The real problem in these scenarios is not lacking a car, having an alcoholic husband, lacking a boyfriend, or having a foreman with poor judgment. The real problem goes much deeper and reminds us of an important Bible principle to understand about change: "Our greatest problems are never *around* us; they are *in* us."[2]

Jesus said it this way in Mark 7:21-23: "For from within, *out of the heart of men*, proceed evil thoughts, adulteries, fornications, murders, Thefts, covetousness, wickedness, deceit, lasciviousness [shameless sensuality], an evil eye [envy], blasphemy [slander], pride [arrogance], foolishness: All these evil things *come from within*, and defile the man."[3]

The apostle James tells us the same thing in James 4:1: "From whence come wars and fightings among you [the outward, visible problems]? come they not hence, even of your lusts [the inward desires of the heart] that war in your members?"

Since the Fall of man in the Garden of Eden, man has attempted to blame someone or something for his trouble. Adam attempted to shift responsibility to Eve, and Eve pointed an accusing finger at the serpent.[4] God's Word is clear, however, that our *real* problems are not the result of pressures from someone or something outside ourselves. We do not sin because of financial, social, medical, or circumstantial pressures. We sin because each of us has a sinful heart.

Lessons from a Tea Bag

We can illustrate this biblical truth this way. When we take a tea bag, place it in a teacup, and fill the cup with hot water, the water activates the tea in the bag, unleashing its taste into the water around it. The hot

---

[2] Bob M. Wood, Bob Jones University. Used by permission.

[3] Throughout this book all italics are mine unless specifically noted.

[4] See Genesis 3:12-13.

water didn't *create* the taste; it merely *revealed*, or drew out, what was already in the bag.[5]

This depicts what happens in the human heart. The pressures around us (the unfavorable circumstances, the temptations, and the commands of God to love Him and our neighbor) merely draw out of our heart what is already in it. We cannot blame the hot water for the taste in the cup. The contents of the tea bag determine the flavor of the tea. If we don't like that particular taste, we need to put into the water a bag containing a different kind of tea.

Similarly, we cannot shift the blame for any bitterness, anger, despair, deception, cruelty, and so forth that we display when we are under pressure. The pressures merely expose how unlike Christ we really are.

Acts 16:22-24 tells us of a "hot water" experience Silas and the apostle Paul had while in Philippi. Because of their preaching, "the multitude rose up together against them: and the magistrates rent off [Paul's and Silas's] clothes, and commanded to beat them. And when they had laid many stripes upon them, they cast them into prison, charging the jailor to keep them safely: Who, having received such a charge, thrust them into the inner prison, and made their feet fast in the stocks."

The "hot water" of suffering revealed the nature of the hearts of these two men. We see their response in the next verse: "And at midnight Paul and Silas prayed, and sang praises unto God: and the prisoners heard them." While other believers might react to such mistreatment with bitterness and anger or with despair and discouragement, Paul and Silas responded with praise and thanksgiving. Why the difference? The hearts of these men had been changed to be like the heart of Christ, who responded in a similar fashion to His suffering.[6]

This book is about change—change that involves warring against this sinful disposition within. As we shall see, this is not a change we can make on our own. Furthermore, we must have God's goal in mind as we seek to change. Remember, not just any change will do.

---

[5] Tea bag illustration adapted from J. Allan Petersen, *Your Reactions Are Showing* (Lincoln, Nebr.: Back to the Bible, 1967), 14-15.

[6] See I Peter 2:21-23.

THE GOAL OF CHANGE

The result of the sanctification process is that the believer looks increasingly like Christ—he becomes a "grown-up Christian." While living on this earth, *Jesus Christ exemplified the characteristics of a man controlled by the Holy Spirit and in perfect fellowship with God.* Remember this statement; we will come back to it. The believer is brought, as Paul said, "unto the measure of the stature of the fulness of Christ" (Eph. 4:13). When the nature of God is reflected fully through the nature of a man, as it was in Christ, the blend produces a person who is the Father's *humble servant.* Spiritually mature humanity is in essence Christlike humility—the humility of a servant.

Please note that this biblical goal of Christlike humility is a far cry from many currently popular, but unworthy, goals of helping someone become well adjusted or develop his "moral consciousness" or achieve personal happiness and success. Our Lord did not come to this planet, live a perfect life, and become a worthy atonement for the sins of the world so that those who become His children can merely be well adjusted, live morally upright lives, and enjoy personal happiness and success. He died to redeem us from the penalty and power of a sinful heart that keeps us from being useful servants of the living God. A truly humble servant of God will be well adjusted, will have a morally sensitive conscience, and will enjoy the blessedness of life with God—but these are *byproducts* of godliness, not primary goals for the Christian life.

The leading passage of Scripture describing the servanthood of Christ is Philippians 2:1-11. Theologian B. B. Warfield said about this passage:

> *A life of self-sacrificing unselfishness is the most divinely beautiful life that man can lead.* He whom as our Master we have engaged to obey, whom as our Example we are pledged to imitate, is presented to us here as the great model of self-sacrificing unselfishness. "Let this mind be in you, which was also in Christ Jesus," is the apostle's pleading. We need to note carefully, however, that it is not self-depreciation, but self-abnegation, that is thus commended to us. If we would follow Christ, we must, every one of us, not in pride but in humility, yet not in lowness but in lowliness, not degrade ourselves but forget ourselves, and seek every man not his own things but those of others.[7]

---

[7] B. B. Warfield, "Imitating the Incarnation," in *The Person and Work of Christ* (Grand Rapids: Baker Book House, 1950), 571.

Only when a believer looks like a humble servant of the Father does he look like Jesus Christ, of whom the Father said, "Behold my *servant*, whom I have chosen; my beloved, in whom my soul is well pleased" (Matt. 12:18).

This change from the self-centered ways of our sinful heart to the self-sacrificing ways of our Lord will require divine assistance. This kind of change is not a do-it-yourself project. We must understand, therefore, the Source of our power to change. Let me illustrate that power this way.

The Power of a "Cat"

I grew up on my grandfather's cattle farm in South Dakota. My father was the mechanic for the many pieces of machinery that were required to farm three thousand acres. Even though my grandfather owned several tractors, two combines, and many other farm implements, my favorite piece of machinery was a yellow bulldozer, a D6 Caterpillar. My grandfather used the "Cat" for such things as moving small buildings, digging a water reservoir on the property, compacting silage in one of several large silage pits, or pulling an eight-bottom disc-plow[8] with thirty-two-inch discs that would turn up new sod a foot deep. If there was a hard job that required much power, the "Cat" was the solution.

Although I loved to ride the "Cat," I didn't get to accompany anyone into the fields because of the danger of having a small boy on such heavy equipment. Dad, however, would let me walk out to the machinery yard with him and ride the "Cat" with him back to the shop when he needed to do repairs.

Sometimes he let me "drive." Watching an eight-year-old boy drive a bulldozer is an interesting sight. Bulldozers do not have steering wheels. Instead, they have two brake pedals—one for each of the operator's feet. Between the two brake pedals are two levers coming out of the floor-board and extending about three feet into the air. To turn left, you have to pull back on the left lever, disengaging the drive train to the left bulldozer track, and push down on the left brake pedal, stopping the left track. The right track would keep going and turn the bulldozer left.

---

[8] An eight-bottom disc-plow is able to plow eight rows in the field at the same time.

"Driving" for me meant that when we needed to turn left, I would stand between dad's knees with *both* feet on the left pedal. At the same time I would grasp the left lever with *both* hands and lean back as far as I could to disengage the clutch. Bulldozers are not much more than very large "toys" to an eight-year-old boy, but to a farmer with a lot of work to do, they are a great assistance.

Now suppose my grandfather wanted to plow an eighty-acre field and went out to the machinery yard to pull the several-thousand-pound disc-plow by hand. What would happen? About all he would be able to do in his own power would be to lift the hitch. He could never move the plow even one inch *in his own strength*. On the other hand, if he were first to start the "Cat's" powerful diesel engine and then hitch the plow to it, he could get out into the field. When quitting time came, he could say, "*I* plowed the field." To make his statement more accurate, he could add, "Yet not I, but the bulldozer did it for me." Without the bulldozer, he would be helpless to get any serious plowing done.

As believers, we can no more please and serve God effectively in our own strength than my grandfather could pull a plow in his own strength. The bulldozer enabled him to carry out his work in the field. In the same fashion, the Holy Spirit is the divine power behind everything the believer does that will count for God. We need, therefore, to understand as much as we can about the Holy Spirit because of the crucial role He plays in biblical change.

THE PERSON OF CHANGE

The Holy Spirit is not some mystical or cosmic impersonal influence or force. He is one of the three *Persons* of the Godhead—God the Father, God the Son, and God the Holy Spirit. He is the Agent who shows us our need of Christ and imparts Christ's life to us at salvation. He then begins the work of changing our lives to become like Christ through sanctification, and He empowers us for service to Christ.

We are changed by Him as we cooperate with His leading. Paul testified that the Holy Spirit's leadership in a man's life is one of the chief evidences of that man's salvation. He said, "For as many as are led by the Spirit of God, they are the sons of God" (Rom. 8:14).

The apostle is not teaching in this verse that we should expect the Spirit of God to give us mystical leadings and nudgings, and thereby direct our lives. That is not what Paul is talking about at all. This verse is in the context of Romans 6-8, which speaks of the work of sanctification that God is trying to work out in our lives—a process initiated and orchestrated by the Spirit of God. He is leading in this process. He is the divine Leader calling attention through His convicting voice to the times when we are intent upon going our *own way*. He leads us into an understanding of the Scriptures and leads us into "paths of righteousness"[9] that will reflect Christ's life in us. Those who experience this kind of leadership—away from sin and toward Christ's likeness—"are the sons of God."

That leadership of the Spirit toward Christlikeness takes place as we obey Paul's admonition in Ephesians 5:18 to "be filled with [controlled by] the Spirit." The Greek verb he uses in this passage for "filled" is an imperative. That means it is a command. God must command us to yield to the Holy Spirit's control because we are not automatically so inclined. We naturally wish to control ourselves.

The Greek verb is also in the present tense. That means it is something that should be continually happening in the present—here and now. It should be an ongoing action. It means "keep on being filled with (controlled by) the Spirit." Lastly, it is a verb that is also in the passive voice, meaning that Someone else does the empowering. It is done *to* us. We do not do it to ourselves. The Holy Spirit is the One who empowers us when we choose to cooperate with Him. The filling of the Spirit refers to the supernatural work of the Spirit within a believer whereby that believer is enabled or empowered to become *like* Christ (sanctification) and become *useful to* Christ (service).

Many believers are virtually powerless to overcome the lusts of their flesh and of their mind because of failure in this very area. They continue for years manifesting the same anger, driven by the same pride, motivated by the same fears, crippled by the same sense of hopelessness, or consumed with the same lusts that they have had for years. How tragic that so many years of blessing and usefulness have been forfeited because these powerless believers never learned how to be or did not practice being controlled by the Holy Spirit. There is no doubt that He is the

---

[9] Psalm 23:3.

8

"Person of Change." Let's look for a few minutes at how He works in the "Process of Change"—sanctification.

THE PROCESS OF CHANGE

Someone has said that sanctification is the "Christianizing of the Christian." Preachers through the years have described it as the process whereby the *Spirit of God* takes the *Word of God* and changes us to become like the *Son of God*.

The Bible teaches that the believer has three main spiritual responsibilities in the sanctification process. God, the Holy Spirit, is the primary initiator in all of these activities, but a believer must cooperate with what the Holy Spirit is doing in his life. Those three responsibilities are listed in the first column of the following chart. Take a minute to look them over and notice the passages from Paul and James that refer to each activity. Notice also in the last column that the Holy Spirit, when He enables a believer in those activities, produces a certain kind of fruit: the flesh is restrained, the mind is renewed, and Christ is revealed through the believer's example and ministry to others.

OUR PERSONAL RESPONSIBILITY	PAUL'S INSTRUCTION (Ephesians 4:22-24)	JAMES'S INSTRUCTION (James 1:21-25)	THE HOLY SPIRIT'S RESULT
1. Mortification of the flesh	"put off [the ways of] the old man [i.e., the old unregenerate self]"	"lay apart [lit., put off] all filthiness"	The flesh is restrained through the Spirit's enablement.
2. Meditation on the Word	"be renewed in the spirit of your mind"	"receive . . . the engrafted word"	The mind is renewed through the Spirit's illumination.
3. Manifestation of Christlikeness	"put on [the ways of] the new man [i.e., the new self in Christ]"	"be ye doers of the word, and not hearers only"	Christ is revealed through the Spirit's fruit.

While every believer has a personal responsibility to carry out these commands, the Bible clearly teaches that these activities can be performed *only* in the power of the Holy Spirit. Keep in mind that sanctification has been designed by God to be a *cooperative venture between God and us*. Notice the joint responsibility in the following verses:

> For if ye live after the flesh, ye shall die: but if ye through the Spirit do mortify the deeds of the body, ye shall live (Rom. 8:13).

I am crucified with Christ: nevertheless I live; yet not I, but Christ liveth in me: and the life which I now live in the flesh I live by the faith of the Son of God, who loved me, and gave himself for me (Gal. 2:20).

In each case, we are commanded to do something: "mortify the deeds of the body" and "live in the flesh [in this body] by the faith of the Son of God." At the same time, God says He is doing something: "through the Spirit" and "Christ liveth in me."

This book is divided into three main parts that correspond to the three personal responsibilities illustrated on the previous page. The understanding and practice of these three personal responsibilities are not incidental in the sanctification process. They are core issues. Failure to cooperate with God in these responsibilities in the power of the Spirit accounts for *every* failure in Christian living.

So essential are these truths in the biblical process of change and growth that they are the touchstone for evaluating any theory or advice offered today in the fields of Christian education, parenting, counseling, and pastoral ministry. Truly biblical counsel will *emphasize* to believers, not merely mention in passing, that to change they must "put off [the ways of] the old [unregenerate] man," "be renewed in the spirit of [their] mind," and "put on [the ways of] the new man [in Christ]." It is for this reason that these three components of sanctification form the structure of this book on change.

We will look at each one in great depth and will especially note the Holy Spirit's role in the sanctification process as the believer yields himself to the Spirit's control. This is *God's* plan! Therefore, it is our only answer and our wonderful hope. It is the continued work of the gospel in us.

SPIRITUAL PARENTING

While this book is about *sanctification*, it is also about *discipleship*. Through the years the term "discipleship" has come to mean different things to different groups. To some, discipleship is a tightly regimented curriculum complete with discussion groups and study guides. Once an attendee has filled in all the blanks and attended all the sessions, he has been discipled. To others, discipleship is something akin to taking monastic vows and moving into a religious commune removed from the rest of civilization. To yet another group, it is merely their denomination's yearly four-week emphasis on daily Bible reading and prayer.

Biblical discipleship is not primarily a program. It is a certain kind of *relationship* between two believers with a very specific spiritual goal in mind. *Discipleship is helping another believer make biblical change toward Christlikeness*—helping others in the sanctification process. It is the spiritual parenting Paul spoke of in Galatians 4:19, when he addressed the members of the church as "my little children, of whom I travail in birth again *until Christ be formed in you.*"

This book on sanctification and discipleship, therefore, can serve as a beginning study for assisting new Christians in their growth in Christ. Perhaps, however, it can best function as a training manual for pastors, Christian educators, counselors, and parents since these leaders are involved in helping others change. Specific sections at the end of each chapter provide the disciple-maker with additional information that will aid him in his ministry to others.

THE CENTRALITY OF DISCIPLESHIP

I want us to look briefly at several common relationships in life that involve biblical change. Perhaps having an idea of how fundamental these principles of change and growth are to every significant area of your life will increase your motivation to master them and practice them at every level of your God-given responsibilities.

When relationships in the following areas are crumbling, you can be sure that biblical responsibilities for discipleship and basic issues of sanctification and life with God are being ignored or defied. You can neither effectively build the following relationships nor troubleshoot them without a biblical understanding of your discipleship responsibilities in each. You must also master God's methods for bringing about change and growth in the lives of His people. We must understand, then, that . . .

Parenting Is Discipleship

Parenting, when understood biblically, is basically a discipling relationship. When God gives a child to a Christian couple, they must realize that their little bundle of joy is essentially a pagan. Their biblical mission is to evangelize him and then to equip him for usefulness to Christ, which is, in essence, discipleship. This is what Paul teaches in Ephesians 6:4

when he tells fathers to "bring them up in the nurture and admonition of the Lord."

Sadly, the goal of many Christian parents is merely "to raise a good kid." Through moral training and consistent discipline, they might even rear a child of whom they are proud. He may never cause them any real heartache but still not be *useful to Christ*. His materialism, impatience, impulsiveness, anxiety, stubbornness, or any other fleshly attitudes and actions can disqualify him from usefulness to Christ. In that case, the biblical parenting goal has not been reached, even though the child never got into serious trouble or never seriously embarrassed his parents. The biblical goal was not reached because their parenting efforts did not produce a disciple of Jesus Christ—someone *like* the Master and, there-fore, someone *useful* to the Master.[10]

Parents who do not understand the role that discipleship and sanctifi-cation play in Christian parenting often find themselves off course when their children reach the teen years. In the early years these parents chart the wrong courses on the sea of early child rearing and, consequently, encounter unnecessary dangers in the teen years. Tragically, they may never reach their anticipated port.

Incidentally, many parenting failures reflect a lack of biblical discipleship between husband and wife and a failure to understand and practice the principles of biblical change and growth within the marriage itself. Husbands and wives who are not actively helping each other grow in likeness to Christ within their marriage will not see the importance of it with their children either. Neither will they know how to apply the issues of sanctification to the lives of their children since they have not had the practice of doing so in their own lives.

---

[10] This is not to say that every failure of a child to follow God's way is entirely the fault of the parents. God Himself said, "I have nourished and brought up children, and they have rebelled against me" (Isa. 1:2). He certainly didn't make any mistakes in His parenting goals or methods. Every child still has within him the inclination to "turn every one to his own way" (Isa. 53:6). God does, however, place a heavy respon-sibility on parents to exemplify godliness and to saturate the child-rearing environ-ment with the ways and the words of the living God lest they "forget the Lord" (see Deut. 6:5-13).

Edification in the Local Church Is Discipleship

The mission of the church is laid out in Ephesians 4:12-16. It is to be a place where God-called and Spirit-gifted leaders help the saints mature "for the work of the ministry" as they grow "unto a perfect man, unto the measure of the stature of the fulness of Christ" (4:12-13). This is clearly a call to disciple the flock.

The New Testament pastoral role is much like that of a Palestinian shepherd in Bible times who led the whole flock to pasture and water but often had to give *individual* attention to sheep that had become ill, injured, or lost. Likewise, the shepherd of the local assembly, through his Bible-preaching ministry, is to "feed the flock of God" (I Pet. 5:2) en masse; but he must also make opportunity to meet with individual members who need personal explanation, encouragement, and exhortation. Whether by public preaching or by private counseling, the pastor's role is that of a disciple-maker.

Of course, his ministry to the flock becomes a pacesetter for every other ministry of the local assembly. Every Sunday school class, special ministries to children and youth, vacation Bible school, and various outreach ministries must also have a passion not only to bring them in but also to help them grow. Christ called His disciples to bring forth fruit that would reproduce itself and would remain.[11] Without a passion to disciple believers to Christlikeness through the ministries of the church, the church will focus merely on perpetuating its programs, and the sheep will grow sickly and unfruitful. The edification ministry of the local church is also, therefore, a discipling effort—helping believers make biblical change toward Christlikeness.

Christian Education Is Discipleship

Christian education, an extension of the Christian home and the church, is also essentially discipleship. The following statements about Christian education point this out.

> In following God they [the students] imitate both His nature and His works. The imitation of God's nature results in holiness of character. . . . The fruit of the Spirit (Gal. 5:22-23) is the expression of the holiness of God in the believer's character. The imitation of God's works results in service. . . .

---

[11] John 15:1-16.

Academic subjects—whether in the humanities or in the natural sciences, whether general or strictly vocational—are studied not as ends in themselves but as means of improving the student as a servant of God.

In endeavoring to fulfill the purpose of Christian education—the development of Christ-likeness in redeemed man—the Christian school teaches, as a consequence of the knowledge of God, the imitation of God. Students learn of God so that they may imitate Him. They are to become "followers of God" (Eph. 5:1).[12]

When principals, teachers, parents, school board members, and students forget this driving motive behind Christian education, the results are disappointing, even disastrous. Well-ordered classrooms, high academic achievement, cultural appreciation, and athletic accomplishment are not the measure of success in Christian education. If those overseeing the sports, fine arts, student discipline, and classroom instruction do not see their arena of responsibility as a means of developing Christlikeness and do not actively and consciously pursue them as such, Christian education will produce only highly trained rebels.

For example, student misbehavior and disinterest at school are not just interruptions in the educational process—they are revelations of the student's heart condition. Spiritual processes of Christian change and growth have been stymied in the student's life and must be addressed biblically. Christian teachers must remember that while the goal of most businesses is to *please* the customer, making him a consumer, the goal of Christian education is to *change* the customer, making him a contributor, a servant. Discipleship must be the driving concern. For that reason, every Christian teacher must understand the principles of biblical change.

Counseling Is Discipleship

Discipleship must be the primary concern in the realm of Christian counseling as well. Too many who attempt to counsel do not have the biblical process of progressive sanctification in mind when they try to help someone. They do not see themselves involved primarily in a

---

[12] Ronald A. Horton, ed., *Christian Education: Its Mandate and Mission* (Greenville, S.C.: Bob Jones University Press, 1992), 8-9.

discipleship relationship of helping their counselee grow in likeness to Christ.

A counselee may come to such a counselor for relief from his despair, anxiety, anger, guilt, or fear. He may want help in getting his spouse back or may desire direction in restoring a wayward teen. He may be struggling with the effects of sexual abuse or the life-dominating clutches of drugs, alcohol, or homosexuality. A woman may be grieving after a miscarriage or the discovery of a malignancy. In each of these cases, change and growth toward Christlikeness are the needs of the hour. When the counselor's mindset is not truly biblical, the counseling process will not intentionally move toward biblical goals.

For example, when a woman who was sexually abused as a child by her uncle comes to such a counselor for help, he may think she needs to recover hidden memories or build her self-esteem. Or he may believe her "damaged emotions" need to be healed or her "inner child" needs to be re-parented. He may suppose that a "Christianized" twelve-step recovery program is the solution or assume that giving her "insight" into why her uncle was abusive in the first place can help her more easily forgive him.

In the process, she may find some temporary relief from whatever was troubling her most. She may even learn some spiritual truths she had not known before. But unless the path of sanctification is clearly charted for her, she will spend months, and perhaps years, steering from one navigational heading to another looking for lasting help. What she needs is a counselor who understands that God's "recovery program" is *sanctification*.[13] She can become godly and useful to Christ as an adult, no matter what her past, if the counselor will help her learn and practice the basics of biblical change. *Any attempt to produce love, joy, peace, endurance, and so forth apart from the Spirit of God is reliance upon strategies that are in competition with God.*

---

[13] By using the phrase "God's recovery program," I certainly do not wish to legitimize any popular obsession with recovery programs. Instead, I want to make the point that any "recovery" for a believer is going to come through following God's plan of sanctification, not through completing some man-made steps. A believer cannot please God by following the teachings of competing, man-made solutions, even if the "solutions" seem to work. Whether something "works" or not is not the issue—obedience to God's plan is the only appropriate goal.

Management in Christian Work Is Discipleship

Paul had an enormous management responsibility on his shoulders—the daily "care of all the churches" (II Cor. 11:28). How did he do it? A look at Ephesians 4:11-13 shows that he expected the "saints" to do the "work of the ministry" as they were brought to maturity by the leadership of the church. Christian leaders today must have the same focus. The work must be done, but the *whole* job isn't done unless the saints are developed in the process.

Some Christian organizations tolerate the anger, disobedience, harshness, or critical spirit of a Christian worker or leader just because he is a productive worker or has an important position. Paul, however, did not hesitate to personally address uncharitable and sinful behavior of the workers and leaders under his oversight.[14] He did not ignore the reports he received from others about selfish behavior within the ranks.[15]

Sometimes he had to address the whole organization for their petty arguments and carnality. He demonstrated that individuals must be addressed and must be disciplined if there is no change. They cannot simply be moved to a less damaging position in the organization. He was concerned that "a little leaven leaveneth the whole lump" (I Cor. 5:6). Entire sections of his epistles were "staff development manuals" to specific groups. He was concerned for the corporate testimony and therefore spent much time addressing individual and corporate problems.[16]

We may speak today within Christian organizations about our "personnel problems." There is nothing at all wrong with this terminology, but we must remember to look at these problems biblically. Paul called the believers with "envying, and strife, and divisions" he saw within the church "carnal" (I Cor. 3:3). He did not pacify or arbitrate divisions. In Philippians 2:1-16, he called the conflicting parties to repentance and

---

[14] See I Corinthians 5:1-7; 6:7-8; Galatians 2:11-16; Philippians 4:2; II Timothy 2:16-18.

[15] See I Corinthians 1:11; 5:1; 11:18; II Thessalonians 3:11.

[16] See how Moses and Joshua dealt with the children of Israel for more examples of how individual and corporate problems were addressed to maintain God's blessing upon the group.

to a like-mindedness that reflected the mind "which was also in Christ Jesus" (v. 5).

Christian leaders must humbly address fleshly actions and attitudes within the organization and help wrongdoers make biblical change through the remedies offered in God's plan of progressive sanctification. This emphasis upon developing Christlikeness within the Christian worker is called discipleship.

YOUR ROLE IN DISCIPLESHIP

As you can see, God's concern about godly living encompasses every area of life. Believers must share that concern and be committed to God's purposes and plans for themselves and for other believers.

Keep in mind as you study this book that you cannot effectively help others change toward Christlikeness unless you adequately understand the basics of biblical change for yourself. You must have a working knowledge of the doctrine of progressive sanctification and must, by God's grace, be *practicing* it in your own life. Paul gave his disciple Timothy the following instructions: "Meditate upon these things; *give thyself wholly to them*; that thy profiting may appear to all. *Take heed unto thyself*, and unto the doctrine; continue in them: for in doing this thou shalt both [spare] thyself, and them that hear thee" (I Tim. 4:15-16).

If you have picked up this book to help someone else, resist the urge to skip over Chapters 2 through 9. Before you can become useful to Christ as a disciple-maker, the fruit of your own walk with Christ must be apparent to others. Humbly study these opening truths, asking God to enable you as you apply them to your life. Then move on to Chapters 10 through 13 about helping others.

Understand that God has called every believer to a ministry of discipleship with those around him. He said we are to be "teaching [others] to observe all things whatsoever [He has] commanded [us]" (Matt. 28:20). Paul told his disciple Timothy, "The things that thou hast heard of me among many witnesses, the same commit thou to faithful men, who shall be able to teach others also" (II Tim. 2:2).

God has placed others around you who need to grow in Christ—your spouse, your children, your friends, your students, your roommate, your congregation, and so forth. All believers are to take up the challenge to "admonish one another" (Rom.15:14) and to "exhort one another" (Heb. 3:13).

The writer of Hebrews warned that those who "ought to be teachers" based on the length of time they have been saved, but who are not actively teaching others, should place themselves under some basic instruction again. He charged them with becoming "dull of hearing" and of being "unskillful in the word of righteousness" (Heb. 5:11-14).

This passage contradicts those who have the unbiblical mindset that "religion is a personal matter; I don't meddle in other people's lives" or "it's their life; if they want to throw it away, that's their business." The apostle insists that those who have this attitude of noninterference in the lives of others need biblical change themselves for their self-centered lack of ministry to others.

The church at Thessalonica was of an entirely different persuasion. They were so grateful for what God had done for them that they ministered to anyone who would listen.[17] May God use this book on biblical change to help you become like the Thessalonians whom Paul commended for becoming "followers of [the apostles], and of the Lord, having received the word" (I Thess. 1:6).

A FINAL WORD

The goal of this book is to give you a thoroughly biblical world-view of the Christian life, of man, and of his relationship with God. When man does not understand God's ways and is not properly related to God, everything is chaos. You will not be able to lead others out of that self-centered chaos unless you understand life from God's perspective, model the proper relationship to God yourself, and know how to lead others to the change that will bring them back to a right relationship with God. There is no true biblical change toward Christlikeness unless life and its problems are handled God's way.

---

[17] See I Thessalonians 1 and 2 for the remarkable ministry of both the apostle Paul and of his converts in this church.

Take Time to Reflect[18]

1. Do you understand the Bible teaching of sanctification? Could you briefly outline its main points for someone who wanted to know how to biblically change something in his life? This question is merely a test of what you already know since a thorough discussion of the concept is the subject of this book.

2. Have you unwittingly accepted unbiblical solutions to solving life's problems (e.g., trying to build your low self-esteem or trying to experience the healing of memories)? Are there concepts you need to rethink and perhaps abandon in light of God's Word? Keep a running list of them as they come to mind throughout this book. Don't let anyone's solution, including your own ideas, go unchecked against the Word of God. If you find that the idea you are espousing is not taught in the Word of God as part of the sanctification process, you must abandon it and learn God's ways of handling the problems of living.

3. What is your attitude toward and involvement in your local church? The Christian home and the local church are God's primary means of providing the instruction, accountability, and practical experience necessary for Christian growth. God intends to use the "assembling of ourselves together" as a means of "exhorting one another" (Heb. 10:25). Would your attendance and service record demonstrate a commitment to spiritual growth and mutual discipleship?

4. What is your attitude concerning involvement in the lives of others? Do you stay out of their problems because you are unprepared to help them? If so, pay close attention to the following chapters. God intends to use *every* believer to help others.

---

[18] Each chapter will close with application questions like these. Take some time to reflect on them, asking God to make His truth operative in your life. Photocopy from Appendix A the study sheet entitled Five Significant Statements/Take Time to Reflect for each chapter, and write out your answers so that you can later review the things you have learned (Prov. 10:14) and share them with others.

5. If you are uninvolved, is it because you think the problems of others are "none of your business"? If so, are you willing to ask God to teach you *His* way of thinking about this?[19]

6. Perhaps you are the kind of person who is always involved in other people's lives (maybe even a busybody who has an opinion about everything), but you never see lasting biblical change take place in them. Are you attempting to help by giving them *your* ideas and opinions? Are you "practicing medicine without a license"? Can you show biblical passages that back up your "prescriptions"? Would the apostle Paul have given the same advice you give?

A WORD TO DISCIPLE-MAKERS[20]

You can use this book in several ways when working with others:

Individual Discipleship

If you are working with an individual, have him read each chapter and then write out the answers to the questions in the Take Time to Reflect section at the end of each chapter. You might also ask him to find and write down five statements in the chapter that had the most significance to him. Tell him you do not want him to write out three or six, but five. Having to search for the five most significant statements will force him to concentrate on the material as he is reading it. If he has more than five, he will have to sift through the ones he previously selected to narrow it down to five. If he has fewer than five, he will be forced to return to the text and add to his list. This process causes him to think

---

[19] Somehow this position of neutrality sounds justified, but often it is merely a way to protect ourselves from the vulnerability that comes in ministry to others (e.g., "If I challenge him about his problem, he will point out some problems and inconsistencies he knows about in my life" or "If I try to help him, he will ask some questions I don't know how to answer"). No matter what our argument, God intends to use this vulnerability to stimulate us to further change and growth ourselves. Avoidance of the responsibility to biblically challenge others is a sure way to remain a spiritual baby.

[20] The term "disciple-makers," as used in this book, refers to anyone who is helping another believer make biblical change toward Christlikeness. Of course, that includes Christian leaders who have *official* responsibilities for others (e.g., parents, teachers, counselors, pastoral staff, and Christian leaders/managers). It also includes Christian laymen who have no official authority over others but, nonetheless, have a *biblical* responsibility to help fellow-believers make biblical change toward Christlikeness (e.g., coworkers, roommates, fellow church members, relatives, classmates).

carefully about what he is reading. Writing them down will reinforce them in his mind one more time. Sharing them with you the next time you meet will further cement them in his thinking. At the same time, the significant statements he chose and his answers to the Take Time to Reflect section will show you where God is working in his life right now. Duplicate the study sheet entitled Five Significant Statements/Take Time to Reflect in Appendix A and have him record his answers for each chapter on a separate copy of the study sheet. If you are having him read one chapter each week, encourage him to read the chapter early in the week so that he has time to reflect on what he has read and to see how his life either measures up to or falls short of what he has just learned.

Small Group Study

Small groups within the local church or Christian school that could benefit from studying this book together include Sunday school classes, deacons, church and Christian school staff members, men's or women's Bible studies, church or Christian school teen leadership councils, church Bible institute classes, and Christian counselor training programs. Organizations that serve the local church, such as Christian camps, can use the book for staff training as well.

If you are working with a small group of people reading through this book, you can ask them to follow the same process described above and then have them share with the group what statements were significant to them and why those statements had an impact upon them. Sharing it with others reinforces the truth they have seen while encouraging others who saw the same ideas. It also highlights that truth for others who missed it in their reading.

Family Bible Study

The small group process described above is a wonderful way for a father to go through this book with his family if the children are of junior or senior high age and can grasp the material—in fact, this was the initial intent of this book. If there is a wide range of ages and abilities, he can study the book with his wife alone or individually with each child who is old enough to understand it. If he is working with one family member at a time this way, he can follow the helps explained in the previous page in the section entitled Individual Discipleship.

Premarital and Early Marriage Growth

Engaged couples and newlyweds can study through the book following the process described in the Individual Discipleship section. Individually answering the questions in the Take Time to Reflect sections, writing out the Five Most Significant Statements for that chapter, and then discussing the results together will pay huge dividends in their relationship. They will find out a great deal about each other while at the same time learning of God's ways of handling the problems of living. If there are areas that seem to puzzle them or points of disagreement between them about something they studied, they can seek out the help of their pastor or other mature Christian friend to clarify the issue. Growing together spiritually in this way will help them launch their marriage with a biblical "like-mindedness" that forms the bedrock of a solid Christian marriage.

PART ONE

RESTRAINING YOUR FLESH

Ye have heard Christ, and have been taught by him, as the truth is in Jesus: That you put off concerning the former conversation the old man, which is corrupt according to the deceitful lusts.
Ephesians 4:21-22

CHAPTER TWO

RECOGNIZING THE EVIL WITHIN

There is a way which seemeth right unto a man, but the end thereof are the ways of death.
Proverbs 14:12

As we saw earlier, Paul starts his threefold discussion of biblical change with a command to "put off [the ways of] the old man" (Eph. 4:22). Although technically the "old man"—all that we were before salvation—has been "crucified with [Christ]" (Rom. 6:6) and sin's absolute rule over us has been broken (as we shall see in Chapter 5), we still possess a residual effect of that "old man" even after salvation. We still have an indwelling principle of sin in us that corrupts every part of us. Paul sometimes calls it "the flesh." It is in constant conflict with the Spirit of God[1] and represents everything within us that attempts to make life work apart from God. It is the source of our tendency to dethrone God and to view ourselves as the ruling entity for our lives. The late Bible teacher A. W. Tozer captures the propensity of the human heart this way:

> The struggle of the Christian man to be good while the bent toward self-assertion still lives within him as a kind of unconscious moral reflex is vividly described by the apostle Paul in the seventh chapter of his Roman Epistle; and his testimony is in full accord with the teaching of the prophets. Eight hundred years before the advent of Christ the prophet Isaiah identified sin as rebellion against the will of God and the assertion of the right of each man to choose for himself the way he shall go. "All we like sheep have gone astray," he said, "we have turned every one to his own way," and I believe that no more accurate description of sin has ever been given.

---

[1] Romans 7:15-25; 8:6; Galatians 5:17.

The witness of the saints has been in full harmony with prophet and apostle, that *an inward principle of self* lies at the source of human conduct, turning everything men do into evil. To save us completely Christ must reverse the bent of our nature; *He must plant a new principle within us* so that our subsequent conduct will spring out of a desire to promote the honor of God and the good of our fellow men.[2]

No honest man can deny that something is desperately wrong with man. In this chapter we want to take a "spiritual MRI"[3] to find out what is going on inside man that causes all his problems. I'm sure by now you may have a feeling that what we will find is not a pretty sight. To be sure, you will be sickened by the sight and perhaps even angered, or you may walk away from the scene very despondent. *Don't stop reading at the end of this chapter.* Don't put this book down in despair or throw it away in anger. The Bible's message not only reveals the extent of man's wickedness but also offers man his only hope—redemption. God not only redeems the believer from the penalty of sin but also continues renewing within him the image of God, a likeness distorted in the Fall in Eden. It is to this end that we are moving. Do not grow faint of heart in the journey, though the portrait of ourselves is not at all flattering.

GETTING THE VIEW OF MAN RIGHT

At the start of Chapter 1, we saw four scenarios. Each person in the scenarios thought his life wouldn't be complete unless something specific changed. One thought he had to have a new car, while another wanted a divorce. The girl yearned for a boyfriend, and the dockworker wanted a new boss. Something did need to change, but not one of them understood his *real* problem—major change was needed in his own *heart*.

Unfortunately, we often do not understand the treachery that lies in our heart. We sometimes think we are pretty good people who "mess up" once in a while. The biblical picture is just the opposite: we are all pretty bad people who do right only by the grace of God. The Puritan writer John Owen reminds us of the danger within our own being.

[Since] there is such a law [of indwelling sin] in Christians, then it is our duty to find it out, as if a fire were in our home. Our earnestness

___

[2] A. W. Tozer, *The Knowledge of the Holy* (New York: Harper-Collins Publishers, 1961), 48.

[3] An MRI (Magnetic Resonance Imaging) is a diagnostic tool used by physicians.

for grace, our watchfulness, and our diligent obedience depends upon this discovery. *Upon this one hinge the whole course of our lives will turn.* Ignorance of it breeds senselessness, carelessness, sloth, self-sufficiency, and pride—all of which the Lord's soul abhors. Eruptions into great, open, conscience-wasting, and scandalous sins are the result of a lack of due consideration of this basic law of indwelling sin.[4]

It is certainly instructive that Paul opens his great Epistle to the Romans with three chapters on the sinful nature of man. He does this before he speaks of salvation in chapters 4 and 5 and before he reveals to us the wonderful truths of progressive sanctification in chapters 6 through 8. Most Christians who have had any training in personal evangelism are familiar with the statement "You must get a man lost before he can be saved." Unless he sees himself as a sinner, he will not reach for the only remedy to that condition—salvation by grace through faith.

Paul's sequence of topics in the book of Romans shows us that the same understanding of the nature of man is prerequisite for rightly understanding the remedy of sanctification in the believer. So essential is a right view of man that Professor Charles Williams writes the following in his historic book *The Fundamentals*:

> *The sin question is back of one's theology, soteriology, sociology, evangelism, and ethics.* One cannot hold a Scriptural view of God and the plan of salvation without having a Scriptural idea of sin. One cannot proclaim a true theory of society unless he sees the heinousness of sin and its relation to all social ills and disorders. No man can be a successful New Testament evangelist publishing the Gospel as "the power of God unto salvation to every one that believeth", unless he has an adequate conception of the enormity of sin. Nor can a man hold a consistent theory of ethics or live up to the highest standard of morality, unless he is gripped with a keen sense of sin's seductive nature.[5]

Those are powerful and foundational statements! Much goes awry in Christian parenting, Christian education, and Christian counseling

---

[4] John Owen, *Sin and Temptation*, ed. James M. Houston (Minneapolis: Bethany House Publishers, 1996), 9.

[5] Charles Williams, *The Fundamentals*, vol. 3 (Los Angeles: The Bible Institute of Los Angeles, 1917), 25.

because of a faulty anthropology.[6] If the nature of man's problem is misdiagnosed, a faulty prescription is sure to follow.

Misdiagnosis in Parenting

For example, all kinds of faulty reasons for the phenomenon of teenage rebellion are "swallowed hook, line, and sinker" by parents because they do not have a biblical picture of their teen's heart. They believe that they are fighting just a hormonal battle or a natural struggle for independence from parental control. Others feel that peer pressure and its resulting worldliness are the main predators upon the family unity, or they feel their teen is suffering from low self-esteem or is merely being "immature."

Of course, the attendant solution to these diagnoses is for parents to "batten down the hatches" while they ride out the storms of raging hormones or, if a teen quest for independence is driving the turmoil, negotiate a "peace accord" with the teen by doling out more freedom in return for some cooperation and civility at home. Those who see peer pressure as the main culprit will try various restrictions to keep him from bad company, while others noticing what they call his low self-esteem will do everything they can to help him feel good about himself. Parents who see their teen as "immature" can hope only that somehow—and, they hope, sometime soon—he "grows out of it."

While some of these diagnoses (e.g., hormones and peer pressure) can certainly influence a teen's thoughts and choices and will need to be addressed, not one of them strikes at the root of the problem—the teen's heart itself. The issues just described are not the cause of his rebellion. Rather, in most cases, they *reveal* what is going on in his heart. That is good news for a parent who understands God's view of the heart, because he can then begin to address the problem God's way.

Incidentally, a parent who does not understand the nature of the human heart will not be aware of how his *own* heart's corruption is a further

---

[6] Anthropology is the study of man. While scientists can determine his physical, cultural, and social development through archaeological, historical, medical, and sociological studies, only the Bible can give an accurate picture of his origin, his true nature, and the remedies for that nature. "Faulty anthropology" here means to have the wrong view of man's nature—a view that does not grow out of a proper study of the Scriptures.

stumbling block to the heart of his child. A parent's own inconsistency, anger, moodiness, materialism, sensuality, or deception can be a far more serious stumbling block to the teen's life than whatever problem (e.g., peer pressure and immaturity) the parent is trying to address.

Misdiagnosis in Counseling

The same confusion of causes and cures exists in the field of Christian counseling. Unbiblical theories of man's problems assert that his problem is his co-dependency, his low self-esteem and insecurities, his "damaged emotions," his unparented "inner child," his dysfunctional upbringing—the list goes on and on. Since none of these theories grow out of a biblical anthropology, none of the attendant solutions are God-honoring or, therefore, truly effective.

In the same way, the labeling of a counselee's problems as one or more of countless psychological disorders points only to a deficient psychological solution that avoids dealing with the inner corruption and deception of the human heart. Without a full understanding of the deceptive and exceedingly wicked nature of the heart, there appears to be no satisfying explanation—and, therefore, no truly effective remedies—for psychotic breaks, deviant sexual behavior (e.g., sexual abuse, homosexuality, or bestiality), eating disorders, the plethora of anxiety disorders, sado-masochistic behavior; again, the list goes on and on. The view from heaven, however, is that the "heart is deceitful above all things, and *desperately* wicked" (Jer. 17:9).

Often, popular Christian theories of change miss the mark as well. So-called deliverance ministries assert that demonic activity is behind the increase in addictions, disorders, conflicts, and struggles of the Christian life. Extensive tests for the presence of demons, methods of exorcism, and "adversarial praying" are presented as means for breaking the "bondage" of the powers of darkness. While the Scriptures are clear about the powerful presence of demonic forces, an obsession with demons is largely a result of a faulty view of the human heart—which can easily enslave and corrupt without any outside help—and a faulty exegesis of Scripture passages dealing with Satan and the spirit world.

Misdiagnosis in the Local Church

In some churches where the true nature of the human heart is not understood and biblical discipleship is not seen as a sanctification issue, wrong means may be employed to help a church member who struggles with some area of his life. For example, a man fighting the lusts of his flesh may be told that he wouldn't have such battles if he were out soul-winning more or if he would get busy helping in the bus ministry. He may indeed need to make better use of his time and influence through evangelistic efforts and other ministries of the church, but local church involvement is not the *primary* means of sanctification of his heart. In addition to his involvement in profitable service, the heart issues of this member must be addressed biblically before the problem of lust can be conquered. The tree itself must be healthy if it is to produce fruit that tastes truly Christlike.

Misdiagnosis in Christian Education

Earlier I quoted from *The Fundamentals*, which stated, "One cannot proclaim a true theory of society unless he sees the heinousness of sin and its relation to all social ills and disorders."[7] Pastors and Christian educators need to take special note here because they are entrusted by God with the leadership and discipleship of a certain "society" of people. Biblical standards for Christian schools and church covenants cannot be forged upon an unbiblical view of man. Man's nature is such that he *will* go astray.

Many believers today believe the lie that whatever a man decides for himself is all right and that no one else should interfere with his decisions. But man needs accountability. He must be made to look at his life through someone else's eyes. Initially those "eyes" are those of his parents, teachers, and church leaders. Eventually, he needs to see beyond those authority figures to the God who "deputized" them to "watch" them on His behalf.[8] Ultimately, he must realize that God is watching him all the time and knows not only his actions but also the "thoughts and intents of the heart" and that his heart is "naked and opened unto the eyes of him with whom we have to do" (Heb. 4:12-13).

Accountability is the constant watchfulness and enforcement behind every effective discipleship effort. School administrators who do not insure the presence of responsible teachers and chaperons in student classrooms and at activities are only reinforcing the inclination of the

---

[7] Williams, *Fundamentals*, 25.

[8] Hebrews 13:17.

student's heart to avoid restraining the sinful impulses of the flesh. The result will be chaos and disorderly conduct at best and perversion at worst. God uses accountability to stimulate change[9] and makes it a primary part of the ministry of the leaders He has appointed—prophets, apostles, parents, and so forth.[10] Please understand, however, that sanctification is not accomplished by keeping rules. The rules for which the student is held accountable are merely the guardrails on the highway that keep him from destroying himself and others while he learns how to drive—how to walk in the Spirit for himself.

Man also needs continual reminding. God constantly repeated His standards and warnings to Israel, who "forgot the Lord" or "remembered not His commandments." God was not above repeating His expectations and penalties for the "society" He led. Like Peter, godly leaders must see the necessity of this "ministry of repetition" (note the progression in II Peter 1:12-13, 15). This does not mean that correction is not given when reminders are unheeded; both reminders and correction are necessary. Teachers and leaders who feel their students are "too mature" to be reminded don't have an accurate picture of the human heart or a biblical picture of their responsibility. Any sensitive believer is aware of this "ministry of repetition" in his own life as well, since the Holy Spirit repeatedly convicts and instructs when the believer is straying.

This section is not by any means a fully developed philosophy of discipline: it merely shows that a biblical view of man is crucial to the leadership of any "society" of believers. It is impossible to have right standards or right remedies for wrongdoing without a right view of man. Through the years, the Christian institutions that have felt that restraint and accountability are passé have spiraled downward spiritually and morally and have become the doors through which countless young people have gone to destruction.

More Misdiagnosis

I have seen in my own thoughts in years past a deficient view of the human heart as I have looked at my own heart. There have been times when I have willfully and foolishly ignored God's ways and have sinned

---

[9] Psalm 10:13; Romans 14:12; II Corinthians 5:10.

[10] Ezekiel 33; Romans 13; Hebrews 13:17.

grievously against Him. When I stopped later to reflect on what I had done, I remember thinking with a mixture of horror and grief, "I can't believe I did that!" But once I learned the truth about my wicked, straying heart, I was truly surprised that I hadn't failed a whole lot more!

The variations on the above theme are numerous. We hear each other say things like "I can't believe anyone would do that!" If we have a biblical view of the human heart, the actions of others will certainly grieve us, but *never* will they surprise us. Another flavor of this same idea is "I trust my kids; they would never do something like that!" It may be true that your child is demonstrating some wonderful spiritual growth in his life whereby an action like "that" would be uncharacteristic at this moment, but it is *never* outside the realm of possibility. Dr. Bob Jones Sr. used to put it this way: "Any sin that any sinner ever committed, every sinner under proper provocation could commit."[11]

Unbelievers often comment with various degrees of contempt, "I can't believe God would damn anyone to hell." Those with a biblical view of man, however, exclaim in grateful humility, "I'm surprised God would *save* any of us!" When we begin to see the human heart as God has been seeing it all along, we are stunned that He would want to redeem the likes of us. We all are truly deserving of nothing but His wrath and judgment.

I also remember times when God had been dealing with my heart about something He wanted me to surrender to Him—the kind of music I would listen to as a teen, whether I would serve Him in a full-time vocational ministry, whether I would forgive someone who had wronged me, and so forth. Once the issue was settled and I had committed myself to God's way of handling the issue, I would begin to have all sorts of trouble doing right. I remember thinking, "The Devil is really fighting me now that I have decided to do right." While Satan certainly wants to see my downfall, it is doubtful that I was experiencing direct attacks from the Evil One; I was more likely experiencing the true strength of my sinful heart whose power was not fully known to me until I resisted it.

---

[11] Dr. Bob Jones Sr., *Dr. Bob Jones Says* (radio talks)—Psalms tape series number 9 (ca. 1949).

Incidentally, this phenomenon (whereby the actual extent of indwelling sin's pull is unknown to us until we begin doing right) is very much like the experience of one who is rowing a canoe. As long as he is going *with* the current, he has no idea how strong the current really is. Only when he decides to turn his canoe around and start rowing *against* the current does he experience its true strength.

A believer who has been giving in to the pull of his sinful heart never learns the extent of its power over him. When he decides to "row upstream," however, he meets the "current" of indwelling sin full force. He quickly realizes that life lived against his sinful bent is not only difficult—it is *impossible*. He must learn how desperately he needs God.

THE NATURE OF OUR NATURE

The apostle Paul testified in Romans 7:21, "I find then a law,[12] that, when I would do good, evil is present with me." Three verses earlier (v. 18) he said, "For I know that in me (that is, in my flesh,) dwelleth no good thing: for to will [to do right] is present with me; but how to perform that which is good I find not." Notice further the unflattering picture God paints of the unredeemed human heart in Romans 3:10-18.

> As it is written, There is none righteous, no, not one: There is none that understandeth, there is none that seeketh after God. They are all gone out of the way, they are together become unprofitable: there is none that doeth good, no, not one. Their throat is an open sepulchre; with their tongues they have used deceit; the poison of asps is under their lips: Whose mouth is full of cursing and bitterness: Their feet are swift to shed blood: Destruction and misery are in their ways: And the way of peace have they not known: There is no fear of God before their eyes.

This is what we are up against. Paul, in this passage, is describing the hearts of unbelievers, but this is also a portrait of every believer's sinful tendency—a tendency that is not exterminated at salvation. Its absolute power over us is broken when we are saved, as we shall see later, but it is still present with us and can still wield its influence upon us.

---

[12] "Law" here is used in the sense of a consistent principle of life, like the law of gravity. Paul is saying, "I find it always true (as if it were a law) that when I do good . . ."

Our natural response to all this ugliness is to cry out with the apostle Paul, "O wretched man that I am! who shall deliver me from the body of this death?" Fortunately, Paul didn't stop on that note. This blessed apostle who knew full well by experience and by revelation the treachery of his own heart followed that cry of desperation with a glorious note of triumphant hope. He exclaims, "I thank God through Jesus Christ our Lord" (Rom. 7:24-25). There is a way out! There is deliverance! There is hope! And with that he launches into the instruction of how to "walk after the Spirit" in Romans 8.

But before we get to a discussion of Romans 8, we need to get a more detailed picture of the nature of our nature. We want a full picture, not just a passing glimpse. We don't want the biblical view of our heart to be soon forgotten. We want it to be burned indelibly upon our minds. With that purpose in mind, let's go back to the start of all this ugly mess. Let's go back to Eden.

Have It Your Way

Years ago a popular fast-food chain advertised its hamburgers by telling customers that they could have any number of options on their burgers. They wanted you to come in and "have it *your* way." I don't know whether the slogan sold more hamburgers, but it certainly appealed to the most basic desire of man's nature. We all, left to ourselves, want life *our* way. It started in the Garden of Eden. Dr. Bob Jones Sr. observed, "The Devil did not tempt Adam and Eve to steal, to lie, to kill, to commit adultery; he tempted them to live independent of God."[13] It is this passion for autonomy, for independence from God, which prompted C. S. Lewis to write, "Fallen man is not simply an imperfect creature who needs improvement: *he is a rebel* who must lay down his arms."[14] As we have seen already, Isaiah exposes the very essence of this rebellion when he declares, "All we like sheep have gone astray; we have turned *every one to his own way*" (Isa. 53:6).

Our biggest problem then is not the environment in which we have been reared; it is not the evil that has been done to us by others; it is not the limitations we feel so acutely. Our biggest problem is a heart that wants

---

[13] *Chapel Sayings of Dr. Bob Jones Sr.* (Greenville, S.C.: Bob Jones University, n.d.), 13.

[14] C. S. Lewis, *Mere Christianity* (New York: Macmillan Publishing Co., 1952), 59.

its *own* way in opposition to *God's* way. Let's take a few moments to reflect upon what God has to say about our heart. Thoughtfully read through the passages listed below and consider how often God targets man's *own way* as his most basic problem.[15]

- "Every man did that which was right in his *own eyes*" (Judg.17:6).
- "So I gave them up unto their *own hearts' lust:* and they walked in their *own counsels*" (Ps. 81:12).
- "Trust in the Lord with all thine heart; and lean not unto thine *own understanding*" (Prov. 3:5).
- "Be not wise in thine *own eyes:* fear the Lord, and depart from evil" (Prov. 3:7).
- "The way of a fool is right in his *own eyes*" (Prov. 12:15).
- "Cease from thine *own wisdom*" (Prov. 23:4).
- "He that trusteth in his *own heart* is a fool" (Prov. 28:26).
- "Woe unto them that are wise in their *own eyes,* and prudent in their *own sight!*"(Isa. 5:21).
- "Be not wise in your *own conceits*" (Rom. 12:16).
- "[Love] doth not behave itself unseemly, seeketh not her *own*" (I Cor.13:5).
- "For all seek their *own,* not the things which are Jesus Christ's" (Phil. 2:21).
- "For men shall be lovers of their *own selves*" (II Tim. 3:2).
- "These are murmurers, complainers, walking after their *own lusts*" (Jude 16).

This *own way* tendency of our flesh is the culprit. Let's look more closely at how dangerous it is and how thoroughly it has penetrated every part of our being.

The Flesh Defies God

God is clear in Isaiah 55:6-9 that *our* natural ways and *His* ways are mutually exclusive. The prophet appeals to God's people to turn back from their *own* way. He says,

---

[15] While several passages are printed here, the Scriptures contain dozens more with the same emphasis.

Seek ye the Lord while he may be found, call ye upon him while he is near: Let the wicked forsake *his* way, and the unrighteous man *his* thoughts: and let him return unto the Lord, and he will have mercy upon him; and to our God, for he will abundantly pardon. *For my thoughts are not your thoughts, neither are your ways my ways,* saith the Lord. For as the heavens are higher than the earth, so are my ways higher than your ways, and my thoughts than your thoughts.

There can be little doubt that God sees our independent spirit—the very thing the world considers a virtue—as the root problem of man. Our heart says, "I will make life work *my own* way!" It raises a clenched fist toward the heavens and asserts, "I will do it *my* way!" Williams says, "Its root principle is the assertion of a will that is not subject to the will of God."[16]

Here then is the defiance of our flesh. Paul says it is "enmity [deep-seated antagonism] against God: for it is not subject to the law of God, neither indeed can be" (Rom. 8:7). This fleshly nature is perpetually at war with God. It *will not* be subject. It *will not* be ruled. It is no wonder, then, that when we begin to submit to the Spirit of God as He works in our lives that our flesh rises up and resists that work of God. We possess within us a clone of Satan's own nature, and it violently opposes God.

If you at the moment are not experiencing this warfare, do not be lulled into complacency. Either you are drifting with its current and, therefore, not feeling its strength as it carries you to ruin, or it is craftily deceiving you by its silence only to strike when you are not watching. Thus, Paul warns, "Wherefore let him that thinketh he standeth take heed lest he fall" (I Cor. 10:12). Peter admonishes us to "Be sober, be vigilant" (I Pet. 5:8) and our Lord Himself says, "Watch and pray, that ye enter not into temptation: the spirit indeed is willing, but the flesh is weak" (Matt. 26:41). Since the Enemy has a base of operation within your own soul, there is never a time when you can let your guard down. He has infiltrated your ranks and will continue both his guerrilla warfare and his outward frontal attacks. His goal is to break your fellowship with your God and render you useless for service to your Redeemer, Jesus Christ. Tozer says,

---

[16] Williams, *Fundamentals*, 44.

The natural man is a sinner because and only because he challenges God's selfhood in relation to his own. In all else he may willingly accept the sovereignty of God; in his own life he rejects it. For him, God's dominion ends where his begins. For him, self becomes Self, and in this he unconsciously imitates Lucifer, that fallen son of the morning who said in his heart, "I will ascend into heaven, I will exalt my throne above the stars of God. . . . I will be like the most High."

Yet so subtle is self that scarcely anyone is conscious of its presence. Because man is born a rebel, he is unaware that he is one. His constant assertion of self, as far as he thinks of it at all, appears to him a perfectly normal thing. He is willing to share himself, sometimes even to sacrifice himself for a desired end, but never to dethrone himself. No matter how far down the scale of social acceptance he may slide, he is still in his own eyes a king on a throne, and no one, not even God, can take that throne from him.

Sin has many manifestations but its essence is one. A moral being, created to worship before the throne of God, sits on the throne of his own selfhood and from that elevated position declares, "I AM." That is sin in its concentrated essence; yet because it is natural it appears to be good.[17]

No wonder the wisest man, Solomon, said, "He that trusteth in his own heart is a fool" (Prov. 28:26). A traitor lives within! It will betray me to the Enemy at every turn. It cannot be trusted. It cannot be appeased. And until we stand in His presence, it cannot be eradicated. Until then its presence must be acknowledged, its tactics studied, its attacks discovered and resisted, and its victories confessed. Charles Williams says,

It scarcely requires stating that modern ideas about sin receive no countenance from Scripture, which never speaks about sin as "good in the making," as "the shadow cast by man's immaturity," as "a necessity determined by heredity and environment," as "a stage of upward development of a finite being," as a "taint adhering to man's corporeal frame," as a "physical disease," "a mental infirmity," "a constitutional weakness," and least of all "as a figment of the imperfectly enlightened, or theologically perverted, imagination," but always as the free act of an intelligent, moral and responsible being

---

[17] Tozer, *Knowledge*, 46.

asserting himself against the will of his Maker, the supreme Ruler of the universe.[18]

The Flesh Defiles Man

Some who will acknowledge the presence of an essential wickedness within, however, fail to realize the pervasive scope of its influence. The Bible teaches that the sin principle has infected every part of man's being. We call this truth "total depravity." Man is depraved—fundamentally crooked, as we have just seen. Total depravity does not mean that an individual man is as wicked as is possible but that his fundamental crookedness has penetrated his total being. No part of his body or of his immaterial being is left untouched.

The sin principle has darkened his *understanding*[19] so that without supernatural intervention he cannot comprehend spiritual things. The *will* has been made stubborn by the influence of indwelling sin,[20] and the *mind and its affections* have been perverted so that we need continual reminders to "set [our] affection [mind] on things above, not on things on the earth" and "seek those things which are above" (Col. 3:1-2). Furthermore, "It dulls the *conscience*, that viceregent of God in the soul, renders it less quick to detect the approach of evil, less prompt to sound a warning against it and sometimes so dead as to be past feeling about it (Eph. 4:19). In short there is not a faculty of the soul that is not injured by it."[21]

We must face it then; we are totally infiltrated by the Enemy. What cautiousness this should bring to our plans and deliberations! How frequently do we rush through our day making decision after decision, touching lives in this way or that, with *no thought* of what corruption has tainted those decisions? Are they decisions that "cannot please God"? How have we defiled those with whom we have companied? This is why God so forcefully asserts,

---

[18] Williams, *Fundamentals*, 10.

[19] Ephesians 4:18; I Corinthians 2:14.

[20] "Blindness of their heart" in Ephesians 4:18 is better translated "hardness" or "stubbornness."

[21] Williams, *Fundamentals*, 14.

For if ye live after the flesh,[22] ye shall die: but if ye through the Spirit do mortify the deeds of the body, ye shall live (Rom. 8:13).

Abstain from fleshly lusts, which war against the soul (I Pet. 2:11).

This I say then, Walk in the Spirit, and ye shall not fulfil the lust of the flesh. For the flesh lusteth against the Spirit, and the Spirit against the flesh: and these are contrary the one to the other: so that ye cannot do the things that ye would (Gal. 5:16-17).

For he that soweth to his flesh shall of the flesh reap corruption (Gal. 6:8).

There is hope for us, but it certainly will not be found by looking within. Paul said, "For I know that in me (that is, in my flesh,) dwelleth no good thing" (Rom. 7:18). The destruction has been an "inside job." Our only hope is for some "outside" intervention. Let us put away, then, any thought of how we must become confident within ourselves or must trust in ourselves. While the absolute power of this sinful bent over us is broken at salvation, the intrinsic corruption still remains as long as we are in this mortal body. It is ever present and ever active. We dare not forget about it or fail to arm ourselves against it.

The Flesh Deceives Man

Perhaps you are saying right now, "Do we have to look at this picture in any more detail? Can't we just leave things here and go on?" We could if God had not wanted us to know anything further. But He has wisely chosen to show us two other aspects of man's sinful tendency that we must consider before moving on to other topics. The first is the deceptive nature of man's heart. We all know by experience the intrinsic pull to be dishonest. None of us had to be taught to lie. It was natural the first time and remains the natural thing now.

---

[22] Romans 8 can be a confusing passage unless you are familiar with the use of the prepositions "in" and "after." Those that are "*in* the flesh" or "*in* the Spirit" are totally immersed in that particular domain. In other words, those "*in* the flesh" are unbelievers, and those "*in* the Spirit" are believers. Those who are "*in* the Spirit" (believers), however, can live "*after* the flesh." Though they have eternal life and are no longer absolute subjects to the domain of the flesh, they can choose to be "minded" after the old ways of the flesh. They were called "carnal" in I Corinthians 3:3. They can expect the conviction and chastening of God.

We are warned in Hebrews 3:13 to "exhort one another daily . . . lest any of you be hardened through the *deceitfulness* of sin." Jeremiah 17:9 warns us that "the heart is *deceitful* above all things, and desperately wicked." James 1:22 speaks of how easy it is for a believer to *deceive* himself. And our key text for this part of our discussion, Ephesians 4:22, says that the "old man . . . is corrupt according to the *deceitful* lusts."[23] It was the Serpent's deception that *"beguiled"* Eve.[24] Deception is one of the two fundamental characteristics of the Devil[25]—the other being the destructiveness of his nature.

We must ask ourselves, then, in what way this fleshly nature within us is deceitful. It is deceptive in that it conceals truth. A fundamental characteristic of God is that He is Truth.[26] Satan wishes to keep the God of Truth hidden from the eyes of men and wishes to conceal from man any of the realities of life (i.e., truths) that would make redeemed man useful to God. Several of those realities are that

- God exists, and He made me.
- My sin is against Him, and He will hold me accountable for it unless I turn to Him for salvation.
- The way of the transgressor is hard.
- There is only one way of salvation, not many.
- Without Him I can do nothing.
- He loves me and skillfully orders my ways for my ultimate good and His ultimate glory.
- His Word is the only trustworthy account of reality.
- He has promised His grace for every trial and challenge of life.

The list could go on and on. I can no more ignore these truths and live a life pleasing and useful to God than I can ignore the reality of gravity and jump over the Empire State Building. Indwelling sin generates lies—fantasies about life that conceal reality. Once sin has deceived the

---

[23] Other passages cautioning us not to be deceived abound. See Luke 21:8; I Corinthians 6:9; 15:33; Galatians 6:7; and Ephesians 5:6.

[24] Genesis 3:13; II Corinthians 11:3.

[25] John 8:44.

[26] John 14:6.

mind, the believer is sure to sin. John Owen effectively portrays the influence of deception on the mind.

> The basis for the efficacy of deceit is its effect upon the mind. For sin deceives the mind. When sin attempts to enter into the soul by some other way (such as by the affections), the mind checks and controls it. But when deceit influences the mind, the chance of sinning multiplies.
>
> The mind is the leading faculty of the soul. When the mind fixes upon an object or course of action, the will and the affections follow suit. They are incapable of any other consideration. Thus, while the entanglement of the affections in sin is often very troublesome, it is the deceit of the mind that is always the most dangerous situation because of its role in all other operations of the soul. The mind's office is to guide, to direct, to choose, and to lead. "If therefore the light that is in us be darkness, how great is that darkness!" (Matthew 6:23).[27]

James 1:14 tells us that the sin principle within us conceals the "hook" (i.e., the consequences of our sin) by deceiving the mind, thus making the bait look entirely good to the affections. It looks like "something to be desired," and so the will chooses it. The will chooses what appears to be good to the affections because the mind has been deceived.

No wonder Paul frequently talked about the mind. He saw how sin "warring against the law of [his] *mind*" could then bring him into captivity (Rom. 7:23). He said, "So then with the *mind* I myself serve the law of God; but with the flesh the law of sin" (Rom. 7:25). Part Two of this book will deal extensively with being "renewed in the . . . *mind*" (Eph. 4:23) so that we are not deceived. You should now be able to see why that renewal of the mind is so crucial—if the mind is deceived, the battle is lost.

The Flesh Destroys Man

The Bible teaching is plain and simple: "And sin, when it is finished, bringeth forth *death*" (James 1:15); "For if ye live after the flesh, ye shall *die*" (Rom. 8:13). Death means separation from something. Of course, the death spoken of here cannot mean eternal separation from God, for these passages are written to believers. It means that the design of the Serpent is to separate the believer from his Master's fellowship, render-

---

[27] Owen, *Sin*, pp. 36-37.

ing him useless in the Master's service. It also means that the Enemy seeks to ultimately separate the believer's body from his soul in physical death so that he can no longer be useful to his Master upon this earth in any fashion.

The toxicity of this heart is so potent that when God wants to judge a man, all He has to do is turn that man over to his own heart.[28] What a frightening thought! You and I have enough evil residing in us that if God were to let us have our *own way*, we would destroy ourselves. Rather than demanding our own way, we ought to be begging God never to let us have what our flesh demands. We ought to pray, "Dear God, limit me, bind me, restrict me. Do whatever you have to, but please don't let me have my own way."

Can you see now why "doing right" is so hard? Can you also see why it is just not possible to live the Christian life on your own without divine assistance? You and I are no match for the enemy that is stationed within. Do you see now why we don't have to look for any causes outside man himself to explain or excuse his behavior? His environment, circumstances, hormones, health, and genetics will never account for the level of wickedness that a man's heart can generate on its own.

The picture is bleak. If there were no help from God, knowledge of this condition would lead only to despair. It ought to lead us rather to repentance and dependence. We will look more specifically in the next chapter at how that sinful heart manifests itself in so many different ways in all of us.

ANTHROPOLOGY AND AUTHORITY

Before leaving this chapter, I want to present one last matter for your reflection. I hope by now you have a healthy fear of the destructive nature of your own heart. Trusting in it and obeying it is to guarantee disaster. When Adam and Eve defied God, their heart was corrupted with a clone of Satan's own heart. You and I have inherited that same sinful bent. A biblical anthropology demands that we understand that if left to ourselves, we think and act just like the Evil One himself. As

---

[28] See Romans 1.

mentioned earlier in this chapter, the worst thing that can happen to a man is for God to abandon him to the desires of his own heart.

Once Adam and Eve fell, God immediately reinforced His structure of authority—not as a punishment but as a protection. Think carefully about this for a moment. Before the Fall, Adam and Eve *instinctively* desired fellowship with their Creator and knew what their place was in His scheme of life. As long as they acted consistently with that reality there was no conflict or chaos. Once they listened to the Serpent's lies and defied God's order, they no longer instinctively desired to be under God. The corrupted heart within them instinctively wanted to rule itself. They now embraced "the way of the Serpent"—do your *own* thing.

After the Fall, God reiterated the human authority of the husband over the wife and later set up the institutions of civil government and the church because, if this evil nature is not restrained, it will destroy itself and everything around it. In addition, He calls each of us as Christian brothers and sisters to submit ourselves "one to another in the fear of God" (Eph. 5:21). He even placed Himself within us in the Person of the Holy Spirit to convict us every time we begin to go our own way.

Why all this accountability? Why all this emphasis upon authority in the Word of God? Because an unrestrained sinful heart is destructive![29] When we are presented with a restriction by some governing authority in our lives, we have the opportunity to face once again our corrupt heart and submit once again to God's ways of handling life. Our tendency is to evaluate merely the *rightness of the rule* we are being told to obey. The real issue is more often our authority's *right to rule* in God's scheme of life. A refusal to acknowledge our authority's right to rule is a rejection of God's ways and an evidence that our corrupt nature is ruling our lives at the moment.

Most people today have the idea that they are not free unless they are making their own decisions. The fallacy of this line of thinking is seen by reflecting on the condition of our society. We have more people making more decisions about their own lives than at any other time in the history of civilization, yet we have some of the worst civil and

---

[29] Romans 3:10-18; 8:13.

personal problems that we have ever seen. You see, the practice of making decisions is not necessarily helpful unless the decisions are *wise*—that is, they are in line with God's scheme of life. If they are not *wise* decisions, they add even more corruption to the decision maker's life and to the society he touches. Remember this: *The same pride in a man that demands the right to make its own decisions will pollute every decision that man makes.* That is why we are told in Proverbs 4:23, "Keep [watch over; guard] thy heart with all diligence; for out of it are the issues of life."

When we have humbled ourselves before God and have acknowledged His right to superintend *all* our choices, we are ready to make the choices that make us truly useful to Him. As long as our old, sinful heart still rules our lives, its choices can only be destructive.

TAKE TIME TO REFLECT

Think carefully about the following questions in light of what you have just learned about your heart from this chapter.

1. How does what we have seen about the human heart fit with a common boast we hear someone make about some sinful habit in which he is engaged (e.g., "Don't worry about me. I can handle it")?

2. For someone who has been engaged in a life-dominating sin such as drinking, drugs, eating disorders, gambling, sexual perversions, and so forth, why won't ten or twelve simple steps to recovery do the job in restoring a man to usefulness to Christ?

3. Why is it impossible to genuinely help someone by encouraging him to feel good about himself?

4. When in your life are you prone to raise a clenched fist to God and demand your own way?

5. How does your heart most often deceive you?

6. In what areas of your life do you see sin's destruction already making headway?

A WORD TO DISCIPLE-MAKERS

Can't Stand the Sight of Blood?

It should be clear to us by now why God is so intent upon convicting us and chastening us. If left alone, we will destroy ourselves. He must confront man about his own sinfulness. You and I, then, are going to interact with many believers who are experiencing that purging work of the Father.

Just as a person who cannot stand the sight of blood will have a hard time being a nurse, so a believer who cannot bear to see someone hurting from God's chastening will have difficulty being an effective disciple-maker. Though no one likes to see someone he loves go through hard and humiliating times, God is very clear in Hebrews 12 that "whom the Lord loveth he chasteneth, and scourgeth every son whom he receiveth" (v. 6). God has a perfect love that wisely arranges chastening "for our profit" (v. 10).

Instead of shielding a child or fellow believer from the consequences of his wrong choices, parents and others who are attempting to help him must not put themselves at cross-purposes to what God is doing in the situation. There will be no biblical change in the one we are trying to help unless he humbles himself when God exposes his sin.

Sometimes a chastened believer will make the statement that he could take the chastening more patiently if he knew it was *God* who was doing the chastening. He may argue that he has a harder time when the correction comes from other people—especially if those other people have some problems of their own or if the correction is not given in a spirit he respects. It is helpful to remind him that one of God's ordained functions for authority is to bear the sword.[30] Authorities are sent by Him "for the punishment of evildoers" (I Pet. 2:13-14). God is fully aware of and has authorized every rebuke and every correction that comes into the life of a believer. It is truly *God* who "worketh in [us] both to will and to do of his good pleasure" (Phil. 2:13), and even when others "thought evil against [us]; . . . God meant it unto good" (Gen. 50:20).

---

[30] Romans 13:1-5.

God's admonition to the chastened believer is (1) "despise not thou the chastening" nor (2) "faint when thou art rebuked" (Heb. 12:5). If we truly want to help bring about biblical change, we will be encouraging the one being disciplined to take the whole situation very seriously instead of "despising" (literally, "to look down upon") or minimizing it. Secondly, we will be encouraging him to endure through the full effects of the situation instead of "fainting." Cutting the corrective process short (e.g., by attempting to deflect the consequences or minimize the situation) violates the instruction of James 1:3-4, which says to let the trial produce the endurance which, in turn, perfects the believer.

If you are a disciple-maker who "can't stand the sight of blood," perhaps you need to examine your own heart for motives that are not God centered. It may be that your *own way* of making life work is to be a "rescuer" with a "soft spot" in your heart. Perhaps you think that if you are firm with someone, you will lose his approval or your reputation for being a compassionate helper. Or perhaps you feel such a great responsibility to turn him around that you think anything negative will keep that from happening.

Remember, we are never anyone's messiah; we are not his savior! We are, like John the Baptist, just a "voice" pointing to the Lamb of God. Our primary responsibility is to be a faithful steward of the opportunity to teach him God's ways. Furthermore, we have a responsibility to do so in a way that does not erect unnecessary stumbling blocks in his path. The responsibility for his outcome, however, is entirely his before the Lord. We certainly may have further concern for him, but we have no responsibility for his outcome.[31] To assume more is to assume a crushing, frustrating burden that God never intended for us to bear.

Jesus Himself said, "As many as I love, I rebuke and chasten: be zealous therefore, and repent" (Rev. 3:19).We cannot be Christlike unless we, like our Lord, are willing to rebuke, chasten, and call to repentance those we minister to. Remember, God did not use David, Peter, or Paul (and countless other Bible characters) because they had "great potential" and, therefore, He "worked with them." He instead exposed their rebellion,

---

[31] I Corinthians 3:5-8.

and when they humbled themselves, He forgave them and gave grace to them as they humbly worked through any lasting consequences.

Now that you understand the danger of this fleshly nature within, perhaps you can more readily see why God is so insistent that we "rebuke" our sinning "neighbour, and not suffer sin upon him" (Lev. 19:17). He commands us to get any brother "overtaken in a fault" involved in the restoration process[32] and to live such self-examined lives that we are ready at any time to help remove a "mote out of [our] brother's eye."[33] We need each other's help. We are too easily deceived and destroyed if sin is allowed to remain unchecked.

Turning Up the Magnification

Often when a believer decides to get serious about his walk with God, the Holy Spirit begins to bring to his conscience all sorts of unresolved sin in his life. This should come as no surprise since our Lord Himself said in John 15:2, "Every branch that beareth fruit, he purgeth it, that it may bring forth more fruit."

Once he has faced the first issues God brings to his mind and has sought the forgiveness of both men and God so that he can have a clear conscience,[34] he may be surprised that God brings to his mind more and more occasions of past wrong behavior and thinking—issues he has not thought about for years. He may tend to become discouraged because it seems as though the more sin he confesses to God, the more sin God reminds him about.

This phenomenon is very much like looking at a microscope slide under 10X magnification (i.e., God is allowing us to see things we never saw about ourselves before). Once these issues are repented of and forsaken, He turns the revolving nosepiece of the microscope to 20X magnification. Now we see more corruption than we had ever noticed before. When that is dealt with, He turns it to 30X, and so forth. Remember that the Lord mercifully keeps exposing the sin in us that would keep us from being productive for Him.

---

[32] Galatians 6:1.
[33] Matthew 7:3-5.
[34] Acts 24:16.

CHAPTER THREE

IDENTIFYING YOUR OWN WAY

But every man is tempted, when he is drawn away of his own lust, and enticed.
James 1:14

As we have seen, all of us are born with the same basic sinful heart that demands to have its own way. If you look around you, however, you will observe that not everyone seems to have the same *own way*. Some people seem obsessed with materialism; other people feel that they will die if they don't have a certain friend; still others think that achievement is the ultimate goal in life.

THE NATURE OF OUR NURTURE

While all of us are born with certain natural desires of the body (food, water, air, and sexual satisfaction when puberty is reached), most of the rest of the things we desire are learned from our surroundings. They have been nurtured (i.e., taught from the earliest stages of life). For instance, a baby comes out of the womb hungry (a natural bodily desire) but is not born with an innate desire for designer clothes or for a certain kind of music. He *learns* from his family, culture, and peers to want those things as he grows older. These desires are called "desires . . . of the mind" in Ephesians 2:3. They are created by the way we *think*.

The field of advertising depends upon this ability of man to learn to desire something. Companies spend much money teaching their audience that life will be happier, more healthful, more successful, and so forth if a member of the audience will buy their products. Someone who begins *thinking* about the benefits of a product and begins *imagining* himself possessing the product begins to desire it. He can think about it so much that he feels he cannot continue without having it. Of course, that is exactly how the product manufacturer wants him to feel. It is a small step from this strong desire to a decision to buy.

Fortunately, desires that are learned can be unlearned. Fashions that were desired by teens a decade ago are no longer desired by today's teens. The desires changed when the thinking changed about the importance or desirability of the fashion.

Many of these nurtured or learned desires are not wrong in themselves. James makes it clear, however, that whenever we have a strong personal desire, we can easily be lured by our flesh to pursue that desire in a sinful fashion or for a sinful motive. Remember, the flesh is that part of us that tries to usurp God's control and replace it with our *own way*. Notice in James 1:13-15 how our desires become the target for temptation: "Let no man say when he is tempted, I am tempted of God: for God cannot be tempted with evil, neither tempteth he any man: But every man is tempted, when he is drawn away of his *own* lust [strong desire], and enticed. Then when lust hath conceived, it bringeth forth sin: and sin, when it is finished, bringeth forth death." James's main teaching here is that the source of our temptation is not from *above*, from God, but from *within* man—from his own lusts.

Notice also in this passage the word "own." In the original Greek language the word is *idias*, a word from which we get "idiosyncrasy," something which is peculiar or unique to an individual. Although everything a believer can experience is "common to man" (I Cor. 10:13), these lusts or strong desires are uniquely our *own* in their strength and combinations. They are as *idias*, or uniquely ours, as are our fingerprints: everyone has them but not in exactly the same swirls and patterns.

Because of this ability to *learn to lust* in unique combinations, we could say we have "designer lusts."[1] Although nothing we wrestle with is new to mankind,[2] no one has desires in exactly the same mixture as the next person. *The rebellion of our own way manifests itself differently in each of us.* That is why we can observe someone whose *own way* is different from ours and wonder, "Why would anyone think *that* is so important? It doesn't make any sense." It doesn't make sense to us, but it makes perfect sense to the other person.

---

[1] Lusts do not have to be sexual. The word "lust" means having an obsessive desire for something. A person can lust for approval, money or possessions, sex, perfection, prestige, and so forth.

[2] I Corinthians 10:13.

To clarify this a bit more in our minds, let us look at some broad categories of rebellion commonly seen in teenagers.[3] We will see that while the essential nature of insisting on his *own way* is common to all, the particular manifestations are different. These examples do not necessarily represent biblical categories, although we could find biblical characters who fit each description. They are simply observations from working with teenagers given to help us understand that not all people desire the same things but that *all* of us are rebels whichever *own way* strategy we adopt. By the way, these patterns are most visible when the teen is responding to authority. The contents of the tea bag are most often revealed in the hot water of supervision and instruction.

We could say that rebellion has many masks. The masks may look a bit different from each other, but underlying them is the same face of rebellion—a demand to have life our *own way*.

THE ASSERTIVE REBEL

This is the person who says, "I won't obey. Nobody is going to tell me what to do." He may

- Do drugs or alcohol, smoke, steal, lie, or gamble.

- Disobey, break curfews, be disruptive, be violent, bully others, or refuse to study.

- Engage in premarital sex, pornography, or other sexual habits.

- Display unacceptable dress or obnoxious behavior, use bad language, or indulge in fleshly music or movies.

- Manipulate, argue, or be "in your face."

The assertive rebel is usually not hard to spot. He is often outspoken, and there is no doubt whose way he is demanding. To some assertive rebels, the only evil is getting caught and the only right is getting his own way. Since the 1960s our culture has tolerated and even encouraged this type of verbal, assertive rebellion. The eventual effect upon our society, as this type of rebellion increases, will be first anarchy and then totalitarianism to squelch the chaos. No societal unit (e.g., family,

---

[3] Alert parents can see the beginnings of a child's *own way* long before the teen years. Unless exposed and changed, this *own way* will dominate his adult approach to life as well.

school, business, church, or country) can survive long when a majority of its members declare, "I won't obey. Nobody tells me what to do."

Example: Craig's parents are at their wit's end. His dad found pornography in the trunk of Craig's car when he was looking for some tools. They also strongly suspect he is drinking, and he won't come home by his midnight curfew. He won't even tell them where he has been or whom he was with. They have tried restricting him, but he defies their word. He speaks to his parents with obvious contempt and is constantly asserting that since he is now eighteen, no one is going to treat him like a kid any longer. His *own way* is to have autonomy and control of his own life.

THE COOPERATIVE REBEL

This person is much harder to spot. He quietly decides, "I will obey since it gets me what I want." This mask has two variations.

One type of cooperative rebel is *compliant,* at best: he is obedient but drags his feet, dawdles, is intentionally inefficient, slams doors, punishes others by his attitude (pouting, sullenness), and thinks, "I'll do what I have to do to get what I want, but I don't agree with this and don't want to do it."

Example: Amy doesn't get into any major trouble at home, but for a fifteen year old, she isn't much help either. She will eventually get her household chores done, but usually not without breaking something or causing additional work for her mother in the process. She is never blatantly defiant, so her parents are at a loss about how to discipline her. She is obedient enough to stay out of big trouble but resistive enough to make life miserable for her parents. Her *own way* is to comply while retaining the right to protest.

Another type of cooperative rebel appears to be driven by a sense of *duty:* as a child he is often called a "really good kid," seems to go out of his way to be helpful, never seems to be a problem, is sometimes perfectionistic and legalistic, and thinks, "I'll do my best because I have learned that life works best this way" or "I'll do my best because I like the image of being a great kid." Perhaps he has often seen a brother or sister who is an assertive rebel resisted by authority and doesn't want the hassle. He may even enjoy the limelight he gets when others compare him to his rebellious brother or sister.

Example: Kevin's *own way* of making life work is to achieve perfection in everything he does. As a child he was surprisingly obedient. As a teen he thinks that if he doesn't make the top grade or isn't on the starting team, life is not worth living. In fact, if he isn't on top, he often spirals into great despair. Winning is an all or nothing issue with him. What he calls a "competitive spirit" is nothing more than a lust (an obsessive desire) for winning. He has decided he has to have first place and nothing less will do. His *own way* is to insure success by being the best.

Surprising as it may seem, there are many of us who really try to be good, not because we are allowing God to work in our lives to produce His fruit, but because it seems that life has fewer snags when we stay out of trouble. We often achieve the accolades and image we want. We can become smug around others who aren't doing right and can become easily embittered during the times when we are being good and don't get what we want. C. S. Lewis warns about the dangers of making life work by just being good.

> If you have sound nerves and intelligence and health and popularity and a good upbringing, you are likely to be quite satisfied with your character as it is. . . . A certain level of good conduct comes fairly easy to you. . . . You are quite likely to believe that all this niceness is your own doing; and you may easily not feel the need for any better kind of goodness.
>
> It is very different for the nasty people—the little, low, timid, warped, thin-blooded, lonely people, or the passionate, sensual, unbalanced people. If they make any attempt at goodness at all, they learn, in double quick time, that they need help. It is Christ or nothing for them. . . .
>
> If you are a nice person—if virtue comes easily to you—beware! Much is expected from those to whom much is given. If you mistake for your own merits what are really God's gifts to you through nature, and *if you are contented with simply being nice, you are still a rebel*: and all those gifts will only make your fall more terrible, your corruption more complicated, your bad example more disastrous. The Devil was an archangel once; his natural gifts were as far above yours as yours are above those of a chimpanzee.[4]

---

[4] Lewis, *Mere Christianity*, 180-81.

As you can see, "being good" can be just our *own way* of making life work without God.

THE PASSIVE REBEL

Lastly, there are others whose *own way* is to passively play the victim. This rebel may say, "I can't obey," or "I forgot to obey," or "I didn't know to obey." Let's look briefly at three variations of the passive rebel.

"I can't obey" implies powerlessness and shows up in indifference or resistance. He won't get a driver's license or a job. He won't try out, reach out, speak out, or move out. He often excuses himself with "I'm not feeling well," or "I have a disability," or "I'm a victim." He may say, "I'm hurting too much," or "My parents weren't good examples," or "I'm too emotional." He is often stubborn and simply won't be put into a vulnerable position.

Example: Perry's *own way* of handling life is to avoid anything that would make him vulnerable. He runs from problems, will not try anything unfamiliar, and spends as much time as he can by himself. He calls himself "laid back" and says he isn't a "people person." Consequently, he is often lonely. His *own way* is to not get involved and not take any risks.

While being "laid back" seems to be a popular posture today, Proverbs calls it by another name—slothfulness. This is the man who should run *to* the problem (e.g., the lion in the streets) instead of away from it (26:13), lives in a "snooze alarm" mode of procrastination (26:14), gets very irritated if someone tries to "push" him (26:15), and is seemingly unteachable about the wrong direction of his life (26:16). The lack of productivity and the deterioration of his life are obvious to any onlooker (24:30-32), but he continues to make excuses (24:33) that will surely lead to disaster (24:34).

The second excuse, "I forgot to obey," is often an indication of laziness and shows up in untidiness and constant sleepiness. He conveniently forgets chores, responsibilities, and appointments. He often appears absent-minded. His mind isn't dysfunctional but is more likely distracted by some other obsession.

Example: Janet wants everyone to accept her. She cannot say no to anyone because she does not want to displease them. Her parents wonder why she always ends up with the wrong friends. They don't know that because of her lust for approval she has already given up her sexual purity. She is obsessed with her appearance. She spends hours shopping and takes forever to get ready in the morning. She carefully plans her wardrobe so that nothing she wears is repeated within a two-week span of time. Though she is meticulous in these areas and can remember every outfit her friends have worn that week, she cannot seem to remember what days she is supposed to come home right after school to watch her younger brother while her mother runs errands. She often forgets where her parents told her to be when they come to pick her up after a game, church activity, or shopping trip. She is courteous and surprisingly helpful at times but has her parents totally baffled. They cannot understand why she is such an airhead when it comes to responsibility. What they don't know is that her *own way* is to have the approval of a select group—nothing else ultimately matters to her.

The last excuse, "I didn't know to obey," is often intentional ignorance. This passive rebel can claim he didn't hear the instructions or didn't think the instructions applied to his situation. A further refinement of this is "I just acted without thinking." He is not, however, acting without thinking. He is acting without thinking about the consequences. He is used to doing what he wants without consideration for others.

Example: Josh doesn't seem to be a really wicked fellow: he just always happens to be in the middle of whatever trouble is brewing at the moment. He loves being a practical joker, even though his pranks have become more daring in recent days and have cost him some money for damages. When confronted about his foolish behavior, he replies, "I guess I just wasn't thinking." His parents are embarrassed by how many times the principal has called them about his class disruptions. They have concluded he is just "immature." They are frightened, however, with the thought of how long they may have to wait until he grows up. In the meantime, his upkeep could be costly. Josh's *own way* is to live for the pleasure of the moment with no thought of God or others.

IS THERE ANY HOPE?

A parent or teacher who is struggling with a teen like one of those discussed above may become quite discouraged when the problems seem to be getting worse. In fact, he may begin to wonder whether his teen is beyond help. Perhaps you even see your spouse—or yourself—in those scenarios. The Bible assures us, however, that we can have great hope. The Scriptures teach us that God has a certain kind of change in mind for *all of us*. That includes these teens, our spouse, ourselves, and every other person who comes to Christ. In I Corinthians 6:9-10 Paul lists a number of behaviors and lifestyles that characterize those who are outside the kingdom of God. The list includes sexual perversions of all kinds. Read slowly over these two verses and notice the breadth of perversion mentioned here: "Know ye not that the unrighteous shall not inherit the kingdom of God? Be not deceived: neither fornicators, nor idolaters, nor adulterers, nor effeminate [male prostitutes], nor abusers of themselves with mankind [homosexuals], Nor thieves, nor covetous, nor drunkards, nor revilers [slanderers], nor extortioners, shall inherit the kingdom of God."

Paul then makes a pretty startling statement in verse 11: "*And such were some of you:* but ye are washed, but ye are sanctified, but ye are justified in the name of the Lord Jesus, and by the Spirit of our God."

Please don't miss this! Here is a group of people whose designer lusts had taken them to the extremes of the behavioral spectrum of wickedness. They were people who did not just occasionally lapse into these sins. The description of their lives as "adulterers," "thieves," and so forth suggests that these sins were the habitual patterns of their lives—their lifestyles. If anybody was going to have a hard time changing, it would be these people in Corinth who had come to Christ out of these lifestyles. Yet Paul did not write them off as hopeless cases. Each one had been fundamentally changed into a "new creature" (II Cor. 5:17). They were not what they used to be, but they still had much growing to do—hence this letter to the church in Corinth about its problems. They were being *changed* by the Spirit of God!

Let's take a look at one more passage about drastic change. In Galatians 5 Paul lists the "works of the flesh" (those manifestations of *own way* living) and then contrasts them with the "fruit of the Spirit" (the manifestations of living life *God's way*). Read these over slowly, taking in the full scope of problems listed by the apostle. These too can be changed!

- Adultery—sexual intercourse between individuals married to someone else
- Fornication—general term for all immoral behavior
- Uncleanness—lewdness; dirty-mindedness
- Lasciviousness—blatant contempt for public decency; shameless sensuality
- Idolatry—obsession with and dependence upon anything other than God to make life work
- Witchcraft—sorcery; use of magical powers; use of mediums and occult practices
- Hatred—hostile attitude toward others
- Variance—contentious spirit; hostile actions
- Emulations—spirit of envy
- Wrath—explosive angry outbursts
- Strife—rivalries coming from a devotion to one's self
- Seditions—feuding, divisive spirit within the group
- Heresies—disunity created by a stubborn opinion[5]
- Envyings—embittered resentment often manifesting itself in hostile, spiteful deeds
- Murders—taking someone's life unlawfully
- Drunkenness—intoxication
- Revellings—debauched, sensual parties

There is no problem that God's Word doesn't address in the Scriptures. All of the masks of rebellion and the sinful behaviors and attitudes listed in these Scripture passages can be changed.

In Chapter 5 we will look at the dynamics involved in resisting the pull of these lusts within us. For now, however, please understand that these attitudes and actions listed in I Corinthians 6 and Galatians 5 are *customized* manifestations of the sinful human heart. We do not all have

---

[5] Please note that "heresy" as used here in the KJV does not have the same meaning as it does today. Here it is simply the holding of an opinion that can divide a group. That opinion may not necessarily be a false doctrine or "heresy" in today's use of the term.

the same lusts to the same degree or in the same combination. All of these, however, are "works of the flesh."

JOHN OWEN ON KNOWING YOUR HEART

The seventeenth-century Puritan preacher John Owen has written much about the nature of the human heart as revealed in the Scriptures. When warning his readers about the propensity of their heart to certain temptations, he wrote,

> It is not enough to *watch our circumstances* to detect the times of temptation. We must also *watch our heart* to know when temptation might approach us.
>
> We need to know our own heart, our natural disposition, and the lusts, corruptions, and spiritual weaknesses that beset us. Our Savior told the disciples, "Ye know not what manner of spirit ye are of" (Luke 9:55). They had ambition and the desire for revenge. Had they known it, they would have watched themselves. David tells us he considered his ways and kept himself from the iniquity to which he was prone (Psalm 18:23).
>
> *Just as people have differing and distinctive personalities, so they are also affected by distinctive temptations.* These relate to their nature, education, and other factors. Unless we are conscious of these propensities, relationships, and dynamic possibilities, temptation will constantly entangle us. This is why it is so important to know ourselves—our temperaments and our attitudes.
>
> If people did not remain strangers to themselves, they would not maintain all their lives in the same paralyzed state. *But they give flattering names to their own natural weaknesses.* They try to justify, palliate, or excuse the evils of their own hearts, rather than uproot and destroy them ruthlessly. They never gain a realistic view of themselves. Ineffective lives and scandal grow like branches out of this root of self-ignorance. How few truly seek to know themselves, or possess the courage to do so.[6]

We need to take good heed to his words. We must become accustomed to looking beyond our own behavior and emotions and ask ourselves, "What is the ruling lust in my heart right now that is driving this behavior or emotion?" Once you have read through the following

[6] Owen, *Sin*, 130-32.

extended case study, which shows a whole family whose ruling lusts need to be challenged, set aside a time when you can prayerfully work through the Take Time to Reflect section. Perhaps it will give you some help in determining what is going on in your own heart.

A CASE IN POINT

Remember Craig, the assertive rebel mentioned earlier in this chapter? Let's examine the *real* problem in his family. He was the teen who defied his parents and was determined that no one would tell him what to do. His folks suspected him of drinking and found pornography in his car. Craig's dad, Frank, during discussions of Craig's problems with his wife, often remarked with angry bewilderment, "I can't believe how arrogant that boy is! What that kid needs is a good dose of humility."

Frank is right; his son has an exaggerated sense of his own importance and has no concern for others. As Craig's rebellion continued, other problems in the home surfaced. Craig wasn't the only one who needed a "good dose of humility."

Craig's father, a successful accountant and a leader in the church, seemingly had his act together, at least in public. He appeared godly and disciplined. He never missed a morning for his own devotions and regularly met with his wife and son for Bible reading and prayer. He wouldn't think of arriving at a deacons' meeting late, and every job assigned to him he completed thoroughly and precisely. Although some people thought he was unnecessarily opinionated, he was usually right in the end, so people generally followed his suggestions.

Craig's mother, Susan, was a great asset to the church as well. She was quiet, joyful, and very giving. She could always be counted on to serve extra time in the church nursery and work tirelessly at every banquet or ladies' retreat. She seemed the epitome of a godly, submissive wife.

Craig saw all of this from another angle at home, however. Frank had managed his family through the years with a heavy hand. Craig appeared to be obedient until eighth grade, when he began "acting up" at school. His public behavior got worse in the next few years. Craig was suspended from his Christian school during his senior year for repeated profanity and then expelled for starting another fight in the boys' locker room; he had shoved a teammate who was standing in front of his locker. Craig's reason was "He got in my way."

Through Craig's growing-up years his mother often pleaded with her husband, sometimes in front of Craig, to let up on the boy. While Frank grew more irritated and angry over his son's behavior, Susan ached inside when she saw her husband tear into Craig. Frank told her she was too soft and would ruin the boy with her pampering. She tried to comfort Craig by excusing her husband's reactions. "Your dad had a hard day at work; don't take his words seriously. He really does love you." When her husband suspended Craig's phone privileges, she even let Craig call his girlfriend when Frank wasn't home. She justified it to herself by thinking that his girlfriend could have a good influence on him.

When Craig got too big to be spanked, Frank became more vicious in his verbal attacks and seemed to gloat over the power he exercised when he restricted Craig. The situation escalated to the present; Craig is a high school dropout in a constant power struggle with his father.

When Craig's expulsion became public, Pastor Williams sat down with Frank and Susan to offer his help. The more they talked, the more the home situation came to light. A conference with Craig later on filled in the rest of the picture. Craig was not the only family member who needed help. Frank admitted he had been out of control with Craig in recent months and had grown to despise his son. Susan revealed that she had let Craig bypass his father's restrictions. Though these admissions were helpful, Pastor Williams could see there were even deeper problems in Frank, Susan, and Craig.

Every family member was guilty of trying to make life work his *own way* instead of *God's way*. Frank's *own way* was to maintain control of everything by diligent oversight. When things began to go out of control, he threw more power at the problem. After all, as a deacon, he had to manage his own household well.[7] He frequently complained to his wife, "If you and Craig would only follow my leadership, we wouldn't be in this mess."

Susan's *own way* was to be a peacemaker. She could not stand conflict and did anything she could to smooth over the relationship between her son and her husband. Craig despised his father for his control and lost respect for his mother because of her obvious duplicity. He took advan-

---

[7] I Timothy 3:12.

tage of her concessions to his restrictions but never loved her for them. He saw her, rather, as weak and cowering—a stance he despised in people.

Dad First

Pastor Williams started in the right place—with the pride of each one's heart that demanded to make life work his *own way*. The pastor took Frank to a passage in I Samuel 15 where the prophet had to confront a king with a similar problem. King Saul felt that he could bypass God's requirements if the cause was a worthy one. Samuel rebuked the king and reminded him that his problem was one of pride: "When thou wast little in thine own sight, wast thou not made the head of the tribes of Israel, and the Lord anointed thee king over Israel?" (v. 17).

Frank began to see his own arrogance when administering correction. There was no doubt that he had provoked his child to wrath.[8] He saw, as well, how he actually taught his son by example that if you have a problem, you can just throw more force at it. His son had learned well and was forcefully pushing back at him. Pastor Williams challenged him to take the leadership in his family, but in a different direction.

"Frank, God wants you to lead your family, but you need to be the leader in humility first. Your family needs to see you humbling yourself before God, before them, and before the assembly at church. You have stepped off God's path of truth and have been leaning to your own understanding and have been wise in your own conceits.

"Craig needs to see you getting into your place under God. The only way you have sought God is to ask Him to help you get your family under control. He will not help you do that; He wants to break you of your controlling ways. You cannot call Craig to a position of submission to you from your position of rebellion against God.

"If you want to see your family turn around, you will have to be the first one to die. In God's pattern of leadership, you, like Christ, have to be the first one on the cross. From there you can call your family to follow you by dying as well. You must lead in following the Father's will of humbling yourself for others."

---

[8] Ephesians 6:4.

Mom Too

Pastor Williams continued, "Susan, you have bypassed God's require-ment that you support your husband. You can, and should, make any biblical appeals to him that will help him be more effective in his ministry at home. But instead, you have taught Craig, by example, that when you do not agree with your leader, you can bypass his commands. Craig certainly didn't need your example to learn *how* to rebel against authority—that comes naturally for all of us—but your example *author-ized* disobedience in this home."

Susan immediately saw her sin against God and against her husband and asked both to forgive her. Several weeks passed, however, before Frank was broken enough by his son's continued rebellion to admit to God and others that what had appeared "so right" to him was actually his *own way* of controlling life to make it work for him. They would learn much more about humility before they would see their son bow in submission to God and to them eighteen months later.

Pastor Williams could have approached this family's problems from many different angles. Other counselors might have seen this as a communication problem or as a child-rearing problem where parents are having problems "letting go" of their only child. Still others may have suggested that Frank and Susan need to show some "tough love." None of these solutions, however, would have addressed the heart of the problem. The contents of *three* "tea bags" have to be changed before the flavor of this family tastes Christlike.

NOT A PRETTY SIGHT

As we saw in the last chapter, Recognizing the Evil Within, a good look at our heart is often pretty gruesome. As we see our flesh manifesting itself through our "designer lusts," which seem so natural to us, we can become even more discouraged. We may think, "There's no hope for me! It looks as though everything I do comes from the wrong motives and desires." There is hope, however. God doesn't show us this picture of ourselves without offering His own wonderful remedy. We will begin to look at that plan in the next chapter, Getting in Your Place. Before going on, however, answer the Take Time to Reflect questions.

TAKE TIME TO REFLECT

1. God says our most basic problem is our propensity to turn "every one to his *own way*" (Isa. 53:6). You have seen the examples of several people's *own way* in this chapter. What are some of the elements that constitute your *own way*? For further help, complete the sentences below.

   - I feel most secure when _____ .
   - All I want to have/be/do is _____ .
   - The thing I worry about most is _____ .
   - The thing that keeps me awake at night is _____ .
   - I go into a panic when _____ .
   - I get most angry when _____ .
   - I tend to get very discouraged when _____ .

2. Do you find yourself depicted in any of the three kinds of rebels discussed in this chapter (assertive, cooperative, passive)? If so, what characteristics do you identify with? Write out your answers. Don't waste time trying to find out exactly which kind of rebel you are. All of us are fairly flexible in the ways we rebel. The goal in answering this question is to identify the ways in which you are most prone to rebel.

3. God exposes the rebellion of our *own way* by placing us in "hot water." What "hot water" situations do you find God placing you into at this time in order to expose your self-centeredness? (Hint: Some "hot water" situations might be physical struggles, struggles with temptations and lusts, pressures at home or work, relational problems with others, etc.)

4. How does the self-centered "tea" taste to others around you (i.e., what kinds of wrong responses come out of you when you can't have your *own way*)?

A WORD TO DISCIPLE-MAKERS

What Is the Ruling Lust?

James 4:1 teaches us that problems have two levels. There is the outward problem, which is easy to recognize and address. In James 4:1 the outward problem is the fighting and warring between two people. Parents and other leaders who address problems only on the outward, visible level are missing important issues of the heart. James says that the underlying problem is a "lust"—a hotly pursued desire.[9] The problem is in the heart of man, not in his circumstances.

Warring children, teens, church members, and so forth certainly need to be confronted about their fighting; but, more fundamentally, they need to be confronted about the underlying desire of the heart that prompted the fight. It may be a desire to be first[10] or a desire to have a possession belonging to someone else[11] or a desire to be accepted like someone else.[12] Merely insisting that the warring parties get along or separating them for a period of time may stop the fight, but it will not solve the *real* problem—their ruling lust, which is a part of their *own way* of making life work.

Not only must that ruling lust be identified and confronted in their lives, but the offenders must also ask forgiveness of it from God and from those they are wronging before lasting biblical change can take place. It is not even enough for the individual to see his ruling lust and acknowledge that he has a problem in that area. Unless he repents with the intention of forsaking, his fellowship with God remains broken and there will be no lasting change. God warned Israel, "Seek not after your *own* heart and your *own* eyes, after which ye use to go a whoring: . . . Remember, and do all my commandments, and be holy unto your God" (Num. 15:39-40).

God was concerned about Israel's heart. Don't miss the heart issues when dealing with the surface problems!

---

[9] Other outward problems that are manifestations of inward heart issues include anger, suicide attempts, shoplifting, wrong friendships, fear, and ungodly speech (cursing, gossip, sarcasm, lying, slander)—virtually any of the behaviors and attitudes listed earlier in this chapter for the various types of rebels.

[10] III John 9 speaks of "Diotrephes, who loveth to have the preeminence among them" (the inner heart problem) and who, therefore, shunned the apostles who received the attention when they came to town (the outward, visible problem).

[11] Jezebel murdered Naboth because her husband coveted Naboth's vineyard. The outward act of murder was prompted by an inward lust for the neighbor's property (I Kings 21). See also Hebrews 13:5.

[12] Jealousy was the heart issue in the first murder (Gen. 4:1-8).

Watch Your Language!

Today the lusts of the heart are addressed in terms that make the lust sound entirely innocent and harmless. For example, someone might say he struggles with a "hunger" to be somebody in other people's eyes. Another might "thirst" for companionship, "yearn" for a better station in life, "need" his ego stroked, or "ache" for someone to lean on. These terms conceal the underlying lust of the heart rather than expose it; they legitimize the lust rather than condemn it. While the Bible uses terms like "thirst" and "hunger" metaphorically, people today use them more or less literally. They think their "thirst" is only natural and, therefore, can't be helped; it must be "quenched" by the thing they long for.

God often used very strong terms to describe the unbiblical "longings" of His people. He called their desires "idolatry," "whoring," "spiritual adultery," and "lust." The pull of indwelling sin has a deadly effect on the human heart. Don't lessen the sense of its treachery by using euphemistic phrases. When one of the phrases described above is used in the Bible, don't remove it from its context. God always makes it very clear that what He is describing metaphorically is something extremely dangerous to man and very offensive to Him.

CHAPTER FOUR

GETTING IN YOUR PLACE

Be astonished, O ye heavens, at this, and be horribly afraid, be ye very desolate, saith the Lord. For my people have committed two evils; they have forsaken me the fountain of living waters, and hewed them out cisterns, broken cisterns, that can hold no water.
Jeremiah 2:12-13

"Gabriel! Michael! All the rest of you in heaven! Can you believe it? Stop and look down there at Israel. Look at what My people have been doing! Doesn't it make you shudder with terror for them?

"These people of Mine have committed two great evils. They first show their rebellion by not coming to drink from My pure springs of water. As if that isn't enough, they further insult Me by trying to quench their thirst with the murky runoff water they catch in their makeshift cisterns. What a sad exchange! Israel doesn't have to live that way. They aren't slaves; they aren't captives! They don't have to drink brackish water from such stagnant, leaking basins; I want them to enjoy living water from Me. Yet, sadly, they have brought this on themselves."

God finishes His address to the heavenly beings and turns to Israel, "What are you doing relying on the waters of Egypt and Sihor and Assyria? Haven't you felt the roar of Assyria? And Egypt has shaved your head in disgrace. You don't have to live this way." God continues in Jeremiah 2:19: "Thine own wickedness shall correct thee, and thy backslidings shall reprove thee: know therefore and see that it is an evil thing and bitter, that *thou hast forsaken the Lord thy God,* and that my fear is not in thee, saith the Lord God of hosts."

While the Scriptures are clear that our *own way,* symbolized by the broken cisterns in the above passage, will not work, the fact that it won't work is God's secondary concern—the second evil. *Forsaking God* is the first and the most wicked of the two evils God enumerates here! We must understand that to look to anything apart from God to make life work is to forsake God.

DEPENDENT BY DESIGN

Trusting in our *own way* defies the most basic fact of man's creation: God made man dependent. Adam was not made autonomous. He *needed* God. He was not self-sufficient. He had to be told who he was and what his job was. He had to be told what to eat and what not to eat. Any attempt to make man a creature who can live independently from God is doomed to failure. Man can no more joyfully and peacefully live independently from God than he can fly by flapping his hands. He was not made a bird. He was made a biped—by design. He was not made an autonomous, self-contained, self-sufficient[1] creature. He was made dependent—by design.

Any change that will ultimately help a man must move him away from autonomy and must move him toward dependence upon his Creator. Any change that gives him the illusion that he is able to make life work his *own way* makes him only a more powerful rebel against God and destroys his usefulness to his Creator. However, God promises satisfaction, hope, security, and joy to those who turn to Him in trusting dependence.[2]

The fact of our creation testifies of our dependence. Psalm 100:3 says, "Know ye that the Lord he is God: it is he that hath made us, and not we ourselves; we are his people, and the sheep of his pasture."

Man can make a space shuttle, build a house, manufacture an automobile, and construct a superhighway; but since none of these items are self-created, none of them are self-sustaining. They are dependent upon

---

[1] Please note that throughout this book the term "self-sufficient" is not used in the positive sense of preparing a child to be able to function independently of his parents and others as he learns the skills of responsible adult living. It is used rather in the negative sense of having an attitude of undue confidence and smugness that avoids and/or scorns the help of others—including God. It is the attitude of self-confidence condemned by our Lord in the parable of the wealthy farmer in Luke 12:16-21. It is also demonstrated in the absence of any God-consciousness in the proud planning of the businessman in James 4:13-16, who goes about his daily routine with no thought of God nor any submission to His plans for him.

[2] Psalms 16, 36, and many others demonstrate the stability and joy that God gives to those who put their trust in Him rather than in their own devices or in other gods.

the one who made them. The space shuttle and the automobile have to be refueled and serviced. The house and the highway have to be repaired. Creation inherently demands dependency. Man can acknowledge this about everything he makes for himself in this world, but he rebels against the thought that somehow he is dependent upon his own Creator. Yet everything around us demonstrates that "a river cannot rise higher than its source." Subordination and dependence are inherent for everything that is made by someone else. God reminds us in Psalm 100:3, "It is he that hath made us, and not we ourselves." The fact of man's creation has enormous implications for the creature. The governing principle here is *if you needed somebody to make you, you need somebody to maintain you.* Man must face his dependency, repent of his proud attempts to make life work his *own way,* and submit to the ways of his Creator. Perhaps a parable can show us how easy it is for us to think we are making life work on our own.

A BOY AND A BIKE

Six-year-old Johnny approaches his father with a request. The dialogue goes something like this:

"Dad, I'm six now. Can I buy a bike?"

"Well, Son, I'm sure you are old enough to learn to ride, but how are you going to buy a bike?"

"I have a quarter, Dad! Remember, you give me a quarter every week when I help you wash the car. This week I saved it because I want to buy a bike. I didn't buy candy with it this week."

"You really are serious about buying a bike if you passed up candy! Well, if you think you are ready for a bike, go get your quarter and let's go shopping."

After checking out several stores, they find a bike that Johnny really likes. Johnny's father looks at the price tag and calculates that with tax the bike will cost one hundred dollars—a far cry from a quarter.

"Son, are you sure this is the bike you want?"

"I sure am! I've always dreamed of having a bike like this. This is the one I want—and I've got my quarter!"

"OK then; wheel the bike up to the counter, Johnny, and let's pay the clerk."

Johnny pushes the bike up to the checkout counter, lays his quarter on the counter, and says to the clerk, "I want to buy this bike." The clerk smiles at him, winks at his father and replies, "Sure, Son, you've made a great choice." Dad turns to Johnny and says, "Son, take the bike outside and wait for me on the sidewalk. I want to talk to the lady." As Johnny leaves the store, his father writes out a check for $99.75 and then joins his son outside. They load the bike into the car, and on the way home Johnny's father commends him for his choice.

> "Son, I just want to tell you how proud I am of you today. Every other week you have spent your quarter on candy and gum—things that would not last. This week you saved your quarter and decided to buy something that would be around for a while. That's a good decision, Son. I can tell you are growing up."

When they arrive at home, they unload the bike and Johnny runs into the house to get his mother. When she comes outside, Johnny exclaims, "Look at my new bike, Mom! Isn't it beautiful! And I bought it with my own money!"

Someday Johnny will gain a better understanding of how life works and will learn that he didn't buy the bike. His quarter was a mere vote in the process saying that he wanted a bike rather than candy. His quarter, however, didn't buy the bike—he was dependent upon his father and didn't even know it. One day, if he remembers his words, he will be humored by his naiveté. Perhaps someday this experience will cause him to reflect on how unwittingly dependent he was upon his dad in so many other ways. Without his dad, he not only wouldn't have had a bike, but he also would have been without many other things. He wouldn't have had a home, food on the table, medical insurance for his broken arm, education, clothes, skill at playing baseball and basketball, a measure of stick-to-itiveness and character his father instilled in him—and a thousand other things, both tangible and intangible. He wouldn't even have life without his father. Without his dad's love, he wouldn't ever have felt that he belonged anywhere. Without his dad's protection, he wouldn't ever have felt really safe. Without his dad's spiritual direction, he might still be lost, without salvation from his sin. He most likely will realize that he was dependent upon his father in ways he never imagined as a six-year-old boy.

Some children never come to realize this kind of dependency, and their ingratitude is a grief to their parents' hearts. The same is true of our relationship with our heavenly Father—only our dependency extends to far more areas and involves far greater issues than the relationship of a mortal father with his children. Colossians 1:16-17 says, "For by him were all things created, that are in heaven, and that are in earth, visible and invisible, whether they be thrones, or dominions, or principalities, or powers: all things were created by him, and for him: And he is before all things, and by him all things consist [hold together]."

These verses and many like them are not just poetry; they are statements of reality. If God were to withdraw His personal superintendence from His creation, it would dissolve into the nothingness from which it was created. It exists only by His continued, wise, powerful, and purposeful will. Hebrews 1:3 testifies that Christ, the Creator, bears up or sustains the universe by His mighty Word. There is no way that man can escape his dependence upon God. He can only rebel against it, which is only to his own destruction.

The account of Nebuchadnezzar powerfully illustrates the destructive nature of man's natural bent toward self-sufficiency. His kingdom of Babylon was at the height of its glory when the following incident took place, as recorded in Daniel 4:29-37.

> At the end of twelve months [King Nebuchadnezzar] walked in the palace of the kingdom of Babylon. The king spake, and said, Is not this great Babylon, that *I* have built for the house of the kingdom by the might of *my* power, and for the honour of *my* majesty? [Notice his self-sufficiency and pride.]

> While the word was in the king's mouth, there fell a voice from heaven, saying, O king Nebuchadnezzar, to thee it is spoken; The kingdom is departed from thee. And they shall drive thee from men, and thy dwelling shall be with the beasts of the field: they shall make thee to eat grass as oxen, and seven times shall pass over thee, *until thou know that the most High ruleth in the kingdom of men, and giveth it to whomsoever he will.* [Notice here the purpose of the humbling that was about to come—to put him in his place under the One who really *does* rule all things.]

> The same hour was the thing fulfilled upon Nebuchadnezzar: and he was driven from men, and did eat grass as oxen, and his body

was wet with the dew of heaven, till his hairs were grown like eagles' feathers, and his nails like birds' claws.

And at the end of the days I Nebuchadnezzar lifted up mine eyes unto *heaven*, and mine understanding returned unto me, and I blessed the most High, and I praised and honoured him that liveth for ever, whose dominion is an everlasting dominion, and his kingdom is from generation to generation: And all the inhabitants of the earth are reputed as nothing: and he doeth according to his will in the army of heaven, and among the inhabitants of the earth: and none can stay his hand, or say unto him, What doest thou?

At the same time my reason returned unto me; and for the glory of my kingdom, mine honour and brightness returned unto me; and my counsellors and my lords sought unto me; and I was established in my kingdom, and excellent majesty was added unto me. *Now I Nebuchadnezzar praise and extol and honour the King of heaven, all whose works are truth, and his ways judgment: and those that walk in pride he is able to abase.*

This response of a man "getting in his place" as a creature having a sense of dependency before his Creator is called humility—a topic we must look at more closely.

HUMILITY—THE HALLMARK OF THE DEPENDENT CREATURE

Andrew Murray, in his classic work on humility, writes, "Humility, the place of entire dependence on God, is, from the very nature of things, the first duty and the highest virtue of man. It is the root of every virtue. . . . Humility is simply [man's] acknowledging the truth of his position as man and yielding to God His place."[3] Man's natural, fallen tendency is to exalt himself as the final authority of his life. One theologian described man's problem this way: "Satan's sin against God in the primal glory was a fivefold expression of the two defiant words: '*I will*' (Isaiah 14:13, 14), and every unyielded life is perpetuating the crime of Satan."[4]

---

[3] Andrew Murray, *Humility* (Springdale, Pa.: Whitaker House, 1982), 10, 12.

[4] Lewis Sperry Chafer, *He That Is Spiritual* (1918; reprint, Grand Rapids: Zondervan, 1967), 95. Italics are Chafer's.

When a man finally recognizes that he is a rebel against God and decides to "lay down his arms," he demonstrates humility by his *repentance*. When he becomes aware that he cannot make life work his own way but desperately needs God, he demonstrates humility by a sense of continued *dependence*. No man who has been humbled before God is self-justifying, self-protective, or self-confident.[5]

The *International Standard Bible Encyclopaedia* says this about humility:

> It by no means implies slavishness or servility; nor is it inconsistent with a right estimate of oneself, one's gifts and calling of God, or with proper self-assertion when called for. But the habitual frame of mind of a child of God is that of one who feels not only that he owes all his natural gifts, etc., to God, but that he has been the object of unde-served redeeming love, and who regards himself as being not his own, but God's in Christ. He *cannot* exalt himself, for he knows that he has nothing of himself. The humble mind is thus at the root of all other graces and virtues. Self-exaltation spoils everything. There can be no real *love* without humility. "Love," said Paul, "vaunteth not itself, is not puffed up" (I Cor. 13:4). As Augustine said, humility is first, second and third in Christianity.[6]

St. Bernard wisely observed that humility is "the esteeming of ourselves small, inasmuch as we are so; the thinking truly, and because truly, therefore lowlily, of ourselves." [7] Humility is the frame of mind a man possesses who is fully aware of his nothingness apart from God and of his sinfulness that would eternally separate him from God were not God willing to rescue him. It says, "I am sinful and need God's mercy," and "I am insufficient and need God's grace."

LIVE THE CHRISTIAN LIFE THE SAME WAY YOU GOT IT

The Christian life starts with this kind of humility.[8] To be saved, a man must realize he has nothing in himself to commend him to God and that he is totally bankrupt before God and unable to do anything about the debt of his sin. He must come to God as a broken, needy sinner

---

[5] See Paul's sense of neediness before God in II Corinthians 3:5 and 4:7.

[6] James Orr, ed., *The International Standard Bible Encyclopaedia*, vol. 3 (Grand Rapids: Wm. B. Eerdmans Publishing Co., 1956), 1439.

[7] Richard C. Trench, *Synonyms of the New Testament* (Grand Rapids: Wm. B. Eerdmans Publishing Co., 1880), 150.

[8] Matthew 5:3; 18:3-4.

dependent upon God for forgiveness. He brings no personal merit to God to bargain with. Ephesians 2:8-9 describes it this way: "For by grace are ye saved through faith; and that *not of yourselves:* it is the gift of God: Not of works, lest any man should boast."

Most Christians understand this and would think it heretical to assume they could do anything to earn God's salvation. They know theirs is the kingdom because they come "poor in spirit" to God (Matt. 5:3). What they are not often ready to accept is that God wants them to have the same dependent attitude *after* salvation. Colossians 2:6 says, "As ye have therefore received Christ Jesus the Lord, so walk ye in him." Humility is not only the start of the Christian life; it is the start of everything godly in the Christian life. Unfortunately, humility is treated as a vice in today's self-assertive, in-your-face culture. In fact, many people would not even know how to describe a humble person. C. S. Lewis put it this way:

> Do not imagine that if you meet a really humble man he will be what most people call "humble" nowadays: he will not be a sort of greasy, swarmy person, who is always telling you that, of course, he is nobody. Probably all you will think about him is that he seemed a cheerful, intelligent chap who took a real interest in what *you* said to *him.* If you do dislike him it will be because you feel a little envious of anyone who seems to enjoy life so easily. He will not be thinking about humility: he will not be thinking about himself at all." [9]

Andrew Murray rightly emphasizes the need for humility for a man to fulfill his purpose as an image-bearer of God. He says,

> Just as Jesus found His glory in taking the form of a servant, so also He said to us, "Whosoever would be greatest among you, shall be your servant" (Matthew 23:11). He simply taught us the blessed truth that there is nothing so divine and heavenly as being the servant and helper of all. The faithful servant who recognizes his position finds a real pleasure in supplying the wants of the master or his guests. When we see that humility is something infinitely deeper than contrition, and accept it as our participation in the life of Jesus, we will begin to learn that it is our true nobility. We will begin to understand that *being servants of all is the highest fulfillment of our destiny, as men created in the image of God.* [10]

---

[9] Lewis, *Mere Christianity*, 114. Italics are Lewis's.

[10] Murray, *Humility*, 7.

Notice further our Lord's words about humility as a continuing attitude of the believer.

> Come unto me, all ye that labour and are heavy laden, and I will give you rest. Take my yoke upon you, and learn of me; for I am meek and *lowly in heart:* and ye shall find rest unto your souls. For my yoke is easy, and my burden is light (Matt. 11:28-30).

> And whosoever will be chief among you, let him be your *servant:* Even as the Son of man came not to be ministered unto, but to minister, and to *give his life* a ransom for many (Matt. 20:27-28).

> And said unto them, Whosoever shall receive this child in my name receiveth me: and whosoever shall receive me receiveth him that sent me: for he that is *least among you* all, the same shall be great (Luke 9:48).

> For whosoever exalteth himself shall be abased; and he that *humbleth* himself shall be exalted (Luke 14:11).

> But ye shall not be so: but he that is greatest among you, let him be *as the younger;* and he that is chief, as he that doth *serve.* For whether is greater, he that sitteth at meat, or he that serveth? is not he that sitteth at meat? but I am among you as he that serveth (Luke 22:26-27).

> Ye call me Master and Lord: and ye say well; for so I am. If I then, your Lord and Master, have washed your feet; ye also ought to wash one another's feet (John 13:13-14).

As we said at the start of this book, not just any change will do. The only change that will ultimately be for our good and for God's glory begins with humility. God says, "Yea, all of you be subject one to another, and be *clothed with humility:* for God resisteth the proud, and giveth grace to the humble" (I Pet. 5:5).

Being "clothed with humility" is a concept that most of us very likely have never considered. We do not think of humility as a dominant characteristic of the contemporary "successful person." Today's athletes, entertainers, politicians, business people, and sadly, many church leaders are not known for their humility, but for their self-confident arrogance, their control over others, or their self-indulgent lifestyles.

Our aversion to the whole idea of humility is testimony of the poverty of our understanding of God's ways. For example, one time I asked a group of college students what had previously held them or their friends back from submitting to God. The responses all indicated that each one felt that if he humbled himself in this way, God would do something to "mess up" his life. When I asked for specifics, they answered with responses like the following:

> I felt that if I surrendered all to God, He would make me be poor the rest of my life. I would not be able to drive a nice car or live in a decent house, and I would have to wear outdated clothes.

> I was afraid that if I made the choice to give my life to God, He would make me confront my friends about their sinful lifestyles. I didn't want to lose the approval of my friends.

> I thought that if I let God run my life, He would make me marry some Christian fanatic whose zeal would always embarrass me or that He would not let me get married at all.

> Having to give up my sensual music and movies kept me from surrendering to Christ. I felt that He was determined to make my life miserable and that I wouldn't have any fun.

> I couldn't imagine what I would do if God were running my life. I thought it meant that I would do nothing but sit around reading the Bible all the time. I guess I feared most that He would call me into the ministry or to the mission field somewhere.

The fear that God would make life *miserable* is just the opposite of the truth. Stop and think about something for a moment. If God were really trying to find some way to "mess up" our lives, He would not need to wait until we finally surrendered to Him to go ahead with His plans for destruction. Since He is God, He could do it any time He wanted to. God doesn't need our permission to "mess up" our lives. In our wickedness, we believe that God is the biggest evil we could encounter and that it is *our* resistance to Him that keeps life from charging headlong into misery! What arrogance that is! What corruption within us it reveals!

Because we have not "glorified him . . . as God" (i.e., have not thought of Him as worthy of our praise) and have not been "thankful," we have become "vain in [our] imaginations, and [our] foolish heart [is] darkened" (Rom. 1:21). This kind of evil thinking has actually changed "the glory of the uncorruptible God into an image made like to corruptible man"

(Rom. 1:23). We actually make God look evil like man and make man look good like God. No wonder Proverbs warns us that "there is a way which seemeth right unto a man, but the end thereof are the ways of death" (Prov. 14:12).

HOW DOES GOD HUMBLE US?

Just as man's pride has many masks for its rebellion, so God has many ways of exposing a man's self-dependence. Our human limitations and our sinful pride must be exposed; we must be humbled to be changed. God doesn't humble every man in the same way. He has wrenches of many sizes in His toolbox to fix whatever problem He finds. Let's look briefly at four means God can use to humble us and to bring us to Himself in dependence.

He can send us a problem we can't handle to expose our helplessness.

In II Kings 5, we read of Naaman, a high-ranking military officer in Syria who had contracted leprosy, a horribly disfiguring and eventually fatal disease. Through the concern of an Israelite slave girl, he learns that Elisha, a prophet in Israel, can cure him of his disease. When he finally approaches Elisha's house, he does not find the welcome he expected for a man of his rank and station. Instead of personally greeting Naaman and showing him the courtesies of hospitality of the day, Elisha sends him a messenger who tells Naaman to go to the river Jordan and dip in its murky waters seven times.

Naaman is furious! He wants a change but on his *own* terms. He wants to choose how the message is delivered,[11] and he wants to choose the river. His own servants finally persuade him that if he had been asked to perform some great task to be healed, he would do it. Certainly he could do a small thing—at least try.

Naaman finally humbles himself and pursues change *God's way*. Isn't it interesting that the command stated he must dip in the water *seven*

---

[11] Naaman was infected with more than just leprosy. He also had the same arrogance we see today when people assert, "I don't mess with the little people; I go straight to the top." Naaman's initial refusal to listen to the "little people" (in this case, Elisha's servant) almost cost him his spiritual and physical well-being. The pride revealed in this philosophy is a bigger problem than is the problem that a man wants to take "to the top."

times! He had to persist in following God's plan even if it didn't seem to be working on the first dip, and the second, and the third. . . . His biggest need was not to be cured from leprosy but to be delivered from his desire to live life his *own way*.

God did not change just his skin, curing him from leprosy; God also changed his heart when he humbled himself. Notice Naaman's response after his healing: "And he returned to the man of God, he and all his company, and came, and stood before him: and he said, Behold, now I know that there is no God in all the earth, but in Israel" (II Kings 5:15).

Like Naaman, we often come to God with an agenda of our own choosing. We think we know best what changes should occur in our lives and how those changes should be brought about. We believe that the blessings of life will be ours if we can just control the circumstances and people in our lives. The tragedy of this is that the only time we bring God into the picture is when we ask Him to help us make life work according to our *own way*. The world around us continually tempts us to think that somehow we have the ability within ourselves to make life work. God mercifully, however, often gives us more than we can handle on our own, to unravel our self-confidence when we have been used to leaning to our *own understanding* (Prov. 3:5). He has made us dependent by design and must humble us, as He did Naaman. There can be no biblical change without it.

He can give us a command we won't obey to expose our self-centeredness.

Another method of teaching humility is seen clearly in the account of Israel's prophet Jonah. Second Kings 14:25 tells us that Jonah had announced to King Jeroboam II that God was going to allow Israel to regain the coastal country they had lost to their enemies. Jonah enjoyed his popularity as a prophet who delivered the good news of God's deliverance. God knew the stubbornness of Jonah's heart, however, and set out to expose it. Perhaps a conversation like the following went on between Jonah and God. We could title this scenario "A Rebel Prophet and a Blubber Sticker."

"Jonah, I see you enjoy delivering messages of redemption to people."

"Oh yes, Lord! You know how much I love to tell people about Your great deliverance on their behalf. That last assignment to the king about regaining the coastal country was a sheer delight. I love being Your messenger!"

"Good, Jonah, because I have a special message of redemption I want you to deliver to the Ninevites. I want to offer them salvation."

"But, God, don't you know how brutal they are? Every group of people on earth hates them. They are barbaric! Why, when they bring their captives home from battle, they dismember them and make piles of their body parts outside their city gates just to show everybody that 'Ninevites rule!' and that 'Nobody messes with a Ninevite!' Besides, they might do the same thing to me. They are awful people, Lord. They really deserve Your judgment. Besides, if I become an ambassador of good will to them, what will my fellow Israelites say? They will think I have betrayed them! I can't do this, God—this is asking too much!"

"I have spoken, Jonah. Your next assignment is in Nineveh."

Although this dialogue is fictitious, it captures the dynamics of Jonah's situation. God is commanding the prophet to demonstrate love for Him by obeying His command. God is also commanding the prophet to demonstrate love for his neighbor by doing what his neighbor needs most. Jonah refuses, exposing his rebel heart. Rather than face his assignment and face his rebel heart, Jonah runs.

Nineveh is due east of Palestine. Jonah gets on a ship headed for Tarshish, which is due west of Palestine. Tarshish is on the coast of Spain, which is the country farthest west in the known world. For all Jonah knew, the world dropped off on the other side of Tarshish.

Of course, it isn't long before God sends a great wind and shakes up his boat. The mariners finally throw him overboard. God sends a great fish with a blubber sticker on its side that reads, "Have You Hugged a Ninevite Today?" Jonah is not into hugging Ninevites. He wants them damned; he does not want them delivered. After three days and nights in the fish's belly, Jonah surrenders to go to Nineveh, and the fish spits him up on the shore.

Jonah makes the five-hundred-mile journey from Palestine to Nineveh and delivers God's message of judgment and redemption. To his chagrin, the people repent—from the king down to the most humble beggar. Jonah is outraged! God has extended mercy to this city of barbarians who had terrorized the nations around them with their brutality.

Jonah throws a pity party for himself under a makeshift shelter of branches, perhaps to wait out the forty days God had given the city to repent.[12] God mercifully provides a large gourd whose speedy growth entertains the moping prophet and whose shade later shields him from the hot Assyrian sun. In one day, however, God destroys the gourd with a worm. Jonah, still pouting, fusses at God for destroying plants. He seizes upon this seemingly just concern for the local ecology as a pretext to vent his anger against God, who will not allow his hatred for the Ninevites to go unchallenged. God, however, is silent and increases the heat until Jonah is about to faint from exposure. The prophet vents his anger at God again and justifies his response to the way this is all turning out. Then God deftly drives home the point that Jonah is obviously more concerned about plants than he is about people and thus exposes the self-righteous pride of the prophet's heart.

Sometimes people ask whether Jonah ever got right with God. I believe Jonah himself wrote this account of his rebellion against God. If that is true, the fact that God used him to write an inspired book and the fact that Jonah was willing to reveal to the world his personal struggle with God are perhaps enough testimony to conclude that he did, indeed, finally humble himself. God often gives us commands that our rebel heart refuses to obey. We insist on going our *own way*. God has made us dependent by design and must humble us, as He did Jonah. There can be no biblical change without it.

He can arrange an outcome we can't control to expose our sinfulness.

It was shocking news to King David when he learned that his adultery with his neighbor's wife, Bathsheba, had resulted in her pregnancy.[13] Her husband had been out of town for months on state business, so it would be obvious the baby was not his. David hadn't counted on this kind of exposure. Everyone thought he was so godly—after all, he had written so many psalms used in the worship of Israel's God. Now everyone would know the wickedness of his secret life. He had to do something! He murdered Bathsheba's husband and waited. But God was determined to expose David. When He did, David was humbled. Sin is pretty heady

---

[12] See Jonah 3-4.
[13] The account is in II Samuel 11-12.

stuff. A man can start thinking that he is invincible, that he can control the outcome of his actions, that he can get away with evil.

God still exposes sin today. Take Jeremy and Chris, for example. They had grown up together. Even though their parents attended different churches, they saw much of each other since they were neighbors and attended the same Christian high school. When Jeremy's parents allowed him to have a car his senior year, they started driving to school together. On the way to school, Jeremy would turn on the radio to a local rock station. Soon both boys were hooked. Their "free spirits" manifested themselves in more frequent cheating at school and eventually in shoplifting in town. The stealing started when they wanted the latest hits but didn't want to be seen buying rock music. The boys became increasingly "independent" and made life rough for their families and their school.

Jeremy was the more daring of the two and could usually talk Chris into anything. They finished high school and anticipated a summer of "good times." Chris's family took an early vacation in June to their church's family camp. Chris detested the thought of it but consoled himself that he might meet some new girls. By Tuesday evening something happened that neither Chris nor Jeremy had counted on. Chris came under deep conviction for his rebellion and asked to talk with one of the counselors after the evening service. Wednesday morning, he could hardly believe what he had done—it was so unlike him. He had repented of his sin to God, had told his parents everything, and now was trying to work out how he would tell Jeremy. Much of his restitution for cheating and stealing that had to be handled when he got home involved Jeremy as well; Jeremy had to be brought into the picture.

To say that Jeremy was upset was an understatement! He was humiliated and outraged. They had always been so careful so that they would never be caught. Unfortunately, he refused to go with Chris to talk with the principal about the cheating, and he refused to go with Chris to the stores where they had shoplifted to make restitution. His pride had been wounded—big time! He quit going to church and within weeks moved out of the house. He never wanted to talk to Chris again.

Both boys faced an outcome they hadn't counted on. Chris never once thought that God would be able to bring him to his knees with conviction. But his sinfulness was exposed to his own conscience at family camp, and he was humbled. Jeremy, as well, had not anticipated anything like this. He had not counted on God's reaching the heart of his friend. He was exposed as well but refused to repent. God has made us dependent by design and must humble us, as He did Chris and King David. There can be no biblical change without it.

He can show us a God we can't comprehend to expose our finiteness.

A certain man was the envy of every rancher in his part of Kansas. His cattle stock was some of the finest in the country, and his crops never failed to bring in bumper yields. Through the years he had become the wealthiest and most respected rancher in the area. Though a man of means, he never thought of himself as superior or asserted himself as such to his neighbors. In fact, because of his godliness, it was not unusual for him to spend an entire evening with a fellow rancher who needed personal advice about his family or who needed direction about a ranching decision. Then things changed!

In one evening, a group of professional rustlers stole his entire stock in one section of the ranch, and a serious electrical storm started a fire on another part of the ranch, destroying the rest of his herd contained in the buildings. As if that weren't enough, the same electrical storm spawned a tornado that hit his oldest son's house, killing all the rancher's children, who had gathered there for a birthday celebration. The rancher and his wife had been delayed coming to the party, or they would have been killed too.

The account you just read is fictional but is based upon the real-life experience of the Bible character Job. He too was known for his wisdom and wealth (Job 1:1-3). He too lost all at once everything he had (1:13-19). Shortly after his calamities, he also lost his health (2:1-10). Yet not until days later did he begin to question God and demand an explanation (23:1-17). He initially responded with unshakable faith in God. He said at the end of chapter 1, "Naked came I out of my mother's womb, and naked shall I return thither: the Lord gave, and the Lord hath taken away; blessed be the name of the Lord."

In chapter 3, Job begins to question why he was born, and in chapter 23, Job longs for an audience with God to plead his case and to discover why he has endured this misery. Job's friends are little comfort to him. Job is not being tried because of his sin, as his friends suppose. His spiritual integrity is being tested by Satan—does he serve God for the person gain he gets from God?

When enduring great pain, we, like Job, can begin to feel justified in our complaints against God and demand an explanation. We feel quite certain that God is entirely wrong in allowing this trouble to come our way. *No attribute of God is more emphasized in Scripture than His loving care for His people. Yet no quality of God is doubted more than His love when we are under the burden of a difficult trial.* We even begin to feel that if we were running things, we would not make the mistake of letting people suffer like this.

God answers Job, not with an explanation of the battle going on between Him and Satan, but with a revelation in chapters 38-41 of the awesome power of the Almighty. God was very strong in His reply to Job. In essence, He said to Job, "Job, you need to get back in your place. If you think you are so smart and know better how to run this world, let's see how you do on a little quiz about how My world is governed. Where were you when I laid the foundations of the earth? Tell me—if you have so much understanding. Have you ever walked on the bottom of the ocean, Job, and explored its depths? Have you ever made the sun rise in the morning? Do you know where I keep the treasuries of the ice and of the snow? Do you know how the stork brings forth her young in the right season?"

For four chapters God questions Job about the universe around him, periodically asking him how he is doing on the quiz. When presented with the awesome power and wisdom of God in the creation around him, Job takes the only action an honest man could do—he humbles himself. Job respectfully replies, "I know that thou canst do every thing, and that no thought can be withholden from thee. Who is he that hideth counsel without knowledge? therefore have I uttered that I understood not; things too wonderful for me, which I knew not. . . . I have heard of thee by the hearing of the ear: but now mine eye seeth thee. Wherefore I abhor myself, and repent in dust and ashes" (Job 42:2-6).

Job was faced not just with circumstances he couldn't understand but with a God he could not comprehend. God exposed Job's finiteness. As a creature, he could never understand the Almighty. In view of the awesome power and wisdom of His God, however, he could—and must—trust Him. No other response is worthy of God. The Almighty has made no mistake and deserves no rebuke. The creature cannot make demands of the Creator without revealing his arrogance. God has made us dependent by design, and Job learned that the only proper response during the puzzling times of life is humility. There can be no biblical change without it.

WHAT IS YOUR NEXT STEP?

Is God dealing with your life in one of these ways? Is He trying to expose your lack of humility in the way you handle life? The first step back to God is repentance for going your *own way*. Note Isaiah's words when he addressed God's people in Isaiah 55:6-7: "Seek ye the Lord while he may be found, call ye upon him while he is near: Let the wicked forsake *his way,* and the unrighteous man his thoughts: and let him return unto *the Lord,* and he will have mercy upon him; and to our God, for he will abundantly pardon."

Here is a people who once followed God's ways. They had abandoned Him, and God is pleading with them to "return." They had once known His fellowship but had become "wicked" and "unrighteous" men by pursuing their *own* ways and following their *own* thoughts. What about you? Do you need to "return" to the Lord? Biblical change starts with "putting off [the ways of] the old man." The first step toward "putting off" is repentance for "putting on" something God forbids—the garment of self-rule and self-sufficiency instead of being "clothed with humility." That is a great offense. It usurps control from God and replaces *His* ways with yours.

In light of the patient "mercies of God" toward you, is it not time for you to surrender yourself as a "living sacrifice" (Rom. 12:1)? Paul says it is "your reasonable service"—it is the least you can do.

As we have seen, this kind of humility—man taking his proper place before God—is the hallmark of the dependent creature. Someone has said, "There is a God in heaven, and you are not Him." Repenting of our self-rule, putting God in His proper place in our heart, and getting in line under His sovereignty are all aspects of the beginning of biblical change *and the chief requirements for usefulness to God.* Remember the following principle:

> **A man's potential for God lies not in his *ability,* nor in his *opportunity,* but in his *humility* before God.**

God is not impressed with our abilities; they came from Him. He is not impressed with our opportunities; they are gifts from Him as well. He is impressed only with our humility; it testifies of our sense of dependency.

TAKE TIME TO REFLECT

1. What application does the parable about the bike have for your dependence upon God?

2. How would you define humility from what you learned in this chapter?

3. Do you have any areas of your life you are asking God to change, but, like Naaman, you think God ought to be bringing about the change in a way different from the way He is apparently doing it? Is He asking you to humble yourself in some way, and are you insisting that the change come about some other way? If so, describe what is happening.

4. Jonah apparently felt he was doing pretty well as God's official prophet in Israel—until God exposed his self-centeredness by giving Jonah a command he refused to obey. Is God perhaps doing the same for you at this time? Are there any "Ninevites" in your life (i.e., people who are hard to love) whom God is commanding you to love? Are there ministries in your church that you are avoiding (nursery, choir, Sunday school teaching, etc.) because they would involve working with certain children, teens, or adults who are hard to love?

A WORD TO DISCIPLE-MAKERS

Stop the Leaks

Pouring more automotive oil into an engine block with leaky seals is only a temporary fix. The engine will run well for several hundred miles. But unless the leaks are stopped, the oil will seep out, the oil pressure indicator will light up on the dash, and the engine will overheat. The driver must plan for another stop to add oil. He will have to plan for regular "pit stops" until he replaces the engine seals and stops the leak.

If you have to continually cover the same ground with a teen or adult you are discipling as you repeat *exactly* the same principles you covered a few days ago and there never seems to be any real progress between meetings, perhaps nothing has changed in his God-ward orientation. He has not humbled himself under his Creator-Master. He is returning for his "oil" to be refilled every time the engine overheats too much for him, but he has never stopped the leaks. Both of you will grow increasingly discouraged (perhaps even irritated) that very little progress is taking place. Here's how God Himself described the phenomenon:

> Now therefore thus saith the Lord of hosts; Consider your ways. Ye have sown much, and bring in little; ye eat, but ye have not enough; ye drink, but ye are not filled with drink; ye clothe you, but there is none warm; and he that earneth wages earneth wages to put it into a bag with holes. Thus saith the Lord of hosts; Consider your ways. Go up to the mountain, and bring wood, and build the house; and I will take pleasure in it, and I will be glorified, saith the Lord (Hag. 1:5-8).

The children of Israel had abandoned their relationship with the Lord. They had built nice homes for themselves but had left the temple in ill-repair after their enemies had destroyed it. When challenged by the prophets about their neglect of the Lord's house, they replied, "The time is not come, the time that the Lord's house should be built" (1:2). They kept procrastinating the most important factor in all of life—their relationship with their God. God very firmly scolds them in verse 4 and says, "Is it time for you, O ye, to dwell in your cieled[14] houses, and this house lie waste?" God says, "Oh! You don't have time to build My house, do you? You seem to find time to build whatever you wish for yourself!" He appeals to them to stop and consider their ways and tells them why their lives are so empty even when they try so hard. He says,

> Ye looked for much, and, lo, it came to little; and when ye brought it home, I did blow upon it. Why? saith the Lord of hosts. Because of mine house that is waste, and ye run every man unto his own house. Therefore the heaven over you is stayed from dew, and the earth is stayed from her fruit. . . . I smote you with blasting and with mildew and with hail in all the labours of your hands; *yet ye turned not to me*, saith the Lord (Hag. 1:9-10; 2:17).

God's chastening actions were designed to bring His people back to fellowship with Him. God goes to great lengths to address the heart issues

---

[14] paneled, covered.

of His people. He is not satisfied with leaving the relationship with Him unreconciled. Don't be satisfied with any change you see if it is obvious that there has been no real reconciliation with and submission to God. There can be no biblical change without humility before God.

Don't Be Sidetracked

A helpful question to ask those you try to help is "What is going on between you and God?" If they look very puzzled at your question, ask them to tell you about their closest friend. What do they do together? How long have they known each other? What interests do they share? What are the likes and dislikes of their friend? Have they ever been "at odds" with their friend? If so, what caused the rift? How did they get it resolved? Why do they like spending time with their friend? These kinds of questions show them that they, indeed, know how to maintain and evaluate a relationship with another person. They can evaluate their relationship with God as well.

When holding a teen or adult accountable for his spiritual growth, don't be sidetracked by statements such as, "I'm really different now; I have done a lot of growing up in the past few months. I realized after all the things that happened to me that I can't be so stubborn. I have to submit to Mom and Dad or I just end up hurting everybody." Statements like this do reflect that the person has done some evaluating, and has, perhaps, even started making some less destructive choices for his life. Remember, however, *unless there has been a reconciliation with his Creator, he is still at war with God.* A spouse or a teen who has decided to change his behavior without changing his fundamental orientation to God may experience a "better life" in many ways (e.g., he doesn't hurt as many people, he has more friends, he is more productive and responsible), but *he still is not reconciled to God,* and a humbling is probably just around the corner. When it comes, he may be greatly disillusioned. He will conclude that he has tried doing right but that it "doesn't work" either.

CHAPTER FIVE

MORTIFYING YOUR FLESH

For if ye live after the flesh, ye shall die: but if ye through the Spirit do mortify the deeds of the body, ye shall live.
Romans 8:13

My father, my two brothers, and I were all avid motorcyclists as I was growing up. We rebuilt, tuned, and customized our own bikes. My brother Denny maintained his interest in motorcycles and even became a world-class motorcycle designer and restorer. I could not begin to count the number of bikes that "lived" in our garage through my growing-up years. Although the combined miles traveled by the four of us would be quite high, I was the only one to have a serious accident.

On the day of my accident I was cruising along at a modest speed on a country two-lane highway near our home. A South Dakota tornado had devastated the area. My passenger, Randy, and I were looking over the damage. My attention was drawn to a demolished farm implement dealership on the left side of the road. I did not notice the pickup that had stopped in my lane just yards ahead of me. The driver was waiting for a break in traffic in the oncoming lane so that he could turn in at the dealership. I noticed him just a split second before I slammed into his tailgate going thirty miles per hour!

I woke up a few minutes later with a badly mangled bike, multiple fractures to my right wrist, and damage to my neck. I had flipped over into the pickup bed and landed on the back of my head. Had I not been wearing a helmet—a requirement of Dad's—I would have been dead. Randy, of course, followed me into the pickup bed and landed on top of me. He walked away without a scratch.

MORTIFYING A MOTORCYCLE

Had I seen the pickup a few seconds earlier, I probably could have avoided the accident. Stopping a motorcycle involves combining three actions in various ways, depending upon the circumstances:

1. Let up on the throttle to cut down on the amount of fuel to the engine.
2. Apply the brakes to reduce forward motion.
3. Disengage the clutch to prohibit the engine's power from driving the rear wheel.

Had I had enough time to initiate these actions at the time of my accident, I would have "killed" the force of the engine that was propelling me to destruction. I would have been able to stop all forward motion and come to a resting stop a few feet behind the pickup. The engine would have been still idling, but because of the combination of actions listed above, all of its ability to ruin me would have been "killed." If I were using Elizabethan terms, like those we find in the King James Version of the Bible, I could say that I had "mortified my motorcycle" or more specifically, "mortified my motorcycle's forward motion."

Today we use the word "mortify" only to indicate a strong measure of embarrassment. We might say, "When Joe told that story about me, I was mortified. I could have died!" The apostle Paul uses the word translated "mortify," however, to indicate a process of "deadening" the power of the flesh. Literally he meant that we are to "drain the life out of" the flesh through the Holy Spirit's assistance. Notice how Paul uses the word "mortify" in the following two verses:

> For if ye live after the flesh, ye shall die: but if ye through the Spirit do *mortify* the deeds of the body, ye shall live (Rom. 8:13).

> If ye then be risen with Christ, seek those things which are above, where Christ sitteth on the right hand of God. Set your affection on things above, not on things on the earth. For ye are dead, and your life is hid with Christ in God. When Christ, who is our life, shall appear, then shall ye also appear with him in glory. *Mortify* therefore your members which are upon the earth (Col. 3:1-5).

John Owen states,

> God has designed this mortification of the indwelling sin that remains in our mortal bodies in order to eliminate the life and power of the flesh. . . . What then is mortification? What does it mean to mortify

sin? . . . Every lust is a depraved habit or disposition that continually inclines the heart toward evil. Unmortified, it is what is described in Genesis 6:5 "Every imagination of the thoughts of [man's] heart was only evil continually." The only reason why an unregenerate man is not under the perpetual pursuit of some lust is because he is distracted by so many more of them. But the general bent is well recognized, for it is the disposition toward self-pleasing. Men are said to have their hearts set upon evil to make "provisions for the flesh" (Romans 13:14). Now the primary task of mortification is to weaken this habit of sin so that its power to express itself—in violence, frequency, tumult, provocation, and unrest—is quelled.

Mortification robs sin of its debilitating, inharmonious, and emotionally distracting influences. Without mortification, sin darkens the mind, while the lusts of the flesh grow like weeds. Mortification is the soul's vigorous opposition to the fruitless self-life.[1]

A derivative of the word "mortify" is also used in Hebrews 11:12 when it speaks of the physical impossibility of Abraham's gendering a son at the age of one hundred. The writer of Hebrews commented that Abraham's body was "as good as dead"—it was "mortified." It was weakened to the extent that it had no more power. Its potency was killed by age. That is the flavor of this word "mortify."

We need to look more closely at the word "flesh" as well. The word "flesh" refers to the indwelling sin principle that remains in a believer after he is saved, although its absolute power over him is broken—as we shall see later in this chapter. In Romans 8:13 Paul seems to equate "flesh" with "deeds of the body," implying that "flesh" could mean both the *source of evil*—indwelling sin—and the *manifestation of evil*—deeds of the body.

Perhaps his meaning is much the same as ours might be if we saw one of our children about to strike a sibling. We might say to our spouse—who is standing near the children— "Honey, stop Johnny!" Do we mean stop the *boy* or stop his *actions?* We mean *both* because they are inextricably linked in practice.

It is in this broader, practical sense that I use the word "flesh" in this book. I believe that is the way Paul uses it in his epistles. When we

---

[1] Owen, *Sin,* 154-59.

"mortify" the "deeds of the body"—kill their action by dealing with the indwelling sin that motivates them—we have mortified the "flesh" or killed its *influence*—not its *existence*—on us at that moment.

"Mortify" is not the only biblical term that shows the proper response to the flesh. There are several parallel designations for indwelling sin and several parallel terms that describe various aspects of the biblical response to it. Take a moment to look them over.

1. The *flesh*—and its resulting deeds—must be *mortified* (Rom. 8:13; Col. 3:5).

2. *Self* and its "ungodly lusts" must be *denied* (Luke 9:23; Titus 2:12).

3. The deeds of the *old man* must be *put off* (Eph. 4:22; Col. 3:9).

4. The indwelling sin nature must not be served (Rom. 6:6, 12-13, 16-19).

The title of this chapter could have come from any of the above statements and have meant the same. Instead of "Mortifying Your Flesh," the title could have been "Denying Self," "Putting Off the Deeds of the Old Man," or "Refusing to Serve Sin." The question before us is "How do I mortify the flesh?" If we answer that question, we really address all of the above statements. Fortunately, God has given us much help in this matter. The most detailed instruction on this issue is given to us in Romans 6, so it is to that chapter we will turn next.

Before we actually discuss the chapter's details, however, I would encourage you to do two things. First, when you finish this paragraph, stop reading this book, pick up your Bible, and read the entire chapter of Romans 6. Notice especially the summary of the chapter in verse 22. Secondly, take some time to identify the battles you are facing right now. Perhaps write them down. You need to have specific struggles of the flesh in mind when you go through this chapter. Note especially those battles that seem persistent or deeply entrenched. As David did, ask God to search you to see if there is any "wicked way" in you (Ps. 139:23-24). Or if you are discipling someone else, you may want to keep their "besetting" sins in mind as you study this chapter so that you will know how it applies to their struggles. The list could include sins such as worry, deception, lack of endurance, destructive bodily habits (such as drugs, drinking, anorexia, bulimia, or overeating), anger, a critical spirit, discontent, profanity and other sins of the tongue, bitterness, laziness, rebellion to authorities in your life, greed and materialism, gambling, or immoral behavior (such as lustful fantasies, pornography, adultery, homosexuality, or incest), and so forth. Of course, the list of possibilities is almost endless. The main point to keep in mind is that *none* of these sinful attitudes and activities are outside the scope of what is being addressed in Romans 6, no matter how strong their pull or how long-standing their practice. With that in mind, read Romans 6, make your list, and then continue with the rest of this chapter.

WE HAVE TO *KNOW* SOME THINGS

To stop my motorcycle I need to know some things. Knowing how to apply the brakes is helpful, but braking is only a part of the stopping process. There are other facts I need to know—such as how to disengage the engine using the clutch and how to cut the fuel to the engine to slow it down. I could be in big trouble if I don't *know* these things or if I don't *apply* them.

Romans 6 deals with an important doctrine of the Christian walk.[2] Bible teachers have called this doctrine by various names, the most common being our union with Christ, our identification with Christ, or our

---

[2] The word "doctrine" simply means "teaching." Many people today minimize doctrine, saying that it is confusing and irrelevant. This growing attitude shouldn't surprise us. Paul said in II Timothy that in the days just before the Lord's return, there will be a population who "will not endure [put up with; listen willingly to] sound doctrine" (4:3). Instead they will run to teachers whose message is more in line with their own desires. The result will be that they will be turned to "fables"—make-believe and skewed views of reality (4:4). Deception is the guaranteed fate of those who do not know doctrine, particularly as we approach the end times. Paul warns that "evil men and seducers shall wax worse and worse, deceiving, and being deceived" (3:13). The only antidote for deception is doctrine taught from the God-inspired book—the Bible (3:16). Paul's admonition is to "preach the word" and to use the teachings of Scripture, the "doctrine," to "reprove, rebuke, [and] exhort with all longsuffering" (4:2).

People today also protest that doctrine is divisive. The apostle John, often called the Apostle of Love, told us that Christians can have unity with only one kind of person—the one who has his doctrine right about Jesus Christ (II John 7-11). There are certain truths (i.e., doctrines) about Jesus Christ that are nonnegotiable. He is God. He came to earth as man and lived a perfect life. He died for the sins of the world. He was buried and rose again the third day. He is the *only* way of salvation. Anybody who teaches that there are many ways to heaven and that there is a little truth in all religions "abideth not in the doctrine of Christ," is not to be received into your fellowship, and is not to be encouraged in any way. It is important for us to understand that you cannot believe a lie and expect things to turn out right for you. Our God is a God of truth, and He calls His truth "doctrine." We must know it and apply it.

co-crucifixion and co-resurrection with Christ. Please understand that trying to resist the flesh without knowing and applying this basic doctrine is like trying to stop a speeding motorcycle by putting on the brakes while leaving the clutch engaged and the engine running full throttle. Many believers try to do just that. They try to resist the force of indwelling sin by sheer willpower and self-discipline.

The motorcycle brakes eventually overheat and give out. The power of the engine must be disconnected from the wheel assembly. Its connection must be "broken" so that it no longer influences the motorcycle's forward motion to destruction. I realize that the motorcycle illustration has its limitations, as do all illustrations. (Technically, you can slow a motorcycle down faster by leaving it in gear while cutting the throttle. Other discrepancies abound as well if you take the illustration too far.) I am using it here to show a motorcycle's destructive effects if the rider does not know how to "mortify" it.

In a similar fashion, Christ has made a way that the pull of indwelling sin can be broken so that it does not have to affect the way we live. Before our salvation, we had no choice but to obey the sinful pulls within. It was as if we were riding a motorcycle without a clutch. The engine was always running, and the wheels were always turning. There was no way to disconnect the engine. The back wheel was a "slave" to the engine. It had to turn when the engine turned.

Romans 6 teaches us, however, that because of Christ's death and Resurrection, we have been "made free from sin" (6:22). We no longer *have* to obey its pull to go our *own way*. How is that possible? Follow Paul's teaching here carefully because this is an especially important doctrine in breaking the power of sin in your life.

Romans 6:3-4 says, "Know ye not, that so many of us as were baptized into Jesus Christ were baptized into *his* death? Therefore we are buried with him by baptism into death: that like as Christ was raised up from the dead by the glory of the Father, even so we also should walk in newness of life." "Baptism" here is not referring to the church ordinance of water baptism. That is our public testimony of new life *after* our salvation. Rather, it is referring to what the Holy Spirit does for us *at the moment* of our salvation. The word "baptism" means to "place into" or "immerse." Paul says here that we are "immersed" or included in all the activities of Christ's death, burial, and Resurrection. The actual details of how that takes place will be a mystery until we reach heaven. The implications now for us as believers, however, are staggering. We are recipients of every benefit of His death, burial, and Resurrection. He considers it as having happened to us—and wants us to consider it the same way.[3]

This means that when He died, *we* died. When He was buried, *we* were buried. When He rose from the dead, *we* were raised to "walk in newness of life" (6:4). Verse 6 says, "*Knowing* this [remember, Paul wants us to know something], that our old man is crucified with him, that the body of sin might be destroyed [its absolute power killed], that henceforth we should not serve sin."

Before our identification with Christ in this way, we, in these earthly bodies, were *required* to serve the flesh. If our sinful bent was better served by lusting, we lusted. If it was better served by lying, we lied. We were truly the "servants of sin" (6:20). Paul tells us, however, that the control of that indwelling sin over us has been destroyed or "nullified." Our flesh itself is not destroyed in our co-crucifixion with Christ, but just as a dead corpse is powerless to respond to anyone's will, so our flesh's absolute power over us has been broken. "For he that is dead is freed from sin" (6:7).

During the first year of our marriage, I worked in a funeral home. I assisted the drivers as they picked up the bodies from the morgue or from a nursing home and then helped later with the family visitation times. The loved ones of the deceased—most of whom were not believers—despaired because the deceased no longer responded to them. No matter how much they cried and grieved, he would not speak to them, hold their hands, or try to comfort them in any way—he was dead! His power to respond was destroyed.

This is the picture Paul wants us to have in Romans 6—dead people don't respond! We no longer have to respond to the pull of the flesh within; we now have a choice! We are free from sin's absolute rule—its "dominion." We are now free to respond to the Holy Spirit who lives in

---

[3] The doctrinal teaching of Romans 6 is so important to resisting the sin nature that I have included in Appendix B the entire text of an article by Michael Barrett entitled "Union with Christ: The Ground of Sanctification." Take time to carefully and prayerfully study it to understand the ramifications of Paul's teaching on "being made free from sin" (6:22).

us. We shall not only "live with him" (6:8) in heaven later, but we can experience a "newness of life" now (6:4).

To illustrate this further, let's say that you have been renting a home from a man named Mr. Brown. On the first of every month he comes to your door to collect the rent. This month Mr. Brown sold the home to Mr. Smith. To your surprise, when the rent is due next month, Mr. Brown shows up at your door again to collect the rent. In months past you were *required* to pay Mr. Brown. You were under his "power." When he sold the house, however, his power to collect the rent was broken. You can pay him if you want, but you don't have to. You are now required to pay the new landlord, Mr. Smith.

In the same way, we are no longer required to obey the flesh. "For [indwelling] sin shall not have dominion [control] over you"(6:14). The flesh's power to demand your obedience has been broken. You can obey it if you want to, but your life is under new management. You are no longer under the power of sin. A new "landlord" has taken over. A new set of requirements from a new Lord is in place—the law of God (7:25). You are a servant to a new master.

Paul says, "This is something you need to *know!*" Resisting the indwelling power of sin starts here. As I mentioned earlier, you cannot stop a motorcycle by merely applying the brakes. Your brakes of self-discipline will give out. The strain will be too much. Your endurance will eventually give out, and you will crash anyway. The power of the engine must be broken. It must be disengaged from the rear wheel. You have to *know* this if you are going to "mortify your motorcycle"—kill its forward motion toward destruction.

WE HAVE TO *RECKON* SOME THINGS

Paul finishes telling us the facts we need to know about our union with Christ and then begins explaining to us the implications of those facts in Romans 6:11. He says, "Likewise reckon ye also yourselves to be dead indeed unto sin, but alive unto God through Jesus Christ our Lord." Paul is saying, "God knows you have been freed from the requirements to obey indwelling sin. Now *you* need to take it personally and quit living as if you *had* to obey it; start living unto God."

We need to understand that if we pay Mr. Brown, we choose to do so. We may have grown used to the previous landlord and his ways. We may have felt the rent was too much at times and that his demands were unpleasant, but we were bound by law to pay him. The *fact*, however, is that our house is under new management. We must now *reckon* that to be true. "Reckon" here means to "consider" it to be true for us.

We "reckon" things every day. When we drive along the highway, we see a speed limit sign that says "55 miles per hour." We are expected to "reckon" or consider that sign to be binding for us. We are to apply it to our lives. We are to believe that it is an accurate statement of the government's expectations on that highway and that it applies to us. That is an act of *faith*. If we don't believe the reality of the law's existence and our accountability to it, we will be duly reminded of that with a speeding ticket. We will be held accountable. Paul says, "God reckons it to be true, and you *likewise* need to reckon yourself to be dead indeed unto sin." You do not have to obey its urges and pulls.

But I Don't Feel Like It!

You may protest, however, "I don't feel free. When those sinful impulses arise in my heart, I feel as though I have to obey!" You are going to have to take it by faith then that these facts are true no matter how you feel. It may *feel* as though you *have* to give in, but you need to *know* better because God said otherwise to "reckon [yourself] to be dead *indeed* unto sin" (6:11).

Many people fail right here. They make decisions about what they will or will not do based upon how they *feel* at the moment—not by the *facts* of what God has said is reality. They don't "reckon" things to be true because God said they were true. They "reckon" a thing to be true only if it feels to them as though it might be true. The result of this kind of living is instability. They are up and down, moody, and unpredictable.

This is the kind of man James describes as a double-minded man. He is "minding" the flesh and his feelings one moment and then "minding" God and His truth the next. James says he is "like a wave of the sea driven with the wind and tossed" (1:6) and warns, "let not that man think he shall receive any thing of the Lord. A double minded man is unstable in all his ways" (1:7-8).

You cannot afford to let your ways be determined by the skewed view of reality that your flesh and its feelings will give you. Paul said that before any of us were saved we "had our conversation [lifestyle] in times past in the lusts of our flesh, fulfilling the desires of the flesh and of the mind" (Eph. 2:3). That was the only way we could live. We no longer have to fulfill those desires—those *feelings* of our flesh and of our mind. Don't give in to *feelings* that are generated by fleshly, selfish thinking. They will not give you an accurate picture of reality. They will keep you trapped in a fantasy world of make-believe. You must "reckon" yourselves "dead indeed unto sin."

Not only must we *know* some things that are facts about our identification with Christ in His death, burial, and Resurrection and *reckon* those things to be true for us, but as Paul tells us, we must also *yield* to the right master as a result of what we know and reckon. Let's look at what it means to "yield [ourselves] unto God" (Rom. 6:13).

WE HAVE TO *YIELD* SOME THINGS

You might again find yourself at this point protesting and saying, "I'm just not good at yielding. That comes hard for me. I'm not sure I know how to yield." Paul reminds us, however, that we are all experts at "yielding." We have done it for years—only, to the wrong master. We are skilled at yielding our bodily "members as instruments [weapons] of unrighteousness unto sin" (6:13). We therefore know what it is like to be "servants of sin" (6:17). The result of this yielding to sin is the "fruit . . . whereof ye are now ashamed" and whose "end . . . is death" (6:21).

After Paul reminds us that we have had much practice yielding to a master, he says, "As ye have yielded your members servants to uncleanness and to iniquity unto iniquity [from one level of sin to the next]; even so now yield your members servants to righteousness unto holiness" (6:19). The result will be "fruit unto holiness, and the end everlasting life" (6:22).

So we are now at a point of decision about how we will respond to whatever pull the flesh has on us at the moment. Are we going to deny God—say no to Him—or deny self? Are we going to mortify the flesh or indulge the flesh? Are we going to walk after the flesh or walk after the Spirit? Are we going to obey God or obey indwelling sin? The choice to obey God (yielding) is a twofold responsibility to resist obeying the flesh and to stop feeding it. Let's look at these two responses.

Don't Obey the Flesh!

We would like to think that in this or that sin, we have been *defeated*. The humbling reality is that we have been *disobedient*. The battle can be expressed as simply as this:

Just two choices on the shelf—pleasing God or pleasing self.[4]

The Christian life is not an easy life to live because of this warring sinfulness that dwells within us. Though it isn't easy, it isn't complicated. Complications are usually the natural consequences of going our *own way*. But even at that, the way out of those complications is always a series of *simple* choices: "In this thing or that thing before me, am I going to please God or please myself?"[5]

Paul defined it as *obeying*. He says, "Know ye not, that to whom ye yield yourselves servants to obey, his servants ye are to whom ye obey; whether of sin unto death, or of obedience unto righteousness? But God be thanked, that ye *were* the servants of sin, but *ye have obeyed* from the heart that form of doctrine which was delivered you" (6:16-17).

Don't miss the point here. Paul does not prescribe some long, convoluted series of therapy steps. He says, "You got yourself into this mess by obeying your flesh and denying God, and the only way out is to start denying the flesh and obeying God." Paul is clear—the flesh *can* be denied, and it *must* be denied!

A Lesson from Kirk

Kirk was a twenty-five-year-old shipping clerk for a local truck line. He came for help about his continual tardiness to work in the mornings. He was consistently thirty minutes late. His boss appreciated the high level of competence and commitment Kirk demonstrated on the job but was growing increasingly frustrated by Kirk's late arrivals. Kirk had been given a verbal job warning and knew he must take action about his habitual failure in this area.

---

[4] Ken Collier, THE WILDS Christian Association. Used by permission.

[5] See the chart God's Love Versus Self-Love in Appendix A for examples of both fleshly self-serving living and godly self-denying living.

Kirk told me that his alarm was set each morning for half past six, that he activated the alarm every night, and that it wakened him every morning. He said that he had even placed the alarm on the dresser across the room so that he would have to get out of bed and walk across the room to turn off the alarm.

Kirk revealed with great embarrassment, however, that once he had turned off the alarm, he went back to bed. He would sleep until about half past seven and then make a frantic attempt to arrive at work by eight o'clock. Of course, he never made it on time. I asked him, "Kirk, on the way from the alarm clock back to your bed, do you ever get under conviction from God about staying up instead of going back to bed?" Kirk replied, "Oh yes! Every day while I shuffle back to the bed I am convicted about it. God reminds me that I should not go back to bed."

I asked him very pointedly, "Kirk, if I come to your apartment for the next couple of weeks, awaken you at half past six and tell you to stay up, will you stay up?" Kirk's face became very serious as he assured me that if I were to awaken him and then tell him to stay up, he would do it. He would not let me down if I tried to help him that way. I then pointed out to Kirk the real issue. He had just revealed that if *I* spoke to him he would stay up, but if *God* spoke to him, he would go back to bed.

The important issue to see here is that what we often call a lack of self-discipline is actually a lack of *obedience* to God. His Spirit is at work convicting and leading, but we often aren't obeying. I told Kirk that if he wanted to become disciplined in this area, he needed to let the Holy Spirit "disciple" him. If he would obey God's Spirit, he would end up being a disciplined person. This is what Paul meant when he spoke about *yielding*. Instead of obeying the flesh's cry to postpone responsibility, Kirk needed to obey the Holy Spirit's conviction to resist the flesh.

Don't Feed the Flesh

Although the flesh must be restrained instead of indulged at the point of temptation, further probing into Kirk's lifestyle revealed other, more grievous matters. When I asked Kirk about his evening schedule, he told me that in addition to his eight-hour day job, he also worked an evening part-time job until half past nine. After work he would go out for coffee with a couple of his coworkers and arrive home about eleven o'clock. Since he felt he owed himself a little pleasure to make up for the day's "rat race," he would usually watch a movie video for another couple of hours. He would often fall asleep on the couch and drag himself to bed when the movie was over about one o'clock. You can now understand why getting up at half past six was hard for Kirk. A major component in his early morning struggle to get out of bed was obviously the fatigued state of his body, but the effect of his lifestyle on his soul was even more destructive. Kirk was feeding his flesh in several ways throughout his daily routine and then was discouraged because he could not overcome his flesh in the morning.

To begin with, his soul was worn down daily by the wickedness of the people around him at work. He was daily exposed to ungodly attitudes, conversation, values, and temptations. Like Lot, his justified soul was "vexed" (literally, worn down or tortured) "from day to day with their unlawful deeds" (II Pet. 2:7-8). God is clear in this passage that a believer who is exposed to the "filthy conversation [sensual lifestyle] of the wicked" will be worn down as he is "seeing and hearing" their "unlawful deeds." If the believer is exercising his will *against* these influences, he is not nearly as affected by them. If, however, he is at all passive to these influences, the result is clear—he will be worn down! Kirk never witnessed to his lost coworkers and never challenged their shameless, sensual talk. He never resisted the evil around him.

Since Kirk was in a weakened spiritual condition, he was not enjoying fellowship with God and constantly felt guilty about his walk with the Lord. Consequently, his work was not a source of joy to him. Rather than punching out at the end of the shift satisfied that he had done his best for Christ that day and grateful for the opportunities for spiritual witness, he was constantly reminded of his disobedience in promptness and witness. The conversations at the coffee shop with his coworkers after work would always drag him further down. He would return home feeling very guilty for his participation in their filthy talk.

Not wanting to go to bed feeling so down, he would watch a movie video he rented on the way home from work. Usually the movie was laced with profanity, adult themes, or violence. Often its content was gratuitously violent or filled with raw nudity and sex. Of course, feeding his flesh in this way sabotaged any hope of resisting its pull in such a small matter as getting out of bed in the morning.

I think the picture here is clear for us. If you wish to restrain the flesh as God commands, you are being foolish to feed it. Peter warned earlier,

"Abstain from fleshly lusts, which war against the soul" (I Pet. 2:11). Paul said, "Be not deceived [i.e., 'Don't kid yourself!']; God is not mocked: for whatsoever a man soweth, that shall he also reap. For he that soweth to his flesh shall of the flesh reap corruption [i.e., ruin, destruction, dissolution];[6] but he that soweth to the Spirit shall of the Spirit reap life everlasting" (Gal. 6:7-8).

We will discuss in Part Two of this book how to "sow to the Spirit." In this part, however, we are discussing how to stop sowing to the flesh. Paul says, "Stop being deceived! This will be your ruin."

We have to exercise self-denial by saying no to the promptings of the flesh, but we also have to say no to *any* pull to feed the flesh, thus making it stronger. Every time we feed it in one area of life, we make it harder to say no to it in *any* area. Its pull and control is stronger. Like the motorcycle we are trying to "mortify," it is no use to merely put on the brakes; we must cut the fuel to the engine. Most believers forget they have a "clutch"—they don't *have* to obey the flesh—and try to stop the bike with the brakes while feeding more fuel to the engine. Cut the fuel! Even then, since the flesh is always with us this side of heaven, the engine never stops. At best it is idling; at worst it is racing!

A most puzzling phenomenon is growing in Christian circles today. Following the world's decline, many believers have the idea that restraint, self-denial, and discipline are passé. In the name of "Christian liberty," they indulge in all sorts of flesh-feeding activities, scoffing at the idea that any behavior could be considered "worldly," while at the same time claiming a new freedom in Christ. The final result is always tragic: destruction. God promised that it would be so in Galatians 6:7-8.[7]

---

[6] William Arndt and F. Wilbur Gingrich, *A Greek-English Lexicon of the New Testament and Other Early Christian Literature* (Chicago: University of Chicago Press, 1979), 865.

[7] Do not grow weary of maintaining restraints against the flesh, no matter how "out of step with the times" your position as a Christian parent, pastor, or school official appears to be. The unrestrained sin nature can produce only corruption followed by destruction. A sure-fire way to produce the necessity for a police state to squelch anarchy is to remove the police from the state when the constituency demands autonomy. This principle holds true for every human institution—the state, the church, and the family. The flesh must be restrained or the people and the institutions will be destroyed.

Whether the modern church is concerned about the effect of the world on believers or not, God is concerned. Carefully consider I John 2:15-17. Personal separation from those elements of the believer's environment that feed his flesh is not optional; it is critical! The more corrupt our culture becomes, the *greater* the need for personal separation from the world. Personal separation from the world does not mean *isolating* ourselves from the world but rather *insulating* ourselves from its toxic, fleshly effect upon our souls. Let me illustrate it this way.

Today physicians and health-care professionals are more careful about protecting themselves from the AIDS virus because the possibility of exposure to it in their line of work has increased enormously. As a result, they do not reuse needles, and they wear surgical gloves and sometimes masks. They are extremely careful about contact with body fluids. They are not *less* careful because "we live in a modern age." They are *more* careful because we live in a "corrupted age." In the same way, believers who are concerned about their spiritual health will be *more* careful in this increasingly corrupt culture. There are more dangers to their souls—not fewer. The pagan, sensual, materialistic environment around them is more contaminated with ungodliness. The need for circumspect living is greater today—not less.

When you seem to be susceptible to every fleshly "bug" in the atmosphere, it is probably because your spiritual immune system isn't functioning. You have been "quenching the Spirit" by indulging in the flesh. You can never get "well" until you stop your contact with contaminating elements around you. That may mean your entertainment habits (movies, music, magazines, recreational habits, etc.) or personal friendships must change. Whatever is dragging you down must be "put off." In addition, your immune system must be built up.[8] Our Lord is serious about our avoidance of fleshly indulgence.

Many in our society who are watching their weight try to eat low-fat foods. They can even become rather obsessed with counting fat grams of intake and measuring calories burned in exercise. To paraphrase a Scripture text, their life verse could be "Make no provision for fattening foods lest you put on the weight thereof."

---

[8] We will look at how to build up our immune system in Part Two, Renewing Your Mind.

Oh, that there would be even a fraction of that kind of concern in believers to be living "flesh-free"—as much as is possible in this world! We are told to "make [no] provision [thinking ahead of time that leads into indulgence] for the flesh, to fulfil the lusts thereof" (Rom. 13:14). Yet the Christian society consumes the world's entertainment and philosophies and embraces its goals and attitudes; consequently, Christians are powerless to make any impact upon the world around them.

The Seat Belt of Self-Denial

As we have seen, the Bible calls this restraint *denying self*. Jesus said in Luke 9:23, "If any man will come after me, let him deny himself, and take up his cross daily, and follow me." Like a seat belt, the restraint of self-denial protects us from danger. A seat belt helps protect us from bodily injury if we are involved in an automobile accident. Self-denial protects us from the danger of giving in to the urges of the flesh. A seat belt, to be effective, must be worn anytime we are riding in an automobile. We are never too young or too old to wear a seat belt. Age has nothing to do with its necessity. *A seat belt is always needed because the danger is always present.*

In the same way, we are never too old to be practicing self-denial. Since the flesh is always with us, *self-denial is always needed because the danger is always present.* There is an unbiblical idea today that the more mature one becomes in age or in spiritual growth, the less he needs to deny himself. I have had unmarried teen couples tell me that the closer they get to the Lord, the more physically involved they can become with one another because they can handle the temptation better. Their thinking was that only weaker Christians needed to establish personal dating standards. Others in the Christian world feel the same way about their music and entertainment standards. Supposedly, the more a believer grows spiritually the more liberty he has to do what he wants. He can expose himself to more of the world's toxicity because he is more immune. The result is unbridled indulgence in the flesh in the name of "Christian liberty."

The world also says that when a person reaches the age of eighteen or twenty-one (i.e., has reached a certain level of "maturity"), he is an adult and can then do what he wants. It is then legal for him to indulge himself in adult entertainment, patronize adult bookstores, order from adult catalogs, and browse adult sites on the Internet. How foolish! The original assumption of "adult" status was that once someone reached the prescribed age he was responsible for his own actions. The present assumption is that once someone reaches a certain age he does not need to practice restraint. He can do what he wants.

For the believer, just the opposite is true. When he is walking in the Spirit and the Spirit is bearing fruit in his life, he will have *more* love, *more* joy, *more* peace, . . . and *more* self-control—not less! The result for the believer will be *more* "freedom" to do what he was intended to do—to fellowship with God unceasingly and to obey God willingly, unhindered by the flesh.

I hope you can see by now that you have to be alert to any manifestation of the flesh in your life. Be familiar with the catalog of the "works of the flesh" in Galatians 5. Colossians 3 and Ephesians 4 discuss many other ways the flesh manifests itself. Don't forget the reason for this *abstinence* from the flesh: "Ye are a chosen generation, a royal priesthood, an holy nation, a peculiar people; *that ye should shew forth the praises of him who hath called you out of darkness into his marvellous light*" (I Pet. 2:9).

BACK TO MORTIFYING

How then do you weaken the flesh? How do you mortify it? Cut the fuel to the flesh "engine" by not feeding the flesh. Disengage the clutch—the power of the engine doesn't have to drive the wheel. The power of indwelling sin has been overruled by Christ—reckon it to be so for you. Lastly, put on the brakes. Deny self! Say no to the flesh.

Please understand, however, that all of this merely gets the motorcycle stopped; it doesn't make it useful in any way. It just keeps it from destroying you. There is much more to be learned than how to "put off [the deeds of] the old man" (Col. 3:9). We must next learn how to be "transformed [changed into something useful] by the renewing of [our] mind" (Rom. 12:2) so that we can demonstrate Christlikeness by having "put on the [lifestyle of the] new man" (Col. 3:10). Such is the subject of our study in Parts Two and Three. Stay with me; we have much ground yet to cover.

TAKE TIME TO REFLECT

How "flesh-free" is your lifestyle? Meditate on David's prayer for God's searchlight to expose corruption in his heart. Here is what David asked for in Psalm 139:23-24: "Search me, O God, and know my heart: try me, and know my thoughts: And see if there be any wicked way in me, and lead me in the way everlasting."

Spend a couple of hours reviewing your schedule and lifestyle. Are there elements in any of the following areas that need to be "put off" because they are high in "flesh content"?

Is your entertainment flesh-free? Examine

the *content* of the movies and television programs you watch;

the *style* and *content* of the music you listen to;

the *atmosphere* of your favorite restaurants and other places where you spend your leisure time;

the *values* you absorb watching or participating in your favorite sports;

the amount of *time* you spend in these kinds of pursuits.

Is your pursuit of possessions flesh-free (clothes, electronics, automobiles, house, etc.)? Examine

the appeal to your *pride* in being "socially correct" with the group you wish to impress;

the *stumbling-block* you are to others who are trying to impress you in the same way;

the *sexual* appeal to others in the way you dress;

the *values* you absorb when studying the latest fashion, lifestyle, sports, and consumer magazines to make sure you are current.

Are your friendships flesh-free? Examine

the *content* of your conversation—sexual, crude, materialistic, or obsessive;

the physical *contact* with others—arousing desires in them and in you that cannot righteously be gratified;

the "iron sharpening iron" *influence* on each other for godliness (living as though God is all that matters) or for worldliness ("living as though this world—*our* world—is all that matters");[9]

---

[9] Erwin W. Lutzer, *How In This World Can I Be Holy?* (Chicago: Moody Press, 1974), 26. Italics are Lutzer's.

the *attitudes* that are fostered—authority versus rebellion, order versus chaos and disorder, and so forth.

A WORD TO DISCIPLE-MAKERS

Watch for Flesh

Lasting change in those you disciple can come only when the flesh is being exposed and restrained. God is very clear about this matter. A quick review of the last four chapters of this book will refresh your mind about the nature and extent of indwelling sin. Be sure, however, when discipling someone about the necessity for self-denial that you do not leave the impression that spirituality is measured by what we *don't* do. If that were the case, the most godly people are the ones already in the cemetery—they don't do anything! Restraining the flesh merely keeps the sin nature that is within us and the sinful world that is around us from corrupting us any further.

The doctor's surgical gloves serve only to keep him from contamination. Although they do not make him a skillful surgeon, they *are* necessary. What would you think of a surgeon who had this attitude?

> I won't wear surgical gloves. After all, they don't make me a great surgeon. Being a doctor is more than wearing gloves. I'm a surgeon because of my love for medicine, because of my medical training, and because of what I do in the operating room—not because I wear gloves. These rules about wearing gloves are just bureaucratic. Gloves are just for those who need something outward to show they are doctors. "Real doctors" don't wear gloves!

A doctor with this attitude is showing either his arrogance—thinking himself invincible—or his ignorance about why he needs to wear gloves. He is so lost in his supposed love for medicine and being a "real doctor" that he is oblivious to the danger lurking around him in the form of the AIDS virus or other contaminants. He would destroy himself and unwittingly contaminate his patients—all while both he and they are confident that he is a good doctor. In the end he would be only a transmitter of death, not a saver of life.

Likewise, restraining the flesh by imposing restrictions on ourselves or others doesn't make us holy. The actual production of spiritual fruit in us is the work of the Spirit of God *alone*. In Part Two we will examine at length how that fruit is produced within us. In the meantime, don't forget your gloves, and teach your medical students to wear gloves! Don't forget, however, to drive home to them why they need to wear gloves. Gloves aren't badges of some elite group. They are lifesavers for everyone in a life-threatening world.

Rescue 911

Don't underestimate the destruction of the flesh when it is allowed to reign unrestrained in a person's life. For example, young people who are indulging their flesh with their music, movies, and lifestyles will *not* "grow out of it." The only thing that will "grow" is the flesh. It is corrupt, it is active, and it is lethal. Time is not on the parent's side; it is advantageous only to the flesh.

Parents who allow their teen to keep his music, his television viewing, or his friends because they don't want to make a "mountain out of a molehill," expecting him to give it up when he is older, will be sadly disappointed. The flesh will not give in that easily. As long as it is being indulged, indwelling sin will expand its operation in the soul, taking over more areas of life and increasing its control and bondage. Dr. Bob Jones Sr. used to say, "You can avoid trouble by having trouble."[10] Address the issues of the flesh when they are in their early stages. Don't wait until they have grown to greater proportions.

The best strategy for any cancer treatment is early detection and treatment. The same is true of the soul. Early detection of the flesh's activity and early treatment are the surest remedy. Sometimes parents take the position that once their teen sees some of the "reproofs of life," he will turn from his rebellion. They fail to understand that while a child is in their care, they are responsible to *arrange* the reproofs of life for him. Study the book of Proverbs to see the parental responsibility to reprove and instruct.

The flesh is far more destructive than cancer. It corrupts the *soul* and then destroys the body. No wonder Solomon warned, "Keep [guard] thy heart with all diligence [and we might add, the hearts of your children]; for out of it are the issues of life" (Prov. 4:23). Sense the emergency nature of the matter and get started with immediate treatment. Rescue from the flesh is truly an urgent "911" matter.

---

[10] Dr. Bob Jones Sr., *Dr. Bob Jones Says* (radio talks), May 21, 1958.

Don't Underestimate the Strength of Sin

Our society has seen an alarming increase in bizarre and enslaving behavior—gambling, psychopathic lying, anorexia, bulimia, cross-dressing, homosexuality, pornography, serial rape, and gruesome psychiatric disorders. Therapists, physicians, and sadly, Christian counselors scramble to find some medical or genetic etiology to explain the extent of today's bondage and perversion. "Surely," they say, "no one in his 'right mind' would do these things!" Some look to a "medical model" of genetic dispositions and chemical imbalances to account for the behavior. Others in the Christian realm opt for a "demonic model" to explain these aberrant activities.

When a "sin model" is preached as the underlying cause, most people—Christian and non-Christian—scoff as if someone were proposing that the earth is flat. What we are seeing in the majority of these situations is actually the result of "full-grown sin." Our understanding of the Bible's teaching about indwelling sin is so deficient that the Christian community is aghast that such behavior could actually take place. A careful study of the first and third chapters of Romans should dispel our "head in the clouds" attitude about the human heart. The individual's problem isn't that he is somehow "out of his right mind." His problem is that he has a "reprobate mind," and he is reaping what he has been sowing.

Initially, you might feel such a diagnosis is unloving and certainly unhelpful. Just the opposite, however, is the case. When the biblical diagnosis is made, the *real* solution can be applied. God has made a marvelous provision for sinners—the gospel. That gospel is more than just a "Romans Road" to salvation. It is not merely the means by which God transfers a man from "the kingdom of darkness" into "the kingdom of His dear Son"—although that alone is far more than we deserve and far more glorious than we can imagine. The gospel—the death, burial, and Resurrection of the Son of God—is also God's provision to transform a redeemed sinner's life of misery here on earth into a life of peace and rest from the power and afflictions of sin so that he can become a useful instrument in the hand of God. Remember, God's "recovery program" is sanctification. Everything else is spiritual quackery.

DON'T FORSAKE THE ASSEMBLY

Again, let me remind you that the primary place where you will be repeatedly taught the blessings of this glorious gospel and its provisions for sinners and saints is in a Bible-preaching, Christ-exalting local church assembly. It is God's means of providing a regular "reality check" for His people. A disciple-maker who does not encourage those he disciples to regularly attend a local Fundamentalist church is short-circuiting God's plan for growth. There he will be taught the things he is to *know*, to *reckon*, and to *yield*. Israel's downfall is often attributed in the Scriptures to the fact that the Israelites forgot the Lord or remembered not His ways.[11] The continual repetition of regular Bible preaching will bring great blessing if it is received with a willing and believing heart.[12]

---

[11] See Deuteronomy 6:10-12; 8:11-20, and Isaiah 51:12-13.
[12] Hebrews 4:2.

PART TWO
RENEWING YOUR MIND

And be renewed in the spirit of your mind.
Ephesians 4:23

CHAPTER SIX

GETTING IN TOUCH WITH REALITY

For in him we live, and move, and have our being.
Acts 17:28

If the *own way* tendency of indwelling sin, as we saw in the last four chapters, is our real problem, what then is the real solution? We ought to be convinced by now that the solution does not lie within us. We are the problem.[1] The world says and, sadly, many Christians say that Bible solutions will not work in the "real" world. The irony of their complaint is that the Bible *alone* gives the only true picture of the "real" world. Sometimes Christian parents and Christian school administrators are asked, "If you teach these young people in a totally Christian environment, how will they be able to function in the real world?" The fact is that if the Christian home, church, and school have done their job well and the student has learned well, *he may be one of the few on the earth who understand the real world.*

Reality (i.e., the truth) is that there is a God in heaven. Reality is that He made us and we are accountable to Him. Reality is that this God has spoken and what He says matters—eternally. Reality is that without His salvation, we are doomed to eternal torment. Reality is that God's Son, Jesus Christ, has died for the sins of the world, that He has risen again, and that whoever believes on Him is given eternal life.

---

[1] The focus of this book does not allow time for discussion of every dissenting view, but every believer in this day needs to become familiar with the philosophies of both postmodernism and New Age thought. While neither grew out of the other, they run on parallel tracks, espousing to mankind that the solutions are within and that man is the creator of his own reality. We are in for the "perilous times" of II Timothy 3 as every individual man and various social groups assert their sovereignty over everyone else. We will see human depravity at its most vicious and perverted level. If you take the Bible's anthropology seriously, you can only shudder if man increasingly looks within his own heart to find his answers.

This is the *real world*, and only a believer walking in fellowship with His Creator and Redeemer can understand it. Everyone else in the world is experiencing a "break with reality." Romans says that those who do not know God "hold [i.e., suppress] the truth in unrighteousness" (1:18). They are not walking in *truth* (i.e., reality). No wonder those who do not know Christ—and believers who are ignoring God's Word—live and act as if they have gone mad. The only world they *can* know doesn't make sense. The reality of life is that life isn't supposed to make sense or bring any lasting peace and satisfaction without God.

AN ALIEN IN TIMES SQUARE

To illustrate the emotional turmoil we can expect in our society when the majority of its citizens do not understand the *real* world (as God has made it and reveals it to us), imagine that you know a missionary in Brazil who works with tribes in the Amazon interior of South America. These tribesmen have never seen an outsider and do not understand the language or the ways of the outside world. Suppose this missionary were to bring one of these nationals out of the heart of the Amazon and abandon him, untutored and unaccompanied, in Times Square in New York City. It would be obvious that this poor Amazonian does not know how to get along in Times Square. He will have experiences that are entirely outside his frame of reference. While he tries to survive and find food and shelter, he will encounter many unsettling events.

Think for a moment about what emotions he might experience and what behaviors he might exhibit during the first several days of his visit to this strange new situation. He will obviously be *fearful* because he does not understand what is going on around him. He will no doubt eventually feel *angry* because he is constantly *frustrated*. Nothing he attempts to do will work as it did back in his homeland. He will not be able to communicate with anyone, and the patterns and behaviors of the people around him will not make sense. He will be filled with *confusion*. He will perhaps be *depressed* as he contemplates giving up, but where will he go to quit? He may become *violent* out of *desperation*. Back home in his own country, he may have been productive and may have enjoyed a measure of security and peace, but Times Square will present him with a reality he does not understand and therefore cannot function in effectively. The result is a man who will soon show many of the "emotional disorders" we see in today's society in general. While the Amazonian tribesman is out of touch with his newfound reality, most of the rest of those in Times Square are just as out of touch with a much greater reality—God—and are experiencing the same emotional struggles and destructive behaviors, but for a different reason.

You see, God is the environment of man. Paul says, "For in him [God] we live, and move, and have our being" (Acts 17:28). For the tribesman to be at peace in his New York environment, he will need someone coaching him about every nuance and characteristic of his surroundings. The more he learns about his environment and brings himself into line with its nature, the freer he will be from the mental and emotional anguish he initially experienced. He cannot simply try to solve his New York problems his *own way*. The Amazonian way will not work in New York. By the same token, man's *own way* will not work in God's world, and the man—believer or unbeliever—who attempts to live independently of the knowledge and ways of God is experiencing a "break with reality."[2]

Having a renewed mind is not just memorizing a few Bible verses about a problem you are having, although that may be a start. It is not just becoming familiar with Christian principles and convictions about godly lifestyles. Having a renewed mind involves a *relationship* with your Creator that actually changes you because of your exposure to deity.

More Than Relief from Problems

The Christian life is first and foremost about God. It is not primarily about escape from everlasting torment or deliverance from life-dominating sins or freedom from unsettling emotions. Our despondency, anger, worry, fear, guilt, bitterness, lust, and so forth are indications that the dependent love *relationship* with God has grown cold—or has never been developed in the first place.

---

[2] The illustration of the Amazonian is an expanded adaptation of a similar illustration in *Knowing God* by J. I. Packer (Downers Grove, Ill.: InterVarsity Press, 1973), 14-15. Please note that the few references to Packer's book *Knowing God* do not imply endorsement of everything Packer says in the book or of the theological positions Packer has taken in recent years. There is much in this book that is correct theologically, and thus, very helpful; but like any other book, including this one you are reading, it must be read with an open Bible beside it.

The primary goal of biblical change is not to gain relief from these problems. These problems remind us of the poverty of our relationship with God, and they are allowed by God to draw us to Himself out of our misery. Christianity is primarily a *relationship* with the Creator, not merely a means to achieve creature comfort. Every trial that ever burdened a mortal man, every temptation that ever stormed a human heart, and every blessing that ever delighted a needy soul have been skillfully designed by the Creator for one purpose: to draw men to Himself. Nothing else ultimately matters to God, and nothing else ultimately satisfies His creatures. God created man to be most satisfied, most joyful, and most useful when there is an ongoing, dependent, life-giving personal relationship with his Creator.

Jesus made this point very strongly while visiting in the house of his friends Lazarus, Mary, and Martha (Luke 10:38-42). Martha felt that Mary should be more involved in getting the house and the meal ready for their Guest. She even fussed at Jesus for engaging Mary in conversation that kept her sister from helping with the chores. Jesus kindly rebuked Martha for her preoccupation with doing things *for* the Guest, when, like Mary, she should have been preoccupied *with* the Guest Himself. Mary knew that her greatest need was to know God.

Most of us have experienced a lost connection between our telephone and that of a friend we were talking to. Perhaps in the middle of our conversation we were disconnected. We re-dialed the number and the connection was restored. Fellowship with God is blocked by the sin of going our *own way* in some aspect of life.[3] The connection is restored upon our repentance. Once restored to fellowship with God, we have the opportunity to develop a dependent, personal relationship with God. Unfortunately, once the connection is restored with God, many people do not know what to say to the Person "on the other end of the line." They do not know how to develop a relationship with God. Let's explore the dynamics involved in any relationship to help us see what needs to be happening between God and us.

---

[3] Isaiah 59:1-2.

More Than Being on Speaking Terms

Man was made to function well only when in fellowship with his Creator. Fellowship, in this context, means more than just having all known sin confessed. A Christian worker may ask a counselee, "Are you in fellowship with God at this moment, or is there a barrier between you and God?" Having "a conscience void of offence toward God, and toward men" is a crucial starting point (Acts 24:16). Fellowship is possible when there is "nothing between my soul and the Savior," as the hymn writer put it; but there must also be much *going on* between my soul and the Savior. The apostle John instructs us to "abide in the vine" and to "walk in the light" (John 15:4 and I John 1:7). Paul also describes it as a "walk" (Eph. 4:1, 17; 5:1-2, 8), being "filled with all the fullness of God" (Eph. 3:19); and he exhorts us to "meditate upon these things" (I Tim. 4:15).

A married couple may live in the same house and get along pretty well with each other. They may go about their daily responsibilities in the home without much friction between them. They may even have great respect for each other. In this sense, they are friends who share *mutual interests*—buying a house, raising a family, getting ahead at work. But marriage the way God planned it includes so much more than mutual interests, goals, and respect.

God intends for that couple to become "one flesh" (i.e., one person). He wants them to develop such a like-mindedness with each other that there is an obvious mutual devotion, admiration, and dependence upon each other. This kind of relationship will be more than just accomplishing goals with the help of the other. This kind of relationship is, first and foremost, about each other. Friends may be described as those who have *mutual interests*. The relationship is primarily about something outside the relationship—goals, projects, and so forth. Lovers are those who have *mutual intimacy*; the relationship is primarily about each other. Lovers find their greatest joy to be the *joy of the other*.[4]

Marriage was created by God to mirror the kind of relationship He wishes to have with us. Intimate fellowship with God, as we can see, is more than just "being on speaking terms." The kind of relationship He

---

[4] Note the concern of Jesus for His disciples' joy in John 15:11 and 17:13. Paul told the Corinthians that the apostles considered themselves "helpers of your joy" (II Cor. 1:24) and that "my joy is the joy of you all" (II Cor. 2:3).

has in mind for us will mean that both the Creator and the creature find their greatest joy in the joy of the other. The obvious questions include these: "How can we know God in this way?" "What does it mean to know God, and how is that relationship developed?" "How is it possible for a creature to have a personal relationship with his Creator?" "What is the difference between knowing God and knowing *about* God?" These are good questions and are worthy of some serious study.

Any person who has read the Bible very much is aware that certain Bible characters seem to stand above their peers in the quality of their relationship with God. For example, Abraham was called "the Friend of God" (James 2:23). Moses spoke with God "face to face, as a man speaketh unto his friend" (Exod. 33:11). Genesis 5:24 tells us that "Enoch walked with God." God Himself called David "a man after his own heart" (I Sam. 13:14). Their relationships with God were not unique experiences that cannot be duplicated by anyone else. Perhaps we can explain the kind of relationship they had by examining what happens in a dating experience.

SOMETHING IS GOING ON BETWEEN THEM!

One of the blessings of working in a college environment is seeing God drawing couples together into a dating relationship and eventually into marriage. In class a teacher will often notice a couple sitting together but will not think anything about it until he sees them consistently walking to and from the class together. As he watches them before class begins, he will notice that they talk to each other in low tones, almost oblivious to the people around them. There is an obvious admiration for each other in their faces. While they may comment to each other about various events around them, most of their conversation is about each other. They discover something else about the other person and then comment on and compliment what they see in that person. They explore each other's opinions, likes, dislikes, family backgrounds, interests, and knowledge about various topics.

In addition to their private conversations, they show their affection by giving each other small gifts, such as a piece of favorite candy, a special card, or a monogrammed key ring. Some of the gifts may have no meaning to an onlooker but have great personal significance to both of them. They seem never to have enough time to be with each other, and they plan times when they can see each other again. At first, each may pursue the relationship because of the delight each one receives from the other. If godly love is central in the relationship, each will become increasingly motivated by how to be a delight to the other.

If they truly delight in each other, they will not be able to keep their joy a secret. They will praise their friend to roommates, family, and anyone else who will listen. In fact, anyone who has much contact with either of them can see that there is something going on between them. Relationships like this are characterized by *continual personal interaction.*

A relationship with God includes the same basic elements of learning *about* Him (revelation), followed by much personal interaction *with* Him. Knowing God in a personal way requires two initial elements.

KNOWING GOD REQUIRES THAT WE HAVE A DESIRE FOR GOD

Our greatest need is for God, yet because of our sinful bent (which is still a part of us, even after salvation), we often resort to going our *own way.* That path leads us directly away from God. God reminds us that the way that "seemeth right unto a man" leads to "death" (Prov. 14:12).

Fortunately, God places within those of us who are His children a desire for a relationship with Him. This is not something we work up ourselves; it is the work of God. Philippians 2:13 says, "For it is God which worketh in you both to will and to do of his good pleasure." He is at work in every believer creating a "will" and an ability "to do" what is "His good pleasure." In Jeremiah 31:3 God speaks of His initiative in drawing men to Himself: "The Lord hath appeared of old unto me, saying, Yea, I have loved thee with an everlasting love: therefore with lovingkindness *have I drawn thee.*"

E. M. Bounds quotes David Brainerd, who testified of the desire God placed within him: "Of late God has been pleased to keep my soul hungry almost continually, so that I have been filled with a kind of pleasing pain. When I really enjoy God, I feel my desires of Him the more insatiable and my thirstings after holiness more unquenchable."[5]

---

[5] E. M. Bounds, *The Weapon of Prayer* (Grand Rapids: Baker Book House, 1975), 136.

In Revelation 3:20 Christ is portrayed as standing outside the door of a believer's heart knocking. It is clear that Christ, not the believer, is taking the initiative for the relationship. Moses told the children of Israel that God was at work in their heart to draw them to Himself: "And the Lord thy God will circumcise thine heart, and the heart of thy seed, to love the Lord thy God with all thine heart, and with all thy soul, that thou mayest live" (Deut. 30:6).

Just as God sought Adam and Eve in the Garden of Eden in order to continue fellowship with them (Gen.3:8-9), so God continues to seek us in order that we can have a personal, dependent relationship with Him. In his account of the battle between his flesh and his spirit, Paul said, "I know that in me (that is, in my flesh,) dwelleth no good thing: for *to will is present with me*" (Rom. 7:18). He is testifying that within him is a continual desire ("will") to do right. That is the work of the Spirit of God and is an evidence of salvation. He states in the next chapter, verse 14, that "as many as are led by the Spirit of God [i.e., led away from the flesh], they are the sons of God." In the next verse, he says that the Spirit of God creates in us the cry of a new child for his new Father. In this way, Paul says, "The Spirit itself beareth witness with our spirit, that we are the children of God" (Rom. 8:16).

God has created in man the desire for Himself and has offered Himself as the object of man's desire! He is the only One sufficient to fill the God-shaped hole within man's soul. Augustine in his *Confessions* writes, "Thou madest us for Thyself, and our heart is restless, until it repose [finds its rest] in Thee."

The psalmist described God's work in his heart this way:

As the hart [deer] panteth after the water brooks, so panteth my soul after thee, O God. My soul thirsteth for God, for the living God (Ps. 42:1-2).

O God, thou art my God; early will I seek thee: my soul thirsteth for thee, my flesh longeth for thee in a dry and thirsty land, where no water is (Ps. 63:1).

Whom have I in heaven but thee? and there is none upon earth that I desire beside thee. My flesh and my heart faileth: but God is the strength of my heart, and my portion for ever (Ps. 73:25-26).

My soul longeth, yea, even fainteth for the courts of the Lord: my heart and my flesh crieth out for the living God (Ps. 84:2).

God is glorified when man takes his place of joyful, grateful dependence because then God is exalted to His place as the only worthy, all-sufficient object of that dependence. David testifies of it this way:

Their sorrows shall be multiplied that hasten after another god: . . . [but] I have set the Lord always before me: because he is at my right hand, I shall not be moved. Therefore my heart is glad, and my glory rejoiceth: my flesh also shall rest in hope. . . . Thou wilt shew me the path of life: in thy presence is fulness of joy; at thy right hand there are pleasures for evermore (Ps. 16:4, 8-9, 11).

Make no mistake about it. If you are God's child, He has placed within you a desire for Himself. If your only desires in life are for yourself and for relief from your problems, and you experience no desire whatsoever for a relationship with God, your first step needs to be a very careful examination of whether or not you even belong to Him. Those who are truly members of His family experience a God-given desire for intimacy with their Father. If you are a true believer, along with your desire to have deliverance from whatever problems seem to plague your life you will have a desire for a better relationship with God. In fact, you may experience a great deal of frustration that the kind of relationship with Him that you desire seems so elusive. An unbeliever never experiences that kind of frustration. He may know he does not have fellowship with God, but it does not bother him. He is content to seek his own solutions to his own problems—apart from God.

The desire for God is, first, an assurance that we are His children. It is, second, the sign that He is at work in our lives, since a desire for God cannot be generated by us on our own. It is also the indication that He is intending to do more in us for our good and for His ultimate glory. Jesus said in the Beatitudes, "Blessed are they which do hunger and thirst after righteousness: *for they shall be filled*" (Matt. 5:6).

When He takes the initiative to create in us a hunger and thirst for righteousness, He intends to satisfy those desires with Himself. He promises we shall be filled! Paul's chief prayer for the Ephesian church was that they would be strengthened in the inner man as they allowed Christ to "dwell in [their] hearts by faith" (Eph. 3:16-17). The word "dwell" in verse 17 has the idea of permanence. It has the idea of someone who is becoming an intimate part of the family by moving in and settling down. As they increased their personal interaction with Christ, they would be able to understand and experience "the breadth, and length, and depth, and height" of Christ's love for them. The result of that increased intimacy with Him would be that they would "be filled with all the fulness of God" (Eph. 3:18-19).

Please understand that the information in this chapter is not incidental to, but is the heart of, biblical change. *Any attempt to solve the problems of life apart from a dependent relationship with God is both arrogant and, in the long run, ineffective.* When Jesus sought to help the harlot at the well in Samaria, He did not offer a recovery program from sexual addiction. Her greatest problem was not her immorality. Her greatest problem was that she sought to fulfill the longing in her soul with something temporal—relationships with mere men. Jesus offered her a relationship with her Creator that would have permanent impact on her thirst for intimacy with another person. He said in John 4:13-14, "Whosoever drinketh of this water shall thirst again: But whosoever drinketh of the water that I shall give him *shall never thirst.*"

Knowing God requires that we first have a desire for God. If you are truly His child, He has already placed within you a "hunger and thirst after righteousness," which He promises to fill (Matt. 5:6). Knowing God requires something else, however.

KNOWING GOD REQUIRES THAT WE SEEK HIM

God promises that those who respond to the desire He places within them by seeking Him will not be disappointed. "But if . . . thou shalt seek the Lord thy God, thou shalt find him, if thou seek him with all thy heart and with all thy soul" (Deut. 4:29). "But without faith it is impossible to please him: for he that cometh to God must believe that he is, and that he is a rewarder of them that diligently seek him" (Heb. 11:6).

The Search for God Must Be a Passionate Search

Deuteronomy 4:29, quoted above, says that we must seek God *with all our heart.* A common complaint about modern Christians is that they are apathetic. That is not entirely true. They are very passionate people. By passionate, I do not mean necessarily that they are sensual. I mean instead that they are wholehearted about something. Notice their passion for sports, entertainment, leisure, adventure, fashions, sex, wealth, and achievement. Everyone is passionate! He either loves himself (thus the passion for those things that please himself), or he loves God and his neighbor.[6] *Apathy toward God is the result of being passionate toward something or someone else.* Jesus was quite clear on this issue. "No man can serve two masters: for either he will hate the one, and love the other; or else he will hold to the one, and despise the other. Ye cannot serve God and mammon [money]" (Matt. 6:24).

Note that He said that while man despises (i.e., considers small) and hates one thing, he *loves* the other thing. If he considers God and His interests a small thing, it is because he is passionate about something else. Jesus directly confronted Peter about his misdirected passion.

> But he turned, and said unto Peter, Get thee behind me, Satan: thou art an offence [stumbling block] unto me: for thou savourest not the things that be of God, but those that be of men. Then said Jesus unto his disciples, If any man will come after me, let him deny himself, and take up his cross, and follow me. For whosoever will save his life shall lose it: and whosoever will lose his life for my sake shall find it (Matt. 16:23-25).

Jesus said in the Beatitudes that only the "pure in heart" could "see God" (Matt. 5:8). "Pure in heart" does not mean the absence of sin, although that is certainly a part of the meaning. It means to have a single, undivided heart. It is free (pure) from other conflicting priorities. God takes our double-mindedness very seriously. He likens Himself to a spouse with an unfaithful partner and likens the believers whose first love is not for Christ to the spouse having an illicit sexual affair.

> Ye adulterers and adulteresses, know ye not that the friendship of the world is enmity with God? whosoever therefore will be a friend of the world is the enemy of God. . . . Draw nigh to God, and he will draw nigh to you. Cleanse your hands, ye sinners; and purify your hearts, ye *double minded.* . . . Humble yourselves in the sight of the Lord, and he shall lift you up (James 4:4, 8, 10).

---

[6] Notice the passionate search for wisdom in Proverbs 2:1-5. God does not reveal Himself to the casual observer but only to the wholehearted and single-minded. What is the result of such a search? "Then shalt thou . . . find the knowledge of God" (v. 5).

We can have a personal, dependent relationship with God if we are willing to seek Him and forsake all other loves. No young lady being sought out by a young man is going to be impressed by his proposal of marriage if he insists on continuing to date other girls in addition to his fiancée. If the relationship is to be lasting and meaningful, each must love the other exclusively and wholeheartedly. Similarly, as Creator and Sustainer of all, God deserves first place in our lives—and demands it—if we are to know Him in any kind of personal, intimate way.

The Search for God Must Be a Search for a Person

Seeking God is not just an exercise in exploring Bible content or studying systematic theology. Those pursuits play an important part in knowing God but are only means to an end—never ends in themselves. The following dialogue illustrates the proper approach when seeking to know God.

Phil played first-string on the soccer team for his Christian high school. One day after soccer practice, Phil jogged over to the bleachers and sat down on the bench next to his coach. They exchanged greetings and talked briefly about the scrimmage the team had just finished. Finally, Phil posed a question.

"Coach, I've been struggling with something in my spiritual life recently and wonder if I could talk to you about it."

"Sure, Phil, what's up?"

"Well, since my decision at summer teen camp to live for the Lord, I have really made an effort to be faithful in reading my Bible and spending some time in prayer every day. It hasn't been easy, but I've been pretty faithful."

"If it's any encouragement to you, Phil, the difference in you this year is noticeable. You used to be far more uptight about things that didn't go your way. I have really been encouraged."

"Thanks, Coach, but I really feel that something is still missing. In addition to my regular devotions, I volunteered to lead singing when the youth group does the Wednesday night service at the rescue mission, and I started the Thursday morning prayer meeting for the seniors before first-hour class. But even with all these things going on, I still feel as if my heart is so cold toward God. I'm doing a lot of the right things now, and I really am glad I'm doing them, but there has to be something more to the Christian life."

"Phil, let me ask you a question about the time you spend reading your Bible each day. When you open your Bible to read every day, what are you looking for?"

"Well, I have been reading through the New Testament, and I usually try to find something that will encourage me for the day or a principle that I can apply."

"That's fine, Phil, but do you have any idea why God gave us the Bible in the first place?"

"I guess He gave it as a guidebook for life?"

"It certainly does teach us how to live, Phil, but it is far more than that. When you get home, look up I John 5:9. It says, 'This is the witness of God which he hath testified of his *Son*.' Your Bible is first and foremost a revelation from God about His Son. There is a *Person* at the center of everything you read in the Bible. If you merely look for principles and encouraging passages, you will find what you are looking for, but you will miss *God* in the process."

"I've never thought about it that way before, Coach."

"Let me give you an example. Since you have been reading in the New Testament, you have probably read the account of Jesus feeding the five thousand in John 6."

"Yes, I read that sometime last week. I'm almost through the four Gospels now."

"God did not put that account in the Bible as an explanation of how we ought to feed large numbers of people when we have a church picnic. It was given to reveal something to us about God's Son, Jesus Christ. You have to stop and ask yourself, 'What does this passage reveal about Jesus Christ?' In fact, you may want to make yourself a bookmark for your Bible with that question on it. You have to look for a *Person* in the Scriptures if you are to have a *personal* relationship with God. When it becomes just a source of principles to you, then you will find your heart cold. This account in John shows us His great compassion for people in need and His great ability to meet that need. It also shows us that He purposefully arranges situations to test the faith of His disciples.

"His compassion and power are two of His attributes. You might stop right there and ask yourself further, 'What is compassion? What else do I know about God's compassion? Who else in the Bible experienced it? Who else in the Bible demonstrated it? How has God personally demonstrated compassion to me? Since I am called to be Christlike, how am I doing at displaying compassion? If it has been lacking in my daily contacts with people, what have others been seeing in me instead of the compassion that would have been Christlike in those situations?'

"You might spend thirty to forty-five minutes on this one attribute, taking notes, praying for God to 'search' you and 'try' you as David prayed[7] and thanking Him for showing you more about Himself. You might make a list of people whom you tend to shun—maybe here at school, maybe at your youth group, or maybe at the rescue mission. You might jot a note after each name, spelling out what you could do to make a difference in each life by showing compassion in some way as Jude 22 teaches. You could then spend time praying for them that God would use you as a channel of His love to them to draw them into a more personal relationship with God as well. You would want to thank God for showing you more of Himself, and you would want to express to Him that it is this kind of excellence in Him that makes you glad that you are His child. You could tell Him about the delight that these verses have been to you as you have meditated upon them. You might even want to write out a special prayer of thanksgiving in a journal to remind you of what you have told Him."

"Wow, Coach! I never thought of my daily devotions like that before; that's pretty exciting! I can see how it makes everything more personal, and it would certainly change me more."

"Phil, what I have just described to you is what the Bible calls meditation. It is not merely studying the Bible to learn more principles, although they are important. It is studying the Bible to learn more about a *Person*—God Himself. The principles you find along the way are manifestations of His character. If you don't see the Person behind the principles, you have missed God's intention for His revelation. Of course, you probably can't take an hour every day for this kind of study, but you should consider setting aside a significant block of time on the weekend that you will spend seeking the Lord in this way. It won't be long before you are looking for ways to spend more time like this with Him throughout the week in addition to your daily Bible reading and prayer. Your daily devotional time becomes an extension of the larger chunks of time you are spending with God on the weekend. Think about the words of William Longstaff's hymn, 'Take Time to Be Holy.' The second stanza says,

---

[7] Psalm 139:23-24.

Take time to be holy; the world rushes on.
Spend much time in secret with Jesus alone.
By looking to Jesus, like Him thou shalt be.
Thy friends in thy conduct, His likeness shall see.

"You really can't find lasting joy or peace any other way. You have to take the Bible *personally* and treat God like a *Person* before your heart will be warmed."

"Thanks, Coach! You've given me a lot to think about. I'll change my approach and let you know in a few days how things are going."

Phil's coach is right. He described to Phil a relationship with God based upon fellowship—personal interactions with God. This kind of interaction with God delights Him because we are finding our delight *in* Him. One of the results of a relationship like this is what the disciples on the Emmaus Road felt "burn" in their own heart, which was just the opposite of Phil's cold heart.

Note the comments of these disciples who walked with Jesus on the way to Emmaus in Luke 24:27-32. They said in verse 32, "Did not our heart burn within us, while he talked with us by the way, and while he opened to us the scriptures?" If you look back at verse 27 you will find out what they saw in the Scriptures that made their hearts burn. Luke says, "And beginning at Moses and all the prophets, he expounded unto them in all the scriptures the things *concerning himself*." They were talking about the Person and work of the Messiah. Jesus Christ is central to the Scriptures. If we miss Him in the process of reading the Bible, we have missed the whole purpose of God in giving us the Scriptures. The Scriptures are about a *Person!* C. S. Lewis said,

> God made us: invented us as a man invents an engine. A car is made to run on gasoline, and it would not run properly on anything else. Now God designed the human machine to run on Himself. He Himself is the fuel our spirits were designed to burn, or the food our spirits were designed to feed on. There is no other. That is why it is just no good asking God to make us happy in our own way without bothering about religion. God cannot give us a happiness and peace apart from Himself, because it is not there. There is no such thing.[8]

---

[8] Lewis, *Mere Christianity*, 54.

One theologian summarized the truths of the coach's conversation with Phil this way:

> Our aim in studying the Godhead must be to know God Himself the better. Our concern must be to enlarge our acquaintance, not simply with the doctrine of God's attributes,[9] but with the living God whose attributes they are. As He is the subject of our study, and our helper in it, so He must Himself be the end of it. We must seek, in studying God, to be led to God. It was for this purpose that revelation was given, and it is to this use that we must put it.

> How are we to do this? How can we turn our knowledge *about* God into knowledge *of* God? The rule for doing this is demanding, but simple. It is that we turn each truth *about* God into matter for meditation *before* God, leading to prayer and praise *to* God.

> We have some idea, perhaps, what prayer is, but what is meditation? Well may we ask; for meditation is a lost art today, and Christian people suffer grievously from their ignorance of the practice. Meditation is the activity of calling to mind, and thinking over, and dwelling on, and applying to oneself, the various things that one knows about the works and ways and purposes and promises of God. It is an activity of holy thought, consciously performed in the presence of God, under the eye of God, by the help of God, as a means of communion with God. Its purpose is to clear one's mental and spiritual vision of God, and to let His truth make its full and proper impact on one's mind and heart. It is a matter of talking to oneself about God and oneself; it is, indeed, often a matter of arguing with oneself, reasoning oneself out of moods of doubt and unbelief into a clear apprehension of God's power and grace. Its effect is ever to humble us, as we contemplate God's greatness and glory, and our own littleness and sinfulness, and to encourage and reassure us—"comfort" us, in the old, strong, Bible sense of the word—as we contemplate the unsearchable riches of divine mercy displayed in the Lord Jesus Christ. . . . And it is as we enter more and more deeply into this experience of being humbled and exalted that our knowledge of God increases, and with it our

---

[9] You may have noticed in the preceding quotation and in the discussion with the coach the mention of the term "attributes." The attributes of a person are those qualities of his nature by which we know him. Everything a person does is a revelation of his nature to those watching him. When the Bible gives us a command or a principle or when it shows us God's intervention in the affairs of man, it is revealing something of the nature of God. It is showing us one or more of His attributes. We look at God's attributes more closely in the next chapter.

peace, our strength, and our joy. God help us, then, to put our knowledge about God to this use, that we all may in truth "know the Lord."[10]

A LETTER TO JOHN

I want to share with you an actual letter from a mother to her son.[11] She knew he would never read it; he had died in an accident on a farm three years before she wrote the letter. She wrote it as a testimony of how she had come to really know God since her son's death.

Dear John,

It's been three years since that night when God called you to Heaven. We have missed you so much, and I'm sure we will until we are together again.

At the time of your death, there was such a searching going on in your heart. I remember our long discussions and your attempts to make us understand what you were looking for. You were searching for a depth that was missing in your life. You had wisdom and insight in your youth. Some of the things you talked about, things that we didn't understand, have become clearer to us. You remarked about the students at college who were so busy serving the Lord yet lacked a personal relationship with Him. In fact, some of them with whom you talked couldn't say for sure they were saved. At the time your daddy and I talked with you I don't think we even understood, but I remember your saying that you wanted something "earth shaking" to show us. Well, when you died it was earth shaking. It tore our very foundations away. I feel that I, especially, took up your searching. I believe the Lord answered your prayer. I don't know why it had to be through your death. I'll never understand that, but through it I have discovered that my foundation was built on a creed more than on a Person. I had accepted the Lord as my Savior, but I was living my life by self-effort. When you died, everything I believed fell apart. I didn't turn from God, but I started questioning what I believed because your eternity rested on what we had taught you to believe. Was it right? Is there a God? Do I believe the Bible? Does God love me, really love me? Is there a Heaven? Are you there with God? What is it like

---

[10] Packer, *Knowing God*, 18-19. Italics are Packer's.

[11] Used by permission of the writer, Mrs. Carol L. Wilkinson.

where you are? What are you doing now? Will I really see you and know you in Heaven?

I can't say I've gotten all the answers to all my questions, but let me tell you some of the things that have happened. In my searching I have come across some of the things you were struggling with. The Bible is more than just a Book of rules. It presents a God Who wants to have fellowship with us. We do have a personal relationship with the God of the Bible. As you said, we do need to see our sins as God sees them. When we see God for Who He is, then we can see our sins as He sees them. Then we can realize the full impact of what it meant to have those sins forgiven through the Cross. Also our emotions do have a part in our Christian life. The Bible says that we worship the Lord "in spirit and in truth." If we don't let our total being become involved in worshiping the Lord, we hinder the Holy Spirit, and we cannot truly worship God. We are to love God with our whole being—body, soul, and spirit. We can know His Spirit's presence. God can be alive to us. We can know His presence in our daily lives. We can have this while we are still here on earth. We can come before His throne and worship Him and in a real sense, be in His presence. I feel that is what you are doing now. Maybe that's why I have a yearning to do the same thing even while I'm still on earth. . . .

Since your death, things have become very simple in my life, and I believe in your daddy's life too. The things we thought were so necessary are unimportant. To get to the basics of Who God is and my relationship with Him is most important. After all, I really want to know the Person Who is now taking care of my son. How well I live by the rules we as Christians have laid down is not so important now. There was a lot of self-effort in my Christian life. God didn't save me by faith and then expect me to live the Christian life by self-effort. I think you were struggling to establish a relationship with God. You had accepted Christ as your Savior and always lived above reproach as a Christian, but you were wanting a real, personal relationship with God. In Heaven you have that relationship now, but I'm still here on earth struggling. I always tried to live right, but it was very "legalistic." I'm afraid that is how we taught you and your sister to live. We taught you how to accept Christ as Savior apart from works but then led you to believe that the Christian life was lived by self-effort, doing everything right. I believe that the element of love was left out of our teaching—accepting God's unchanging love and loving Him with your total being. This should come before works and lead to good works which are done out of a heart full of love for Him.

I'm writing this "open letter" to you as a testimony of an answer to your prayer, even after your death. If there is anything I have learned, it's that no matter how straight the line we walk in our Christian life is, it is empty self-effort without an attitude of worship and without allowing the Spirit of God to involve our total being in a loving relationship with Him. Out of that love will flow good works, a desire to fellowship with Him, a desire to please Him and serve Him. His love will compel us to be witnesses of His love to others. As the saying goes, I think I've had "the cart before the horse" by trying through self-effort to please the Lord and serve Him without letting His love fill my being in a very real, everyday sense. This realization is just beginning. Now I have to let it become an experience in my life. My prayer is that now I will live what I have learned.

Remember when I used to take you by the shoulder, tell you to look at me, and then say, "I love you, John"? I remember the sheepish look you would give me when I said that. Well, John, I still love you very much.

Your Mother

This mother picked up her son's search for a relationship with his Creator. She sought her God and was not disappointed. She was "in touch with reality." May it be true for all of us.

LIVING IN THE *REAL WORLD*

The dictionary defines "reality" as

1. The quality or state of being actual or true. 2. A person, entity, or event that is actual. 3. The totality of all things possessing actuality, existence, or essence. 4. That which exists objectively and in fact.[12]

The *real world* ("that which exists objectively and in fact"), as we have just read, is one that is created by and for the pleasure of the God of heaven. A man who is not seeking God ("a person, entity, . . . that is actual"), and who consequently is not seeing God, is living in the world

---

[12] *The American Heritage Dictionary of the English Language*, s.v. "reality."

without a full picture of reality ("the totality of all things possessing actuality, existence, or essence").

Paul instructed the pagan philosophers on Mars Hill in Athens about the *real* (true) God:

> God . . . made the world and all things therein, . . . [and] giveth to all life and breath, and all things; . . . For in him we live, and move, and have our being; . . . [He] now commandeth all men every where to repent: Because he hath appointed a day, in the which he will judge the world in righteousness by that man whom he hath ordained; whereof he hath given assurance unto all men, in that he hath raised him from the dead (Acts 17:24-31).

Ignorance of this truth—this reality—is not only eternally fatal but also a guarantee that life itself will be filled with emptiness, restlessness, and frustration.

The book of Ecclesiastes presents a powerful argument for precisely this point. Solomon said that God has "set the world [eternity] in their heart, so that no man can find out the work that God maketh from the beginning to the end" (3:11). This verse teaches that God has created within every man a desire to know the end from the beginning (the eternity) of everything he sees, yet God has withheld the solution to the mysteries. Solomon learned that he cannot control life (3:1-10) and that he cannot even comprehend life (3:11). God's purpose in human limitations is "that men should fear before him" (3:14). Unless man, with his natural, sinful bent, experiences some mysteries beyond his comprehension and some experiences beyond his power, he begins thinking that he is pretty much in control of his life, and in the process, he forgets God. That is a dangerous "break from reality." God mercifully prompts man to return to reality.

When someone at our house is experiencing a particularly difficult trial and is asked how he is doing, he often will reply, "I'll be OK once I take some time to argue myself back to reality." It is very easy when in a trial to get a distorted view of reality. It may appear that God isn't concerned or that He isn't able to keep His world running on schedule for us. Those are *illusions*. They are not true. They are not *reality*. This is why Peter warns those experiencing difficulty to "gird up the loins of [their] mind" (I Pet. 1:13). Like a Greek warrior tying his loose skirts tightly around his waist so that they do not impair his movement, a believer in a trial must restrain all sloppy thinking about life and about God during those times of difficulty. He must "argue himself back to reality." He must renew his mind about the central part God plays in every aspect of life.

CONCLUSION

Living in the real world requires that a man know the God who has revealed Himself to us. Man cannot create within himself a desire for God. *God* must take the initiative if man is to know Him. The good news is that God *has* taken the initiative—He has revealed Himself to us and created within us a desire to know Him, allowing us to know Him and His truth (i.e., the real world). Renewing the mind starts right here—with God!

TAKE TIME TO REFLECT

The old hymn writers had a keen sense of their need for God and of His all-sufficiency. Find a church hymnal that contains the following songs and meditate on the words. Make them a part of your personal praise to God by singing them to the Lord. Begin building your relationship with Him by putting Him into the center of your thoughts. We so easily become consumed with our own problems and obsessed with the search for the things we have decided we must have to make life work. In the process, we abandon God. That is a great "evil," according to Jeremiah 2:13. Put God on the forestage and turn the spotlights on Him! He is all that matters and the only One who can help. Let the words of these hymns help you.

"Constantly Abiding" (Mrs. Will L. Murphy)

"Draw Me Nearer" (Fanny J. Crosby)

"Fairest Lord Jesus" (German, seventeenth century)

"How Sweet the Name of Jesus Sounds" (John Newton)

"I Am His, and He Is Mine" (George Wade Robinson)

"In the Garden" (C. Austin Miles)

"I've Found a Friend" (James G. Small)

"Jesus, I Am Resting, Resting" (Jean S. Pigott)

"Jesus Is All the World to Me" (Will L. Thompson)

"Jesus, Lover of My Soul" (Charles Wesley)

"Jesus, the Very Thought of Thee" (Bernard of Clairvaux)

"Near to the Heart of God" (Cleland B. McAfee)

"Nothing Between" (Charles A. Tindley)

"Oh, to Be Like Thee!" (Thomas O. Chisholm)

"O Thou, in Whose Presence" (Joseph Swain)

" 'Tis So Sweet to Trust in Jesus" (Louisa M. R. Stead)

Write out your observations about the thoughts and desires for God expressed in these hymns. Do any of them reflect your own thirst for God? Do the ambitions of these hymn writers seem too lofty, or are they expressing something that any child of God can know? Do they stir you to have a greater desire for God, or do they discourage you? Summarize your thoughts on paper.

A WORD TO DISCIPLE-MAKERS

The Bible introduces us to three critical relationships between man and God and outlines the appropriate response to each. These relationships define "reality." They can be summarized as follows:

THE "REAL WORLD" AS GOD SEES IT		
RELATIONSHIP	RESULT	ESSENTIAL QUESTION OF LIFE ANSWERED
Creator-Creature	Humility	Where did I come from?
Father-Son	Security	Where am I going?
Master-Servant	Productivity	What am I here for?

Creator-Creature

God is immeasurably superior to man in every conceivable way. When man contemplates God and His works, he is aware of the enormous *distance* between himself and his Creator. Theologians call this distance "transcendence."

> When we speak of God as transcendent we mean of course that He is exalted far above the created universe, so far above that human thought cannot imagine it. To think accurately about this, however, we must keep in mind that "far above" does not here refer to physical distance from the earth but to quality of being.[13]

---

[13] Tozer, *Knowledge*, 107.

> We must not compare the being of God with any other. . . . We must not think of God as highest in an ascending order of beings, starting with the single cell and going on up from the fish to the bird to the animal to man to angel to cherub to God. This would be to grant God eminence, even pre-eminence, but that is not enough; we must grant Him *transcendence* in the fullest meaning of that word. Forever God stands apart, in light unapproachable. He is as high above an archangel as above a caterpillar, for the gulf that separates the archangel from the caterpillar is but finite, while the gulf between God and the archangel is infinite. The caterpillar and the archangel, though far removed from each other in the scale of created things, are nevertheless one in that they are alike created. They both belong in the category of that-which-is-not-God and are separated from God by infinitude itself.[14]

Reflecting on God's transcendence accentuates in our minds His *greatness*—a favorite theme of the psalmists and of the prophets.

There are those today who wish to exalt man's position to be something worthy of great esteem. Yet compared to his Creator, the psalmist cries out in wonder that God should even notice him. He exclaims, "What is man, that thou art mindful of him?" (Ps. 8:4).

Truly man was made in the image of his Creator, but even in his pristine glory in the Garden of Eden, each attribute he possessed was a mere shadow of the perfect archetype inherent in God. The Fall of man further distanced him from God and has distorted man's reflection of his Creator's image.

Chapters 2 through 5 in this book present man's true condition before God. Reflecting on the enormous distance between man and his Creator will produce a *humility* that expresses itself in a spirit of *dependency* upon God. That dependence replaces any confidence man is tempted to place in himself or in any other part of God's creation.

When you are discipling someone who is self-confident, self-assertive, or self-protective, or who is manifesting any other form of pride, you must bring him face to face with the truth of who he *really* is—a creature, not a god—who his Creator is, and the implications of those realities. Every philosophy of life attempts to answer three basic questions, the

---

[14] Ibid., p. 109. Italics are Tozer's.

first of which is "Where did I come from?" The Creator-creature relationship answers that question once and for all and puts man in his proper place.

The Psalms are replete with passages in which David contemplates the work of the Creator and responds with *worship*—the creature taking his place of humility before his Maker and praising Him because of His worthiness. In addition to meditating upon Psalms 8, 19, 29, 95, 104, 136, 139, and 148, study Genesis 1-2; Job 38-41; Isaiah 40, 45; John 1:3; Romans 1:19-20; Colossians 1:16; and Revelation 4:11.

Father-Son

Once a man has faced his sinfulness and has come to God in humility and repentance, he becomes a son of God (John 1:12). Part Two of this book presents how to develop a personal relationship with God and how to be changed by exposure to God. The New Testament introduces us to the reality that God is the Father of those who believe on Him. As a Father, He is certainly their Source of life and likeness, but the New Testament writers also use this term to teach us His tender care for His children. In the Creator-creature relationship, we see an immense *distance* between the essential nature and power of God and that of His creatures. That realization spawns *humility* in the creature. In the Father-Son relationship, we have a *nearness* that fosters *security*.

This powerful, sovereign Creator is also our loving and wise Father. We can speak to Him intimately and call Him "Our Father which art in heaven" (Matt. 6:9). Jesus said that in His Father's house He was preparing places for us in which we would dwell with Him forever (John 14:2). In the meantime He deals with us as *children*—disciplining us (Heb. 12:5-11), addressing us as "little children" who need to heed His instruction and admonition (I John), and constantly prompting us to "grow up" to be like our Elder Brother, Jesus Christ (Eph. 4:13, 15).

The result of understanding the Father's complete and perfect love for His children will be a growing sense of *security* in the believer. The apostle Paul assures us that in place of the "spirit of bondage" and "fear" we had before salvation, we have "received the Spirit of adoption, whereby we cry, Abba, Father [Daddy!]" (Rom. 8:15). John testifies of this security when he says that "perfect [mature] love casteth out fear" (I John 4:18). The security extends not only to our eternal home with the Father—answering the second philosophical question of life,

"Where am I going?"—but also applies to our temporal walk in the Father's ways in this life. As a loving Father, He gives both protection and direction to His children. A believer who is plagued by fears, anxieties, worries, obsessions, addictions, and other dependencies has not yet learned the liberating truth of the Father's love for His children. He has not learned the *goodness* of God.

The "Bad Dad" Syndrome

Please note here that many today insist that they have a hard time accepting God's fatherly care for them because they have never had a good father. They say they cannot understand what a good father would be like because they have never seen it in their own homes. Occasionally someone teaches that a person's view of his own father shapes his view of God. We need to understand the true dynamics underlying this idea and be able to dismiss any fallacies within it.

First, a person's view of his father does not necessarily shape his view of God. He is not without a basic view of a good father, or he would not have a standard in mind against which he compares his experience with his own father. He cannot know that his own father was *bad* if he does not know what a *good* father is like. More likely, he does not have a good view of God because he has not learned from the Scriptures who God is and what *He* is really like. In addition, a person can have the best of earthly fathers and still not know what God is like if he has not been exposed to biblical teaching about Him.

Another likely dynamic involved in the "I've-never-had-a-good-father-so-I-can't-understand-how-God-is-good" rationale is the propensity of man's heart to make excuses for its own misbehavior—a strategy that started in Eden—and man's arrogant habit of prejudice.[15] By prejudice I

---

[15] Don't dismiss this statement because it sounds too harsh—especially if you are thinking about yourself or someone you know who has suffered at the hands of another. You might think, "How could he say something so terrible—Joan is a victim! How could he make life harder by that kind of accusation!" Don't let your emotions dictate your theology. Remember that the picture of the human heart that God paints is not a pretty one. Don't "touch up" His portrait of man because you do not like how it looks. The snapshot God shows of man never lies. If your doctrine of man, anthropology, is off, your doctrine of change, sanctification, will be skewed as well. The biblical portrait of man's great depravity will drive us to God in greater dependency upon God's wonderful grace (Rom. 5:20).

mean the inclination to prejudge everyone in a certain category by our experiences with a representative of that category. For example, if a driver feels that he has been treated unkindly by the police officer who wrote him a speeding ticket, his heart will have a tendency to assume the worst—that the officer is on a "power kick" and that all officers operate from the same tainted motive.

It is also quite possible that the one who has not had the blessing of loving relationships in his home has never learned how to respond to love. He perhaps has *learned* to view every kindness as a step of manipulation. For example, an abused daughter soon learns that any special attention and kindness from Dad means that he is setting her up for another sexual favor.

An individual may also be threatened by genuine acts of love and goodness to him because it would require some sort of response from him—one with which he is yet unfamiliar because he was not taught at home how to graciously receive and respond to kindness. Therefore, he is threatened by any expression of love toward him. He can be taught from the Scriptures what a proper response to God's lovingkindness is.

The crucial need in any case is for the believer to *learn from God Himself* what He is like. Jesus presented to the Jews a totally new concept of God when He presented God as His Father and the Father of those who followed Christ. His Sermon on the Mount in Matthew 5 through 7 introduced an entirely new dimension of relationship with God that was different from any they had previously known. Study the Gospels, especially Matthew and John, and the First Epistle of John to see this relationship of the believer to his Father. The result is a great sense of *security* at being objects of the Father's love and a great *devotion* to the One who has loved us so.

Master-Servant

Reality is that God has redeemed His children. We have experienced deliverance from the penalties of sin and are being delivered from the power of sin as we are sanctified. The logical response to this kind of love is a grateful surrender to be His bondslave, translated as "servant," a term Paul often used to describe himself (Rom. 1:1; Gal. 1:10; Phil. 1:1) and that other apostles applied to themselves (James 1:1; II Pet. 1:1; Jude 1). Paul called this choice our "reasonable service" (Rom. 12:1). John says that we will love Him as we contemplate His love for us (I John

4:19). The result of reflecting on His great love for us will be a *dedication* of our lives to Him that motivates us to *productivity* for Him. We will explore that productivity in Part Three of this book. Our purpose in life is service for Christ, a purpose that answers the third major philosophical question of life, "What am I here for?" A believer who resists this surrender is resisting the *grace* of God shown to him at his salvation.

Your responsibility as a disciple-maker is to be alert to areas of need in the lives of those you work with. Do they lack humility? Teach them their place as a creature under the Creator. They must know the *greatness of God*. Are they fearful and lack security? They must know the *goodness of God*. Teach them how to have a personal relationship with their loving heavenly Father. Are they living for themselves instead of demonstrating productivity for Christ? They must know the *grace of God*. Teach them the obligations of a servant to his Master.

Don't miss the opportunities to teach them more about these essential relationships whenever possible. This is especially important in parenting. A major responsibility of parents is to teach their children who God is and what the appropriate response to that knowledge is. Parenting does not accomplish biblical goals merely by teaching children the disciplines of the Christian life without nurturing them in the essentials of a relationship with God. These essentials must be lived and taught by every disciple-maker. They are reality. Any attempt to make life work without them is an exercise in fantasy and futility.

CHAPTER SEVEN
BECOMING LIKE CHRIST

For with thee is the fountain of life: in thy light shall we see light.
Psalm 36:9

Since this book is about biblical change, you may be asking right now, "How does a search for God and a study of His attributes, as you mentioned earlier, change me and make me more like Christ? What does this have to do with renewing my mind?" Those are good questions that are at the heart of what this book is all about. Exposure to God brings about profound change in a believer—the kind of change to Christlikeness we need.

MORE ABOUT GOD'S ATTRIBUTES

To understand biblical change we must understand the Bible doctrine of illumination. We shall look at it in some detail in this chapter. But first we will learn how God's attributes fit into our study of sanctification. Some theologians divide the attributes of God into communicable and noncommunicable attributes. We use these two terms more commonly to talk about diseases. A communicable disease, like measles, is one you can "get" from someone else. A noncommunicable disease, like cancer, is one that cannot be passed from one person to another through normal contact. A noncommunicable attribute is one that no creature of God can "get." These attributes include the following:

- **Omnipotence**—God is all powerful.
- **Omniscience**—God innately knows everything.
- **Omnipresence**—God is everywhere at all times.
- **Immutability**—God's nature will never change.
- **Transcendence**—God is distinctly different from His creation.
- **Eternality**—God has no beginning or end.

Being like Christ does not involve acquiring any of these attributes. That is impossible. Being Christlike, rather, means acquiring His communicable attributes—those generally known as the "fruit of the Spirit." Galatians 5:22-23 lists several facets of the Spirit's fruit.[1] It lists the following:

- **Love**—genuine self-sacrifice for the good of others
- **Joy**—a feeling of great pleasure and delight in who God is and in what He has provided
- **Peace**—a sense of well-being; rest; tranquility; contentment
- **Longsuffering**—stability under pressure; self-control under provocation from people
- **Gentleness**—kindness toward others; reasonableness; flexibility
- **Goodness**—benevolent thoughts and actions toward others; generosity
- **Faith**—faithfulness; reliability
- **Meekness**—willingness to be governed; submissive attitude toward authority and circumstances
- **Temperance**—self-control, especially of one's passions

These are all communicable attributes of God. That means that God possesses these qualities and that any believer can "get" them as he is controlled by the Holy Spirit. When Jesus walked on this earth, these were characteristics of His life. These are what comes out of the "tea bag" of a Spirit-filled believer when he is put into "hot water" situations. When he manifests these characteristics on a consistent basis, even under pressure, we say he has Christian (Christlike) character.

CHANGED BY HIS GLORY

Second Corinthians 3:18 is a key verse in understanding biblical change: "But we all, with open face beholding as in a [mirror] the glory of the Lord, are *changed* into the same image from glory to glory, even as by the Spirit of the Lord."

---

[1] Most Bible teachers would say the list in Galatians 5:22-23 is representative, not exhaustive. Other passages outlining godly qualities include the Beatitudes in Matthew 5:1-12, the qualities of love in I Corinthians 13:4-8, the great virtues of II Peter 1:3-11, and the characteristics of godly wisdom in James 3:17-18.

Paul, in the verses preceding this one, has been showing the benefits of the new life in Christ as opposed to the former life of the Jews under the law of Moses. He said that those who insist on remaining under the Jewish system of laws in order to try to please God are spiritually blinded[2]—as if a veil were over their face.

He teaches that, by contrast, believers have an "open" or "unveiled" face—that is, the veil of blindness has been lifted, and they can perceive what God's Spirit wants to teach them about Himself.[3] As God shows them His glory in His Word, they experience a very specific change. By God's Spirit, they display an ever-increasing reflection of those "glories" in their own lives.

God's glory is the manifestation of His many-splendored excellencies. It was shown in the Old Testament as a Shekinah—a radiant reflection of God's nature too brilliant for any mortal to view directly. It was the overwhelming presence of His perfection.

When we look up at the sun, we see its white light—all of its colors mixed together. If we look at sunlight through a prism, we see the white light broken up into its individual colors of the rainbow.

A few men saw the "white light" of God's glory. They were almost blinded by the manifestation, as if looking at the sun directly, and fell on their faces in stunned humility.[4] For example, when Ezekiel the prophet told of the experience later, he almost stammered trying to come up with words to describe the experience. He said,

> And above the firmament that was over their heads was the *likeness* of a throne, as the *appearance* of a sapphire stone: and upon the *likeness* of the throne was the *likeness* as the *appearance* of a man above it. And I saw as the colour of amber, as the *appearance* of fire round about within it, from the *appearance* of his loins even upward, and from the *appearance* of his loins even downward, I saw as it were the *appearance* of fire, and it had brightness round about. As the *appearance* of the bow that is in the cloud in the day of rain, so was the *appearance* of the brightness round about. This was the

---

[2] See also II Corinthians 4:3-4 regarding the blindness of unbelief.

[3] See I Corinthians 2:9-16.

[4] Exodus 24:12-18; Revelation 1:12-18.

appearance of the *likeness* of the glory of the Lord. And when I saw it, I fell upon my face, and I heard a voice of one that spake (Ezek. 1:26-28).

Most people in the Scriptures who saw God, however, did not see this kind of blinding vision of the Lord. Rather than the "white light" of His glory, they saw individual "colors"—individual attributes. God revealed some aspect of Himself by giving people one of His names, which stands for some part of His character. Sometimes the way He dealt with the nation Israel or with an individual was to show some part of Himself—perhaps His faithfulness, His compassion, His power, His mercy, His covenant love, and so forth. His law given to Moses revealed the holiness of His nature. The behavioral codes of the Pentateuch showed aspects of His righteousness and His wisdom.

In the New Testament, God's specific "glories" or attributes were demonstrated more clearly in the earthly life of Jesus Christ. John 1:14 says, "And the Word [speaking of Jesus Christ] was made flesh [came to this earth], and dwelt among us, *(and we beheld his glory, the glory as of the only begotten of the Father,)* full of grace and truth."

Second Corinthians 3:18 tells us that we are "changed" when we are exposed to God with an "open [unveiled] face" (unobstructed contact). Paul is saying that no one who is exposed to the glories of God as they are revealed by God's Spirit through the Scriptures will remain the same.

ILLUMINATION: WHEN GOD TURNS ON THE LIGHT

Let's look at the actual process of this change more closely. We must not think that reading the Bible alone changes a man. God's Spirit must personally show the realities of God to that man as he ponders the Scriptures. This divine work is called "illumination." Let's look at a couple of biblical examples of this experience.

In Matthew 16:13 Jesus asked His disciples, "Whom do men say that I the Son of man am?" They replied that some thought He was John the Baptist and that others thought He was one of the prophets—perhaps Elijah or Jeremiah. He asked them a more pointed question in verse 15: "But whom say ye that I am?" Peter answered with a powerful statement of reality: "Thou art the Christ, the Son of the living God" (v. 16). Jesus' reply to Peter is instructive to us at this point in our study. Our Lord said,

"Blessed art thou, Simon Bar-jona: *for flesh and blood hath not revealed it unto thee, but my Father which is in heaven*" (v. 17).

Jesus said in effect, "Peter, you have experienced something that is not common to all men. You cannot learn what you learned by natural means. My Father Himself showed you this truth. He opened your eyes and you were illuminated."

Read Luke 24 and note the accounts of the two disciples traveling with the resurrected Christ on the road to the city of Emmaus (vv. 13-35) and of His subsequent appearance to a larger group of disciples (vv. 36-48). You will find that the disciples did not understand the significance of His death, burial, and Resurrection until they were illuminated. Jesus reminded them of the "things . . . which were written [about Him] in the law of Moses, and in the prophets, and in the psalms. . . . Then opened he their understanding, that they might understand the scriptures" (vv. 44-45).

Here is how C. H. Spurgeon described illumination when commenting on Psalm 36:9, "In thy light shall we see light."

> Purify flesh and blood by any educational process you may select, elevate mental faculties to the highest degree of intellectual power, yet none of these can reveal Christ. The Spirit of God must come with power, and overshadow the man with His wings, and then in that mystic holy of holies the Lord Jesus must display Himself to the sanctified eye, as He doth not unto the purblind [blinded] sons of men. Christ must be His own mirror. The great mass of this blear-eyed world can see nothing of the ineffable glories of Immanuel. He stands before them without form or comeliness, a root out of a dry ground, rejected by the vain and despised by the proud. Only where the Spirit has touched the eye with eye-salve, quickened the heart with divine life, and educated the soul to a heavenly taste, only there is He understood.[5]

A. W. Tozer expresses the same thought this way:

> For millions of Christians . . . God is no more real than He is to the non-Christian. They go through life trying to love an ideal and be loyal to a mere principle. . . . A loving Personality dominates the Bible,

---

[5] Charles Haddon Spurgeon, *Morning and Evening* (Peabody, Mass.: Hendrickson Publishers, 1991), 619.

walking among the trees of the garden and breathing fragrance over every scene. Always a living Person is present, speaking, pleading, loving, working, and *manifesting Himself whenever and wherever His people have the receptivity necessary to receive the manifestation.*[6]

It remains for us to think on [these truths] and pray over them *until they begin to glow in us.*[7]

If we cooperate with Him in loving obedience, *God will manifest Himself to us, and that manifestation will be the difference between a nominal Christian life and a life radiant with the light of His face.*[8]

TANNED BY THE SUN

Most fair-skinned people working in the sun for an extended period of time in their garden or in their vocation must shield themselves from the sun lest they be burned by it. Direct exposure to the sun will have an automatic effect on their skin. Tanning is not something they do *to* themselves. If the tan is a "vacation tan"—one that they got while on a vacation where they spent more time in the sun—it will gradually disappear when they return to their normal routine out of the sun.

Change into Christlikeness, likewise, is not something we do *to* ourselves. It is something that happens supernaturally through the agency of the Holy Spirit when we expose ourselves to God's Word and He reveals to us His glory. A light-skinned man who is not tanned as much as he would like can do only one thing—spend more time in the sun.[9] In fact, if a dark tan is truly important to him, he will not be watching the clock to see whether his "fifteen minutes" of time in the sun is up; he will be watching his skin to see whether it has the color he wants. If he wants a darker tan than his time in the sun gave him today, he will look at what he has to do tomorrow to see whether he can delay or eliminate anything so that he can spend more time in the sun.

---

[6] A. W. Tozer, *The Pursuit of God* (Camp Hill, Pa.: Christian Publications, 1993), 46.

[7] Ibid., 56.

[8] Ibid., 58.

[9] Please do not consider this illustration an endorsement of some people's fascination with tanning. Tanning can be fraught with all sorts of medical problems (e.g., cancer) and raises spiritually questionable issues (e.g., partial nudity). The effect of the sun on human skin, however, has some direct parallels to the effect of the glory of God on the believer's soul.

In the same way, a believer who is not manifesting godliness in some area of life can do only one thing—spend more time in the Word asking God to illuminate his mind and heart. Believers who have very little "tan" are revealing their limited exposure to the glory of God. We are called by God in I Peter 2:9 to "shew forth the praises [attributes] of him who hath called [us] out of darkness into his marvellous light." If we aren't spending time "walking in the light," our "untanned" (i.e., un-changed) lives show that our walk has been mostly "in darkness." If we truly want more change in our lives, we will look at what is on our agenda today to see whether anything can be postponed or eliminated so that we can spend more time being exposed to the glory of God. We won't be watching the clock; we will be watching for the effect of the glory of God on our lives.

Youth directors and pastors are aware of a phenomenon common to young people who go to a summer Bible camp and make decisions for the Lord. The decisions to give up their ungodly friends, habits, music, and so forth seem to last for only a couple of weeks. The teen's desire and resolve seem to weaken over time. He eventually returns to his former lifestyle very discouraged and perhaps even cynical because he loses hope that change is possible for him. Onlookers note the slide back into his old ways and comment that he made just a "camp decision." Unfortunately, many adults (and consequently, many teens) come to expect this phenomenon—an attitude that betrays a shallow under-standing of biblical change.

Suppose we were to take the same attitude toward a coworker who came back from a vacation at the ocean three weeks ago. He came back very tanned because of the time he and his family had spent in the sun, but now his tan is fading. We would not look scornfully at him and chide him for his "vacation tan." We wouldn't say that the tan he had when he returned wasn't real because it didn't last! We would all understand that unless he keeps up the same level of exposure to the sun that gave him the tan in the first place, he will not keep the tan. Rather than looking contemptuously at teens (or even adults) who make "camp decisions," we who understand how the Christian life works should immediately get involved helping them structure their lives to include generous amounts of time exposed to God's Word, while we pray that the Holy Spirit will continue to illumine their heart.

EVIDENCES OF EXPOSURE TO GOD

All of us know the most obvious effect of time spent in the sun—darker skin—but what happens when a man is exposed to the glory of God? What are the effects of illuminated truth upon a believer? Not all the effects we will discuss are present in the same proportion every time for every person who is illuminated, but there *will* be some effect. No man can see God or His truth and be unaffected by it. He will be moved in some way by the experience.

Illuminated Truth Moves the Believer Intellectually

Often when God's Spirit illumines some Scripture passage, the believer sees afresh the *validity* of the truth. He is moved to have a steadfast confidence, an inner assurance. He says to himself, "This is right; I must believe it!" An illuminated man is divinely persuaded that he has seen something from God and that what he has seen is right. He will boldly defy every assault of hell and will burn at the stake if necessary before he will deny the truth of what he has seen and knows to be true.

While the believer is intellectually convinced of the truth, he is also *humbled* by the experience. He is not cocky or arrogant in his knowledge. Every man in the Bible who truly saw some aspect of God and His nature was found "on his face." Whenever we see some area of our own life in contrast to God's nature, we will see our own great deficiency and rebellion in that area. We will be humbled and repentant.

In a teen leadership camp, Chris and the rest of the teens were given an assignment to memorize and meditate upon Philippians 2:3-16 to learn about the servant nature of their Lord. They were challenged to look at how Christ denied Himself in order to be a servant to others. Jesus did not concern Himself about His reputation among His peers. He obeyed His Father to take the lowest form of created, rational beings—a man. He further obeyed His Father and submitted to His human authorities to the point of death, even death by a humiliating and excruciating form of Roman torture—crucifixion.

In a personal conference with one of the leadership speakers, Chris shared how God had humbled him as he spent several hours during the week meditating on the text and thinking of its ramifications for Christ and for himself. As part of the exercise, he was to list seventy-five ways he was selfish at home, at work, and at school. It was humbling enough to see how much he looked out for himself at the expense of others throughout his daily routine; it was painful for him to realize his own selfishness compared to the self-sacrifice of his Lord on his behalf. He sought the Lord's forgiveness and was ready for help on how to be more like Christ at home. He had been *humbled* when his illuminated heart saw the glory of the Lord.

When we behold the glory of God and see some aspect of His nature, we are taught what that virtue truly looks like. In this illustration, Chris had thought he was a pretty good teen. In fact, if you were to ask his parents or his youth director what he was like, they would tell you that he was a model teen. He was leader of the youth group and had a good testimony at home and at school. Without doubt Chris had been responsive to his earthly authorities and to God in the areas he knew about, but it was not until he had been exposed to some aspect of the glory of God that he learned what self-sacrificing love really looks like. When he saw it manifested in the Person and works of God's Son, he was shown a new, higher standard. When compared to the teens around him, Chris always came out on top. When he considered the self-sacrificing humility of God's Son, Chris realized how much further he had to go to be Christlike.

Jesus taught His disciples a similar lesson when He washed His disciples' feet. Peter thought he was doing pretty well until he was exposed to this level of servant activity by his Master. After His actions, Jesus instructed them.

> So after he had washed their feet, and had taken his garments, and was set down again, he said unto them, Know ye what I have done to you? Ye call me Master and Lord: and ye say well; for so I am. If I then, your Lord and Master, have washed your feet; ye also ought to wash one another's feet. For I have given you an example, that ye should do as I have done to you. Verily, verily, I say unto you, The servant is not greater than his lord; neither he that is sent greater than he that sent him. If ye know these things, happy are ye if ye do them (John 13:12-17).

No man can be proud of his level of spiritual maturity or theological understanding when he has been exposed to God's nature. We "all have sinned, and *come short of the glory of God*" (Rom. 3:23). He may have made some progress on his spiritual journey, but he will quickly be *taught* by the glory of God that he has many more miles to cover before he can say he has "arrived."

Such are the impressions on the intellect of man when he sees God. He is at the same time taught, humbled, and made bold. How can it be otherwise—he has seen God!

Illuminated Truth Moves the Believer Emotionally

An illuminated believer viewing the glory of God sees the *beauty* of the truth. He declares, "This is wonderful; I must praise it!" The Word becomes attractive to him and he finds himself admiring it. It may even be breathtaking. There is a new loveliness and worthiness about the truth to him. He cherishes it and delights in its splendor.

The result emotionally is twofold. First, there is great *joy* within him. Notice how David almost explodes with delight over the law of God in Psalm 119. The psalmist sees the glory of the Word, loves its taste, and praises its beauty. He sees the excellency of it. Peter called the effect "joy unspeakable and full of glory" (I Pet. 1:8). An illuminated believer drinks deeply of this wellspring of joy, and others look with envy upon his continual feast of joy. Sometimes he is even overwhelmed by the hymns he sings. Their truth reminds him of what he has seen from God Himself, and he experiences a silent sense of camaraderie with the hymn writer who, he knows, has truly seen God himself.[10] This joy of which I speak is far more than the lightheartedness of a naturally exuberant, bubbling personality. It is the effect upon the soul of an illuminated man who has seen the glory of God.

---

[10] The lump in his throat and the tears in his eyes as the illumined believer sings are not the result of having worked himself into an emotional high by the mood-altering tunes and mantralike repetitions of many praise and worship songs. Neither is he experiencing merely the delight and sense of oneness and unity with hundreds—perhaps thousands—of others lifting their voices together with him as he sings in a large meeting or concert. Unfortunately, the emotions many experience during these times are mistaken for being "close to God." Rather, the truly illumined believer can hardly contain himself as he sings because the words of the hymn have reminded him of the truths he has previously seen from the Word when the Holy Spirit showed him the glory of God. The sight of God is as stunning to him at the time of this new reflection—when he is *thinking* about what he is singing—as it was at the moment of the initial illumination of that truth as he studied his Bible. He has never recovered from the experience of seeing God in His Word, and he hopes he never will.

Second, there is in him a great *peace*. Seeing God brings a great stability and steadiness to the soul. A man who is seeing truth illuminated by the Spirit of God is not agitated, restless, irritable, worried, or moody. He is at rest! He has seen God and that is enough. He is satisfied that nothing shall separate him from the love of his God[11] and that God will use His power on his behalf as He wisely sees fit. Paul called it the "peace . . . which passeth all understanding" (Phil. 4:7).

Joy and peace melt together to show an effect in man greater than the sum of its two parts. The believer is *satisfied*. He is like a person who has just pushed his chair back from the Thanksgiving dinner table at his grandmother's home after stuffing himself with turkey, dressing, gravy, sweet potatoes, hot rolls, cranberry sauce, and pumpkin pie; he cannot be tempted with an invitation to eat a bologna sandwich. He is just too full to eat anything else.

God made us to be completely satisfied with Himself. A believer who is beholding the glory of the Lord finds "fulness of joy" (Ps. 16:11). Such was the experience of the psalmist David. He was a "satisfied customer" because he had "tasted" and seen "that the Lord is good" (Ps. 34:8).

Many Christian organizations and churches are filled with discontented, frantic believers. Many of them are driven, perfectionistic, controlling people who never seem to be able to get everything checked off their lists. There is always something more to do. They never experience any real peace or rest because there is always something else out of control at the moment. If for some reason life quiets down for a few moments, they worry about what could go out of control if they don't keep an eye on everything. It is not long before these on-the-go, high-energy people turn into relational terrorists. When they are irritated, people keep their distance.

This sad state of affairs is a revelation that these believers have not spent much time "in the sun." Here's how our Lord expressed this in Matthew 11:28-30: "Come unto me, all ye that labour and are heavy laden, and I will give you rest. Take my yoke upon you, and learn of me; for I am meek and lowly in heart: and ye shall find rest unto your souls. For my yoke is easy, and my burden is light."

---

[11] See Romans 8:35-39.

Jesus made it quite clear that a man who spends time learning of Him will be a man known for the peace in his soul. Prayerful reflection on God's wisdom, power, and sovereignty calms the heart. Peter reminds us that "grace and *peace* [are] multiplied [to us] through the knowledge of God" (II Pet. 1:2). A person without peace—constantly agitated or restless—does not know God well.[12]

Centuries ago the prophet Isaiah promised that the man who would "seek . . . the Lord while he may be found" would "go out with *joy*, and be led forth with *peace*" (Isa. 55:6, 12). Illuminated truth surges with an unspeakable joy and an unquenchable peace that totally satisfies the believer. How can it be otherwise—he has seen God!

Illuminated Truth Moves the Believer Volitionally

When God's Spirit illumines the mind with truth, the believer is shown the *urgency* and the *responsibility* of the truth. He cries, "This is compelling; I must do it!" He is energized and motivated. He immediately wishes to become a witness of these things. He has something to testify about—he has seen God! The prophet Isaiah, when he saw God, exclaimed, "Here am I; send *me*" (Isa. 6:8). The apostle Paul, upon beholding the glory of God, asked, "Lord, what wilt thou have *me* to do?" (Acts 9:6).

Chris's response at camp, upon seeing the Lord's humility and obedience, was to humble himself in repentance, ponder how Christ's humility would look if manifested in his life, and cheerfully throw himself into whatever service for others he could find around him. The attitude of willing service is the natural result of seeing the glory of God. There is no grudging service here—no clock-watching laborers—only a burning passion of the believer to "present [his body] a living sacrifice, holy, acceptable unto God." He feels it is his "reasonable service" (Rom. 12:1). How can it be otherwise—he has seen God!

This Is Revival!

This effect of illuminated truth upon the heart of a believer is the essence of revival. When the Holy Spirit reveals the glory of God to him, the believer's response is always, "This is right; I must believe it! This is wonderful; I must praise it! This is compelling; I must do it!" A man

---

[12] See Psalm 119:165.

moved in this manner by what he is seeing of God is being revived, and others cannot help noticing the profound change. Those around him see his "light so shin[ing] before men, that they . . . see [his] good works, and glorify [his] Father which is in heaven" (Matt. 5:16). The change in him is the direct work of the Spirit of God upon the soul of a man who is seeking God in His Word.

Believers must take the time and effort to hike into the forest of God's Word and harvest the logs of truth from that massive timberland. They must by reflection split the logs and stack them in the fireplace of their own heart while they pray for the illumination from God to set the logs ablaze. The resulting fire will provide the light that directs their paths and the heat that fuels their passion for God.

Unfortunately, most people accumulate only a few sticks of kindling from their pastor's Sunday sermons—not because he doesn't present great truths from God's Word but because they think little upon those truths, even during the message. Even when God *does* ignite those splinters of truth, their fire blazes only momentarily because there is so little truth for the Holy Spirit to burn.

Solomon's burden in Proverbs 2 is that men would embark on this earnest and diligent search for truth. He says that the man who will do so will "find the knowledge of God" (2:5). He is the one who God says will "*receive* my words, and *hide* my commandments" (2:1). He will "*incline* [his] ear" and "*apply* [his] heart" (2:2). He is the one who "*criest* after knowledge" and "*liftest* up [his] voice for understanding" (2:3). He "*seekest* [wisdom] as silver" and "*searchest* for her as for hid treasures" (2:4). This is no casual "I'll-pursue-God-if-I-have-the-time-and-if-I-remember-to-do-it" attitude. It is the wholehearted pursuit of God within His revelation that is rewarded with a view of God Himself!

This is revival! This is the crying need of our day! Our preaching, counseling, and writing must point people to the God whose glories fill eternity. We must teach people to pursue *Him* in the Word while they beg the Spirit of God to illumine their eyes so that they can be "changed into the same image from glory to glory, even as by the Spirit of the Lord" (II Cor. 3:18).

THE RIGHT DIAGNOSIS

We can look around us and see so many disheartening problems. The violence, crime, poverty, and educational deficiencies grieve anyone sensitive to the plight of those around him. The family, which should be the greatest refuge for a child, has become a domestic battlefield where a child is often caught in the crossfire of his parents' warfare. The time and energy that should be spent giving him the direction and training he needs to prepare him for life are drained by each spouse's preoccupation with protecting his "territory" from the other spouse.

At the same time that social ills and marital troubles are escalating, we witness an increase in the amount of personal instability of even the average, middle-class citizen. The sale of prescription drugs for supposed psychiatric disorders is at an all-time high, and it is almost in vogue to be seeing a psychiatrist or to be in counseling for marital or personal problems. However, attempts to achieve emotional stability, recover from disorders, fix the family, restructure society, upgrade education, eliminate poverty, and rehabilitate criminals will continue to fall short of their intended goals because they never address the root cause of the problem—man is estranged from God and, therefore, "out of touch with reality."

Sadly, even those who have experienced the redemption of God's salvation from eternal torment are ignorant of most of reality as God defines it because they do not know God well. Most believers know God only as well as tourists whose sole knowledge of the country they are visiting is from the information they have acquired at their destination airport. They have arrived in the country and have listened to the receptionist at the information booth "preach" about the wonders of the local scenery. They have glanced through the brochures, studied the maps, and talked with some of the nationals. They have even "raised their hands" that they would be interested in a tour, but other distractions have kept them from actually getting out of the airport and seeing the country for themselves. They may know more *about* the country than they did before their arrival, but they don't really *know* the country. They have not explored its coasts, penetrated its mainland, and gazed upon its natural beauty. They are merely tourists—and poor ones at that. In much the same way, many believers simply do not know God in any kind of personal, ongoing, intimate relationship. Their hearts are, for the most part, unilluminated. Consequently, they are not "changed into the same image." Biblical change starts with God, is orchestrated by God, and is accomplished by His Spirit entirely for the glory of God.

WHAT IS YOUR VIEW OF GOD?

We have touched very little on the actual disciplines involved in "beholding" the glory of God in this chapter. We will devote more time to discussing those elements in the following two chapters. For now, it is crucial that you at least understand the *importance* of beholding the glory of God as God illuminates His truth by His Spirit. There can be no change to Christlikeness without it. To further impress upon our minds this truth, I will conclude this section with an extended quotation from A. W. Tozer.

> What comes into our minds when we think about God is the most important thing about us. . . .
>
> For this reason the gravest question before the Church is always God Himself, and the most portentous fact about any man is not what he at a given time may say or do, but what he in his deep heart conceives God to be like. We tend by a secret law of the soul to move toward our mental image of God. This is true not only of the individual Christian, but of the company of Christians that composes the Church. Always the most revealing thing about the Church is her idea of God, just as her most significant message is what she says about Him or leaves unsaid, for her silence is often more eloquent than her speech. She can never escape the self-disclosure of her witness concerning God.
>
> Were we able to extract from any man a complete answer to the question, "What comes into your mind when you think about God?" we might predict with certainty the spiritual future of that man. Were we able to know exactly what our most influential religious leaders think of God today, we might be able with some precision to foretell where the Church will stand tomorrow. . . .
>
> A right conception of God is basic not only to systematic theology but to practical Christian living as well. It is to worship what the foundation is to the temple; where it is inadequate or out of plumb the whole structure must sooner or later collapse. I believe there is scarcely an error in doctrine or a failure in applying Christian ethics that cannot be traced finally to imperfect and ignoble thoughts about God.

It is my opinion that the Christian conception of God . . . is so decadent as to be utterly beneath the dignity of the Most High God and actually to constitute for professed believers something amounting to moral calamity.

All the problems of heaven and earth, though they were to confront us together and at once, would be nothing compared with the overwhelming problem of God: That He *is*; what He is *like*; and what we as moral beings must *do* about Him. . . .

Let us beware lest we in our pride accept the erroneous notion that idolatry consists only in kneeling before visible objects of adoration, and that civilized peoples are therefore free from it. The essence of idolatry is the entertainment of thoughts about God that are unworthy of Him. It begins in the mind and may be present where no overt act of worship has taken place. "When they knew God," wrote Paul, "they glorified him not as God, neither were thankful; but became vain in their imaginations and their foolish heart was darkened." . . . The idolater simply imagines things about God and acts as if they were true.[13]

If our view of God is not right, nothing can ultimately be right in our lives. To live in the *real world*, God must be central in our thoughts. We must embrace Paul's perspective of God's role in all of this:

For by him were all things created, that are in heaven, and that are in earth, visible and invisible, whether they be thrones, or dominions, or principalities, or powers: all things were created by him, and for him: And he is before all things, and by him all things consist. And he is the head of the body, the church: who is the beginning, the firstborn from the dead; *that in all things he might have the preeminence* (Col. 1:16-18).

TAKE TIME TO REFLECT

Spending a Day with God

I'm sure by now you realize that you cannot change any part of your life without a growing relationship with your Creator. You must first be reconciled with and submissive to God. In addition, something must be "going on" between you and God for any real progress to be made.

---

[13] Tozer, *Knowledge*, 1-3, 5. Italics are Tozer's.

Everything God allows in our lives is designed by Him to draw us to Himself in humble submission and dependence. You grow only when you are moving toward that end.

Furthermore, you cannot help others come to know God in this way if you are not walking in this kind of fellowship yourself. If you have not seen much progress in your own walk with Christ, let me suggest that you plan to take a day or weekend off and spend it alone with God. Married couples find it necessary to get alone together on a regular basis to improve their relationship with each other and to build their marriage. Sometimes they annually attend a couple's conference where, in addition to the sessions on marriage topics, they are able to spend some quiet time together reflecting on their marriage and planning ways to make their relationship stronger. Other couples plan a weekend away on their anniversary for the same purpose. The main idea is to remove themselves from the daily distractions so that they can devote their thoughts and attention to each other and their relationship. Plan a similar "retreat" alone with God.

If your responsibilities will not allow you to take an entire weekend away, at least plan for quarterly outings with God. For example, arrange to free up several hours of a Saturday. Pack a lunch and drive to a local or state park or somewhere else where you will not be around many people. Take your Bible, a notebook, your prayer list, a hymnal, and perhaps a devotional book. Spend your time reading lengthy sections of the Scriptures and writing down what you are learning about God or about your own heart condition. Allow God to bring to your mind any matters that need to be reconciled with Him or others. Write down the names of the people you need to see to make reconciliation so that you do not forget to do so once you return home. Confess your sin to God and praise Him for the promises of His forgiveness.

Take some time to sing praises to Him out of your hymnal. (Go ahead and sing out loud if no one is around, even if you can't "carry a tune.") If you absolutely cannot sing, read the words out loud slowly and reflectively so that their meaning can sink into your heart. If you play the guitar, take it with you to accompany yourself, but don't get side-tracked by getting caught up on the practice time with your instrument or "performing" for anyone close by who might hear you. If it will become a distraction in any way to your worship of God, leave it home.

Set aside some time to get "caught up" on your intercessory prayer for family members, coworkers, spiritual leaders in your life, missionaries, and those enduring great affliction at this time because of illness or disaster. Make note of any "errands of mercy" you could do for them when you return home or spend a few minutes writing a letter of encouragement right then.

Choose a Scripture passage of several verses and meditate on it using the Becoming God's Kind of Person and How to Meditate: The MAP Method study sheets in Appendix A of this book. Memorize the passage and spend time prayerfully reflecting on its meaning and application for you. Write out what changes you will need to make in your life to carry out what you learned from God's Word. You must take time for God to speak to you. Ask Him to illumine you by His Spirit. Listen to Him and reflect seriously on what He says.

By now I think you get the idea. You cannot know God "on the run" any more than you can know any other person that way. Personal relationships are not built "efficiently." They take enormous amounts of time devoted to interaction with the other person. (This is why we call our time with God "devotions"; it is time "devoted" to Him.) You will find that your "day with God" will have a significant effect upon your regular, daily devotional time with Him. When you spend time with Him each day, though it be only thirty to forty-five minutes, the depth and quality of the interaction with God will be profoundly different. When you sense the shallowness creeping back in, schedule another "day with God." You cannot become an effective disciple-maker of others if you do not spend this kind of time with God on a regular basis. You will soon lose sight of the place God must play in your ministry to others. You will not be passionate about their need for God since you are experiencing no passion for God yourself. Also, you will not know how to help them develop their relationship with God since you have not done it yourself.

Consider these admonitions from C. H. Spurgeon at the age of twenty as he began his Sunday morning sermon at the New Park Street Chapel on January 7, 1855:

> It has been said by some one that "the proper study of mankind is man." I will not oppose the idea, but I believe it is equally true that the proper study of God's elect is God; the proper study of a Christian is the Godhead. The highest science, the loftiest speculation, the mightiest philosophy, which can ever engage the attention of a child

of God, is the name, the nature, the person, the work, the doings, and the existence of the great God whom he calls his Father.

There is something exceedingly improving to the mind in a contemplation of the Divinity. It is a subject so vast, that all our thoughts are lost in its immensity; so deep, that our pride is drowned in its infinity. Other subjects we can compass and grapple with; in them we feel a kind of self-content, and go our way with the thought, "Behold I am wise." But when we come to this master-science, finding that our plumb-line cannot sound its depth, and that our eagle eye cannot see its height, we turn away with the thought, that vain man would be wise, but he is like a wild ass's colt; and with the solemn exclamation, "I am but of yesterday, and know nothing." No subject of contemplation will tend more to humble the mind, than thoughts of God. . . .

But while the subject humbles the mind it also expands it. He who often thinks of God, will have a larger mind than the man who simply plods around this narrow globe. . . . The most excellent study for expanding the soul, is the science of Christ, and Him crucified, and the knowledge of the Godhead in the glorious Trinity. Nothing will so enlarge the intellect, nothing so magnify the whole soul of man, as a devout, earnest, continued investigation of the great subject of the Deity.

And whilst humbling and expanding, this subject is eminently consolatory. Oh, there is, in contemplating Christ, a balm for every wound; in musing on the Father, there is a quietus for every grief; and in the influence of the Holy Ghost, there is a balsam for every sore. Would you lose your sorrows? Would you drown your cares? Then go, plunge yourself in the Godhead's deepest sea; be lost in His immensity; and you shall come forth as from a couch of rest, refreshed and invigorated. I know nothing which can so comfort the soul; so calm the swelling billows of grief and sorrow; so speak peace to the winds of trial, as a devout musing upon the subject of the Godhead.[14]

A WORD TO DISCIPLE-MAKERS

Something True About God

When teaching biblical principles, commands, or examples, be sure you teach the attribute of God that lies behind each principle, command, or

---

[14] C. H. Spurgeon, *The New Park Street Pulpit*, vol. 1 (1856; reprint, Grand Rapids: Zondervan Publishing House, 1963), 1.

lesson from a biblical example. Everything in the Scriptures is given to teach us something about God. When your child asks you, "Daddy, why does Uncle John smoke cigarettes and we don't?" you need to have a solid answer anchored in the nature of God. Depending on your child's level of understanding, you should be able to tell him something like this:

"Son, God says our bodies are the temples of God (I Cor. 6:19-20). Since God has chosen to live in us when we become Christians, we should keep our temple healthy and clean. If God were a sinner like us, He wouldn't mind; but since He is holy and deserves our very best, we want to be as clean and healthy as we can be. Smoking hurts our bodies and wastes our money, so we don't do it. Uncle John isn't a Christian yet, so he doesn't understand how important it is. We need to keep praying for him and witnessing to him.

"But we have to remember something, Son. Smoking isn't the only thing that hurts our bodies. Staying up late and not getting enough sleep, eating foods that are not good for us, and eating too much food aren't good for us either. God is a special person, and we want to make our bodies a special place for Him to live in."

Behind every truly godly practice and principle is something true about God—an attribute that requires a certain response from His creatures. We don't want those we disciple learning just a code of moral conduct or ethics; we want them to know their God and to respond to *Him* in each situation.

How God's Attributes Affect Christian Standards

The chart on the following page shows how our personal standards (the bottom box) must flow out of God's attributes (the top box). Study the chart carefully, noting the flow of examples one and two throughout the entire chart. Once you have studied the chart, read the explanatory paragraphs that follow.[15]

---

[15] General concepts taken from "Standards vs. Convictions," unpublished outline by Tony Miller. Used by permission.

| **ATTRIBUTE** |
| "Something true about God"[16] |
| *Example: God is love* |

PRECEPT	**PRINCIPLE**
A specific command reflecting an attribute of God	A general law or concept about an attribute of God
Example: Matt. 23:37-40—love the Lord your God and your neighbor as yourself	*Example: Rom. 8:35-39—nothing shall separate us from His love*
Comes from **Outside Man** *(revelation)* ⬇	⬇ Comes from **Outside Man** *(revelation)*

| Is developed **Inside Man** *(meditation)* |
| **CONVICTION** |
| A personal belief about how an attribute of God relates to me |
| *Example 1: I will deny myself in order to show my love to God and my neighbor.* |
| *Example 2: Since nothing shall separate me from God's love, I can trust His actions.* |

| **STANDARD** |
| A personal guideline that reflects my conviction |
| *Example 1: I will stop being critical of John, although he aggravates me by his pickiness and ill-temperedness. Instead I will look for ways to do good to him, including planning a way to lovingly confront him so that he can be restored and once again become useful to God.* |
| *Example 2: I will reject any thought that questions God's character and love for me, and I will remind myself of what I learned about His love when I memorized Romans 8:35-39.* |

Notice that every precept (specific command from God) is a revelation of His nature. He commands us to be holy because *He* is holy. He commands us to be merciful because *He* is merciful. We are to forgive others because *He* has forgiven us. He commands husbands to love their wives because *Christ* loved the church. Behind each of His commands is a specific concept about God's nature that compels Him to issue that command. We will honor His commands if we honor Him as a person.

The same is true for every principle (a general law) we find in the Scriptures. For example, we are to do everything "decently and in order" because God is a God of order and design (I Cor. 14:40). He does everything according to plan and on time. He does not do anything haphazardly or halfheartedly.

---

[16] Tozer, *Knowledge*, 19.

From these *precepts* and *principles*, which are based upon *attributes*, we form *convictions*—personal beliefs about how an attribute of God relates to me. As a result of the principle of God's orderliness and purpose that we see in His creation and in His redemptive works, we might come to this conclusion: Since I want to be like God, I must strive to have an affinity for order and stop living chaotically. I must start planning what I am going to do with my time instead of impulsively doing whatever comes to my mind and appeals to my flesh at the moment.

The application of that newly formed conviction shows up in various standards I might impose upon my life. To apply the conviction for order in the previous paragraph, I might come up with the following personal guidelines—*standards*: I will establish and maintain a personal budget so that my spending reflects godly priorities instead of impulse buying. I will sit down on Sunday afternoon and decide how I will spend my evenings during the coming week. I will keep a running list of jobs that need to be done around the house or for others, and I will work on these a little bit at a time instead of letting them pile up while I vegetate on the couch watching television every night.

Again, it takes reflective time to go through this process, but it is the only way to bring your life into conformity to the nature of God. Remember, this whole process starts with meditation upon the attributes of God and a study of the Word that highlights for us His precepts and principles. Everything above the thick black line in the middle of the preceding chart comes from God and is the product of God's revelation to us. Everything below the thick black line comes from the time we spend with God meditating on His Word and asking Him to show us how His revelation should affect our daily lives.

We need to be sure, as we said in the illustration about the boy's curiosity over his uncle's smoking, that we do not merely pass on our standards to our children and others we are discipling. We must take the time to show them the biblical precept or principle behind the conviction and standard, and even more important *we must show them the God behind the precepts and principles.*

CHAPTER EIGHT

SEARCHING FOR WISDOM

Let this mind be in you, which was also in Christ Jesus.
Philippians 2:5

Wisdom is the principal thing; therefore get wisdom: and with all thy getting get
understanding. Exalt her, and she shall promote thee: she shall bring thee to
honour, when thou dost embrace her.
Proverbs 4:7-8

In the last chapter we looked at how we are changed into the image of Christ by beholding the glory of God. There are still a few gaps that must be filled in, however, if we are to have a working understanding of how this change takes place as God's Spirit uses God's Word to renew our mind.

Part Two of this book is entitled "Renewing Your Mind." Another title for this section could have been "Developing the Mind of Christ." It could also have been called "Getting Wisdom from God" since the Old Testament forerunner and equivalent to Christlikeness is "wisdom." In fact, Jesus Christ is called "the wisdom of God" (I Cor. 1:24). Many Bible teachers believe that Lady Wisdom in Proverbs 1:20 ff. and Proverbs 8 is a personification of Christ. Furthermore, the fruit of the Spirit and the characteristics of wisdom are the same. That shouldn't surprise us, however, since they have the same Source. A study of how we become wise, therefore, will clarify for us many of the actual basics of how we become Christlike by renewing our minds.

In the first sermon of His public earthly ministry, Jesus Himself preached that a man must have two specific heart responses to His words to be wise. That inaugural sermon was like nothing His audience had ever heard. It was brief but potent. Within minutes He had swept away centuries of sloppy thinking about God and man's place before Him. He articulated the nature of godliness in a few short phrases that came to

163

be called the Beatitudes. He penetrated old concepts of "thou shalts" and "thou shalt nots" and exposed the heart issues of each one with His authoritative "But I say unto you."

He said His people should not only refrain from murder but also seek reconciliation with the person they would kill if they could. They should abstain from adultery—even in the mind. They should learn to take insults graciously and love their enemies. He said that spiritual disciplines of praying, fasting, and giving should be done secretly, not for show, and that worry over temporal matters was to be replaced with a passion for eternal matters. His audience was stunned with His obvious authority and His uncommon grasp of truth. Jesus closed this first sermon, the one we call the Sermon on the Mount, with the following invitation:

> Therefore whosoever heareth these sayings of mine, and doeth them, I will liken him unto *a wise man,* which built his house upon a rock: And the rain descended, and the floods came, and the winds blew, and beat upon that house; and it fell not: for it was founded upon a rock. And every one that heareth these sayings of mine, and doeth them not, shall be likened unto *a foolish man,* which built his house upon the sand: And the rain descended, and the floods came, and the winds blew, and beat upon that house; and it fell and great was the fall of it (Matt. 7:24-27).

These final words of His sermon have several important implications for the believer that will be the focus of our study in this chapter and the next. First of all, they teach that wisdom is found in the context of a *relationship* with Him—the hearer's response to *His* words. These are not the words of a fellow mortal. They are the words of the living God. No man can have a "take it or leave it" attitude about anything God says without significantly affecting his relationship with Him.

Second, this passage teaches which actual *responses* to His words will make a man wise. Jesus clearly defined two—hearing and doing. We shall see later how these two responses must become habitual practices for a man's heart to remain fertile soil for truth. They are the primary disciplines of wisdom and, thus, of a Christlike, renewed mind.

Third, He made it clear that whether or not a man responds by hearing and doing will determine the usefulness of his life to God. The foolish man who ignores His words will come to a predictable result: *instability* and, therefore, *uselessness*. A house that cannot withstand the pressures of a storm is useless as a shelter for a man and his family. In the same way, a man who is unstable, up and down, and inconsistent is useless as a servant for God. Conversely, a man who is faithfully hearing and doing will have the stability of life to be useful to his Master, just as a solidly built house is useful to the owner.

These closing remarks in the Sermon on the Mount concisely and powerfully state the nonnegotiable, bottom-line requirements for wisdom—the mind of Christ. They are not at all like the lengthy and contradictory teachings of the religious leaders of Jesus' day. Imagine how His audience of ordinary people must have felt after hearing His words. Now anyone—young, old, blind, poor, unlearned, man or woman alike—could be wise. No wonder "the common people heard him gladly" (Mark 12:37). His simple requirements should put hope in our heart as well. We, too, can be wise!

WHAT IS WISDOM?

Before we look at the actual disciplines of wisdom—hearing and doing—we need to have in our minds a good idea of what wisdom is. We want to avoid some misconceptions about it.

Some people have the idea that possessing wisdom is having some kind of bird's-eye view of all that God is doing in the world—and particularly in their own lives. They think of wisdom as the view of the rush-hour traffic snarl from the traffic helicopter. From that vantage point the pilot and news broadcaster can view the whole area and can see the exact cause and effect of every automobile's activity. These people think that, with wisdom, life should be equally understandable. It is not uncommon for people who believe that wisdom is a "helicopter view" to become quite discouraged when they come to a crisis and cannot see the whole picture.[1]

Example: Carolyn was quite distraught when complications developed during her infant son's surgery to correct a birth defect. Her anxiety went beyond the normal motherly love and concern for her baby. She began to question her own walk with God. She was known in her circle of

---

[1] The two descriptions of wisdom (dashboard and helicopter) are adapted from concepts suggested by J. I. Packer in *Knowing God*, pp. 91-93.

friends as a spiritually minded woman and seemed to know how to interpret the circumstances of life to know what God was trying to do. She said, "I could see how God was using my own illness last year to teach me more of His love and care, but I can't see any good that will come out of this for little Timmy. What is he going to learn? He's only eight months old. And why would God do something to Timmy to teach me anything? It seems that God should be doing something to *me*—not my son—if He wants to teach me something."

We can all certainly understand Carolyn's concern for her son's welfare and perhaps even identify with her questions. Part of the struggle Carolyn is having, however, is a result of her faulty view of wisdom and godliness. She truly believes that if she is walking with God she will understand the "whys and wherefores" of everything that happens in her life. If she cannot figure out how "all things work together for good" (Rom. 8:28) in her life, she feels that somehow she has disqualified herself from some "inner circle" with God where He shares all the secrets of His providence.

A quick survey of the Scriptures will reveal, however, that most of God's saints never knew much of His plan at all. That certainly was the case with Abraham, who was told to leave home and just follow God. It was the experience of Joseph, Daniel, Job, and hosts of others as well. Very seldom did they have a "big picture" of God's providence. Wisdom, then, is not the view of the road from the helicopter *above* the traffic snarl.

The View from the Dashboard

A more fitting illustration of wisdom is to view it as the skill exercised by a driver caught *in the middle* of the traffic snarl. He must know the *next right response* when someone slams on the brakes in front of him or cuts him off unexpectedly or when a child in the back seat lets out a bloodcurdling scream. His response to dilemmas like these reveals his real skill (wisdom) as a driver.

He does not have to know *why* his car blew a tire at that time, but he needs to know how to skillfully get his disabled vehicle off to the side of the road without injury to people or property. He does not have to know *why* the lane ahead of him is barricaded, but he must know how to skillfully merge with the cars in the lane next to him.

In Genesis 39 Joseph did not know *why* he had to spend time in prison on a trumped-up charge of attempted rape, but he knew and practiced *responses* that kept him usable to God anyway. The patriarch Job never knew *why* all of his children and properties were wiped out in God's providence, but he knew and practiced *responses* that kept him usable to God anyway. The apostle Paul never knew *why* God refused to remove his "thorn in the flesh" (II Cor. 12:7), but he knew and practiced *responses* that kept him usable to God anyway. The important lesson here is that *wisdom is not having God's perspective of the whole matter before us, but having God's perspective about what next response will honor Him while keeping us still usable to Him.*

The goal of safe driving is to stay on the road in order to reach the destination. A skillful driver knows how to do that in most of the conditions that may confront him. Similarly, the goal of the Christian life is to stay on the path of usefulness to God no matter what the circumstances. Christians who are thrown off the road of usefulness by indulgences in their own flesh or by ungodly reactions to calamity or to the fleshly actions of others are not living wisely.

Incidentally, parenting, as well as any other discipleship effort, is essentially this kind of spiritual "driver's training"—teaching and training that prepare the child to stay on the path of usefulness to Christ no matter what comes from without or within. As I have already explained, the goal is not to rear a "good kid" or have students who are excelling academically, and so forth. The goal is to equip these young saints "for the work of the ministry" (Eph. 4:12) to help them stay on the road of usefulness. If, in the end, they are unusable to Christ—they are not handling life wisely—both we and they have failed.

A Day of Judgment Is Coming
We must not forget how critical this matter of usefulness is to God. Many Christians today have the idea that they will appear at the Judgment Seat of Christ to be judged for their sin. That is not the case. All our sin—past, present, and future—was judged at Calvary. The total payment was made and the wrath of God was propitiated by Christ's atonement.

The Judgment Seat of Christ will be an examination of our usefulness or fruitfulness for God. Our works—not our sin—will be exposed as either "good or bad" (II Cor. 5:10). The word "bad" in this verse does not mean "evil." It means useless or good for nothing. Since He fully paid our sin debt and bought us for Himself, He is entitled to a full measure of usefulness from us. That is why we are called His servants.

The whole point of our Lord's teaching about abiding in the vine in John 15 is that He is interested in our fruit-bearing ability. He said, "Ye have not chosen me, but I have chosen you, . . . *that ye should go and bring forth fruit, and that your fruit should remain*" (John 15:16). He is speaking here of the fruit of our service (converts) and of our sanctification (Christlike character). In the Sermon on the Mount, He expressed His plan that we be the "salt of the earth." He warned that if we lose our "savour"—our saltiness—we are "good for nothing" as far as use to His kingdom is concerned (Matt. 5:13). He further stated that we are to be the "light of the world," but that we will be useless unless the light can be seen. It would do no good to be hidden (Matt. 5:14-16). A man out of fellowship with God because of unconfessed sin in his life is contributing to the darkness around him. His life has no redemptive influence. Since he is not working "with" the Lord in His purposes, Jesus said that man is actually "against me" (Matt. 12:30). Our Lord is serious about our usefulness to Him.

A believer who practices "already-paid-for sin" disqualifies himself from that usefulness because he is grieving the Spirit of God, who must empower him for service. He will be held accountable for that "good for nothing" condition—not for the sin which disqualified him from that usefulness. That sin was judged fully and forever at the cross.[2] Walking in wisdom, as the Bible defines it, is the only way for a man to be useful to God. It is the only way we avoid being "ashamed before him at his coming" (I John 2:28) when we shall stand before Him to give an account of our usefulness.

THE PATH TO WISDOM

As we have seen, Jesus set forth the twin disciplines of hearing and doing as foundational to the acquisition of wisdom. His statement at the end of the Sermon on the Mount is not the only passage where God links these two disciplines together. Consider carefully the following passages:

---

[2] See Romans 14:12; I Corinthians 3:13-15; II Corinthians 5:10; and I John 2:28; 4:17 for teaching about the Judgment Seat of Christ.

And the king of Assyria did carry away Israel unto Assyria . . . Because they obeyed not the voice of the Lord their God, but transgressed his covenant, and all that Moses the servant of the Lord commanded, and would not *hear* them, nor *do* them (II Kings 18:11-12).

And they come unto thee as the people cometh, and they sit before thee as my people, and they *hear* thy words, but they will not *do* them: for with their mouth they shew much love, but their heart goeth after their covetousness. And, lo, thou art unto them as a very lovely song of one that hath a pleasant voice, and can play well on an instrument: for they *hear* thy words, but they *do* them not (Ezek. 33:31-32).

And [Jesus] answered and said unto them, My mother and my brethren are these which *hear* the word of God, and *do* it (Luke 8:21).

But be ye *doers* of the word, and not *hearers* only, deceiving your own selves. For if any be a *hearer* of the word, and not a *doer*, he is like unto a man beholding his natural face in a glass: For he beholdeth himself, and goeth his way, and straightway forgetteth what manner of man he was. But whoso looketh into the perfect law of liberty, and continueth therein, he being not a forgetful *hearer*, but a *doer* of the work, this man shall be blessed in his deed (James 1:22-25).

God's concern is that His people will often fail to *hear* His words, or they will *hear* but will fail to *do* them. This twofold responsibility is the foundation for usefulness in God's plan for man. Study carefully the chart on the following page so that you can see where our study in wisdom is headed. Make sure the map is clear in your mind before we start the journey. We divide each of the two master disciplines of hearing and doing into two more basic disciplines so that we can look at them more closely. We call these components of wisdom "disciplines" to underscore the need for them to become habitual responses of life. They are developed on purpose and with diligent practice. They are developed in submission *to* God with a dependence *on* God to carry them out. We call hearing and doing "master" disciplines in order to show their higher order in relationship to their basic components (attention, meditation, etc.). The rest of this chapter will be spent discussing the master discipline of hearing. Chapter 9 will cover the master discipline of doing. Now that you know where we are headed, study the chart carefully, and let's get started.

THE GOAL	WISDOM (THE MIND OF CHRIST)			
THE MASTER DISCIPLINES	Hearing		Doing	
THE BASIC DISCIPLINES	**Attention** Choosing to listen to God	**Meditation** Choosing to think like God	**Obedience** Choosing to obey God	**Endurance** Choosing to persevere for God

THE MASTER DISCIPLINE OF HEARING

One of the first parables our Lord told focused on the importance of hearing.[3] In Luke 8:4-21 He set forth what has been called "the parable of the sower" or, more accurately, "the parable of the soil." He told how a farmer spreading seed on the ground could expect various results depending upon the condition of the soil. Only one kind of soil was truly productive and bore fruit. The four kinds of hearers were these:

The Indifferent Hearer—The soil of the "way side," the footpath that borders the field, is packed hard because of constant traffic and frequent rains; and the seed is left exposed to the wild birds that quickly devour it. This man's heart is totally unreceptive to truth—indifferent. It bears no fruit and is, therefore, useless to the farmer.

The Impulsive Hearer—The soil in this part of the field is shallow because of underlying bedrock. The heat of the sun quickly bakes the seed, and it does not bring forth any fruit. The heart described here is emotional and insincere. This man does not count the cost of receiving the Word and is unwilling to pay the price. Initially he seems to be open and receptive, but the tests of life reveal that no seed has really taken root. His reaction often is "All that sounds good to me, but not if I have to . . ." An underlying bedrock of stubbornness keeps God's Word from deeply penetrating the soil of his heart. This ground, too, is basically useless to the farmer because it bears no lasting fruit.

---

[3] "Hear" is used nine times in this parable.

The Infested Hearer—Fruit does not grow well in this soil either because it is infested with weeds that crowd out the seed. This person seems receptive to the Word but is unwilling to "weed out" the distractions that consume his life—anxieties, riches, pleasures. Like the previous type of soil, it is almost useless to the farmer because its yield is almost nonexistent.

The Ideal Hearer—The good soil receives the seed and produces "an hundredfold." It is the heart that hears the Word and keeps it. Jesus said it is "honest" (truthful with itself) and "good." "Good" here does not mean morally good but means "free from defects." It is a heart that has not let anything crowd out or hinder the growth of the seed of the Word. These are the Marys who sit at Jesus' feet, the Corneliuses who wish to "hear all things that are commanded" (Acts 10:33), and the Bereans who "received the word with all readiness of mind, and searched the scriptures daily" (Acts 17:11). This kind of soil keeps the Word. This heart goes to whatever extent necessary to nurture the seed to fruit-bearing maturity. This kind of soil is truly useful to the farmer.

In this parable Jesus admonished the audience, "He that hath ears to *hear*, let him *hear*" (Luke 8:8). A few verses later He says, "Take heed therefore how ye *hear*" (8:18). Notice that He places the main responsibility for fruitfulness on the condition of the soil. The sower, here speaking of Christ, always does His part.[4] The seed is always of highest quality. The only deciding factor is the soil—the heart of man. "Hearing" in the Scriptures always means more than just auditory reception. It describes a high quality of attention and retention. It is fitting that the book of Proverbs should open with the statement "A wise man will hear" (Prov. 1:5). What does it mean, therefore, to hear?

THE BASIC DISCIPLINE OF ATTENTION

Biblically, hearing means first of all that we are choosing to listen to God. As we said earlier, wisdom is found in context of a *relationship* with Christ. His words are not the words of a fellow mortal. They cannot be

---

[4] While Christ is here referring to Himself as the Sower, He commissioned all believers to be His agents in spreading the truth of the gospel to every creature (Matthew 28:19-20).

ignored or disobeyed without seriously changing the relationship of the believer with the speaker of the words.

Spiritual Junk Mail?

Most of us find our mailboxes cluttered with junk mail these days, and it is not uncommon to receive "junk" phone calls—usually during the six o'clock dinner hour. If we subscribe to a computer on-line service, we are further barraged with "cyber-junk" advertising. It seems that someone is always trying to persuade us to buy something.

Imagine for a moment that you have received an oversized envelope in the mail soliciting your subscription to a national news magazine. Like most of us, you open the envelope, briefly scan the offer, and throw the whole thing into the trash can. As far as you are concerned, your actions are appropriate because you have decided you do not need that particular magazine. You do not for a moment imagine that four weeks later an executive in the magazine's publishing headquarters will be distraught as he ponders, "I sent one of our packets to [your name], and an entire month has gone by without a response from him. I wonder what I did wrong? Did I offend him in some way? Why would he ignore me this way? Why doesn't he respond?"

The scene, of course, is ludicrous. We don't expect any publishing executive to be upset over our failure to reply. There is no personal relationship involved. The scenario is entirely different, however, if the piece of mail we received four weeks ago was from a parent or from a grandparent. Ignoring *their* letters will certainly have some effect on the relationship.

By now I'm sure you see the application to our walk with God. Too many of us hear the words of our God and ignore them. We don't respond in any particular way to Him, and then we wonder why there seems to be so much distance between us and God. The answer is simple: His words to us demand and deserve an appropriate response. His words cannot be ignored or discarded as if they were a piece of junk mail.

Jesus said, "Whosoever heareth these sayings of *mine*" can be wise (Matt. 7:24). Godliness is not the result of responding to Bible principles but responding to a *Person*. The beginning of wisdom certainly entails giving attention—but that attention must be directed to God! The Christian life is not merely maintaining biblical rules but maintaining a *relationship* with God, as we have seen in previous chapters. Whom you listen to is the first issue to settle in gaining wisdom. That is why Solomon says, "The fear of the *Lord* is the beginning [the choicest part, the foundation] of wisdom" (Prov. 9:10). A man who is not in his proper place of reverence for and submission to God *cannot be wise*. He can listen only to his own sinful heart or to the sinful hearts of others and will become a greater fool.[5]

Adam was not created autonomous. *He was designed to listen to someone for direction in life*. That direction was to come from God as Adam fellowshipped with Him in the Garden. When he stopped listening to God and listened to the Serpent, the sinful desires of the Serpent's own nature were implanted within him, furnishing him with a constant flow of information antagonistic to God. This is not a new theme to us since we have studied the sinful bent of man's heart in Part One of this book, but it has important implications for us here. If we are to move out of the "foolishness" of our own heart and develop a renewed mind, we must make it a habit of life, a discipline, to listen to *God* rather than to our *own heart*. Notice how often Proverbs directs the attention of the learner to his God and to his elders.[6]

> My son, hear the instruction of thy *father*, and forsake not the law of thy *mother* (1:8).
> *Wisdom* [Christ Himself] crieth without . . . turn you at my reproof (1:20, 23).
> My son, . . . receive *my* words, and hide *my* commandments with thee (2:1).
> The *Lord* giveth wisdom: out of *his* mouth cometh knowledge and understanding (2:6).
> *He* [God] layeth up sound wisdom for the righteous (2:7).
> My son, forget not *my* law (3:1).
> Trust in the *Lord* (3:5).
> Be not wise in thine own eyes: fear the *Lord* (3:7).
> Hear, ye children, the instruction of a *father* (4:1).
> Hear, O my son, and receive *my* sayings (4:10).

---

[5] For a more thorough study of the fool as he is described in the book of Proverbs, see Fools by Default in Appendix A.

[6] I use "elders" in this chapter and the next to refer to the spiritual leaders God has placed over us.

My son, attend to *my* words; incline thine ear unto *my* sayings (4:20).

My son, attend unto *my* wisdom, and bow thine ear to *my* understanding (5:1).

My son, keep thy *father's* commandment, and forsake not the law of thy *mother* (6:20).

My son, keep *my* words, and lay up *my* commandments with thee (7:1).

Hearken unto *me* now therefore, O ye children, and attend to the words of *my* mouth (7:24).

Doth not *wisdom* [Christ Himself] cry? . . . Hear; for I will speak of excellent things (8:1, 6).

Wisdom hath builded her house. . . . She crieth . . . Come, eat of my bread. . . . Forsake the foolish (9:1-6).

A wise son heareth his *father's* instruction (13:1).

Hear thou, *my* son, and be wise (23:19).

The list could go on, but I think you get the point. Never in Proverbs is a man advised to listen to his own heart or to the heart of his peers. He is warned not to listen to seductive women, to crowds and mobs, to companions bent on being destructive and wasteful, or to evil men. He is exhorted often to listen to his God and to his elders. Understand then that the cornerstone of wisdom is a dependent and submissive heart that shows itself by giving its attention to God and to spiritual leaders—primarily our godly parents and our pastor.

THE BASIC DISCIPLINE OF MEDITATION

In addition to calling a man to listen to God, Proverbs exhorts the believer to *retain* the words of God and of his elders. The goal is to *think* like God. He is to make these words a permanent part of his life so that they actually direct his steps, preserve him from evil, and make his life fruitful. Notice Solomon's exhortation toward this end.

Forsake not the law of thy mother (1:8).

Apply thine heart to understanding (2:2).

My son, *forget not* my law (3:1).

Let not mercy and truth forsake thee: bind them about thy neck; *write* them upon the table of thine heart (3:3).

My son, *let not them depart* from thine eyes: *keep* sound wisdom and discretion (3:21).

Forsake ye not my law (4:2).

Let thine heart *retain* my words (4:4).

Get wisdom, get understanding: *forget it not* (4:5).

Forsake her [wisdom] *not* (4:6).

Take fast hold of instruction (4:13).

Let them not depart from thine eyes; *keep* them in the midst of thine heart (4:21).

Bind them continually upon thine heart, and *tie* them about thy neck (6:21).

My son, *keep* my words, and *lay up* my commandments with thee (7:1).

Bind them upon thy fingers, *write* them upon the table of thine heart (7:3).

Again, the list could go on and on. These words from God must become so much a part of us that we do not forget them in the day-to-day activities of life. They can then dictate the *next right responses* we must make to life's challenges.

Some Things You Just Don't Forget

So many believers protest at this point that if we are talking about memorizing Scripture, we must exempt them because they don't have good memories. I would assert, however, that they can remember anything that is important enough to them if they have rehearsed it enough times. Most people never forget their name, phone number, and names of their children. They can remember these things because they have repeated them often and because these pieces of information have a high personal priority with them.

To illustrate this further, let's suppose that a boy beginning to date a girl in college finds out that she is allergic to daisies. That bit of information about her nature becomes a governing principle for him. It dictates his actions toward her. If he wishes to show her his affection through a gift of flowers, he will not do so with a bouquet of daisies. If he truly cares about protecting her from the uncomfortable reaction she would have to daisies, and if he values his relationship with her, he will always remember to bring her something other than daisies. *There are some things you just don't forget because of the importance of the person to you.*

If I can say it reverently, God is allergic to some things too. His Word teaches us what He loves and what He hates. The psalmist David was very intent upon knowing God's nature so that he would not damage his relationship with God in any way. David understood that the laws and words of God are reflections of His nature. In order not to violate the relationship, David was intent upon knowing what God had said. Notice in these familiar verses from Psalm 119:4-16 David's concern for the *personal* relationship he had with God.

> *Thou* hast commanded us to keep *thy* precepts diligently. O that my ways were directed to keep *thy* statutes! Then shall I not be ashamed, when I have respect unto all *thy* commandments. I will praise *thee* with uprightness of heart, when I shall have learned *thy* righteous judgments. I will keep *thy* statutes: O forsake me not utterly.

> Wherewithal shall a young man cleanse his way? by taking heed thereto according to *thy* word. With my whole heart have I sought *thee:* O let me not wander from *thy* commandments. *Thy* word have I hid in mine heart, that I might not sin against *thee.* Blessed art *thou*, O Lord: teach me *thy* statutes. With my lips have I declared all the judgments of *thy* mouth. I have rejoiced in the way of *thy* testimonies, as much as in all riches. I will meditate in *thy* precepts, and have respect unto *thy* ways. I will delight myself in *thy* statutes: I will not forget *thy* word.

Much of the motivation to *remember* the words of God is tied to the kind of relationship we have with Him. If we view His words like the words of our state's highway department printed in a motor vehicle manual, we may have a difficult time being motivated to remember them unless we are taking the driver's test soon. If we view the words of God, however, as the self-revelation of One we love, our motivation to know and keep them increases dramatically. We want to know how the One we love thinks so that we can become like-minded with Him.

We cannot soon forget the words of One in whom we take delight. If the *relationship* with God drives our desire to know His words, their mastery will be neither tedious nor burdensome. Without this relationship, however, the knowledge of the Word becomes merely an academic pursuit or an exercise in duty-driven self-discipline. The first chapter of James speaks to us about the approach to the Word that keeps us from becoming a "forgetful hearer."

How to Remember Not to Forget

James tells us that when trouble comes we are to be "swift to hear, slow to speak, slow to wrath" (1:19). It is so easy when pressures mount for us to be quick to speak, quick to blow off steam, and very slow to listen to God. Peter, James's copastor of the church in Jerusalem, had similar words for this congregation. He told them that in times of trial they must be diligent to "gird up the loins of [their] mind" (I Pet. 1:13). Pressured times are not the times to give in to sloppy thinking. Yet those are the times when it is especially easy to "forget" what kind of *next right response* keeps us usable to Christ during the trial.

After admonishing us to be "swift to hear," James outlines for us the procedures to master the Word, or rather, to let it master us. Here are his words (1:21-25):

> Wherefore lay apart [put aside] all filthiness and superfluity of naughtiness [all that remains of wickedness], and receive with meekness the engrafted word, which is able to save your souls. But be ye doers of the word, and not hearers only, deceiving your own selves. For if any be a hearer of the word, and not a doer, he is like unto a man beholding his natural face in a glass [a mirror]: For he beholdeth himself, and goeth his way, and straightway forgetteth what manner of man he was. But whoso looketh into the perfect law of liberty, and continueth therein, he being not a forgetful hearer, but a doer of the work, this man shall be blessed in his deed.

The last verse in this section tells us how to avoid being a "forgetful hearer." It says we are to look "into the perfect law of liberty," which refers to the Word itself. It is the liberating "truth [which] shall make you free."[7] The word "looketh" (Greek *parakupto*) is the operative word in this passage. It means "to bend over (to see something better)."[8]

---

[7] John 8:32. Sadly, John 8:32 has been misapplied in many counseling situations. When John the Apostle said, "Ye shall know the truth, and the truth shall make you free," he was not referring to the truth about yourself, your past, your family history, and so forth. The only liberating "truth" is the revelation from God *about Himself*. The "truth" from God changes man. Jesus said, "Sanctify them through thy truth: thy word is truth" (John 17:17). It is in this sense that the truth sets us free—free from the bondage of our sinful hearts. John is not teaching that we cannot be free until we know or face some truth about our past or about others who have harmed us, as is commonly taught today.

[8] Arndt and Gingrich, *Lexicon*, 624.

If you have ever been around someone who has lost a contact lens on the carpet, you can understand the force of this word. There your friend is, on all fours, his eyeballs only inches from the floor scanning the carpet. He is peering intently at the carpet, systematically covering a section at a time, trying to catch a glimpse of his lens. He is careful to ward off others who would come near the search site lest they step on his contact. He has one goal—find the contact! This is no casual, haphazard glance at the floor from a standing position. This word communicates the kind of single-minded, systematic search for something valuable that has us bending over in order to see better.

This illustrates as well the force of Proverbs 2 where we learn the normal means of getting wisdom.[9] Proverbs 2:2-6 says,

> *Incline* thine ear unto wisdom, and *apply* thine heart to understanding; Yea, if thou *criest* after knowledge, and *liftest* up thy voice for understanding; If thou *seekest* her as silver, and *searchest* for her as for hid treasures; *Then* shalt thou understand the fear of the Lord, and find the knowledge of God. For the Lord giveth wisdom: out of his mouth [His words] cometh knowledge and understanding.

Notice again the intensity and the single-mindedness about this search. This is what is involved in biblical meditation. Meditation is not hard to understand. Anyone who knows how to worry knows how to meditate. A worrier takes one thought (e.g., "I just know I'll never get married"; "I'm afraid my husband will leave me"; "We don't have any money left") and looks single-mindedly at that thought from every possible angle, examining every possible implication and application of that thought to him personally. Worriers are skilled in the meditation process but are meditating on the wrong kind of thoughts.[10]

---

[9] James 1:5 says we get wisdom by asking for it. I believe that this is God's "fire-extinguisher wisdom," which we need when we are in the midst of the trial of verse 2. This is when we ask God to bring to mind the truths we have learned that will help us make the next right move in the trial. The normal way of discovering that truth that God can bring to mind in a trial is found in Proverbs 2. Every student knows that he will not have the right answers during a test unless he has diligently studied them ahead of time with the intent of remembering them for the time of testing.

[10] For biblical help on how to think right instead of worrying, see Basics for Worried Believers in Appendix B.

Biblical meditation involves the same process, but the reflective thought must be on the truth from God and not on a lie from our own heart or from Satan. We must start with truth revealed to us from the Word and then examine it from every possible angle, asking God to show us its implications and applications for us and our relationship with Him. We will "bend over to see it better." For some that will mean looking up the verses in commentaries or studying the individual words in Bible dictionaries or word studies. It may mean looking up cross-references to other passages in the Scripture that shed more light on the passage being studied. For someone who knows Greek or Hebrew, it will mean examining the words in their original languages.

Above all, it will mean an ongoing interaction with God Himself, asking Him to reveal to us the truth He wants us to know and practice so that our fellowship with Him can increase and our fruitfulness for Him can grow. He will most often respond to us first by convicting us of unconfessed sin. "The entrance of [His] words giveth light" (Ps. 119:130) and the light will expose our sin. Notice the sequence in Proverbs 1:23: "Turn you at my reproof: behold, I will pour out my spirit unto you, I will make known my words unto you."

Remember, the aim of this meditation is to help us behold our God and think like our God so that we can know and, therefore, "do those things that are pleasing in his sight" (I John 3:22). The barriers that hinder our fellowship with Him must be removed before He will reveal His words.

This kind of reflection does not necessarily follow the same pattern for every believer. You can gain some ideas for your own meditation by reviewing again several portions of this book and its appendices. Review the following sections:

- How to Meditate: The MAP Method in Appendix A
- Phil's conversation with his coach in Chapter 6 in the section entitled "The Search for God Must Be a Search for a Person." Reread the entire section down to the heading entitled "A Letter to John."
- "Spending a Day with God" at the end of Chapter 7 in Take Time to Reflect
- A Word to Disciple-Makers at the end of Chapter 7

The passage in James 1 that exhorts us to look into the "perfect law of liberty" says we are to continue in it. The next question might be "How long do we continue peering intently into the Word?" The twofold answer is found in the next phrase: "He being not a forgetful hearer, but a doer of the work." *We are to continue as long as it takes to make sure we do not forget what we have heard.* That often means meditating on the same passage, studying and reflecting on it, for several weeks. That certainly doesn't mean we cannot read other passages or keep up with a "through-the-Bible-in-a-year" schedule, but it does mean that our focused attention must continually come back to the passage at hand until it becomes a permanent part of our thinking.

That is not as impossible as it seems. The Holy Spirit wants to teach the Word to us. In addition, the constant repetition and concentration of the meditation process will firmly entrench God's words in our heart.

The second indicator of the thoroughness of our meditation is when we actually become "a doer of the work." *We are to continue as long as it takes to actually begin to show a difference in our lifestyle and practice.* Here is how Paul describes it in I Timothy 4:15-16: "Meditate upon these things; give thyself wholly to them; *that thy profiting may appear to all.* Take heed unto thyself, and unto the doctrine; continue in them: for in doing this thou shalt both save thyself, and them that hear thee."

In the first psalm David testifies of the fruitfulness and stability that meditation will produce in the life of a believer who continually reflects on God's Word.

> Blessed is the man that walketh not in the counsel of the ungodly, nor standeth in the way of sinners, nor sitteth in the seat of the scornful. But his delight is in the law of the Lord; and in his law doth he meditate day and night. And he shall be like a tree planted by the rivers of water, that *bringeth forth his fruit in his season*; his leaf also shall not wither; and whatsoever he doeth shall prosper (Ps. 1:1-3).

This, then, is the first discipline of wisdom—hearing the Word of God. We must choose to listen to *God* instead of to our own heart or to others who listen to their own heart. In addition, we must choose to *think* like God. The reflective time we spend will yield a lasting like-mindedness that increases our affection for God and controls our decisions. We will know *the next right response* in any given circumstance because we are beginning to have a renewed mind—the mind of Christ.

TAKE TIME TO REFLECT

Ask yourself whether you have developed the habit of *listening*. The most searching tests of your willingness to learn are threefold. Do you have a regular time of Bible reading, meditation, and prayer; are you regular in attendance at a Fundamentalist, Bible-preaching church; and do you willingly receive instruction and correction from the spiritual leaders in your life? Proverbs depicts the fool as one who will not listen to God, to rebuke, or to reason. Be brutally honest with yourself on this point. Do you listen on purpose to God and to the elders in your life?

Second, ask yourself whether you have developed the habit of *remembering* what you are told. Wise men figure out ways to make sure they do not lose what they have been told. The sluggard in Proverbs offers many reasons that explain why he does not have the time, the opportunity, or the inclination to work his field so that his crop will grow. He comes to spiritual poverty while the wise man flourishes.[11]

Perhaps the following exercises will help you develop the habit of listening to God and then *reflecting* on what He has said.

1. Earlier in this chapter you were exposed to a brief portion of Psalm 119 with the second person personal pronouns (thou, thine, thy, etc.) italicized. If you read the passage emphasizing the italicized words, you saw that David took his relationship with God very seriously. Psalm 119 is the lengthiest chapter in the Bible, but it is also the most instructive about the kind of attitude we should have toward the words of our God.

   Take a pen, colored pencil, or highlighter and shade or underline the second person personal pronouns—thee, thou, thine, or you, yours, and so forth—for the entire Psalm 119. Once you have done this, read it reflectively and audibly (if possible) as a prayer to God affirming your desire to hear and heed His words.

2. Another project that will reinforce the need for hearing God's Word to be wise is to go through the book of Proverbs and mark

---

[11] Proverbs 24:30-34.

or underline the words "wise" and "wisdom." Study the context of each occurrence to see the benefits of wisdom and to learn the process of acquiring it.

3. Finally, to further reinforce the truths you have studied in this book so far, go back and reflect on the Take Time to Reflect section after each chapter. Systematic and purposeful review will help solidify in your mind the truths you have studied. Wisdom does not come by merely desiring it. It takes diligent effort to know God and His ways. Note the warning in Proverbs 13:4: "The soul of the sluggard desireth [he wants a harvest], and hath nothing: but the soul of the diligent shall be made fat."

A WORD TO DISCIPLE-MAKERS

Be Cautious About the Culture

Examine the lifestyle of the one you are trying to disciple to see whether he is involved in activities that tear down the habits of the heart he needs to be wise. As we have seen, he needs to know how to *listen* (i.e., pay attention, specifically to God and his elders) and how to *reflect*. Neither of these basic disciplines of hearing is cultivated automatically by the culture in which we live.

For example, the video entertainment medium, whether through movies, music videos, or video games, actually tears down the powers of concentration and the ability to reflect. It does not enhance them. That may seem like a contradiction of reality since a teenager can sit for three hours watching a video or can spend all night in his room playing video games. Aren't these activities to be commended for helping him give attention for extended periods of time? No, not at all. In fact, his concentration ability is diminished because he is being trained to have an attention span of only a few seconds before an image change captures his attention again. The plot itself is not usually complicated enough to demand genuine powers of concentration. *A person who is not skilled at being attentive and reflective can never be biblically wise; he cannot be godly.*

A separate but related issue is that so much time that could be spent listening and reflecting is spent daydreaming and being amused. In many cases, the silence of reflection is too painful and the discipline of listening to others is too humbling. Modern culture anesthetizes the mind while mainlining the soul with emotional experiences that keep the worldling believing he is really living.

Furthermore, a believer whose life is dominated by his present culture will have a harder time resisting the evils of that culture than a person whose life is dominated by a world-view that transcends his culture. In other words, if his thoughts are not continually directed to a transcendent world (a view of the world as God sees it), he will be far more likely to give in to the temptations of the culture he lives in.

Start Early

Parents can begin to develop the proper habits of the heart—attention and reflection—at a very early age. Reading to a child while he sits on his parent's lap, coaching him as he learns a new skill, and playing problem-solving games with him (puzzles, strategy games, etc.) are ways parents can encourage these disciplines. In addition, helping him biblically solve problems regarding friends or school as he gets older teaches him to listen and reflect.[12]

Parents should not consider interaction with their child to be biblical discipleship, however, unless they are actually teaching him biblical content and a biblical world-view while developing the disciplines of attention and reflection. For example, music lessons and sports training can be useful tools for training a child in these disciplines *if* the parents will make the necessary applications. Both of these activities can teach a child to listen to his teachers and coaches, pay attention, solve problems, and work with others. If the parents, and consequently the child, however, become so focused on the *result* of his effort rather than the disciplines he is developing in the *process*, the spiritual effect will be only pride. The parents have then produced only a more highly skilled rebel. Greater attention must be given to the kind of *person* he is becoming rather than to the *performance* level he is achieving. If God cannot use him because his pride disqualifies him from fruitfulness for

---

[12] Some parents seem to take pride in teaching their child to "think for himself." In real life that usually translates into a pride in the child that makes him unteachable. His *own* thoughts become the standard against which he measures the ideas of others. Unwittingly, he is being taught a humanistic tenet—that man is the measure of all things. The parental goal must be to teach our children to "think like God." He must measure everything he is taught and the ideas he hears against what *God* says is true. Of course, that requires that he *know* what God says.

Christ, all the training has been in vain, no matter what levels of accomplishment he reaches.

You Are Being Watched

Perhaps the most powerful influence in this area, however, is the model of the disciple-maker himself. Do those who follow you see that you are serious about listening to God? Do they see your regular church attendance? Do they ever see you taking notes during sermons, see you studying the Bible on your own so that you actually *think* like God, or hear you talking about what you learned from God? When you try to help them solve a problem, is it obvious that you have scriptural foundations for your advice, or are you just giving them your own ideas? Does your own attendance and participation at church reveal a genuine desire to listen to God and think like Him?

Many children reach their teen years never having been trained to pay attention to anyone, let alone God or their elders, nor have they been taught how to reflect on truth in such a way that they are not "forgetful hearers." Without these basic disciplines of hearing, they cannot be wise. It is never too late to start discipling someone in these disciplines, but like any parental training—and discipleship is spiritual parenting—the process will be greatly accelerated if the disciple-maker involved will hold the trainee accountable and will "practice what he preaches."

These habits of the heart are developed by a combination of example, exhortation, rebuke, and explanation. All of these teaching tools are found in the book of Proverbs, and every disciple-maker should become proficient in their use.

CHAPTER NINE
WALKING IN WISDOM

But be ye doers of the word, and not hearers only, deceiving your own selves.
James 1:22

THE MASTER DISCIPLINE OF DOING

In the last chapter we looked at the first master discipline of wisdom—hearing. We learned that hearing consists of two basic disciplines of attention and meditation. We also saw that Jesus taught in His Sermon on the Mount that doing is the second master discipline of those who would be wise. Our chart in the last chapter also divided doing into two basic disciplines of obedience and endurance, the subjects of our study in this chapter.

Doing Versus Being

While I will say much in this chapter about doing, I want to be sure you understand that Christianity is not made up of just the things we do or do not do. Please don't misunderstand this issue. It should be clear by now that Christianity is essentially a *relationship* with God, not a system of *rules*.[1] At the same time, it should be clear to us that every relationship produces its own rules. We saw that illustrated in the last chapter with the rule "Thou shalt not bring her daisies." *Every relationship generates laws consistent with the nature of the person we are relating to.*

---

[1] There is debate in Christian circles about whether we are supposed to concentrate on being a certain kind of person or doing certain kinds of things. The truth embraces both. You are always going to be some kind of a person or another, and you are always going to be doing one thing or another. You cannot cease to be nor cease to do. Furthermore, the two are interdependent. You have to do certain things to be a certain kind of a person. Conversely, you have to be a certain kind of a person to do certain things. I am not trying to muddy the waters with needless philosophical statements, but I am trying to help you see that the matter cannot be so neatly divided as some would have us believe.

As we saw in the first chapter, sanctification is a *cooperative venture between God and us*. That is not man's idea and does not in any way detract from God's sovereignty. God set it up that way. We need to get it straight, then, that God Himself has determined that those who will be like His Son and, therefore, wise, will be doing certain things.

The Key Player

We must remember that we cannot do any hearing unless the Holy Spirit teaches us God's Word as we are "bending over, peering intently" at it. We see this in I Corinthians 2:9-16. The Holy Spirit is the One who illuminates our minds.

Just as the Holy Spirit is the key player in the hearing aspect of gaining the Christlike wisdom of a renewed mind, He is also central to the doing aspect. Our flesh, as we have seen, often begs us to obey its lusts. Galatians 5:16-17 captures the nature of that battle: "This I say then, Walk in the Spirit, and ye shall not fulfil the lust of the flesh. For the flesh lusteth against the Spirit, and the Spirit against the flesh: and these are contrary the one to the other: so that ye cannot do the things that ye would."

Paul and other biblical writers speak much of doing, but doing is to be a response of obedience to God the Holy Spirit and is to be energized by Him. We call this *obedience* to the Holy Spirit, *walking* in the Spirit, or *being controlled* by the Holy Spirit.

We must have a fuller understanding of the Holy Spirit's role in our lives if we are to understand the kind of doing Jesus is calling for in Matthew 7:24-27. (See Chapter 8.) There is much confusion today about the Holy Spirit's ministry in our lives.

From the moment of salvation, the Holy Spirit is God's resident agent personally handling every transaction that goes on between us and God. His continuous presence gives the believer the opportunity for fellowship with God at all times. His presence within us is also the permanent *seal* (mark of ownership) that we are indeed God's child.[2] In addition, His presence within us is the *earnest* (guarantee, down payment) that

---

[2] Ephesians 1:13; 4:30.

assures us that God will bring us to the total likeness of Christ when we finally stand in His presence in heaven.[3]

From that base of operation within us, He *convicts* of sin that would hinder our fellowship with the Father.[4] He *teaches* us more of Christ so that our fellowship with Him is enriched, and He *assists* us in our work for Christ.[5] The word "Comforter" in these verses has the idea of someone who "comes alongside to help." It could be better translated "helper" in these passages. How blessed we are to have within us God's personal agent who serves as arresting officer, private tutor, and personal assistant or helper in order to carry out His mission of establishing and maintaining our fellowship with God!

There is much more, however. His permanent presence not only allows continual fellowship with God as we respond to His conviction and heed His teaching but also empowers us to be what we ought to be (sanctification) and do what we ought to do (service) when He fills us. Just as my grandfather needed the power of the "Cat" to do his work in the fields, so every believer needs the power of the Spirit to do the work of God and to reflect His nature. Since these cannot be done by any man on his own, every Christian needs to understand and practice what it means to be controlled by or filled with the Spirit.

Controlled by the Spirit

The indwelling of the Spirit, which is the birthright of every believer, should not be confused with this control of the Spirit, which is conditional. Every believer has the Spirit's *presence* in his life, but not every believer has the Spirit's *power*. One of the New Testament expressions of the Holy Spirit's empowering work is found in Ephesians 5:18, which says, "And be not drunk with wine, wherein is excess; but be filled with the Spirit."

The word "filled" here is not speaking of possessing a certain *quantity* of the Spirit as we might speak of a glass "filled" with water. It expresses, rather, the idea of "control," as when we speak of someone being "filled with rage." We mean by that phrase that anger is such a dominant part

---

[3] II Corinthians 1:22; 5:5; Ephesians 1:14.

[4] Galatians 5:17; I Thessalonians 4:7-8.

[5] John 14:26; 15:26.

of his life at that moment that he is controlled by it. We might speak of someone being "filled with fear" or "filled with lust" in the same way. The person described as "being filled" with these passions is so consumed by the fear or lust that his behavior is noticeably affected.

Paul compares being filled with the Spirit to being drunk with wine. A man who is filled with wine to the extent of drunkenness behaves differently when he is under the influence than when he is sober. He is transformed into a destructive, wasteful person. The alcohol affects every part of the man's life, but in a destructive way. That is why Paul says the effect of drunkenness is "excess" (literally "wastefulness").

A Christian under the control of the Holy Spirit is also transformed, but in a useful way. He, too, comes "under the influence"—the controlling influence of the Holy Spirit. It transforms him so that he "walks" differently. The Bible says that God "worketh in you both to will and to do of his good pleasure" (Phil. 2:13). Notice this is a work "in you." That means it is something the Holy Spirit does.

Notice also that He does two things in us. First, He creates within us a "will"—a desire—to do what pleases Him. If you have any desire to please God, if you have any desire to do what is right, God's Spirit put that desire there. We have already learned that left to ourselves "there is none that seeketh after God" (Rom. 3:11). He *wants* us to please God, and He wants us to *want* to do so as well.

Second, we see that He creates in us an ability to do God's good pleasure. You can be assured that if He puts a desire in you to please God, He is doing so because He expects to enable you to do just that. He doesn't create a desire in us for something that can't be accomplished. The Greek word for "do" in this verse is the word from which we get the word "energy." He gives us the divine energy—the power—to please God.

Amazing Grace!

This divine help in creating a desire and giving us power to please God is called "grace." It is His undeserved help to accomplish what pleases Him. And what's more, He is willing to give us all the grace—the divine help—we need to do whatever He requires. Look at Paul's encouraging words in II Corinthians 9:8: "And God is able to make all grace abound toward you; that ye, always having all sufficiency in all things, may abound to every good work."

This is a powerful promise! He will *always* give us *everything* we need to do *whatever* He asks us to do. What battle are you facing with your flesh right now? What habit are you struggling with? What bitterness or anger stays unresolved in your heart? God promises to always give you everything you need to do whatever it is that pleases Him in that situation. With His help you can always make the *next right response*. His grace is mediated to us by His Spirit as we say no to the flesh and say yes to God. Here's how Peter puts it: "God resisteth the proud [the one insisting on his *own way*], and giveth grace [divine assistance] to the humble [the one submitting to God's *way*]" (I Pet. 5:5).

As long as we are insisting that we have our *own way*, we can expect God to resist us. When we get in our place as a submissive creature, however, He immediately gives us sufficient grace so that we can always make the *next right response* of obedience.

THE BASIC DISCIPLINE OF OBEDIENCE

Let's see how this relationship of obedience to the Spirit of God works out in a real life situation. Let's suppose that your Christian friend John has been convicted by God from His Word that he must stop his lying. It must be "put off" or laid aside. He realizes that he is especially susceptible to lying when his image before others is at stake. Suppose he says to himself, "I must stop this bad habit of lying. It always gets me into more trouble than it's worth. I may look better at first, but it seems I always get found out, and I end up looking like a real idiot. Therefore, I must remember not to lie when I am tempted to do so."

Let's look at this scenario for a moment. Here John is trying to stop lying for the same selfish reason he started lying—to enhance his image before others. His motive for now telling the truth is as self-centered as his motive for lying in the first place. His primary concern is still his image. He will not be successful long. In the end he will always choose to do what advances his own cause the most. He will, no doubt, be quite discouraged because he cannot seem to give up his bad habit of lying.

Notice that there is no personal submission to God in this situation. Your friend John cannot lie without showing enormous disrespect for the very nature of God. Jesus described Himself as "the way, *the truth*, and the life" in John 14:6. The Holy Spirit is called the "Spirit of *truth*" in John 14:17. Suppose that John knows that you, his friend, are allergic to a certain cologne. Let's further suppose that even though he knows this, he wears it around you anyway. He is not showing any concern about how his behavior will affect you. He is thinking only of what *he* likes. In much the same way, because of *His* nature, God is "allergic" to lies. Even more fundamentally offensive to God is the whole mindset that *John's way* (in any part of life) should take precedence over *His way*, since He is John's Creator and Redeemer.

God is a Person who dwells within us in the *Person* of the Holy Spirit. He is "personally" wronged when His nature is violated. That is why Paul warns us, "And grieve not the holy Spirit of God" (Eph. 4:30). His work in us is quenched (hindered) by our selfishness.[6]

Let's go over again the scene with John from the standpoint of a person desiring to be controlled by the Spirit of God. John knows from the Bible that lying is wrong. He has been convicted by the Holy Spirit when he has lied in the past. He says to himself, "I cannot continue to grieve God in this way. My lying shows that I am more concerned about myself and what I want than about God and what He deserves and demands." John might then express his heart's desire to God in a prayer like this:

"Dear God, You are so patient with me. You have watched me lie over and over again, and yet you have not dealt harshly with me for violating Your very nature of truth. You have faithfully convicted me by Your Holy Spirit. I know I have grieved You by my deception. Forgive me for my selfish concern for *my own image*. I want to be concerned only about how I portray the *image of Christ* to others through my life.

"I will need the help of Your Holy Spirit to renew my mind as I meditate upon Ephesians 4:15 and 25 and other passages about Your hatred for lying and deception. May He enlighten my heart with an understanding of Your ways. Continue to convict me by Your Spirit and help me to be sensitive to His conviction. Help me to 'speak the truth' at all times no matter what the cost. Help me to be willing to deny everything—including a good image before others—in order *not* to deny You what is rightfully Yours: a life that represents You well. Help me to that end. In Jesus' name, Amen."

---

[6] I Thessalonians 5:19.

When John comes to God with the kind of heart demonstrated in the prayer above, he will receive divine help—grace—from the Holy Spirit to resist the temptation. The Holy Spirit will, in the process, be helping him become a "truth-teller."

The key element shown in John's heart is humility. Notice what David says about God's response to humility in Psalm 34 and in Psalm 51, David's psalm of repentance.

> The Lord is nigh unto them that are of a broken heart; and saveth such as be of a contrite spirit (Ps. 34:18).

> For thou desirest not sacrifice; else would I give it: thou delightest not in burnt offering. The sacrifices of God are a broken spirit: a broken and a contrite heart, O God, thou wilt not despise (Ps. 51:16-17).

God Himself showed His high esteem for such a heart in Isaiah 66:1-2. He said that He is not looking for any dwelling that a man can build. After all, heaven itself is His throne, and He rests His feet upon the footstool of the earth. How can man impress Him with anything man can build? He said, however, that there is one thing that always arrests His attention and causes Him to look with interest and offer willing assistance—a man who humbles himself before his God, a man who will take His Word seriously. He put it this way:

> Thus saith the Lord, The heaven is my throne, and the earth is my footstool: where is the house that ye build unto me? and where is the place of my rest? For all those things hath mine hand made, and all those things have been, saith the Lord: *but to this man will I look, even to him that is poor and of a contrite spirit, and trembleth at my word.*

The kind of humility reflected in John's prayer showed itself in three ways. John was repentant—he knew he needed God's forgiveness. He was submissive—he knew he needed to subject himself to God and *His* ways. He was dependent—he knew he couldn't resist sin effectively without supernatural help from God.

At that moment of repentant, submissive, dependent humility, John received God's attention and assistance. The Holy Spirit was pleased—not grieved. The Spirit of God was also now free to give John the power he needed since He did not need to resist John any longer.

That same expression from his heart would need to be offered to God many times in the days ahead—and many times during each of those days—for John to see any lasting change in his pattern of lying. John is practicing "putting off" the ways of the flesh, and as he is hearing and doing what the Holy Spirit says, he is developing the "mind of Christ." He is being "renewed in the spirit of [his] mind" (Eph. 4:23). He is handling life wisely. His life will demonstrate an increasing stability and fruitfulness for Christ.[7]

Biblical obedience is not just compliance to some abstract law or rule. It is the submissive response to the Person of the Holy Spirit who has revealed the will of God to us through His Word. It means saying yes to God as we say no to self. It means denying self instead of indulging self. It means pleasing God instead of pleasing self. It means walking in the Spirit instead of grieving the Spirit. It is the way of wisdom instead of the way of the fool.

Biblical obedience is more than just commandment-oriented living versus desire- or feeling-oriented living, however. While commands must be obeyed and feelings may need to be ignored, the issue can be more fundamentally stated as a flesh versus Spirit issue. We are either obeying our flesh and pleasing ourselves or obeying the Holy Spirit and pleasing God. A love relationship is at the heart of our obedience. "We will always please the one we love the most."[8] If we love God the most, we will please Him. If we love ourselves the most, we will please ourselves. Deuteronomy 6:5 commands us to love God "with all [our] heart, and with all [our] soul, and with all [our] might." Paul emphasizes this kind of wholehearted obedience in Colossians 3:23-24: "And whatsoever ye do, do it heartily, as to the Lord, and not unto men; Knowing that of the Lord ye shall receive the reward of the inheritance: for ye serve the Lord Christ."

In the small Old Testament book of Malachi, God confronted the Israelites about their lack of devotion for Him. He said, "A son hon-

---

[7] "A Lesson from Kirk" in Chapter 5 demonstrated some of the same principles in the illustration here about John. The lesson from Kirk was that what we often call a lack of self-discipline (Kirk's failure to get up when his alarm went off) is most often a lack of *obedience* to the Holy Spirit.

[8] Ken Collier, THE WILDS Christian Association. Used by permission.

oureth his father, and a servant his master: if then I be a father, where is mine honour? and if I be a master, where is my fear?" (Mal. 1:6).

The people replied with surprise, "Wherein have we despised thy name?" God answered that their less-than-wholehearted devotion to Him was evidenced by the quality of sacrificial lambs they were bringing to Him each day. He chided them with these words: "And if ye offer the blind for sacrifice, is it not evil? and if ye offer the lame and sick, is it not evil? offer it now unto thy governor; will he be pleased with thee, or accept thy person? saith the Lord of hosts" (Mal. 1:8).

The Lord's test here is simple and foundational. *We will always reserve the best for the one we love the most.* A child picks out for himself the biggest piece of cake with the most frosting because he loves himself most. He will enthusiastically defend himself when accused of wrong-doing—even if he is guilty—because he loves himself most. He will want to be *first* in line in the cafeteria at school, *first* to be picked for the team on the ball field, and *first* to be out the door at recess. This love for himself is evidenced by the way he *wholeheartedly* looks out for himself and gives himself the best options.

Notice God's rebuke to Israel in Malachi's day. When they reserved the best lamb in the flock for themselves instead of offering it to God, God challenged them about their lack of love for Him. He said in essence, "If you offered to your civic leaders the kind of diseased, crippled gifts you give to Me, they would throw you out. You are treating your governors better than you are treating your *God!*" He then pronounced the coming punishment upon those who tried to "get by" with inferior sacrifices. "But cursed be the deceiver, which hath in his flock a male, and voweth, and sacrificeth unto the Lord a corrupt thing: for I am a great King, saith the Lord of hosts, and my name is dreadful among the heathen" (Mal. 1:14).

Anyone who watched an Israelite lead a crippled lamb to the sacrificial altar had every right to judge the devotion of that Israelite to God. His inferior gift to God meant that he was keeping the best lambs at home for himself. The quality of his sacrifice betrayed whom he loved most—himself or God. It was a simple test: whoever got his best lamb—himself or God—was the one he loved most. Such is the nature of obedience: it is a reflection of the heart.

THE BASIC DISCIPLINE OF ENDURANCE

Endurance is continued obedience to God even under pressure. It is the obedience of the heroes of the Faith in Hebrews 11, who continued doing right even though it cost many of them their lives. Endurance is the crowning virtue of character. In fact, when we comment about someone, "My, he really has some character to him," we are usually referring to his endurance in the midst of some hardship. Our Lord Himself demonstrated the sustained obedience that lies at the heart of endurance. We find it described in Philippians 2:5-11.

> Let this mind be in you, which was also in Christ Jesus: Who, being in the form of God, thought it not robbery to be equal with God: But made himself of no reputation, and took upon him the form of a servant, and was made in the likeness of men: And being found in fashion as a man, *he humbled himself, and became obedient unto death, even the death of the cross.* Wherefore God also hath highly exalted him, and given him a name which is above every name: That at the name of Jesus every knee should bow, of things in heaven, and things in earth, and things under the earth; And that every tongue should confess that Jesus Christ is Lord, to the glory of God the Father.

We looked at this passage in Chapter 1 to discover the Christlike humility that God honors. It is a submission to the Father that demonstrates itself in obedience. The obedience, however, is a specific kind of obedience. It is a "cross-death" kind of obedience. This passage says Jesus remained obedient "unto death, even the death of the cross." He said, "I'll die before I disobey My Father." This kind of endurance that the Father honored is not the stubborn self-will of a person who refuses to give in because he believes he is right. It is absolute submission to the One who loved us most. It is the believer's refusal to betray the Father by looking out for himself. It is the Christlike mindset that denies everything dear to itself—even life—before it would ever deny the Father. Notice again the *relationship* that drives this kind of loyal endurance in our Lord as He spoke these words:

> My meat is to do the will of *him* that sent me, and to finish *his* work (John 4:34).
> For I came down from heaven, not to do mine own will, but the will of *him* that sent me (John 6:38).
> I do always those things that please *him* [the Father] (John 8:29).

> I honour my *Father*. . . . And I seek not mine own glory (John 8:49-50).
> I must work the works of *him* that sent me, while it is day: the night cometh, when no man can work. As long as I am in the world, I am the light of the world (John 9:4-5).
> I lay down my life. . . . This commandment have I received of my *Father* (John 10:17-18).
> Now is my soul troubled; and what shall I say? *Father*, save me from this hour: but for this cause came I unto this hour. *Father*, glorify thy name (John 12:27-28).

This same response to the Father is the heart cry of the believer that takes up the cross of suffering and follows Christ. In its maturity this "cross-death" kind of obedience is driven by something that is much deeper than mere duty. It is motivated by a devotion of the believer to his heavenly Father. It is the cry of the Savior to the Father in the messianic statement of Psalm 40:7-8: "Then said I, Lo, I come: in the volume of the book it is written of me, *I delight to do thy will, O my God:* yea, thy law is within my heart."

You might protest, "God can expect that of His Son, but He cannot expect that of us, can He?" Yes, He can, and He does. *This* delight to *do* the will of the Father is what Paul is commanding when he says, "Let this mind be in you, which was also in Christ Jesus" (Phil. 2:5). This kind of endurance that is honored by God in His Son, as explained in Philippians 2, is the same endurance God says He honors in us. "Blessed is the man that *endureth* temptation [trials of any sort]: for when he is tried [has passed the test], he shall receive the crown of life, which the Lord hath promised to them that love *him*" (James 1:12).

Notice the love for Christ, the *relationship*, that fuels the endurance in the trial. This kind of Christ-centered endurance is what the writer of Hebrews is calling us to when he says,

> Wherefore seeing we also are compassed about with so great a cloud of witnesses, let us lay aside every weight, and the sin which doth so easily beset us, and let us run with patience [*endurance*] the race that is set before us, *Looking unto Jesus* the author and finisher of our faith; who for the joy that was set before him endured the cross, despising the shame, and is set down at the right hand of the throne of God. For *consider him* that endured such contradiction of sinners

against himself, lest ye be wearied and faint in your minds (Heb. 12:1-3).

For examples of many others who have endured this way, study Hebrews 11, the Hall of Faith. These believers looked beyond the trial to the face of their Master. Moses, one of the heroes listed in Hebrews 11, "endured, as seeing *him* who is invisible" (11:27).

He would not let the temptations of affluence and ease or the possibility of persecution and suffering turn his gaze away from God. This "gaze of a soul upon a saving God" is the essence of faith.[9] All the believers listed in Hebrews 11 kept their face turned toward God for fellowship, comfort, and strength during difficult times. They would let nothing pull their heart away from Him. This is why they are called heroes of the Faith. We could rename them "heroes of the Godward gaze" and mean the same thing. Their endurance—sustained obedience under pressure—was fueled by a sustained look at their God and at things eternal. Paul also exhorts us to "see" the invisible by faith in order to endure.

> For which cause we faint not; but though our outward man perish, yet the inward man is renewed day by day. For our light affliction, which is but for a moment, worketh for us a far more exceeding and eternal weight of glory; *While we look not at the things which are seen*, but at the things which are not seen: for the things which are seen are temporal; but the things which are not seen are eternal (II Cor. 4:16-18).

This endurance is the fruit of a Christlike, renewed mind. It is more than having a head filled with Bible passages and scriptural principles. A renewed mind must start with that kind of hearing, but it is far more. It is a mind that is beholding "those things which are above, where Christ sitteth on the right hand of God" and is setting its "affection on things above, not on things on the earth." It is a mind that is "renewed in knowledge after the image of him that created him" and that is letting "the word of Christ dwell in [it] richly in all wisdom." This is why Paul could exclaim, "And whatsoever ye *do* in word or deed, *do* all in the name of the Lord Jesus, giving thanks to God and the Father by him" (Col. 3:1-2, 10, 16-17).

---

[9] Tozer, *Pursuit*, p. 81.

This endurance with its face toward God and its eye on the eternal is Christlikeness! When listening to God is followed by reflection on God's words so that we begin to think like God, we are then hearing. When obeying His words and enduring in them because they are His words drive us to being "faithful unto death" (Rev. 2:10), we are doing His will and are living wisely. There is a certain biblical role God used to describe how all of this blends together into a usable life on this earth. It is a role that describes mature, grown-up Christianity.

GROWN-UP CHRISTIANITY

As we have seen, Christlikeness is not the same as following a moral or ethical ideal. It is not simply possessing more knowledge of Bible content or Bible principles. It is not merely replacing old habits with new ones or being and doing good. Furthermore, it is not becoming well-adjusted or recovering from some life-dominating sin. Christlikeness is the manifestation of the fruit of God's Spirit in the life of a believer beholding the glory of God. The result of the process we have been looking at in this book is a person who looks increasingly like Christ—the grown-up Christian.

Paul said God's goal for believers is to come "unto the measure of the stature of the fulness of Christ" (Eph. 4:13). I made this statement in Chapter 1: While living on this earth, *Jesus Christ exemplified the characteristics of a man controlled by the Holy Spirit and in perfect fellowship with God.* His submission to and dependence upon His Father and His sacrificial ministry to others blended those characteristics into a perfect ideal Paul called "the form [nature] of a servant" (Phil. 2:7). *Servanthood is grown-up Christianity.* We will close the second part of this book with a brief look at how all we have learned about having a renewed mind prepares us to be Christlike servants. The designation "servant" means little to modern man, but to a first-century believer the term was filled with meaning. Slaves in the ancient world were valued for two basic qualities, which are also characteristics of our Lord.

First-Century Slaves Were Responsive to the Needs of Others

The concept of being responsive to the needs of others is set forth in the New Testament word *diakonos* (servant), which appears over sixty times in the New Testament in its various forms. It is the Greek word from which we get the word "deacon" and describes someone who is actively involved in meeting the needs of others. Jesus used the word in the following passages:

> But Jesus called them unto him, and said, Ye know that the princes of the Gentiles exercise dominion over [lord it over] them, and they that are great exercise authority upon them. But it shall not be so among you: but whosoever will be great among you, let him be your minister [diakonos]; . . . Even as the Son of man came not to be ministered [verb form of diakonos] unto, but to minister [same word again], and to give his life a ransom for many (Matt. 20:25-26, 28).

> But he that is greatest among you shall be your servant [diakonos]. And whosoever shall exalt himself shall be abased; and he that shall humble himself shall be exalted (Matt. 23:11-12).

> And he sat down, and called the twelve, and saith unto them, If any man desire to be first, the same shall be last of all, and servant [diakonos] of all (Mark 9:35).

> If any man serve [verb form of diakonos] me, let him follow me; and where I am, there shall also my servant [diakonos] be: if any man serve [verb form again] me, him will my Father honour (John 12:26).

In these passages our Lord taught that those most exalted in His scheme of events had an attitude of "otherness." Their energies and concerns were not with themselves and how others could serve them but on how they could become a blessing to someone else.

A *useful* first-century slave did not hang around in the shadows hoping he would not be called upon to perform a task. He was right in the middle of the action—washing feet, filling water pots, tutoring children, working in the fields, running errands, and so forth. *God's attributes of love, compassion, kindness, patience, and mercy, when manifested in the life of a believer beholding the glory of God, result in Christlike service for others.*[10] This servanthood is grown-up Christianity!

---

[10] See also John 13:12-17 and Romans 15:1-7.

This aspect of servanthood is familiar to most of us. We admire people who are constantly doing things for others. But if the servanthood is indeed Christlike, it has yet another quality about it.

First-Century Slaves Were Responsive to the Will of Another

Another Greek word, *doulos,* emphasizes the second aspect of slavery—being responsive to the will of another. In the classical world this word spoke of someone who was enslaved to another. It emphasized the total ownership and sovereignty of the individual by someone else.[11] It is used 125 times in the New Testament and eventually took on a different meaning in the Christian use of the word. Paul used it in Romans 1:1 and elsewhere when he called himself "a servant of Jesus Christ." John the Apostle used it in the same way in Revelation 1:1. These men were stressing their total submission to their Master, Jesus Christ. They were testifying of their responsiveness to His *will*—to His commands. In fact, Jesus Himself said, "And why call ye me, Lord, Lord [implying that I am your Master, and you are My slave], and do not the things which I say?" (Luke 6:46).

This aspect of servanthood is often overlooked in our freethinking, democratic society. By this definition, many believers are not very good servants. They do not respond well to the will of their masters. They do not obey speed limits, parking restrictions, tax laws, and a host of other civil and institutional laws. They do not cheerfully submit to parents, husbands, employers, church leaders, and other authority figures in their lives. The spirit of our age preaches that if you do not like the will of your master, it is all right to ignore or defy it. Nothing is more un-Christlike! A serious look again at Philippians 2:1-11 shows our Lord's spirit to the earthly authorities who sentenced him to death—"even the death of the cross."

Paul gave very serious instructions to the New Testament slaves, who made up a large part of his congregations. Many of them were owned by "unworthy" masters who severely mistreated them. Carefully and reflectively note his words to them.

---

[11] Examine Matthew 8:9; 22:1-14; Mark 12:1-5; and Luke 12:41-47; 14:16-23 to see how first-century slaves were quick to respond to the will of their masters.

Servants *[doulos]*, be obedient to them that are your masters according to the flesh, with fear and trembling, in singleness of your heart, as unto Christ; Not with eyeservice, as menpleasers; but as the servants *[doulos]* of Christ, doing the will of God from the heart; With good will doing service [verb form of *doulos*], as to the Lord, and not to men: Knowing that whatsoever good thing any man doeth, the same shall he receive of the Lord, whether he be bond or free (Eph. 6:5-8).

Servants *[doulos]*, obey in all things your masters according to the flesh; not with eyeservice, as menpleasers; but in singleness of heart, fearing God: And whatsoever ye do, do it heartily, as to the Lord, and not unto men; Knowing that of the Lord ye shall receive the reward of the inheritance: for ye serve [verb form of *doulos*] the Lord Christ. But he that doeth wrong shall receive for the wrong which he hath done: and there is no respect of persons (Col. 3:22-25).

Let as many servants *[doulos]* as are under the yoke count their own masters worthy of all honour, that the name of God and his doctrine be not blasphemed. And they that have believing masters, let them not despise them, because they are brethren; but rather do them service [verb form of *doulos*], because they are faithful and beloved, partakers of the benefit. These things teach and exhort (I Tim. 6:1-2).

Exhort servants *[doulos]* to be obedient unto their own masters, and to please them well in all things; not answering again; Not purloining, but shewing all good fidelity; that they may adorn the doctrine of God our Saviour in all things (Titus 2:9-10).

There was no doubt about the obedience required of first-century slaves. They belonged to someone else and were expected to carry out the wishes of their master without complaint or back talk. They were to submit even to unreasonable masters with a single-minded humility that "adorned" the gospel they professed. Our Lord Himself played by His own rules; He came to this earth and responded to His human authorities the same way.

Christlikeness, then, will be evidenced in doing good for others; but just as important, it will be evidenced by submission to authority. Those who want the image of being a "good Christian" but who are not good servants will have a fierce struggle with submission. They will contest that they have learned to "think for themselves" or will protest that there is no way to succeed in modern times without asserting themselves. Our Lord slashes through all the rationality of every age by reminding us not to call Him Lord if we refuse to do the things He says (Luke 6:46). And He says, "Obey them that have the rule over you" (Heb. 13:17).[12] God takes our disobedience to human authorities personally.[13]

By contrast, Christ's attributes of meekness (willingness to be governed), humility, faith (confidence in His Father), and temperance when manifested in the life of a believer result in a Christlike submission to authority. Here is the testimony of Peter about how Christ suffered at the hands of human authority: "Christ also suffered for us, leaving us an example, that ye should follow his steps: Who did no sin, neither was guile found in his mouth: Who, when he was reviled, reviled not again; when he suffered, he threatened not; but committed himself to him that judgeth righteously" (I Pet. 2:21-23).

These two issues—being responsive to the needs of others and being responsive to the will of our masters—are the litmus tests of Christlikeness. This is grown-up Christianity! This is why the Father gave the highest commendation to His Son in Matthew 12:18 when He said, "Behold my *servant,* whom I have chosen; my beloved, in whom my soul is well pleased."

He called His Son a servant because He was responsive to the needs of others. He was known for His *sacrifice.* He denied Himself to stay *involved.* But He was also responsive to the will of His Father. He was known for His *submission.* He denied Himself to stay *in line.* May we hear the same commendation when we stand before Him: "Well done, thou good and faithful servant *[doulos]:* . . . enter thou into the joy of thy lord" (Matt. 25:21).

We *can* hear Him say those words to us if we will "let this mind be in [us], which was also in Christ Jesus" (Phil. 2:5). We will become *living*

---

[12] This is not an isolated command. See also Romans 13:1-7 and I Peter 2:13-17.

[13] It is true that human authority can overstep its God-ordained limits. We are not called to obey human authority that demands that we defy one of God's own commands.

advertisements of Christlikeness, true servants, when we have a renewed mind that is hearing and doing the will of the Father.

TAKE TIME TO REFLECT

The Tests of Wisdom

Reflect upon the following questions that are based upon the four basic disciplines we have studied in the past two chapters. Examine yourself to see whether you are truly hearing and doing or whether you are self-deceived and not becoming truly wise.

1. Do you *listen* to what God says through His Word and through your elders? Or do you more often listen to your own heart or to others who listen to their own heart? Your inclination to listen to God and your elders will be revealed most often by how well you take correction from them. A wise person will welcome reproof and instruction because he wants to become wiser. A fool will reject correction and instruction and will remain a fool.

2. Do you *reflect* on and *remember* what God and your elders say? What kind of soil are you? Being "good soil" is no accident. If you truly are "good soil," you should be able to list the things you do *on purpose* to make sure you "keep" the seed so that it bears fruit. Biblical meditation is one such activity and is not done on the run or on the spur of the moment. If you are truly reflecting on God's Word, you should be able to point to extended periods of time in your schedule that are devoted to time with God.

3. Do you do what God and your elders say? Do you find yourself using your mind to think of reasons not to obey God or your leaders? Are you quick to find excuses like the following that, in your mind, justify your lack of compliance?

   - "Dad told me to get off the phone in five minutes, but since he didn't come back to check on me, I can keep talking."

   - "Since no one saw me cheat, it isn't really cheating. I knew the answers anyway; I just couldn't think of them at the moment."

   - "I don't have to obey that regulation since I don't agree with it. It really is better stewardship of my time not to go through that procedure anyway."

   - "It's OK to disobey the speed limit because I can't ruin my testimony by being late for the meeting."

- "I have to discipline my children in anger or they don't pay attention to anything I say."

- "It's OK for me to take my daily lunch break with Shelley at the office since my wife isn't really meeting my needs, and Shelley is such an encouragement and is so much fun to be with."

Every person in the above situations has meditated upon a lie until he has begun to believe it. He has rationalized disobedience to God and other authorities and has become self-deceived. Each one is proving that he loves himself most because he is pleasing himself rather than God and others. *Obedience is always an act of love toward someone; it is never merely compliance with a rule.*

Remember, even obedience can be an act of self-love, however, if you obey to get what you want—esteem in other people's eyes, freedom from hassle, and so forth. If this concept is just beginning to dawn on you, go back and re-read Chapters 2 through 5 to get a better look at what is really going on in your heart.

4. Do you *persevere* in what God and your elders say?

    Do you follow through even though you must pay an unexpected price for enduring? An unwillingness to pay the price is most often the reason spouses bail out of marriages, teens bail out of their families, families bail out of their good Bible-believing churches, and employees bail out of their jobs. They encounter difficulties they did not anticipate and eventually decide that they should not have to deny self any longer. They do not endure and, consequently, will not be crowned.[14] The question is never what will please me in this decision but what will please the One who loved me most.

A WORD TO DISCIPLE-MAKERS

Fostering Obedience

Rebuking and disciplining others has never been a popular activity for most people—even less so in today's individualistic and relativistic culture. The tragic result is that few parents rear truly wise children, few

---

[14] James 1:12.

Christian schools develop truly wise students, and few Christian counselors produce truly wise counselees. Wisdom cannot be developed in anyone when robbed of its training tools of rebuke and corrective action. The entire Bible is replete with examples and exhortations that teach the necessity of using these tools.

Obedience is fostered in an atmosphere of loving accountability. Most often that accountability is provided from God-ordained authority in our lives at home, at church, at school, and at work. First Peter 2:13-25 teaches what spirit a believer ought to have toward authority—whether good or bad. It specifically says that authorities are "sent by [God] for [1] the punishment of evil*doers*, and for [2] the praise of them that *do* well" (v. 14). Authorities are to both enforce and encourage.

Think with me for a moment about the effect that correction administered in a godly fashion has upon a person. First, the rebuke or penalty gets the offender's *attention*. Second, with the proper kind of confrontation, it can cause him to stop and *think*. Third, it reinforces what the offender is supposed to be *doing*. And finally, the surety of a penalty will be a motivator to *persevere* in obedience the next time he is tempted to disobey. Did you notice that in each of these four effects of correction is one of the basic disciplines of wisdom—attention, meditation, obedience, and endurance? Parents, pastors, and others who are unwilling to correct those they lead in a biblical fashion are abandoning one of God's most important tools for developing the disciplines of wisdom. No one becomes wise who has not become skilled in using all these tools through much practice.

James 1:22-23 says clearly that a man who is only a hearer of the word, and not a doer, is self-deceived. Though he may have given his *attention* to something from God and may have even *meditated* upon it, if he has not followed through with *doing* it, he is kidding himself to think that he is making spiritual progress. In fact, he is headed for trouble. This is why Paul almost seems to shout when he says, *"Be not deceived;* God is not mocked: for whatsoever a man soweth, that shall he also reap" (Gal. 6:7). This is why the writer of Hebrews commands us to "exhort one another daily, while it is called To day; lest any of you be hardened through the *deceitfulness* of sin" (Heb. 3:13). James 1:13-15 also pictures the deception and destruction of sin.

Sometimes fellow Christians who refuse to get involved protest, "I didn't want to get him into trouble, so I didn't do anything." Their spirit betrays a faulty view of sin and its effects. A man who is hearing but not doing is *already in trouble!* The principle of sowing and reaping is already activated. The time bomb is ticking, and his destruction is sure. The involvement of one who will rebuke and chasten is a mission of mercy to rescue someone who is *already in trouble*. Don't let a fellow believer continue in his downward spiral of self-deception and destruction. Rescue him by your involvement of rebuke and correction.

Of course it isn't easy, but you have to decide whether you yourself will be a hearer and a doer in this matter of rebuking and correcting. James says that "to him that knoweth to *do* good, and *doeth* it not, to him it is sin" (James 4:17). You are being deceived if you think you do not have to get involved with others. We will look at this matter more in a later chapter, but for now, seriously consider God's mandate for you to get involved restoring a brother "overtaken in a fault" (Gal. 6:1).

Fostering Endurance

Continuing to do what is right in the face of pressure to disobey often requires generous doses of encouragement. But again, notice how *God* encourages. He does not encourage His children by reminding them about something good about *themselves*. He does not say, "Now you have been a good boy, so I think things should turn out all right if you just hang in there." Nor does He say, "You haven't done anything wrong that deserves that kind of mistreatment. You don't have to take it from them. Just stand up for yourself." Much so-called encouragement given today is sentimental at best and unbiblical at worst.

God encourages us by revealing to us something good about *Himself*. For example, note these passages:

> Blessed be God, even the Father of our Lord Jesus Christ, *the Father of mercies*, and the *God of all comfort*; Who comforteth us in all our tribulation, that we may be able to comfort them which are in any trouble, by the comfort wherewith we ourselves are comforted of God (II Cor.1:3-4).

> There hath no temptation taken you but such as is common to man: but *God is faithful*, who will not suffer you to be tempted above that ye are able; but will with the temptation also make a way to escape, that ye may be able to bear it (I Cor. 10:13).

> The Lord is not slack concerning his promise, as some men count slackness; but is *longsuffering* to us-ward, not willing that any should perish, but that all should come to repentance (II Pet. 3:9).

Often in the Old Testament when He wanted to encourage a believer, God revealed one of His names or some aspect of His nature. Notice how God does this with Job in chapters 38-42 or with Israel in Isaiah chapters 40-66. In the Psalms, David often comforted himself with what he knew about God. Study these passages and meditate upon the names of God so that you can comfort and encourage others with some truth about God.

PART THREE

REFLECTING YOUR LORD

And . . . put on the new man, which after God is created in righteousness and true holiness.
Ephesians 4:24

CHAPTER TEN

BEING A GOD-LOVING EXAMPLE

And thou shalt love the Lord thy God with all thine heart, and with all thy soul,
and with all thy might.
Deuteronomy 6:5

WHERE WE HAVE BEEN

Congratulations on coming this far in your study of biblical change![1]
We have seen that we have three basic personal responsibilities in the
sanctification process. These are summarized for us by the apostle Paul
in Ephesians 4:22-24. I want to review them briefly for you so that you
can see where we have been.

The first was the responsibility to restrain the flesh through the enablement of the Holy Spirit. We learned how to recognize the evil within
us, how to identify our *own way* of making life work, how to get into our
place of submission to God, and how to mortify the flesh.

Second, Paul taught us that we are changed when our mind is illumi-
nated and renewed by the Holy Spirit as He teaches us from God's Word.
We learned how to know God and how to become like Him by beholding
His glory in the Word of God. We also learned how to become wise by
hearing and doing His words. Our cooperation with God in these
responsibilities will prepare us to be servants who are more useful to our
Master because we are more like our Master. These were the thrusts of
Parts One and Two of this book.

---

[1] If you have jumped to this part of the book without reading the earlier chapters,
I urge you to go back and work through Parts One and Two. What we are about to see
in Part Three is the fruit of the life I have been describing in the preceding chapters.

209

WHERE WE ARE GOING

Part Three will now take our growth in Christ one step further. In Ephesians 4:24 Paul exhorts us to "put on the new man." That means that our changed lives must be revealing Christ to others. God uses the first two responsibilities of restraining the flesh and renewing our mind to establish a *Christlike character within us*. God intends next to use what He has produced in our lives to have a *Christlike influence on others*. Christ made it clear that we are to be "salt of the earth" and are to shine as "the light of the world." Notice this mandate in Matthew 5:13-16.

> Ye are the salt of the earth: but if the salt have lost his savour, wherewith shall it be salted? it is thenceforth good for nothing, but to be cast out, and to be trodden under foot of men. Ye are the light of the world. A city that is set on an hill cannot be hid. Neither do men light a candle, and put it under a bushel, but on a candlestick; and it giveth light unto all that are in the house. Let your light so shine before men, that they may see your good works, and glorify your Father which is in heaven.

These verses are a call to spiritual leadership. Please do not be distracted by the word "leadership." The call to spiritual leadership does not mean that every believer must hold some official position in the church or must have a certain kind of personality. J. Oswald Sanders says in his classic work *Spiritual Leadership*, "Leadership is influence, the ability of one person to influence others to follow his or her lead."[2] We sometimes call this spiritual influence ministry, discipleship, shepherding, spiritual parenting, or mentoring. Whatever name we use, the purpose is the same—challenging others to change and to grow into Christlikeness.

Servant-Leaders

We learned in the last chapter that Christlikeness shows itself most notably in servanthood—being responsive to the needs of others and to the will of our masters. It is this kind of character—that of a servant—that provides the backdrop for our influence (leadership) in the lives of others. We are called to make a difference spiritually in the lives of others as the servants of God, the One who has commanded us to serve others.

---

[2] J. Oswald Sanders, *Spiritual Leadership* (Chicago: Moody Press, 1994), 27.

How to Make a Difference

The principle of influence—of making a difference in the lives of others—is easily stated and easily understood.

You have to *be* different to *make* a difference.
You cannot change anything by adding more of the same.

Suppose you have in front of you a glass of unsweetened iced tea, but you do not like unsweetened tea. You wish, therefore, to add something to your glass of tea to change the taste. You cannot change the taste by pouring more unsweetened tea into the glass. You must add something *different* to the glass, such as sugar, lemon, or ginger ale.

To have an influence on other people, you cannot be just "more of the same" kind of people they are. You must be different to make a difference. This is the significance of our Lord's command that we be salt and light. A first-century housewife who wished to preserve a piece of meat without the benefits of refrigeration could not wrap the meat in another piece of meat to store it. She needed to preserve it with salt—something different from the meat itself. If a first-century man needed to walk to his neighbor's house at night in the darkness, he had to take a lamp of some kind to light his way. The darkness could be changed only by light—something different from the darkness.

Likewise, the greatest spiritual impact is made upon people by someone who is *different* from them. Others must see someone like Christ in us—not someone like the rest of the world—if we are to have any godly influence on them. We can catch some of the flavor of this mandate by examining a very important passage in the Old Testament written to Israel's leaders—primarily its fathers. In it we find the three specific functions of spiritual leadership that will be the subject of our study in this chapter and the two to follow. Notice Moses' words:

> And thou shalt love the Lord thy God with all thine heart, and with all thy soul, and with all thy might. And these words, which I command thee this day, shall be in thine heart: And thou shalt teach them diligently unto thy children, and shalt talk of them when thou sittest in thine house, and when thou walkest by the way, and when thou liest down, and when thou risest up. . . . lest thou forget the Lord (Deut. 6:5-7, 12).

When Moses spoke these words, he was about to pass the torch of leadership to Joshua, his God-appointed successor. The people of Israel stood assembled on the east bank of the Jordan River. Moses delivered his farewell address and took them on a "scrapbook tour" of the past forty years. He recounted the Lord's hand upon the nation. While his memory surveyed the wilderness wanderings, his prophetic eye visualized the pitfalls that lay before the children of Israel in the yet-to-be-conquered land of Canaan. Canaanite influence and paganism could easily swallow up the people of God and render them useless in representing Israel's holy God before the nations.

The dangers to God's people have not changed in the few thousand years since that day on the Jordan bank—nor have God's strategies. If God's name is to be proclaimed to the unbelieving world and His ways passed on to the next generation of believing children, it will be done only by those who take seriously the charge given in Deuteronomy 6. Parents and leaders addressed by Moses in this passage could not be laid-back or cavalier about their spiritual responsibilities. Moses charged them to be God-loving examples, Word-filled teachers, and ministry-minded overseers.

These three characteristics are the fruit of the kind of life we have been discussing in the previous chapters of this book. A man who has been exposing himself to God cannot help being filled with devotion to the Lover of his soul. The Word of his Lover will be his daily delight, and he will be obsessed with calling others to "taste and see that the Lord is good" (Ps. 34:8). A believer who is "putting on the new man" will be passionate about his God and passionate about making disciples of others. Let's look more closely at what it means to be a *God-loving example*. In the next two chapters we will examine what it means to be a *Word-filled teacher* and a *ministry-minded overseer*.

LOVING GOD WITH ALL YOUR HEART

Moses instructed the people that to have any lasting influence upon their children, they must "love the Lord [their] God with all [their] heart, and with all [their] soul, and with all [their] might" (Deut. 6:5).

I sincerely hope that you have not come this far in your study of this book without having spent much time pursuing a personal relationship with God. I am afraid, like most of Israel in Moses' day, we too have very little impact for God upon others because we have very little passion for God. Like the rest of the world, we are too often passionate about matters of little consequence. By our actions and reactions we betray that we have ascribed great value and worth to many things other than God. Dr. Bob Jones Sr. used to say, "What you love and what you hate reveal what you are."[3] Our loves easily become our idols. Those things that have become idols are exposed in a number of ways.

For example, a man worries only about things that are of great importance to him. No one worries about things that do not matter to him. Determine what a man worries about, and you have discovered his treasures. Does he worry most about his appearance and dress before others, his acceptance by certain individuals, his financial security, his pecking order among his peers, or his performance in his work? His anxieties reveal his priorities.

Similarly, how he chooses to spend his resources of time, money, and energy reveals his priorities. Are they spent primarily—if not in amount, at least in preoccupation—on his leisure and recreational activities, his work, or his family? While not one of these has to be evil in itself, none is worthy of first place in any believer's life.

A man's anger is another indicator of his priorities. Find out what highly displeases him, and you have exposed what he values. No one is displeased if something he values little is taken away or is threatened. But begin to rob a man of his treasures, and you will have a fight on your hands. It may be his control, his reputation, his possessions, his position, or his health. A man's anger reveals what areas of life are most precious to him. His anger exposes what he has not yet surrendered fully to God to deal with as He wishes for His glory and for the man's good.

We hear much today about the apathy of the church. No one is ever apathetic! Every man is passionate about something—be it his autonomy, his pleasures, his sports, his wardrobe, his solitude, his control, or any one of a countless number of idols. Those who have influence for God are passionate about *God*. They love *Him* with heart, soul, mind, and body!

Please do not miss the thrust of the previous four chapters about renewing the mind. Those who are thus pursuing their God will find

---

[3] Dr. Bob Jones Sr., *Word of Truth* (radio broadcast), number 337 (ca. 1952).

they are not ill rewarded. Biblical change leads to a passionate relationship with the God of heaven that makes every other love pale in comparison. Notice the words of C. S. Lewis: "We are half-hearted creatures, fooling around with drink and sex and ambition when infinite joy is offered us, like an ignorant child who wants to go on making mud pies in a slum because he cannot imagine what is meant by the offer of a holiday at the sea."[4]

John Piper echoes the sentiment: "The irony of our human condition is that God has put us within sight of the Himalayas of his glory in Jesus Christ, but we have chosen to pull down the shades of our chalet and show slides of Buck Hill—even in church."[5]

Moses instructed the people of Israel that the next generation would "forget the Lord" unless they saw before them examples of those who obviously loved God with all their heart, soul, and mind. The process for developing that kind of passion has been explained in Chapters 6 and 7. The result is a God-exhilarated lover, and like all true lovers, he is extravagant. Think with me about some of the lovers of God in the Scriptures.

MARY'S EXTRAVAGANT GIFT

Jesus had entered the home of a leper in Bethany just days before He was to hang in public shame at Golgotha. He was soon to experience the desertion of His disciples, the mocking scorn of the Jewish establishment, and the sin burden of the entire world. Mary of Bethany, the sister of Martha and Lazarus, in an extraordinary act of devotion, breaks the seal on an alabaster box of spikenard and lavishes it upon the feet and head of her blessed Lord Jesus. The perfumed oils slowly fill the room with fragrance as the disciples are quickly filled with anger. "What extravagance!" they cry. "This ointment is worth an entire year's wages; it could have been sold and the money given to the poor!"

---

[4] C. S. Lewis, *The Weight of Glory and Other Addresses* (Grand Rapids: Eerdmans, 1965), 2.

[5] John Piper, *Desiring God* (Portland, Oreg.: Multnomah Press, 1986), 83.

Jesus' rebuke to the disciples was penetrating. "Why trouble ye the woman? for she hath wrought a good work upon me" (Matt. 26:10).[6] Such extravagance is the sign of a lover—someone who has an intense devotion toward and delight in another.[7] The gifts of lovers to each other are often misunderstood by others—lovers often appear to overdo it.

A similar incidence of devotion by another woman, this one a former harlot, is recorded in Luke 7:36-50. The Lord comes to her defense and praises her extravagant gift as a demonstration of her love. She had experienced extravagant forgiveness. No other gift but an extravagant one would be appropriate in return.

Do those following us see our devotion to our Lord in our extravagant gifts, or do they see us give to the Lord in a miserly and reluctant fashion? Perhaps that is why our joy is so small. Did not Paul teach us, "He which soweth sparingly shall reap also sparingly" (II Cor. 9:6)? What if those who follow us were to see us as cheerful givers instead of grudging givers?

I submit that the reason we do not love Him passionately—as did these devoted worshipers who gave their extravagant gifts—is that we have not contemplated often the extent of His "unspeakable gift" to us (II Cor. 9:15). Those who have reflected much on His forgiveness may even be accused of overdoing it in their giving, but that is to be expected—they are lovers!

MARY'S EXTRAVAGANT ATTENTION

In Luke 10:38-42 we find Mary at Jesus' feet again. This time she is giving extravagant time to the Lord. Martha thinks she is overdoing it and should be doing something useful and practical. I say again, however, that lovers are extravagant! They cannot get enough of each other's time. Thoughts of the loved one return to their mind often throughout the day and even invade their dreams at night. They take the time to

---

[6] The accounts by Matthew (26:6-13) and Mark (14:3-9) do not name the woman. John (12:1-8), however, records a similar incident, which many commentators believe is a parallel to the synoptic accounts, and names Mary the sister of Martha and Lazarus as the devoted worshiper.

[7] "Lover" as it appears in this chapter is used entirely in the sense of strong affection, devotion, and adoration toward another. The usage here is devoid of any sexual attraction or involvement.

mull over every action and word of the loved one, seeking to savor each one to the fullest.

Such was the experience of David, the lover of God. He found great *delight* in the testimonies, words, commandments, and statutes of his God.[8] Ponder the extravagance in David's longing to spend time with his God.

> O God, thou art my God; early will I seek thee: my soul thirsteth for thee, my flesh longeth for thee in a dry and thirsty land, where no water is; To see thy power and thy glory, so as I have seen thee in the sanctuary. Because thy lovingkindness is better than life, my lips shall praise thee. Thus will I bless thee while I live: I will lift up my hands in thy name. My soul shall be satisfied as with marrow and fatness; and my mouth shall praise thee with joyful lips: When I remember thee upon my bed, and meditate on thee in the night watches (Ps. 63:1-6).

God-loving examples to the next generation are people who cannot get enough time with God. They can miss the evening newscast, the day's sports scores, the stock-market report, the latest office gossip, and the night's feature television special; *but they cannot miss their time with God!* They will be found consistently in the Word and in the house of God. They may be accused of overdoing it, but that's to be expected—they are lovers!

DAVID'S EXTRAVAGANT PRAISE

David, the sweet psalmist of Israel, had a lot of time to think. He spent most of his early life on hillsides watching sheep or in caves watching out for his enemies. He didn't waste the time, however. He thought much of God. And the more he thought, the more overwhelmed he was with Israel's God. The book of Psalms bursts with the extravagant praise of a man who had seen God. Read Psalm 145, the last of David's writings, and note the exuberance of "a man after [God's] own heart" (I Sam. 13:14). Notice how many times he uses the word "all" to make sure he doesn't leave anything out. Here is a God-intoxicated man who cannot find the words to express the greatness of the God whose "greatness is unsearchable" (v. 3).

---

[8] Psalm 1:2; 119:16, 24, 35, 47, 70, 77, 174.

His extravagant praise was misunderstood, however—even by his own wife! The occasion was the return of the ark of the covenant to Jerusalem. Its possession by the Philistines had brought great shame upon Israel. David's earlier attempt to bring it back had ended in bitter tragedy because God's methods for carrying the ark had been ignored. The time finally came when David ventured to bring it back again. The Scriptures describe the event in II Samuel 6:13-15. "And it was so, that when [the priests] that bare the ark of the Lord had gone six paces, he sacrificed oxen and fatlings. And David danced before the Lord with all his might; and David was girded with a linen ephod. So David and all the house of Israel brought up the ark of the Lord with shouting, and with the sound of the trumpet."

Then follows in verse 16 the sad commentary on the heart of his own wife. "And as the ark of the Lord came into the city of David, Michal Saul's daughter looked through a window, and saw king David leaping and dancing before the Lord; and she despised him in her heart."

How tragic! She misunderstood his praise because she did not share David's gratitude. His heart was full of thoughts of God's deliverance from his enemies and of God's selection of him as king. This was not the heated dance of the pagan Philistines nor the flesh-induced gyrations of a believer doing whatever came naturally when "letting go" in the name of worship. Neither was he performing for anyone's entertainment. The one-time celebration of the return of Israel's ark warranted an extraordinary display of praise to Israel's God. He was accused of overdoing it, but that was to be expected—he was a lover!

PAUL'S EXTRAVAGANT SERVICE

It was the apostle Paul's last stop before his final trip to Jerusalem. There he would be arrested, accused, imprisoned, and eventually escorted to Rome where he would die for his Lord. He addressed the elders of the church at Ephesus and fondly recounted his previous visits. The Holy Spirit had already told him that "bonds and afflictions" awaited him in Jerusalem (Acts 20:23). He remained resolute, however. "But none of these things move me, neither count I my life dear unto myself, so that I might finish my course with joy, and the ministry, which I have received of the Lord Jesus, to testify the gospel of the grace of God" (Acts 20:24).

He reminded them of "the words of the Lord Jesus, how he said, It is more blessed to give than to receive" (v. 35). They prayed together, "wept sore, and fell on Paul's neck, and kissed him, Sorrowing most of all for the words which he spake, that they should see his face no more" (vv. 37-38).

Just before he reached Jerusalem, he stopped in the home of the evangelist Philip. While Paul was there, the prophet Agabus informed him that he would be arrested in Jerusalem and turned over to the Gentiles. As might be expected, his friends wept and begged him not to go to Jerusalem. "Then Paul answered, What mean ye to weep and to break mine heart? for I am ready not to be bound only, but also to die at Jerusalem for the name of the Lord Jesus" (Acts 21:13).

Here is extravagant service! He was accused of overdoing it, but that's to be expected—he was a lover!

THE EXTRAVAGANCE OF OUR GOD

No one's extravagance of any type can outdo, however, the extravagance of our God! His love is extravagant, His sacrifice was extravagant, His promise to do "exceeding abundantly above all that we ask or think"[9] is extravagant, and the reception of His saints "into the everlasting kingdom" will be an abundant, extravagant entrance.[10] He is that kind of God! He may be accused of overdoing it, but that's to be expected—He is the Lover of our souls!

How can we be anything but passionate toward God if we spend any time at all beholding His works and His glory? Jonathan Edwards in his treatise on religious affections writes, "We are nothing if we are not in earnest about our faith, and if our wills and inclinations are not intensely exercised. The religious life contains things too great for us to be lukewarm."[11]

He further laments the condition of his day—how he would grieve if he knew the condition of ours.

---

[9] Ephesians 3:20.

[10] II Peter 1:11.

[11] Jonathan Edwards, *Religious Affections*, ed. James M. Houston (Minneapolis: Bethany House Publishers, 1996), 8.

We find that people exercise the affections in everything else but religion! When it comes to their worldly interest, their outward delights, their honor and reputation, and their natural relations, they have warm affection and ardent zeal. In these things their hearts are tender and sensitive, easily moved, deeply impressed, much concerned, and much engrossed. They get deeply depressed at worldly losses, and highly excited at worldly successes. But how insensible and unmoved are most men about the great things of another world! How dull then are their affections! Here their love is cold, their desires languid, their zeal low, and their gratitude small. How can they sit and hear of the infinite height, depth, length, and breadth of the love of God in Christ Jesus, of His gift of His infinitely dear Son offered up as a sacrifice for the sins of men, and yet be so insensible and regardless! Can we suppose that the wise Creator implanted such a faculty of affections to be occupied in this way? How can any Christian who believes the truth of these things not realize this?[12]

Is it any wonder then that so few believers of the next generation want what we purport to possess? Who would want to be like us? *If we are not known to be God-loving believers by our obvious extravagance for the Lover of our soul, why should those who follow us bother with Him either?*

Let us put away our obsessions with anything but Christ! Let us fill our souls with His life-giving Word, listen obediently to the promptings of His Spirit, and delight ourselves in extended times of fellowship with the One who has loved us with an everlasting love. Then, and only then, can we expect the next generation to be attracted to Him rather than to the world. Oh believer, "love the Lord thy God with all thine heart, and with all thy soul, and with all thy might" (Deut. 6:5)!

To Know Him Is to Love Him

I have spoken much already about the necessity of reflection and meditation upon the Word. If the fire that burns within us is from God, it will have both the heat of passion and the light of truth as revealed in God's Word. May God deliver us from academic studies that have not penetrated the heart. Light without heat warms no one. May we be spared, as well, from the heat of supposed Holy Spirit movements that are not based upon the clear teaching of Scripture. Heat without light is a darkness that destroys. John Piper so astutely observes,

---

[12] Ibid, p. 27.

"True worshipers will worship the Father in spirit and truth." True worship does not come from people whose feelings are like air ferns with no root in the solid ground of biblical doctrine. The only affections that honor God are those rooted in the rock of biblical truth.

Else what meaning have the words of the apostle, "They have a zeal for God, but it is not according to knowledge" (Romans 10:2)? And did not the Lord pray, "Sanctify them by the truth; your word is truth" (John 17:17)? And did he not say, "You will know the truth and the truth shall make you free" (John 8:32)? Holy freedom in worship is the fruit of truth. *Religious feelings that do not come from a true apprehension of God are neither holy nor truly free, no matter how intense.*[13]

There can be no true enjoyment of God except that which is based upon His own revelation of Himself. Mere poetic fantasies or imaginary dialogue with God will not suffice. Those who have great impact for God are those who have a great passion for Him fueled by meditation upon His Word. They are also those who "are strong" and "have overcome the wicked one" because "the word of God abideth in [them]" (I John 2:14). Take a few moments to ask yourself what your present experience with God and His Word is. What does your example reveal about your passion for God? No one can know Him intimately and not love Him passionately.

Are You Thirsty for God?

If the discussion in this chapter of the God-loving heart has stirred any desire within you to pull up the shades of your chalet and view the Himalaya Mountains for yourself, then you have experienced the "hunger and thirst after righteousness" of which our Lord spoke in Matthew 5:6. It is the same longing for rest that Jesus spoke of in Matthew 11:28 when He said, "Come unto me, all ye that labour and are heavy laden, and I will give you rest." It is a thirst He intends to quench and a rest He intends to give to those who come to Him and who stop searching for relief in other sources.

It is this thirst that God will use to draw us to His Word. In it we will find the Living Water. We will find Rest for our souls. In short, we will find God. When He is revealed to us as we behold His glory, we will be

---

[13] Piper, *Desiring God*, 80.

stunned by His mercy to us, humbled by His grace, and thirsty for knowledge of Him.

Have You Been Tasting God?

Scriptural sermons, biblical Christian music, short readings of the Scripture, and books like this on the Christian walk will allow you to "taste and see that the Lord is good" (Ps. 34:8). But even these aren't enough. These brief exposures to God and His ways are nothing more than the pizza or sausage samples offered at the end of the supermarket aisles. They offer only a small taste of the product; they are not the meal. You may have "tasted" the Lord in recent days, but you will not be full until you have feasted at His banquet hall and filled yourself with the knowledge of who He is.

Do You Know the Joy of Abiding in Christ?

After you have spent a day with God reflecting on what He has revealed about Himself, confessing your sin, turning your heart toward Him in praise, and offering yourself to Him to use as He wills, you will begin to experience the joy of abiding in Christ.[14] Others will take notice that you have been with Jesus.[15] As the hymn writer said, "Thy friends in thy conduct, His likeness shall see."[16] This kind of God-loving believer makes a difference in the lives of others because he is filled with "all joy and peace in believing" (Rom. 15:13). Even Christian circles are filled with believers who are not filled with joy or peace. They are an unhappy lot and just as agitated and restless as the unbelievers around them who know not God. Who wants to follow their unhappy examples? On the other hand, the best advertisement is a satisfied customer. Think of the woman in John 4 who, after she had met the Lord at the well in Samaria, returned to call the entire city to drink of the same Source that had quenched her thirst.

MASTERS AT MEDITATION

You may protest, "I understand what you wrote about meditation in earlier chapters, but I am not good at that kind of thing. I could never learn how to reflect on God's Word that way." The truth is that *all* of us

---

[14] John 15:11.
[15] Acts 4:13.
[16] William Longstaff, "Take Time to be Holy."

are masters at meditation. We all are very skilled at taking one thought and mulling it over and over in our mind. We do it every time we experience a temptation of any sort. Consider the first temptation in the Garden of Eden, recorded in Genesis 3:6. When Satan presented Eve the option of eating the forbidden fruit, the Bible says, "And when the woman saw that the tree was good for food, and that it was pleasant to the eyes, and a tree to be desired to make one wise, she took of the fruit thereof, and did eat, and gave also unto her husband with her; and he did eat."

Notice what happened here. Eve listened to the *word* of the Serpent: "Ye shall not surely die: For God doth know that in the day ye eat thereof, then your eyes shall be opened, and ye shall be as gods, knowing good and evil" (vv. 4-5). Eve's next move was to reflect on that information and consider how the fruit would be beneficial for her.

When we hear preaching on this passage in Genesis 3, our attention is often drawn to the appeals to the lust of the flesh ("the tree was good for food"), the lust of the eyes ("it was pleasant to the eyes"), and the pride of life ("a tree to be desired to make one wise"). Perhaps there is a parallelism here with the threefold appeal John presents in I John 2:16, but I feel that an emphasis upon these draws attention away from the real dynamics of this situation.

Eve was drawn into this temptation because she began to consider that the fruit was *good* and *delightful* (pleasing) and *desirable*. The next logical action was for her to take it. Her passions were inflamed by meditating upon the virtues and benefits of the fruit. She was then only a short step away from actually choosing to take it. She saw it eventually as something "desired to make one wise." Notice, too, how the qualities she ascribed to the fruit were qualities that belonged to God Himself. He only is truly *good*. He only is truly *delightful*. He only is *"to be desired to make one wise."* Here is idolatry in its purest form. She was replacing God as the object of her passions with a piece of fruit! How did this happen? She meditated upon a lie. This is the essence of temptation.

Sin starts with a deception—often a twisted truth. We mull over and over in our mind the deception, considering the benefits of indulgence until we are so convinced of its virtues that we choose to embrace it. Only then do we find that a hook is imbedded in the lure.

Understand then that *we will meditate!* We will meditate on truth, inflaming our desires for God; or we will meditate upon lies, inflaming our desires for things that will become idolatrous replacements for Him. Meditation is not an option. We *will* meditate. Our only option is the choice of fuel for our reflection.

This book is my effort to tempt you with God. I want you to see that *He* is good, *He* is delightful to the eyes, and *He* is "desired to make one wise"! If you will spend enough time reflecting on Him and considering His virtues, it will be but a small step for you to *choose* Him as the satisfaction for your thirsty soul. I think now you can see why people who are passionate for God spend much time listening to and reflecting upon the words of their Lover. They have refused the lies of the Serpent and have filled themselves with the truths of their Creator.

Let us then put away our preoccupation with lesser things. The next generation must be tempted with God. They must see by our passionate, God-loving lives that He is *good*, that He is *delightful,* and that He is *desirable to make one wise.* I am afraid that those who observe our lives may be led to the delusion that other things—such as prestige, money, sports, recreation, control, or relationships with others—are the ultimate good, delightful, and desirable pursuits of life. We must tempt them with God!

TAKE TIME TO REFLECT

God's Love Versus Self-Love Study Sheet

For a thorough discovery of how others see you, use the study sheet God's Love Versus Self-Love in Appendix A. Go through the entire sheet yourself, underlining the phrases on both sides of the chart that you know apply to you. Give your underlined paper to your spouse, child, or coworker and tell him that you are sure there are items you have missed. Ask him to go through the sheet and underline in another color of ink or pencil the additional areas from both sides of the chart that he sees apply to you. If there are areas that you have already underlined that he wishes to underline in his own color to let you know he heartily agrees with your evaluation, encourage him to do so.

Assure him that no matter what he underlines, you will not be defensive or argumentative. In order for you to have honest feedback, he must feel that you will not retaliate or challenge him. You may ask him for a clarification of his choices so that you can know specifically how to improve, but he must not feel threatened by your follow-up questions. You must approach this assignment with him in genuine humility. Any self-protective and self-serving responses on your part will only confirm with him any previous suspicions on his part that you are out to please yourself instead of God and others.

Rate Your Example Study Sheet

The apostle Paul exhorts Timothy, "Let no man despise thy youth; but *be thou an example* of the believers, in word, in conversation, in charity, in spirit, in faith, in purity." To evaluate your example, use the questions in the study sheet Rate Your Example in Appendix A to rate yourself in the categories suggested by I Timothy 4:12 and expanded further with specific applications. If you are open to finding out how others perceive your leadership, photocopy the checklist and give it to your spouse, coworker, children, friend, and so forth. Ask them to honestly fill it out and return it to you.

Of course, there are many other larger issues that you should have addressed as you went through Parts One and Two of this book. The Rate Your Example questions are intended to help you fine-tune your example. They do not address any major issues.

You might also ask yourself the following questions:

- What extravagant gifts have I recently/ever offered to God?
- When was the last time I gave God any extravagant attention?
- When was the last time I gave God any extravagant praise?
- Am I known by those who follow me as one who gives God extravagant service?
- What extravagances of God regularly occupy my thoughts?

A WORD TO DISCIPLE-MAKERS

The Power of Example

In Mark 3:14, Jesus "ordained twelve, that they should be with him." Through exposure to their Lord, the disciples gained His vision of the lost, learned the lessons of servanthood, and acquired a desire for personal godliness as they observed His life and character.

People have a difficult time doing or being something they have not seen modeled in some way. For example, it is much easier for a child to learn to water-ski if he has grown up watching his parents and older brothers and sisters doing it than it would be if he had never seen a water-skier and had to learn to water-ski by reading a book or watching a video on water-skiing. The information gained through the book or video may be extremely helpful and logical, but seeing it carried out again and again by an experienced skier and trying it out under the skillful eye of a veteran skier is by far the best way to learn.

Jesus gave many lectures (discourses) to His disciples, but He was always an example of what He was teaching. When He wanted to teach them about servanthood, He washed their feet. When He wanted to teach them to respect God-ordained authority, He paid His taxes. God wants each one of us who is maturing in his relationship with Him to be close-up illustrations of godliness to those around us.

But This Is Scary!

Of course this is frightening. Anyone in a position of being an example has a very vulnerable position. Not one of us comes equipped with a "bulletproof" life. We are going to be disappointed, hurt, and misunderstood by those we try to help. Because of this vulnerability, many avoid leadership positions and consequently never grow. God is grieved when He finds this attitude. He says, "For when for the time [taking into consideration how long you have been saved] ye ought to be teachers, ye have need that one teach you again which be the first principles of the oracles of God; and are become such as have need of milk, and not of strong meat" (Heb. 5:12).

Paul testifies that he learned to rejoice in vulnerability because it gave him an opportunity to see God work firsthand in his life. He said, "Therefore I take pleasure in infirmities, in reproaches, in necessities, in persecutions, in distresses for Christ's sake: for when I am weak, then am I strong" (II Cor. 12:10). The vulnerable situations in life compelled him to look more steadfastly at Christ, who strengthened him in the difficulties.[17] Consequently, he grew.

---

[17] Philippians 4:13.

Although vulnerability is scary for us, our Lord greatly values our ministry to others. He said that "whosoever shall do [His commandments] and teach them, the same shall be called great in the kingdom of heaven" (Matt. 5:19). He puts a high priority on living out what we know and being an instrument of influence on others.

The Badge "Speaks"

A dad who drives faster than the speed limit says something to his child about himself—dad is inconsistent. He skews the boy's view of his father. A dad who wears a police badge and breaks the speed limit when off duty says something to his child about the entire realm of law enforcement. He skews the boy's view of everything the dad represents by his badge. Sometimes we wonder why the children of pastors or Christian workers "go bad." Perhaps by percentage there are no more failures than in the church congregation, but maybe there is a dynamic here that Christian leaders overlook. Their example to their children is important, not just for their own integrity as parents, but for the integrity of everything they represent as ambassadors of Christ.

The apostle Paul was very cautious not to cast a reflection on the gospel ministry by his own life. He said that he lived in such a way as to be "Giving no offence in any thing, *that the ministry be not blamed:* But in all things approving ourselves as the ministers of God" (II Cor. 6:3-4). Paul wore a "badge" that said he was the minister of God. He knew that any personal actions would be either a credit or a discredit to the ministry. All of us should be concerned about our example, but if you are a disciple-maker with a "badge" (e.g., father, deacon, pastor, teacher, or person with any position of spiritual leadership), you must be doubly aware of how your example affects others. You represent more than just yourself when you wear a "badge."

CHAPTER ELEVEN
BEING A WORD-FILLED TEACHER

And these words, which I command thee this day, shall be in thine heart: And
thou shalt teach them diligently unto thy children.
Deuteronomy 6:6-7

In the last chapter we saw that "putting on the new man" means having
a Christlike influence that makes a difference in the lives of those around
us. We saw from Deuteronomy 6:5 that God's first concern for spiritual
servant-leaders is that they become *God-loving examples*.

In the two verses that follow, Moses set forth the second function of
Israel's leaders. They were to become *Word-filled teachers*. He commanded them to saturate their *own* heart with the ways and the words
of the living God. They were then to saturate the minds of their children
with the same. Here are his instructions to that end, followed by the
apostle Paul's parallel emphasis in the New Testament.

> And *these words*, which I command thee this day, *shall be in thine*
> *heart: And thou shalt teach* them diligently unto thy children (Deut.
> 6:6-7).

> Let *the word* of Christ *dwell in you* richly in all wisdom; *teaching* and
> admonishing one another in psalms and hymns and spiritual songs,
> singing with grace in your hearts to the Lord (Col. 3:16).

All of us are teaching all the time. We teach by our example, as we saw
in the last chapter. We also teach whenever we open our mouth and give
advice, comment, or instruction. God's concern is not just that we teach,
for we will always be doing that, but that we be *Word-filled* teachers.

GET READY FOR DANGEROUS DAYS

In II Timothy 3, Paul warns his disciple Timothy that "in the last days
perilous times shall come" (v. 1) and that to survive these dangerous days
Timothy must continue in the things he has been taught from "the holy

scriptures" by his godly mother and grandmother (v. 15). Paul warned Timothy that he would see an increase in false teachers, who would be "ever learning, [yet] never able to come to the knowledge of the truth" (v. 7). These "evil men and seducers [would] wax worse and worse, deceiving, and being deceived" (v. 13). Timothy would need to remain assured of the truth—his only protection against faulty thinking and error.

In order to bolster Timothy's confidence in the things he had learned, Paul reminds him that the Scriptures have a particular nature that sets them apart from other kinds of knowledge. Notice his words:

> All scripture is given by inspiration of God, and is profitable for doctrine, for reproof, for correction, for instruction in righteousness: That the man of God may be perfect, throughly furnished unto all good works (II Tim. 3:16-17).

These verses teach four important functions of the Word. The Bible teaches us what is right for us ("doctrine"), teaches us what is wrong with us ("reproof"), teaches us how to make it right ("correction"), and teaches us how to keep it right ("instruction in righteousness"). God uses the Word in these ways to equip the believer for ministry to others ("furnished unto all good works"). A Word-filled teacher will skillfully use the Scriptures for these purposes in the lives of those he disciples. Let's look at each function in more detail.

THE SCRIPTURES TEACH US WHAT IS RIGHT

Today's religious climate tolerates anyone except those who claim that doctrine is important for biblical unity. Modern ecumenists pronounce that the sole test of faith is whether one loves Jesus. The question to be asked is "Which Jesus?" Paul was fearful that the believers of his day would be deceived by men who were "false apostles, deceitful workers, transforming themselves into the apostles of Christ" (II Cor. 11:13). He said,

> But I fear, lest by any means, as the serpent beguiled Eve through his subtilty, so your minds should be corrupted from the simplicity that is in Christ. For if he that cometh preacheth *another Jesus*, whom we have not preached, or if ye receive *another spirit*, which ye have not received, or *another gospel*, which ye have not accepted, ye might well bear with him (II Cor. 11:3-4).

I marvel that ye are so soon removed from him that called you into the grace of Christ unto *another gospel:* Which is not another; but there be some that trouble you, and would pervert the gospel of Christ. But though we, or an angel from heaven, preach any *other gospel* unto you than that which we have preached unto you, let him be accursed. As we said before, so say I now again, If any man preach *any other gospel* unto you than that ye have received, let him be accursed (Gal. 1:6-9).

The apostle John had the same concern when he wrote,

Beloved, believe not every spirit, but try the spirits whether they are of God: because many false prophets are gone out into the world. Hereby know ye the Spirit of God: Every spirit that confesseth that Jesus Christ is come in the flesh is of God: And every spirit that confesseth not that Jesus Christ is come in the flesh is not of God: and this is that spirit of antichrist, whereof ye have heard that it should come; and even now already is it in the world (I John 4:1-3).

Whosoever transgresseth, and abideth not in the doctrine of Christ, hath not God. He that abideth in the doctrine of Christ, he hath both the Father and the Son. If there come any unto you, and bring not this *doctrine*, receive him not into your house, neither bid him God speed: For he that biddeth him God speed is partaker of his evil deeds (II John 9-11).

Doctrine was important to these men, and it must be important to us if we are to be Word-filled teachers. What the Scriptures say is important because of what the Scriptures are.

The Scriptures Are Inspired

To survive the dangerous days ahead, we and our children, like Timothy, must understand that the Word of God is inspired by God—literally, "God-breathed." The Scripture writers were not setting forth their own ideas or parroting the mythology of their day. They were writing the exact words that God desired to have preserved for every generation to follow. Peter said that "the prophecy [revelation from God] came not in old time by the will of man: but holy men of God spake as they were moved [borne along] by the Holy Ghost" (II Pet. 1:21).[1]

The Scriptures Are Infallible

Since the Scriptures are God-breathed, they take on the nature of the Author. He is omniscient—knowing all things—and, therefore, is not ignorant of anything. He hasn't left out anything important, nor has He revealed anything that can be contradicted by new information in the future. He has revealed *completely* and *truthfully* everything necessary for man to know. He cannot make a mistake.

Not only is He wise enough to be without error in all that He said, but He is also omnipotent—all powerful—and, therefore, competent enough to make sure His will is transmitted without error to His creatures. His infinite perfections insure that all His purposes—including His purpose of transmitting His words to man without error—will be fulfilled.

The Scriptures Are Authoritative

The founder of Bob Jones University affirmed the Bible's authority with the declaration "Whatever the Bible says is so!"[2] Today, man in his rebellion to God's authority takes the position "Whatever *I choose* to believe is so!" He sets himself up as the final authority—the final decision maker—about what is true and what is not. His arrogance is astounding! The Bible stands in judgment upon man's beliefs and behavior—not vice versa.

The Bible is the final authority about salvation. It is the exclusive source of information about how a man can be redeemed from his lost condition. No church, religious group, government, or well-intentioned individual can add to or subtract from the Scripture's clear teaching without usurping God's authority. Listen to the following words of the apostle Peter: "*Neither is there salvation in any other: for there is none other name under heaven given among men, whereby we must be saved*" (Acts 4:12).

---

[1] For a more thorough discussion of inspiration, see Edward J. Young, *Thy Word Is Truth* (Grand Rapids: Eerdmans, 1957) and Louis Gaussen, *The Inspiration of the Holy Scriptures* (Chicago: Moody, 1949).

[2] Dr. Bob Jones Sr., *Dr. Bob Jones Says* (radio talks), June 17, 1957.

The Bible is also the final authority about how man is to live after his salvation. It is the final authority about sanctification. The apostle Peter speaks regarding this as well. "According as his divine power hath given unto us *all things* that pertain unto [eternal] life and godliness [the way we live in this life], through the knowledge of him that hath called us to glory and virtue" (II Pet. 1:3).

In this passage Peter echoes what we have seen in Acts 4:12—namely that the Bible is the exclusive source of information about how to have eternal life. But he also declares that the Bible is the only source of information about how to live a godly life on this earth while we wait for heaven. Some might protest, "Why should I believe that the Bible is the final authority regarding the way I live when I don't believe it is the final authority on other topics—like history, chemistry, space exploration, nutrition, welding, and so forth?" That is a fair question and has a simple answer.

The Bible does not claim to say everything there is to know about history, although everything it says about historical events is entirely accurate. Therefore, we can go to other sources of information to learn other facts about history. The Bible does not claim to say everything there is to know about astronomy, although everything it says about the heavens is entirely accurate. Therefore, we can go to other sources of information to learn other facts about astronomy. The same is true about many other subjects mentioned in the Bible.

The Bible *does* claim, however, to say everything there is to know about how to live on this earth with a sense of well-being, contentment, peace, and joy. It covers "all things that pertain unto life and godliness." Therefore, to go to sources that do not point you to the God of the Scriptures for help to solve the problems of living is to rely upon a competing source of information for help. According to God, this is a great "evil" (Jer. 2:13). While science may discover some things that may be *helpful* to a man's well-being, nothing man can discover outside of the Bible is *essential* to man's well-being.

Second, if what man has discovered on his own is truly helpful, it can already be found in the Word of God in a much purer form. Our problem, however, is that when we attempt to help others, we are often at a loss to know what the Bible says about the issues that confront us from day to day. We are *not* Word-filled teachers!

How to Handle Hurt

Let's look at an issue about which the Bible teaches us authoritatively what is right but for which Christians are prone to come up with their own solutions.

Our hearts are increasingly heavy in these "perilous times [dangerous days]" (II Tim. 3:1) when we meet so many who have been abused and hurt at the hands of others. Incidents of childhood sexual abuse continue to rise. The frequency of divorce and the resulting single-parent homes have wreaked untold emotional, economic, physical, educational, and spiritual disaster in the lives of today's children. The result is that more and more of us who minister to others are dealing with people who carry with them much excess emotional or spiritual baggage.

How are we to address their hurt and pain? Is God silent about it? Must we search through the rubble of secular psychology to discover something that we might use to help them? Should we look for drugs to alter their moods, agitation, and loss of well-being? Need we turn to alternative Eastern religions to find some way to calm their troubled souls? Do we teach them to look deep within themselves for the solution? I hope by now in our study of biblical change that you can see the futility of all of these options. The Bible will teach us correct doctrine; it will teach us what is right.

God is the Expert at addressing people in pain. *Most of the Bible was written to hurting people.* The Old Testament Scriptures were written about and to hurting people who were in the chains of slavery at the hands of Egyptians, Assyrians, and Philistines. The New Testament Gospels are records of our Lord's words to Jews living under the cruel rule of Roman Gentiles. The Epistles were written to small, largely Gentile churches whose congregations often contained many slaves. Many were owned by evil masters.

Think with me for a moment about the conditions in which the believers in the first church in Jerusalem lived. Early in the first century as the gospel began to make its impact in that capital city, the believers were increasingly targeted for persecution because of their newfound faith in Jesus Christ. Acts 7 testifies of Stephen's martyrdom at the hands of the Jewish religious leaders—one of whom was Saul of Tarsus. Acts 8 tells of Saul's continued terrorist actions against the church. These early believers were finally driven out of Jerusalem into Judea and Samaria and eventually into Asia Minor. They were rejected in their Jewish homeland because they were Christians. They were further persecuted in the Gentile-ruled cities of Asia Minor because they were Jews. No matter where they went, they suffered greatly. They were denied jobs, land, and status. Their families were ridiculed and maligned. Often they were jailed or killed because they were believers.

James and Peter, copastors in Jerusalem who wished to encourage their scattered flock, wrote James and I and II Peter to these hurting people. Notice their God-inspired counsel:

> My brethren, count it all joy when ye fall into divers temptations; Knowing this, that the trying of your faith worketh patience. But let patience have her perfect[ing] work, that ye may be perfect and entire, wanting nothing (James 1:2-4).

> Blessed be the God and Father of our Lord Jesus Christ, which according to his abundant mercy hath begotten us again unto a [living] hope by the resurrection of Jesus Christ from the dead. . . . Wherein ye greatly rejoice, though now for a season, if need be, ye are in heaviness through manifold temptations: That the trial of your faith, being much more precious than of gold that perisheth, though it be tried with fire, might be found unto praise and honour and glory at the appearing of Jesus Christ (I Pet. 1:3, 6-7).

Don't miss the thrust of these apostles' writings: Allow God to use these times of great pain to refine your soul and to prepare you for the day when you will stand before your Lord.

Think with me for a moment about this advice. Is that the emphasis you would get from most of today's Christian self-help books on helping hurting people? Would they tell you to "gird up the loins of your mind, be sober, and hope to the end for the grace that is to be brought unto you at the revelation of Jesus Christ" (I Pet. 1:13)? You see, we are right back where we started in Chapter 1: God's recovery program is sanctification.

How then do we deal with great pain? Peter tells us to *grow* out of it. We are to increase our intake of the Word and be doubly careful that we are "not fashioning [our]selves according to the former lusts in [our] ignorance" (I Pet. 1:14). Instead, during times of increasing affliction, we are to "desire the sincere milk of the word, that [we] may *grow* thereby"

(I Pet. 2:2). Notice how many times in his two epistles the apostle Peter uses the words "know," "knowing," "knowledge," "known," "remember," "remembrance," "mind," and "grow." This is the kind of counsel from divine inspiration that Peter and James gave their scattered flock. If we are to be Word-filled teachers, our counsel must echo theirs, or we must ask ourselves some important questions: Did God forget to tell us the things we need to know in these "perilous times"? Should we expect Him to send us a supplement to our Bible to fill in the holes where He forgot to say what we need to know to handle today's kinds of problems?

The answer, of course, is obvious. He reminds us that His Word is entirely sufficient to equip every believer for *every* good work.[3] Our problem is that we do not know Him and His Word well enough to know His ways. We must become *Word-filled teachers*. That means that when we are advising anyone about the problems of living, we must be saying *exactly* what God Himself said! As we have seen in II Timothy 3:16-17, God's inspired Word will always tell us what is right. It is the *only* infallible source of truth. It accurately contains "*all things* that pertain unto life and godliness" (II Pet. 1:3).[4]

THE SCRIPTURES TEACH US WHAT IS WRONG

Second Timothy 3:16-17 also informs us that the inspired Scriptures have a second function. They are used by God to teach us what is wrong with us and how that wrong is to be addressed. Word-filled teachers must know what the Bible says about how to reprove others who are not right. Telling someone he is wrong certainly goes against the grain of these times in which every man feels he alone is the determiner of what he should or should not do. The truth of the matter, however, is that man—even believing man—is prone to go his *own way*, as we have seen. The believer, therefore, must "reprove, rebuke, exhort with all longsuffering and doctrine. For the time will come when they will not endure sound doctrine; but after their own lusts shall heap to themselves teachers, having itching ears; And they shall turn away their ears from the truth, and shall be turned unto fables" (II Tim. 4:2-4).

---

[3] II Timothy 3:17.

[4] See Basics for Hurting Believers in Appendix B for more help in working with someone who is suffering.

The Bible gives specific instructions on how to address someone who is wrong in doctrine or in practice. Perhaps the most important element in confronting is the necessity of prayerful self-examination before dealing with the sins of others. Notice this emphasis in the following passages:

> And why beholdest thou the mote that is in thy brother's eye, but considerest not the beam that is in thine own eye? Or how wilt thou say to thy brother, Let me pull out the mote out of thine eye; and, behold, a beam is in thine own eye? Thou hypocrite, *first cast out the beam out of thine own eye*; and then shalt thou see clearly to cast out the mote out of thy brother's eye (Matt. 7:3-5).

> Brethren, if a man be overtaken in a fault, ye which are spiritual [i.e., those walking in the Spirit as Galatians 5:22-26 teaches], restore such an one in the spirit of meekness; *considering thyself*, lest thou also be tempted (Gal. 6:1).

God does not give us permission to remove splinters from the eyes of others—even our children if we are parents—until we have done some spiritual "lumberjacking" and have removed the logs from our own eyes. We cannot be used of God to call anyone to obedience to us or to God if we are doing so from a position of our own disobedience. I will not labor this point here because it has been illustrated extensively earlier.[5] Again, this is why Moses commanded Israel's leaders to be sure that the words of God had saturated their own heart before they attempted to teach them to their children.

Please note that Jesus Himself considered this willingness to rebuke and chasten an expression of His love for His people. He loved them too much to allow them to continue in their sin. In Revelation 3:19 He wrote the following to the Laodicean church: "As many as I love, I rebuke and chasten: be zealous therefore, and repent."

The rebuke must be done in such a way that the loving heart of the rebuker is evident. A believer who is allowing the Word of God to convict his own conscience about his relationship with God and with his neighbor will not be mean-spirited as he deals with others. He knows

---

[5] Review "A Case in Point" in Chapter 3, in which Pastor Williams had to reprove Frank and Susan for going their own way.

all too well the sinfulness of man as he has seen it exposed within his own heart and will desire to help others be rescued from the storms of the flesh as well. Many problems that arise from the *manner* in which believers confront one another will be eliminated if the "teacher" himself is *Word-filled*. If he is not, the issues of concern will most likely be wrong and so will the manner of confrontation.

God's Greatest Concern for His People

We must let the Scriptures not only prescribe the *manner* in which we rebuke wrongdoing but also define for us the true *nature* of the problem we are addressing. As we have seen before, we must deal with both the surface sin and the heart issue. We can learn some important lessons about rebuke by examining God's rebukes of His people.

Notice God's rebuke of Moses for striking the rock in Numbers 20:1-13. There is no doubt that Moses is angry with the people. In fact, the Scriptures teach us much of the nature of anger in this passage.[6] When God deals with Moses for mishandling this situation, however, God does not rebuke Moses for his anger, but rather for his *unbelief* (20:12). God is the ultimate Reality. Any evaluation of a situation that leaves Him out of the picture is going to result in wrong conclusions because not all the facts are being considered.

Acts 17:28 reminds us that "in [God] we live, and move, and have our being." He is our environment. A man's ignoring the nature and ways of the God who surrounds and sustains him is as dangerous as a swimmer's ignoring the nature and ways of the water around him. If the swimmer does not consider the absence of oxygen underwater, he will destroy himself either by his ignorance or by his stubbornness in ignoring the nature of water.

Ignoring God is not just dangerous; it is offensive to God. Notice again Jeremiah 2:13, the passage we looked at in Chapter 4. God says, "For my people have committed two evils; they have forsaken me the fountain of living waters, and hewed them out cisterns, broken cisterns, that can hold no water." God says in effect, "You sin against Me in two ways. First you forsake Me as the essential component of life. Then you further

---

[6] For a more complete discussion of the causes of anger revealed in this passage, see Basics for Angry Believers in Appendix B of this book.

insult Me by looking elsewhere for a solution." The root of this abandonment of God for other solutions is *unbelief*. Thus, most of God's rebukes to man in the Bible are leveled at their unbelief. Note the following examples:

Ye rebelled against the commandment of the Lord your God, and ye believed him not, nor hearkened to his voice (Deut. 9:23).

For they are a very froward [perverse] generation, children in whom is no faith (Deut. 32:20).

God often reproved His people in the Old Testament for their unbelief, even though the more obvious problem seemed to be their complaining, covetousness, fear, or immorality. They indulged in sin because of their failure to see God in the picture. They were "out of touch with Reality." The writer of Hebrews puts his finger on the problem of the children of Israel. He says, "But the word preached did not profit them, not being mixed with faith in them that heard it" (Heb. 4:2). Notice that they were refused entrance into the Promised Land "because of unbelief" (Heb. 3:19). From a human standpoint we might say they could not go in because they were afraid. God called it unbelief. The writer was concerned that his New Testament audience might also "fall after the same example of unbelief" (Heb. 4:11).

The same pattern unfolds in the New Testament when Jesus rebukes His disciples. Jesus saved Peter from sinking after Peter walked on the water, and then He rebuked him in Matthew 14:31: "O thou of little faith, wherefore didst thou doubt?" When the disciples panicked in the storm, he said, "Why are ye so fearful? how is it that ye have no faith?" (Mark 4:40). To the disciples who could not cast out the demon he replied in Matthew 17:17, "O faithless and perverse generation, how long shall I be with you? how long shall I suffer you?" And to the two disciples He spoke with on the road to Emmaus he stated, "O fools, and slow of heart to believe all that the prophets have spoken" (Luke 24:25). Of course, these rebukes are only representative; there are many others.

Please note that Jesus did not chide His disciples for their lack of gratitude. Often parents of wayward teens will rebuke them for their ingratitude. In desperation, and perhaps in sorrow, they may feel—and say—"After all I've done for you, you don't appreciate it. How could you be so ungrateful?" The teen's problem is only superficially ingratitude. The problem is more fundamentally unbelief. His picture of life does not include God. Jesus could have rebuked His disciples for their ingratitude but didn't. Instead, He cut to the heart of the matter and asked, "After all the times you have seen Me work, how could you still not believe?" Wise parents will ask the same question. They will not reprove their teen for his ingratitude when his real problem is his unbelief.

The apostles had the same concern. Paul summarized the believer's proper mindset when he restated the Old Testament truth "the just shall live by faith."[7] He set forth Abraham as the model of faith because "he staggered not at the promise of God through unbelief; but was strong in faith, giving glory to God" (Rom. 4:20). The writer of Hebrews reminds us that "without faith it is impossible to please [God]" (11:6), and then he catalogs in the same chapter many examples of those who walked by faith. These were honored in this chapter, God's Hall of Faith, because they saw the promises afar off and saw "him who is invisible" (11:27). They did not live as mere worldlings—unaware of the greater realities of God and His ways. We too are exhorted to "hold fast the profession of our faith without wavering" (10:23). We are exhorted to "Take heed, brethren, lest there be in any of you an evil heart of unbelief, in departing from the living God. But exhort one another daily, while it is called To day; lest any of you be hardened through the deceitfulness of sin" (3:12-13).

This faith—this eye that sees the invisible—is at the heart of godliness. It should come as no surprise then that God's people are rebuked more for their unbelief—their failure to see God in their circumstances—than for anything else. In fact, as we have seen, unbelief rests at the core of anger, depression,[8] covetousness, immorality, and all other vices; for the believer has taken his eye off his God as the Source of all delight and provision and has looked elsewhere—and has always been disappointed in the long run.

The lesson here for disciple-makers is obvious. Don't just rebuke some-one for his outward sin. Be aware of how that sin is a manifestation of a

---

[7] Habakkuk 2:4; Romans 1:17; Galatians 3:11.

[8] See Basics for Depressed Believers in Appendix B to see how facing the losses of life without a faith in God's promises strips away hope during the trial and spirals us into depression.

heart of unbelief. This is the pattern of the prophets, the apostles, and the Lord Himself. The Scriptures truly tell us *what is wrong*.

THE SCRIPTURES TEACH US HOW TO MAKE THE WRONG RIGHT

Paul told Timothy that the inspired Scriptures have a third function in the life of a believer—correction. That is, they teach us how to make the wrong things in our lives right with God and others. The word "correction" comes from a Greek word that means to make something stand up again or to right something again.

Suppose that while backing out of a parking lot at your church Sunday morning you hit a car parked behind you, denting its fender. If you put your immediate plans for dinner on hold for a few minutes while you located the owner, made arrangements for the dented fender to be repaired to the owner's satisfaction, and then followed up in the weeks ahead to be sure the fender was indeed restored to its original condition, you have fulfilled the meaning of this word "correction."

Much is wrong with man. We saw his desperate condition in Part One of this book. He must be restored. The process involves more than saying, "I guess I need to be more careful in the future so that I don't sin in that area again." Proverbs 28:13 captures the two most crucial elements of this process—confession and forsaking. It says, "He that covereth his sins shall not prosper: but whosoever confesseth and forsaketh them shall have mercy."

The first part of making any offense right with God or others is *confession*. Confession involves agreeing with your accusers—God or any other person you wronged—that you are indeed guilty of the charges that have been brought against you. The most direct manner for confessing your sin is to say to the one you have wronged, "I was wrong when I (name or describe the offense so that he knows that you see it the way he sees it). Will you forgive me?" By asking forgiveness, a statement like this assumes full responsibility for the wrong and seeks a reconciliation between the estranged parties. Statements of "I'm sorry" or "I apologize" never address the matter fully. One can be sorry that something happened yet not assume any responsibility for it. For example, I might be sorry that you hit Joe's car in the parking lot last Sunday, but I'm not willing to take responsibility for it. An apology, though it can include a full acceptance of responsibility, often does not.

Although God is willing to forgive anyone who comes to Him in repentance, He does not extend forgiveness to any man until that man agrees with God's charges against him and takes full responsibility for his sin.[9] This confession of sin makes reconciliation possible. Being reconciled to someone means that the former estranged relationship has been exchanged for one of peace and favor. Notice God's response to a repentant sinner:

> I, even I, am he that blotteth out thy transgressions for mine own sake, and will not remember thy sins (Isa. 43:25).

> Let the wicked forsake his way, and the unrighteous man his thoughts: and let him return unto the Lord, and he will have mercy upon him; and to our God, for he will abundantly pardon (Isa. 55:7).

There is much confusion today about confession, reconciliation, and forgiveness. I challenge you to make a thorough Bible study of these topics so that when you disciple others in these areas, you can give them *Word-filled* advice.

The second part of correction, according to Proverbs 28:13, is *forsaking*, which means a willingness on the part of the offender to make restitution, as did Zacchaeus.[10] It may mean accepting certain restrictions—some temporary, some permanent. For example, Adam and Eve *never* were allowed back in the Garden of Eden after their sin. Moses *never* got to go into the Promised Land until Jesus Himself called him to the Mount of Transfiguration for a conference about the exodus of Christ. The prodigal son of Luke 15 was restored to fellowship and honor with his father but *never* received another inheritance to spend. Luke 15:31 says that all the remaining estate of the father had been willed to the elder brother. There was nothing left to give the repentant prodigal.

The difference in the attitude of King David when he was confronted by Nathan about his adultery[11] and the attitude of King Saul when he

---

[9] See Psalms 32:5; 38:18; 51:1-3; Luke 15:18; I John 1:7-10.

[10] Luke 19:8.

[11] II Samuel 12:1-25, especially verse 13.

was confronted by Samuel about his rebellion against God[12] is instructive. David accepted every consequence *without protest*. Saul wanted to negotiate any negative outcomes, whereas David grieved over his estrangement from God and was willing to accept whatever measures God chose to counter the tendencies of his lustful heart. He wanted his fellowship and usefulness to God restored to its former condition.

Reconciliation is the heart of the gospel! God specializes in it. If we are to reflect Him, we must also become masters at staying reconciled to God and others. Our heart should break when we see those around us unreconciled to God and others. We truly have been given a ministry of reconciliation.[13] Study this great doctrine. Become a *Word-filled teacher* on the subject of reconciliation.

THE SCRIPTURES TEACH US HOW TO KEEP IT RIGHT

Finally, Paul says that the inspired Word of God is useful for "instruction in righteousness." The word for "instruction" here is very picturesque. It is the Greek word *paideia*, which means "upbringing, training, instruction, chiefly as it is attained by discipline, correction."[14] It "denotes the training of a child, including instruction; hence, discipline, correction. . . . [It is] the Christian discipline that regulates character."[15] From this Greek root we get the word "pedagogy"—the study of how to teach and instruct. It is the kind of instruction and structured oversight that should characterize any godly parenting effort. We could accurately translate it *child training*.

Children do not effectively rear themselves. Someone must provide the instruction and structured oversight that insist that the right principles and practices be learned and diligently applied. This is what a mother does when she sees to it that her grade-school child comes home from school and practices the piano for the required thirty minutes. The child may need some instruction about fingering, counting out the meter, or finding the correct notes. If the mother has any musical background, she

---

[12] I Samuel 15:10-35, especially verse 30.

[13] II Corinthians 5:18-21.

[14] Arndt and Gingrich, *Lexicon*, 608.

[15] W. E. Vine, *An Expository Dictionary of New Testament Words* (Old Tappen, N.J.: Fleming H. Revell Company, 1940), 183.

can help with this part of the pedagogic process. In addition, her child training in music will include generous doses of encouragement. Her training will also include warnings, rebukes, and chastening actions when the child is not cooperating or is disobeying. This process remains in force until the job is done—until the child is becoming skillful in playing the piano and is practicing on his own without external prodding.

All of this is implied in the rich word *paideia*. Paul does not say here that it is "instruction in piano playing," however. His thrust is "instruction in *righteousness*." The disciple-maker, like a creative mother who trains her child in piano, must bring to bear all the instruction, accountability, and discipline necessary to see that his disciple is growing in his skill of right living—righteousness. That will require specific instruction in the aspects of life that are particularly difficult at the moment, along with whatever encouragement, correction, and discipline are needed to spur the learner on to continue his "practice" of right living on his own.

Much parenting and other forms of discipleship fail right here. For a mother to train her child to have the discipline necessary to practice the piano on his own, the mother herself must have a strong measure of discipline in her own life. If she gives in easily when the child complains or whines or if she responds to the child's complaints by yelling or by firing off a sharp lecture, she exposes her own lack of character. In the same way, a pastor, teacher, or other disciple-maker who responds with impatience and browbeating to his church member's or student's failures is not giving godly "instruction [i.e., child training] in righteousness." He is rather teaching that there are some matters that are so grievous that a person cannot help losing control.

The actual process of giving structured oversight will be discussed at length in the next chapter. The important concept to understand here is that a Word-filled teacher is skillful in providing this kind of direction for his followers. Sometimes students in a Christian high school or university complain that rules or instructions are repeated too often. They may protest that "the principal or administration is treating us like children." That is true! They are being treated just as God treats *His* children. He uses whatever repetition, instruction, and methods of chastening are necessary to get the job of perfecting His children accomplished. If we are to reflect Christ to others, we can do no less.

Word-filled teachers, then, know what is right. They possess a thorough understanding of Bible doctrine. Second, they can recognize what is wrong and know how to humbly yet directly confront those who are "overtaken in a fault" in order to "restore such an one in the spirit of meekness" (Gal. 6:1). Word-filled teachers, third, know how to guide a person in making the wrongs right. They can teach the offending brother how to confess his sin to God and others and how to forsake its practice. Last, they know how to provide the diligent instruction and oversight that will enable the ones they are leading to persevere in godly practices until their lives are characterized by "righteousness"—consistent right living.

I hope you are beginning to see the powerful impact that you can have on others for Christ if you are a *God-loving example* and a *Word-filled teacher*. There is yet one more characteristic of a godly disciple-maker—one I have alluded to. He must be a *ministry-minded overseer*. That is the topic of our next chapter.

TAKE TIME TO REFLECT

1. Are you seriously studying the Word and doctrinally sound books about the Word in order to become a Word-filled teacher? Chapters 8 and 9 in this book are extensive discussions about the importance of biblical meditation. Review them and put them into practice.

2. Does your advice echo the words of the Scriptures? Does the Word of God control your thinking so much that your advice flows out of your mouth in the actual words of Scripture, or does your advice sound more like whatever counsel is popular at the moment in evangelical Christianity or in the secular mainstream? Are you better known as a ____-filled teacher—fill in the blank with whatever author or speaker you follow most closely—or are you known as a *Word*-filled teacher?

3. Do you have regular, planned times of study, or is your study a more haphazard, "catch as catch can" approach? Word-filled teachers become Word-filled on purpose.

A WORD TO DISCIPLE-MAKERS

DOUBLE-CHECK YOUR ADVICE BY THE BOOK

It will not do for us to pass on to our children—or to others we are trying to help—what *seems* to have worked for us or what *appears* to be a good idea. Many today will attend a seminar or read a book and will become excited about something they learned that promises to solve major problems in their life. Unfortunately, they often do not stop to think about whether the advice is biblical.

Looking for Needles in Haystacks

For example, perhaps a young couple in a parenting seminar is taught that a child's personality is developed before age five and that there is very little possibility of change after that. If their little Johnny is already age seven and has become the neighborhood bully, the parents will be tempted to resign themselves to living with a budding terrorist since supposedly there is nothing they can do to change him. This unbiblical theory strips away all hope from such parents.

There is no doubt that much developmental groundwork is laid—or is not laid—by age five, but to state that the concrete hardens by that age and that the results are binding ignores the Bible's clear teaching that *any* person at *any* age can change from his old lifestyle to a pattern that pleases God and can then be useful to Him. There is no doubt that the longer someone lives in his self-centered, bullying ways, the harder the change will be to become a God-loving, others-serving individual. The Spirit of God, nonetheless, can use the Word of God to change *any* of us at *any* time we decide to begin cooperating with His program of sanctification. God's power isn't rendered ineffective once a child passes the tender age of five.

On the other hand, these parents might attend a parenting seminar that suggests that the reason their eighteen-year-old Jimmy never takes risks or steps out of his comfort zone is that his "inner child" never grew up. They must "re-parent" their son's "inner child" until its developmental age is the same as the boy's chronological age.

By attending two seminars—one that says you *can't* change a child after five and one that says you *must* at least change his "inner child"—they have been given conflicting opinions, neither of which is biblical. Parenting for serious-minded people like those who attend such seminars becomes a search for child-rearing needles of truth in psychological haystacks. Even if parents find something that looks like a needle, unless they diligently search the Scriptures to see whether God calls it a needle, they can only experiment with it to see whether it does indeed work. Pragmatism then becomes the standard for recognizing needles. If they do spend the time examining the needle against God's standard of truth in the Word, they will discover that, if it is indeed truth and vital for "life and godliness" (II Pet. 1:3), it is already taught in the Word of God in a much purer form than the seminar could ever give them. They are much more likely to find needles in a needle factory than in a haystack. What they need is a biblical understanding of the nature of man, the nature of God, and the doctrine of sanctification. That will be found only in the Bible, God's divine "needle factory."

Don't Get Stuck in a Stage

Consider the teaching that says that every person who has suffered major tragedy in life—for example, the death of a loved one or news of cancer—must go through five stages of grief if he is to emerge emotionally balanced in the aftermath. It is quite possible, so the teaching goes, that a person can get "stuck" for an undetermined amount of time in any of the five stages and allegedly cannot progress to the final stages until he has successfully weathered the first ones.

It is noteworthy that the Bible, which claims to give us "all things that pertain unto [eternal] life and godliness" (II Pet. 1:3), never once mentions this seemingly crucial five-step phenomenon for handling a problem as universal as death. Every tragedy of life can tempt a believer to anger, denial, or any of the other so-called stages of grief. The Bible, however, calls both anger and denial sinful responses to our circumstances. Anger and denial are both direct opponents to godliness and are problems that are the particular jurisdiction of the Scriptures. There is hope when these responses are removed from the so-called stages of grief and placed back into their biblical framework of works of the flesh. There is always a biblical solution when we define the problem in its biblical terms.

We must be doubly careful then that we teach others to look at life's problems through the lens of the Scriptures. Just as we learned in the first chapter that not just any *change* will do, it is also true that not just any *advice* will do. Our teaching must move others toward God's goals of loving Him preeminently and of loving our neighbor as ourselves and must move them toward that goal in God's predetermined path of change—sanctification. As you can see, our teaching must be driven by the Scriptures. We must be able to show that we have dipped our counsel from the mainstream of revealed truth, not merely parroted the untenable observations of fallen man.

To develop the analogy a bit further, please note that our counsel must be dipped from the *mainstream* of divine revelation. Too often an entire counseling or parenting strategy is built on isolated passages of Scripture. Those passages are indeed part of the river but were never intended by God to be used to provide a complete system of counseling or parenting. It is noteworthy that God says, "My word . . . shall not return unto me void, but it shall accomplish that which I please, and it shall prosper *in the thing whereto I sent it*" (Isa. 55:11).

God promises to bless His Word—but only to accomplish the purposes He originally designed it for. The mainstream of truth about change and growth is the doctrine of sanctification—the topic of this entire book. The advice of this book, and of any other human instrument, must flow from the center of God's stream of truth about sanctification if it is to have God's blessing when dealing with the subject of change.

The Ministry of Repetition

I mentioned in Chapter 2 that the human heart must be reminded of God's ways since it has a tendency to drift to its *own way* when left unchecked. When I was working toward a private pilot's license while in college, my instructor introduced the class of student pilots to two essential directional aids on the aircraft. One was the magnetic compass that is positioned in the cockpit at the same place in the windshield that a rear-view mirror is fastened in a car. Its main limitation is that it bounces around with the aircraft's movement, thus making it difficult to get an accurate reading. The second directional aid is called a DG—directional gyroscope. It gives a steady readout under all conditions. Its limitation, however, is that with the passing of time it drifts. After a couple of hours of flying it is possible for it to be several degrees off. My flight instructor advised us to reset the DG just before every takeoff. Positioned at the end of the runway, which was clearly marked by numbers representing the runway's orientation on the compass—28 for 280 degrees, 36 for 360 degrees, and so forth—we could accurately reset the DG to a known compass heading. Since our small single-engine aircraft carried only enough fuel to stay in the air for a few hours, we were assured of taking off rather frequently and thus regularly resetting the DG.

This is very much like the human heart. Without a continual check against a known standard, it tends to drift. This is why regular, daily times with God and regular attendance at a Bible-preaching, doctrinally sound church are crucial for the survival of every believer. Those who are "forsaking the assembling of [them]selves together"[16] will find that spiritually they are drifting off course. The human heart needs a constant exposure to God's Word to reprove the heart's current direction and show it to be off course.

---

[16] Hebrews 10:25.

CHAPTER TWELVE

BEING A MINISTRY-MINDED OVERSEER

And [thou] shalt talk of [the words of God] when thou sittest in thine house, and when thou walkest by the way, and when thou liest down, and when thou risest up. And thou shalt bind them for a sign upon thine hand, and they shall be as frontlets between thine eyes. And thou shalt write them upon the posts of thy house, and on thy gates.
Deuteronomy 6:7-9

In the last two chapters, we looked at Deuteronomy 6 and saw in verse 5 that Moses taught Israel's leaders to be *God-loving examples*. In verses 6 and 7 he called them to be *Word-filled teachers*. Moses continued his instruction with a third responsibility for them to be *ministry-minded overseers*.

There are two thrusts in this third emphasis. First, Israel's leaders were to be *ministry-minded*—intentionally interacting with their followers for the purpose of stimulating spiritual growth. Like our Lord, who illustrated truth from every possible angle of daily life—fishing, farming, wildlife, housecleaning, shepherding, building, and military strategic planning—they were to be alert to both the incidental and the intentional opportunities to have a spiritual influence on others. Second, they were to be ministry-minded *overseers*. It was their responsibility to *structure* the daily experiences and environment of their children so as to *saturate* them with the ways and the words of the living God so that they achieved spiritual goals.

Consider for a moment the conditions in your circle of Christian friends, your church, and your ministries. How many of the spiritual leaders are known for being God-loving examples, Word-filled teachers, and ministry-minded overseers? Tragically, there are often glaring holes in the consistency of the example, shallowness in the level of biblical teaching and application, and very little personal involvement of the leader in the spiritual direction and accountability of those under his authority.

The unhappy result is that the people of God in general, and children of Christian families in particular, are not being discipled into useful servants for Christ. We need to see the urgency of our condition today, be broken by our failure, and earnestly endeavor to get our mission of discipleship back on track.

Before we go any further, please note that the emphases in Chapters 10 through 12 of this book are sequential. You cannot effectively *oversee* others unless you are the right kind of *example*—one known for being God-loving—and are a *teacher* whose mind is saturated with the Word of God. If you are not making strong progress in these first two areas yourself, you will not have a ministry mindset as you oversee others. Your interactions with them will not focus on stimulating their growth in Christlikeness because you are not experiencing that growth yourself. Your efforts to manage others will focus on lesser goals of achieving a certain level of production and attainment, or of controlling behavior and results.

What does God mean when He commands spiritual leaders to be overseers? All of us can think of leaders who have been tyrannical, cultic, or authoritarian; and we shudder at the damage that has been done in the lives of countless saints who have followed such leaders. Thankfully, that is not what God asks us to be. In fact, He warns against having this kind of self-serving mentality—certainly the opposite of *servant*-leadership. He tells church leaders, "Feed the flock of God which is among you, taking the oversight thereof, not by constraint [not because you have to], but willingly; not for filthy lucre [not because of what you get out of it], but of a ready mind; Neither as being lords [as those who overpower others] over God's heritage, but being [examples] to the flock" (I Pet. 5:2-3).[1]

Jesus warned His disciples about adopting the Gentile mentality of seeking power over the lives of others. He said, "The kings of the Gentiles exercise lordship over them [overpower their followers]; and they that exercise authority upon them are called benefactors [a title of

---

[1] Notice in Ezekiel 34 the scathing rebuke of the spiritual leaders in Israel, the shepherds, who used their position of leadership for personal gain. God does not take the misuse of spiritual leadership lightly. James 3:1 warns that "masters" will "receive the greater condemnation [judgment]."

honor]. *But ye shall not be so:* but he that is greatest among you, let him be as the younger; and he that is chief, as he that doth serve" (Luke 22:25-26).

SPIRITUAL PARENTING

God provides the perfect picture of oversight in spiritual matters—parenting. God deals with us as His children. He presents Himself as our Father. When we *parent* others the way God *parents* us and when we are truly *God-loving* and *Word-filled*, we will stay away from the excesses of Gentile, self-serving lordship. As Christlike servant-leaders, we can have genuine spiritual influence on others.

The apostle Paul used the imagery of child rearing often. He saw himself as a spiritual parent who took responsibility for the growth of others until they demonstrated Christ to others by their lives. Notice his passion in Galatians 4:19: "My little children, of whom I travail in birth again *until Christ be formed in you.*"

He knew his job of oversight was not finished until his followers were "put[ting] on the new man, which after God is created in righteousness and true holiness" (Eph. 4:24). This theme of *parental supervision* for the spiritual development of others is a common thrust throughout the entire Bible.

For example, the writer of Proverbs instructed and warned his "son" by his brief cause-and-effect reality bites of life. The apostle John acknowledged that his readers were at various stages of development. Some were "little children" in the Faith; others were "young men" who were effectively engaged in spiritual battle; and still others, who were reproducing their lives in others, were called "fathers."[2]

With the paradigm of spiritual parenting in mind, I want to propose a simple developmental model for discipling others. These three emphases follow roughly the major outline of this book and are best illustrated through the actual parenting process within a Christian home.[3] We can summarize them in the following way.

---

[2] I John 2:1, 12-14, 18; 4:4.

[3] This chapter is intended to present the overall discipleship *themes* of parenting at various stages. For help in specific aspects of biblical parenting at different age

In Part One we learned about restraining the flesh. This is the first item of business in any discipling/parenting endeavor. In the home a child in his preschool years must be taught how to obey. In the same manner, the first major step in spiritual growth for *any* believer is learning the *meaning* of self-denial—he cannot have his *own* way. He must yield instead to God and to the authorities God has placed in his life.

Second, as we saw in Part Two, the disciple must learn how to live wisely. That will require the development of a renewed mind—one that thinks as God thinks. He must be taught the proper *applications* of self-denial in the various arenas of life. He must also learn the biblical *motivations* for his self-denial—love for God and others. He must learn to turn his face to God for help and thereby exercise faith that trusts God for the power to say no to himself. Parents of school-age children who are truly discipling their offspring will be alert to the *increased* opportunities to train their children in these finer points of God-dependent self-denial during the grade school and junior high years. These lessons can be introduced even in the preschool years, but as the child increasingly interacts with those outside his home during the school-age years, his opportunities to apply these lessons increase as well and become a primary discipleship emphasis in the school-age years.

Finally, during the teen years the discipling/parenting focus should be able to move to a coaching role as parents see their teen consistently *practicing* God-dependent self-denial on his own. He is thus becoming a useful servant for Christ. A teen—and any other disciple—who has moved effectively through the first two discipleship emphases will be bearing fruit in the lives of others. This corresponds to Part Three of this book—reflecting Christ to the world around him.

---

levels, see the following: Fugate, J. Richard. *What the Bible Says About Child Training.* Tempe, Ariz.: Aletheia Division of Alpha Omega Publications, 1980. Jones, Bob, III. *Who Says So?!: A Biblical View of Authority.* Greenville, S.C.: Bob Jones University Press, 1996. Ray, Bruce A. *Withhold Not Correction.* Phillipsburg, N.J.: Presbyterian and Reformed, 1978. Sorenson, David. *Training Your Child to Turn Out Right.* Independence, Mo.: American Association of Christian Schools, 1995. Stormer, John A. *Growing Up God's Way.* Florissant, Mo.: Liberty Bell Press, 1984. Tripp, Paul David. *Age of Opportunity: A Biblical Guide to Parenting Teens.* Phillipsburg, N.J.: Presbyterian and Reformed, 1997. Tripp, Tedd. *Shepherding a Child's Heart.* Wapwallopen, Pa.: Shepherd Press, 1995.

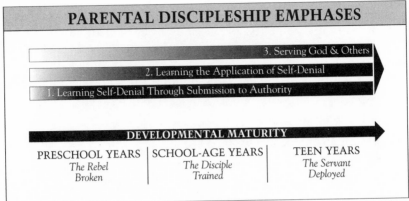

Examine the relationship of these thrusts in this chart. First, note that these emphases build one upon the other. Second, notice that although each emphasis can be started in the very earliest times of a child's life, some concepts cannot be fully understood or practiced until the child has developed more fully mentally and physically. This is indicated on the chart by the fact that the arrows become solid about the time of life that we can expect the child to be consistently practicing the emphasis.

Third, notice that every emphasis must be maintained throughout life. Although submission is the first lesson to be learned in any discipling endeavor, it can *never* be put aside. It is the foundation for the training that is to follow. Likewise, the submissive heart introduced in the preschool years and the training in biblical motivations and practical applications of God-dependent self-denial learned in the school-age years must both be continued for effective service to be a reality in the teen years.

THE ATOMIC STRUCTURE OF CHRISTIANITY

Before we look at these emphases in detail, we need to realize the *importance* of God-dependent self-denial in our Christian walk. Consider for a moment how a wrong view of the chemical makeup of the world crippled science for centuries. We will continue to experience a similar "dark ages" in Christianity today if we do not grasp this basic component for godliness.

In the sixth century B.C., Greek philosophers proposed that everything in the universe was composed of four basic substances: earth, air, fire, and water. As early as the fifth century B.C., other philosophers became convinced that there must be something unseen that was even more basic than these four substances. In 1803 John Dalton wrote a series of postulates that became the foundation of our modern atomic theory. Continued scientific discovery supports the atomic theory and has led to a much better understanding of the most basic particles of matter. These discoveries propelled mankind into the present nuclear age. Not understanding the basic building blocks of matter greatly hindered scientific progress.

The Main Principle of Discipleship

Christianity has a similar basic component that lies at the heart of everything godly. That component is *death*. Jesus told His disciples,

> If any man will come after me, let him deny himself, and take up his cross daily, and follow me. For whosoever will save his life shall lose it: but whosoever will lose his life for my sake, the same shall save it (Luke 9:23-24).

> Verily, verily, I say unto you, Except a corn of wheat fall into the ground and die, it abideth alone: but if it die, it bringeth forth much fruit. He that loveth his life shall lose it; and he that hateth his life in this world shall keep it unto life eternal (John 12:24-25).

In the biblical world-view, *life* comes only from *death*. This theme of death was a common one for our Lord. He Himself stated that He came to die. His death made eternal life a *reality* for all who trust in Him. His death also made freedom from the power of sin a *possibility*, as we saw in Chapter 5 when we discussed how the believer is to mortify his flesh. Christ's work *for us* at Calvary demanded His death. Our work *for Christ* on this earth demands our death to self in return. We must then become skillful at dying—to self. That daily dying must be done in the right way and for the right reasons, however, if it is to produce the right result.

A *ministry-minded overseer* will never forget the absolute necessity of this atomic-level component as he disciples others. Matter cannot be explained without atoms, and the Christian life cannot be understood, nor reproduced, without the ongoing death to self that Jesus called self-denial. With this reality in mind, let's look at how we can effectively oversee the discipleship of others as they grow in Christ.

THE PRESCHOOL YEARS—THE REBEL BROKEN

As we have seen, our Lord said that a disciple who is following Him must *deny himself*. In the first step of any discipleship effort, the disciple must be taught the meaning of self-denial: you cannot have your *own way*.[4] A child in his preschool years should be taught the meaning of the word "no." He must learn that someone other than himself is in charge and that he is not his own master. Paul underscored this in the familiar verse "Children, obey your parents in the Lord: for this is right" (Eph. 6:1). Parents who insist on obedience from their children have an opportunity to begin laying the foundation for teaching self-denial.

Keep in mind that obedience and self-denial are not necessarily the same. Obedience can be just the outward compliance to the demand of an authority. Self-denial is the practice *within the heart* that says no to what the sinful heart wants for itself at that time. We are practicing self-denial when we treat *self* as if it were dead—no longer having any influence on us.

Of course, preschool-age children cannot understand the difference between obedience and self-denial, but it isn't necessary at this early age. They can—and must—learn, however, as early as possible that there is an *order* in life and that they are *subordinates*. They are not *rulers* but *obeyers*.

They must also be taught as soon as possible to ask God for help to obey. The self-denial that must become a regular practice of life must eventually become a *God-dependent* self-denial. A parent can reinforce this as he prays with his preschooler at structured teaching times and at times of correction. A parent can pray, "And dear Jesus, help Johnny to obey Mommy and Daddy. It will be too hard for him unless *You* help him to please *You* instead of himself." This teaches Johnny early on that *God* is the most important component in his obedience. Later you can teach him the principles covered in Part One of this book that outline the more complete aspects of this God-dependent self-denial.

Kindergarten Christianity

Sometimes parents of a youngster who is not behaving in school will tell school officials, "Yes, Johnny is a little hard to control. He always had a hard time taking no for an answer." What that generally means is that

---

[4] If it has been some time since you read Chapters 2 and 3 in this book, take a moment to review them. Remember that any man left to his *own* way will destroy himself and will probably take others down with him.

Johnny was not consistently given no for an answer when he was at home or that his parents did not consistently make the no stick. He did not learn God-dependent self-denial *as a way of life*. He did not learn to say no to himself and yes to his masters. Without a basic attitude of submission to authority, he cannot be delivered from his own flesh and ignorance, nor can he be trained to become useful to God or anyone else. He is sabotaging his own future. This lesson of self-denying submission to God and authorities is the primary lesson of "spiritual kindergarten." It is kindergarten Christianity. He can make no real progress until this lesson is in place.

This is why Christian teen camps place so much emphasis upon salvation and surrender with the teens. Until these issues are settled, nothing else of eternal consequence can be accomplished in their lives. The same is true in Christian education. Unless the chapel messages, classroom instruction, and interactions with the faculty are used of God to bring the students to a point of submission to God and other authorities, no real discipleship for Christ can be accomplished. Without students whose hearts are gladly submissive to God, the training and education by the Christian school can produce only more highly skilled rebels. The student will be better educated in his field of interest but will use his education to serve only himself. All Christian counseling must start here as well. If the couple struggling with problems in their marriage or the individual overwhelmed with some difficulty is not submissive to God and His ways, no significant progress is possible. This lesson of God-dependent self-denial isn't optional. It is foundational!

These early lessons in self-denial can be effectively taught, however, only by "masters" who have the self-denial to persevere in their supervision *until the lesson is learned.* Preschool children can be trained to obey immediately and sweetly.[5] A one year old can be trained to stop arching his back in protest while he sits in his highchair or to come to his mother when she calls his name or to stop reaching out for a forbidden object

---

[5] Obviously the "immediately" comes first; the "sweetly" part comes a bit later. Early on children can be taught to answer Mom's directive of "Please bring me your dirty clothes so I can wash them" with "I will be happy to, Mommy." While they may not always have the proper delight in obedience, they will be learning that God's standard is not grudging obedience but glad surrender. Nothing else truly glorifies Him because no other response is worthy of Him.

when his father states, "No, Johnny." A three year old can be taught to sit attentively in his parent's lap for a few minutes while his parent reads to him out of a colorful book of Bible stories. A four year old can learn to pick up his toys and put them in the toy box when it is time for him to go to bed.[6]

Be Not Weary in Well Doing

These lessons—and dozens like them—will require that a parent consistently and calmly both repeat the command *and* carry through with the appropriate consequences if the command isn't obeyed. The child must learn he cannot have his *own* way. You must be aware of this basic *ministry* thrust of discipleship at this developmental level and must consistently and competently *oversee* that discipling relationship in the preschool years until he knows he cannot have his own way.

A young mother can grow very weary of telling her toddler the same thing over and over again. It is very frustrating to have to interrupt whatever she is doing to stop him from getting into trouble or to insist that he obey her in some matter or to administer correction when he disobeys her. Consider this, however. If she works in a factory placing a part on an automobile body on an assembly line, she will not grow frustrated if more car bodies that need a part keep coming down the line for her to assemble. Even though she has already put plenty of parts on car bodies, she *expects* to continue to do the same task as long as that is her job.

Training a toddler—or a child at any age—is the same. A parent should *expect* to be giving the same instructions, the same reminders, and the same corrective measures over and over and over again. That is a parent's job. It is *paideia*—child training—and the repetition of these matters is a primary teaching tool.

---

[6] A young child faced with a floor covered with toys to pick up, however, may not know where to start. We taught our daughters to play a cleanup game we called "Where Does This Go?" We helped them start cleaning up by picking up a toy, handing it to them, and telling them, "Now ask yourself, 'Where does this go?' " It made them focus on one toy at a time—not a roomful of toys. They always knew the answer to the question and could put each toy in its place. The point is that we had to *oversee* the task, playing it with them often at first, and even later reminding them of the question to ask themselves. Eventually, they could do it on their own.

After Paul introduces the principle of sowing and reaping in Galatians 6:7-8, he encourages us to persevere with the exhortation of verse 9: "And let us not be weary in well doing: for in due season we shall reap, if we faint not."

So you see, parenting—or any other discipling relationship—is not primarily about controlling behavior and teaching good Christian habits. It is the process whereby a God-loving, Word-filled leader *structures* and *supervises* the experiences and environment of those he leads so that they come face to face with God and His ways and His Word. It is about *ministering*—intentionally interacting (through conversation, instruction, correction, chastening, etc.) with those he leads for the purpose of stimulating spiritual growth.

In the early years of childhood—and in the early days of any spiritual discipleship effort with others—the spiritual growth will come in the form of learning to take no for an answer from God and other authorities and learning to give immediate and cheerful obedience. That is the foundation for everything else in the Christian life. In the next level your disciple or child can learn the *reasons* behind each limitation and can learn a higher motive for obedience, but in his early years he must be trained to submit to the will of those who are discipling him. There is no life without death in God's world-view. It is your job as the *overseer* to make sure this component of God-dependent self-denial is given its appropriate place in the daily experiences of those you lead. It is the foundational principle for spiritual growth. Again, let me encourage you to master the truths of Part One of this book (Chapters 2 through 5) if self-denial still does not seem a paramount issue to you. You can build nothing godly in your own life or in the lives of others unless you and they are practicing God-dependent self-denial.

THE SCHOOL-AGE YEARS—THE DISCIPLE TRAINED

The flesh when manifesting itself will produce chaos. The apostle James said that the result of listening to fleshly "wisdom" is "*confusion* and every evil work" (James 3:15-16). Paul said that "God is not the author of *confusion*, but of peace" (I Cor. 14:33). In both of these passages the Greek word for "confusion" means "a state of disorder, disturbance, confusion, tumult, . . . commotions."[7] The Bible teaches that when the flesh is not restrained by structure and authority, it can produce only *chaos* and "every evil work."

In the preschool years, "The Rebel Broken," the child is trained to cheerfully *take orders*. In this second time of life, "The Disciple Trained," he is taught to *value order*. He cannot become a *productive* citizen of your household or of his church and community unless he is abandoning the chaotic lifestyle of selfish living.

We will look at the motivations for this orderliness later in this chapter and will learn in the next chapter how to keep this orderliness in life from becoming a legalistic straitjacket. For now I want you to see the importance of orderliness if the disciple you are training is ever to be productive for God or for anyone else.

Learning Law and Order

Children who are given responsibilities to clean their room, rake the leaves, pick up their toys, clear the table, vacuum the floor, take out the trash, and wash the car are being trained to bring order out of chaos. To participate in these chores, they must learn to cheerfully *take orders*, which is the first major thrust of discipleship, and they must learn to *value and practice orderliness*. They are learning "law and order"—foundational principles of civilized and productive people. They are learning to be constructive instead of destructive.

Please understand that we are not to *live* for order. We are to live for Christ and *value* order. Order in our lives does not make us *godly*; rather, it makes us *useful* to God. A person whose life has order is constructive in his deeds and words instead of destructive. He determines his activities by priorities, not by what pressures him most at the moment. He knows how to schedule his time and work toward worthy goals. He knows as well that anything worthwhile in life comes through processes of "sowing and reaping" and "cause and effect." That means he is willing to put continued effort—repetition—into something and is willing to wait for the outcome. An ordered person understands and lives out the principles embodied in such old sayings as "A place for everything, and everything in its place" and "Failing to plan is planning to fail."

---

[7] Vine, *Dictionary*, 227.

By contrast, the chaotic person's life is characterized by haphazard efforts to accomplish the things that press him most and by the spontaneity of doing whatever he feels like doing at the moment. He lives for whatever pleases him the most at that moment and hopes for the best in the future.

Unfortunately, many parents live such chaotic lives themselves that these lessons are never taught at home. Nobody lives by any set schedule in such homes. Mealtimes when family members sit around the table and fellowship with each other are nonexistent. Everyone eats whatever he wants whenever he is hungry. The family does not make decisions based on any order of priorities—spiritual, financial, or otherwise. Bedtimes vary from night to night, and the lives of family members are filled with crisis and calamity.

Tragically, the child-training responsibility is approached with the same mentality as is the pile of dirty dishes on the kitchen counter. Instead of attending to them on a regular, systematic basis, they are ignored until they are out of control. Then both the dishes and the children are handled with grudging disgust. The lack of structured, principled, and godly problem-solving habits in homes like these leads to all sorts of emotional upheaval in the family members. The rule of life in homes like these is "every man for himself," which only reinforces the natural bent of everyone to live for himself. Children growing up in such homes do not learn to be productive citizens, and more tragically, they do not learn to become useful disciples of Jesus Christ because no one with a ministry mindset is *overseeing* their training and development.

The grade school years (approximately ages six through twelve) provide wonderful opportunities for parents to build upon the lessons of the preschool years. A child who has learned the *meaning* of self-denial ("you cannot have your *own way*") in his preschool years can now be taught the *applications* of God-dependent self-denial in the expanded experiences of life, particularly as he becomes more active in his interaction with others outside his own home. These are the years when he will become a part of many other social settings and experiences outside of home and school—scouts, church groups, 4-H clubs, Bible clubs, little league sports, summer camps, children's choirs, and overnight stays at the homes of friends and relatives. He is no longer under the continual, watchful eye of his parents as he was when a preschooler. Other adults now supervise increasingly greater portions of his life.

Parents must carefully *oversee* the selection of those authorities so that a biblical thrust of self-denial is reinforced and maintained in these extended settings. A child will not be helped if he spends large amounts of time at the home of a friend whose parents allow the children to fight and pick on each other, to be rude and disrespectful to adults and other family members, to watch videos and television programs that are sensual or teach worldly values, or to play without adequate supervision of their activities.

Sending him to a school classroom, summer camp, vacation Bible school, or soccer practice that is loosely run and poorly supervised will undermine what he needs to be taught at this age as well. If the child returns from these activities more out of control, more disrespectful, and more self-serving than is usual for him at this time in his life, then a wise parent will discreetly probe to find out what went on and counter the effects of it with instruction and, if necessary, reproof and correction. If the negative influence continues to have its chaotic effect, you may need to curtail and perhaps eliminate the activity from the child's life.

Children who play games in which they have to wait their turn and play by the rules will benefit from the reinforcement to practice self-restraint and will experience the need for and the benefits of orderliness. In elementary schools, orderliness is taught and reinforced when the children walk with other class members to the bathroom and to the drinking fountain in single file without talking, raise their hand to ask a question, stack their books neatly in their desk at the end of the day, abide by a dress code, address teachers and other adults respectfully, and say excuse me when they bump into someone. All of these practices help teach children to *take orders* and to *value orderliness*.

These examples about chaotic versus orderly living are not techniques that in themselves guarantee godly and orderly children and disciples. They are merely examples of the kinds of structures and strategies that a God-loving, Word-filled, ministry-minded disciple-maker will use as he *oversees* the restraint of the fleshly impulses of those he leads. The disciple can thus be trained in the day-to-day *applications* of God-dependent self-denial. Remember, the goal by the teen years is to have a child who is useful to the Lord in productive service. That means that he should have had much practice in self-restraint.

The *empowerment* for godly living, as we have seen in Parts One and Two already, comes from walking in the Spirit. These times provide many opportunities to teach your child/disciple to look past both discouraging and exhilarating events to the all-seeing God, who enables the believer to do right and judges the heart. He records not the temporal score or the placement in the contest but rather notices the humility of heart that accepts the outcome as coming from God. Teach the child to look to God for strength to think and do right in both his losses and in his victories. He must learn *God-dependent* self-denial.

The *motivation* for denying self is found in the first and second great commands—demonstrating love for God and our neighbor. Even young children can be taught to examine their motivation for their actions. For example, if eight-year-old Johnny and his six-year-old sister Susan are fighting, most parents simply separate them into different rooms, make them take some time out, or punish them in some other fashion without ever addressing the real issues of their children's heart. How much better it would be if the parent dealing with the situation would stop the fight and then address the *heart*. "Johnny, let me ask you a question. When you were treating your sister the way you were just now, were you pleasing God or pleasing yourself? And Susan, when you hit Johnny when he teased you, were you pleasing God or pleasing yourself?" Even a six year old like Susan will already have a sense of awe and respect for God and will recognize that she is definitely pleasing herself and not God in the way she treats her brother if she lives in a home where her parents are God-loving and Word-filled.[8]

The next step in this parenting scenario is to use the situation to teach the process of biblical reconciliation. A sinning child—and that's what he *and you* need to see him as—needs to be reconciled to God *and* his sibling. Johnny, in the situation above, can learn to say to his sister, "I was wrong when I teased you. Will you forgive me?" His sister, even at six, can learn to say, "I forgive you, and I was wrong when I hit you. Will

---

[8] You don't have to wait until Susan is six years old, however, to teach this. Two- and three-year-old preschoolers have already developed a keen sense of what is "mine"—a concept that must be firmly in place in order to "please self." They can also have a good grasp by this time that the God who made them wants them to share and to be kind. A three year old can choose to do right because it "makes Jesus happy."

you forgive me?" They can then both pray and ask God to forgive them for pleasing themselves instead of Him. This approach certainly takes longer than sending them to their room—and they still may need to be separated for a period of time—but it addresses the real problem: the heart. This kind of parenting is done by a ministry-minded overseer. He is not just overseeing the behavior of his children but is sensitive to every opportunity to have a spiritual *ministry* with his children.

Not for Kids Only

Often when discipling adults who are just beginning to put their lives back together after their recent conversion or after repenting of going their own way for a period of time, you will need to help them bring a measure of order back into their lives. Their lives reflect the chaos of fleshly living—usually in several areas. For example, you may have to help them establish some rules in their financial lives—perhaps destroying credit cards or setting up a budget or contacting all their creditors and arranging for payments on past due debts. You may have to help them set up some principles of communication that will help them solve problems with other family members without blowing up or clamming up.

They may need to establish some consistent penalties for the misbehavior of their children instead of doing whatever they feel like doing at the moment. They may need to establish some regular routines of exercise and rest or work out a diet that will help them lose the weight that is endangering their health. They may need to switch jobs, eliminate corruptive friends, forsake sensual music, or address ungodly habits. Most important, they may need similar structure in their devotional time with the Lord and in their personal Bible study. Without regular and generous exposure to the glory of God, they cannot be changed into the image of Jesus Christ.

I think you get the picture. A person whose life is not useful to the Lord at the moment has a great need for some structure and order so that his life does not continue to spiral out of control and into greater chaos. Again, bringing these areas into subordination to scriptural principles alone does not make a person godly by itself. Only the Spirit of God working through the Word of God can make someone godly. These attempts to eliminate the chaotic effects of fleshly living in the past only keep him from further corruption and make him more useful in service for Christ when he does begin walking in the Spirit again.

How Well Do You Smell Smoke?

Before moving on to the third emphasis in disciple-making, I want to make one last comment about your interaction with your children or your disciples. You cannot establish rules that will cover every possible manifestation of fleshly living—in fact, the fewer rules you can have while getting the job done, the better. The real culprit that hinders your child's or your disciple's usefulness to God is any manifestation of the flesh in his life. You have to be a "flesh-sniffer." You will not be sensitive to the rule of the flesh in his life, however, if you are living a fleshly life yourself.

Most people who smoke do not realize how keenly nonsmokers can smell cigarette smoke. A smoker may go into a nonsmoking building and try to light up in the restroom for a couple of quick puffs. He does not think that others will smell it because of the exhaust fans in the bathroom. Every nonsmoker in the area can tell within minutes, however, that someone has lit a cigarette. The smoker doesn't smell smoke as keenly as the nonsmoker.

When we who lead are indulging in the flesh, not only do we hurt our impact by our poor example, but we also do not "smell" the fleshly indulgence of our children or those whom we disciple. We will not pick up on the attitudes, words, and choices that reveal his self-centered heart. Fleshly living will only become further entrenched, making any change in the future that much harder to make.

A God-loving, Word-filled, ministry-minded leader will not need all kinds of techniques to get his discipleship of others on track. He will already know *what* God has dealt with him about and will know *how* God has delivered him from his own self-centered ways. He will have plenty of wisdom (he will know the *next right move*) because God has already parented him in that area. We are to rear our children the way God rears us. Our problem is often that we do not know what to do with our children or disciple because we have not been listening to God as He has tried to disciple us by His Spirit into a life of spiritual usefulness for Him.

THE TEEN YEARS—THE SERVANT DEPLOYED

The Bible does not present maturity as a result of reaching a certain age but of becoming fruitful for Christ.[9] By now, I think you can see that the purpose for the training in God-dependent self-denial and for the renewing of the mind toward Christlikeness is that the one you are discipling will become *useful* to Christ. He can actually be an effective *servant* for Christ. You want him during his teen years to be a God-loving, Word-filled, ministry-minded believer himself—a servant-leader.

Ideally, a Christian teen (ages thirteen through nineteen) who has been biblically discipled by God-loving, Word-filled, ministry-minded parents should be consistently *living* the applications of God-dependent self-denial by this time of his life. He will be away from home much of the time at school or work and should evidence a commitment to doing the loving action toward God and others at his own expense. If the teen has learned well the lessons in the previous years, his parents can now function more as coaches who provide wisdom for new situations and problems and as cheerleaders who give generous doses of encouragement to persevere in God-dependent self-denial. He should be increasingly active in *service* at school and church, influencing others for Christ.

A welcome trend in Fundamentalist churches and Christian schools is to take groups of teens and adults on short-term mission trips. When those trips are to areas of the world where the team has to experience hardship of one sort or another, they can be wonderful tools in teaching the satisfaction and joy that can come from denying self for God and others. Many teens return excited about seeing God use them when they stopped thinking about themselves and started giving themselves in service for Christ.

The tragedy of these situations is that it is often the *first* time a teen has really had to deny himself for God and others. He could be many more miles down the road toward genuine usefulness to Christ had his heart's selfishness been exposed earlier through other service opportunities arranged by the spiritual leaders in his life. Teens can be greatly used of the Lord in nursing home and rescue mission services and ministries of

---

[9] John 15:1-6.

helps to others in the congregation.[10] During the summer months they can serve as support staff at a Christian camp—working in the dining hall, helping on the grounds crew, or serving as a counselor.

Often, however, a steady job keeps the teen out of church and youth activities throughout the school year and ties up his summers, making participation at camps and mission trips impossible. A teen may truly need a job to save for college, but many teens are working simply to pay for the latest fashions or for an automobile—often one he doesn't need except to get to work and often a model that is more a status statement than a means of transportation. Parents who encourage this are taking the risk of producing a savvy consumer and not a God-dependent, self-denying servant.

Ministry-minded parents who feel their teen must work will carefully oversee where he works, how much he works, with whom he works, and why he works. They will be sure that his work outside the home reinforces the discipleship thrusts they are attempting to make in his life. A wrong job worked for the wrong reason can unravel years of Christian parenting in a teen's life and stifle attempts of his parents and church leaders to teach him Christian service.

Once when my wife and I were holding a family conference at a church, an eighth-grade girl came to us just before Sunday school and gave us a container of cookies she had baked for us. I visited with her for a few moments and expressed our gratitude for her thoughtfulness. I learned later from the youth pastor that she is part of a small group of the teens who call themselves the Doulos Group: Servants for Christ.[11] He told me that they prepare treats like these for visiting preachers and missionaries

---

[10] Incidentally, a child's participation in ministry outreach can begin much earlier than his teen years. When our daughters were elementary school age, we involved them in occasional nursing home services for which they had to prepare a simple piano piece and sing together with the family. They protested at that age that they did not know what to say to the residents because often they could not understand what the elderly person was saying. Our girls would say that they did not *like* to go. We reminded them that we were not doing this because *we* liked it but because *the residents* liked it and *God* liked it. When they became teens, they willingly and cheerfully participated in a nursing home ministry. They had learned the joy of ministry to these dear folks who were in their latter years of life.

[11] *Doulos* is the Greek word for "servant."

and do service activities for needy families in the church. They will often do a work of ministry and leave a card that says simply "Servants for Christ." They are becoming servant-leaders.

The parents who are encouraging this kind of activity and the youth pastor who is helping coordinate their efforts are teaching these teens the joy of service. The young people are becoming *useful* to Christ. They are learning to demonstrate their love for God and others in concrete ways. They are being equipped "for the work of the ministry" (Eph. 4:12).

On a broader scale, this is the kind of opportunity that needs to be available to anyone in the church. It is not my goal in this chapter to give you an encyclopedia of ideas for working with teens. I am rather trying to demonstrate that the kind of spiritual leaders God uses are overseers who provide structure and accountability with a ministry mindset—they desire to see their disciple change and grow in Christlikeness.

GETTING THEM READY FOR THE BIGGEST DAY OF THEIR LIVES

Why should we go to such effort to teach our children and disciples the principles, applications, and motivations of God-dependent self-denial? One day as I was thinking about my responsibilities to disciple my wife and daughters, I realized that "the biggest day" of my daughters' lives will not be the day they get married or the day that one of them has our first grandchild. And though my wife and I consider the day we were married a stellar day, it was not "the biggest day" of our lives. That day is yet to come. It will be the day when we all stand before Jesus Christ to give an account of our usefulness to Him during this earthly pilgrimage. The significance of that day is defined by the significance of the One before whom we will appear.

All of our work on earth—every thought and action—will be tried by the fires of His omniscience, and the degree to which we lived to please ourselves or lived to please our Lord will be exposed. Everything we have done will be evaluated for its effect upon His purposes on the earth and will be consequently discounted and disqualified or rewarded and celebrated. It will be a momentous, awe-inspiring day for us! It will eclipse every other day any of us have ever had up to that time.

My greatest joy in that day will be in seeing *His* joy if my wife and children can give a good account to Him. The apostle John urged his "little children"[12] to continue in what he had taught them so that "when [Christ] shall appear, [they could] have confidence, and not be ashamed before him at his coming" (I John 2:28). Paul was driven by the same forward look. He said in I Thessalonians 2:19, "For what is our hope, or joy, or crown of rejoicing? Are not even ye in the presence of our Lord Jesus Christ at his coming?"[13]

May we too be driven by a passion to delight our God by preparing for Him another generation of God-loving, Word-filled, and ministry-minded disciple-makers who can stand before Him and hear "well done, thou good and faithful servant: . . . enter thou into the joy of thy lord" (Matt. 25:21). This is our mission—getting them ready for the biggest day of their lives!

TAKE TIME TO REFLECT

The Epistle of II Corinthians is Paul's autobiography of the ministry. To gain a biblical perspective of his ministry mindset, read through the entire book and note the verses in which he speaks of his concern for the spiritual growth of others. Either underline or shade them in your Bible or write them out in a notebook. Notice the following examples from chapter 1:

"That we may be able to comfort *them* which are in any trouble" (1:4). Notice Paul's concern for the comfort of *others* in this verse.

"And whether we be afflicted, it is for *your* consolation and salvation" (1:6). Italics show you his concern for others again.

"And our hope of *you* is stedfast" (1:7).

"And more abundantly to *you*-ward" (1:12).

"That *ye* might have a second benefit" (1:15).

"Not for that we have dominion over your faith, but are helpers of *your* joy" (1:24).

---

[12] I John 2:1, 12, 13, 18, 28; 3:7, 18; 4:4; and 5:21.

[13] See also I Corinthians 1:8; II Corinthians 1:14; 5:10; Philippians 1:9-11; and 2:16.

This Epistle is filled with references such as these that show Paul's continual burden for the spiritual growth and development of others. Our lives should reflect the same concern.

A WORD TO DISCIPLE-MAKERS

Ministering in the Milieu

The mandate of Deuteronomy 6:7 to "talk of [the words of God] when thou sittest in thine house, and when thou walkest by the way, and when thou liest down, and when thou risest up" underscores the necessity for spiritual leaders to take advantage of informal times to teach the ways and words of God. These mundane activities of normal living are also the cauldron in which many problems of living with others come to the boiling point. The ministry-minded leader will be alert to his follower's failures, conflicts, weaknesses, habits, strengths, and temperament. Those will be uncovered in the milieu—in the midst of the normal events of life—as he watches the one he is discipling relate to the daily ups and downs of living on a fallen planet with fallen people.

Each of us learns best when a need or weakness in our life has been exposed in some way. It is at that point of need that we are most teachable. A wise disciple-maker will personalize his discipleship "curriculum" as he sees a need arise. The lesson will be more potent and, in most cases, the disciple will be more open to help because he has just been exposed.

This ministry in the milieu is why family living is such a wonderful "workshop" for discipleship. Wise, alert, ministry-minded parents will not lack opportunities to bring God and His ways into the picture of everyday events. This same "up close" contact is why experiences at a summer camp and the dormitory life at a Fundamentalist Christian college can be such powerful aids to spiritual growth if the spiritual leader or counselor has a ministry mindset. He will also not lack opportunities to address new challenges.

Nothing exposes our own spiritual deficiencies—and sometimes outright spiritual poverty—more than parenting and disciple-making. If you are buckling under the pressure, study Basics for Pressured Believers in Appendix B. Resist the urge to just "get away from it all" as a solution to the pressure unless by that you mean to remove yourself from the milieu temporarily for a few hours to "argue yourself back to reality" by an increased interaction of meditation and prayer with God Himself.

Don't think that just a change of scenery or pace will solve the problem. There is no doubt that these can be temporarily restorative—that is part of the reason for the "day of rest" Sabbath commanded by God in Exodus 20:8-11. The greater benefit for the cessation of normal activities, however, was to devote oneself to the contemplation of God. That, as you have seen from Chapters 6 and 7, is the greatest refreshment available to any person.

Often parents who use their work, television, sports, hobby, or other escapes as ways to get away from the pressures of family living will be heartbroken when their teens use a similar "get away from it all" strategy to avoid home once they have the mobility to do so. We must not teach them that to "get away from it all" is a valid way of handling problems. They must learn by our example and by our coaching to "get to the God of it all" when under pressure.

CHAPTER THIRTEEN

LABORING TOGETHER WITH GOD

"I have planted, Apollos watered; but God gave the increase. . . . and every man shall receive his own reward according to his own labour. For we are labourers together with God."
I Corinthians 3:6, 8-9

What a privilege that God has called us and equipped us to be God-loving, Word-filled, ministry-minded disciple-makers—"labourers together" with *Him!* We are humbled by the responsibility and cry out with Paul, "Who is sufficient for these things?"[1] How can *we* "serve God acceptably"?[2] How can *we* give Him the "reasonable service"[3] of which He is worthy?

Before we close our study in this book, we must ask ourselves some penetrating questions about ministry. What is *God's* part in the work, and what is *our* part? What will keep us from the excesses that have plagued the church through the centuries? We dare not teach on the one hand simply a passive approach to "let go and let God," nor can we merely impose a rigid system of discipline upon others and expect biblical change to take place in their lives. As always, God gives us clear teaching—sound doctrine—that when "rightly divid[ed]" will allow each of us to stand before Him at the Judgment Seat as "a workman that needeth not to be ashamed" (II Tim. 2:15).

Lessons from the Farm
Let's consider how we are laborers *together* with God. God chose to reveal His written Word and send His Son, the incarnate Word, to a nation called Israel—largely an agricultural nation of farmers and shepherds.

---

[1] II Corinthians 2:16.
[2] Hebrews 12:28.
[3] Romans 12:1.

Even the New Testament Epistles, while written to metropolitan populations like those in Corinth, Ephesus, Philippi, and Colosse, contain much agricultural imagery because of everyone's familiarity with vineyards, shepherds, and farms. The Bible's imagery of planting, watering, fertilizing, pruning, and harvesting was not chosen, however, because of the nature of the *people* (they were an agricultural community) but because of the nature of the *truth* that God was communicating to man. Since God created *all* growth processes—physical and spiritual—we should expect them to bear a remarkable resemblance to each other. The physical laws of God reflect the spiritual laws of God.

Paul teaches us in I Corinthians 3:5-9 that if we can understand the role of God and the role of man in the activities and responsibilities of a "plant grower" (a farmer), we can understand the role of God and the role of man in the activities and responsibilities of a "people grower" (a disciple-maker). This passage teaches us two different responsibilities.

Our Part: We are to be "faithful farmers," planting and watering as God's laws of nature dictate and as God's grace enables us—practicing God-dependent self-denial.

God's Part: He is the sovereign Lord of the harvest, giving the increase as He sees fit.

It should not surprise us that we again encounter the paradox of divine sovereignty and human responsibility. Paul says, "I have planted" (Paul did his part), but he readily admits that "neither is he that planteth any thing" (I Cor. 3:6-7). In I Corinthians 15:10 Paul testifies that *he* labored, yet he said it was "the grace of God . . . which was bestowed upon [him]" that made him what he was. God frequently attributes some work to *Himself* that He also commands *us* to do. Jonathan Edwards expressed the paradox this way:

> We are not merely passive, nor yet does God do some, and we do the rest. But God does all, and we do all. God produces all, and we act all. For that is what he produces, *viz.* our own acts. God is the only proper author and fountain; we only are the proper actors. We are, in different respects, wholly passive and wholly active.

In the Scriptures the same things are represented as from God and from us. God is said to convert (II Tim. 2:25), and men are said to convert and turn (Acts 2:38). God makes a new heart (Ezek. 36:26), and we are commanded to make us a new heart (Ezek. 18:31). God circumcises the heart (Deut. 30:6), and we are commanded to circum-cise our own hearts (Deut. 10:16). . . . These things are agreeable to that text, "God worketh in you both to will and do (Phil. 2:13)."[4]

We can expect, therefore, to learn that even in our disciple-making oversight of others we are to do something and can expect God to do something. Paul teaches that "we are labourers together with God" (I Cor. 3:9).

Three Kinds of Farmers

As I have already mentioned, the Bible frequently illustrates truth by way of farming imagery. For example, the Word is presented as seed and the heart of man is represented by soil in Luke 8. The Word is also presented in Isaiah 55:10 as rain and snow that "cometh down . . . from heaven, and returneth not thither, but watereth the earth, and maketh it bring forth and bud, that it may give seed to the sower, and bread to the eater." The blessing of God is represented in verse 13 of that same chapter by the appearance of the fir and myrtle trees rather than the desert briars and thorn bushes. In the passage before us—I Corinthians 3:5-9—Paul presented himself and Apollos as farmers and his audience, the Corinthian church, as the field.

In order for you to understand more accurately your role as a God-loving, Word-filled, ministry-minded disciple-maker, I want us to consider in this chapter three kinds of farmers. They each represent one kind of approach to life and ministry. Two of them represent the wrong extremes. Only one of them honors God. Study the following chart to get an overview of where we are heading.

UNDISCIPLINED FARMER	DISCIPLINED FARMER	
The Gambling Farmer (Slothful)	The Controlling Farmer (Legalistic)	The Trusting Farmer (Faithful)
Pleases Self		Pleases God

In the last chapter we discussed the diligent oversight that ministry-minded disciple-makers must have. The question before us now is "How can I provide biblical oversight for others by imposing structure and

---

[4] Sereno Dwight, *Efficacious Grace*, in *The Works of Jonathan Edwards*, ed. S. Dwight (1834; reprint, Edinburgh: Banner of Truth, 1974), 2, 557.

accountability upon them without putting them into a legalistic strait-jacket, which dishonors God?"

Often, if anyone imposes any discipline upon the life of another in this day, he is called a legalist. Certainly legalism is a danger we must avoid, but I propose to you that the danger in legalism is not the discipline itself. A person who is pleasing self by imposing discipline upon himself and others is just as destructive as a person who is pleasing self by ignoring the discipline of himself and others. The first leads to the fleshly self-discipline of a legalist, and the other produces the fleshly self-indulgence of a sluggard. Neither pleases God.

With that brief overview, let us move on to look more closely at each of the three kinds of farmers. We will specifically note how they respond to God's laws of nature. They represent the various responses believers can have to God's laws of any sort—natural or revealed.

THE GAMBLING FARMER

The first farmer we want to study we will call the Gambling Farmer. This farmer *ignores* the laws of nature and gambles on the outcome. God has created His world with certain built-in laws. God's laws are statements of reality—the way things are in God's world. His laws in the natural world are often self-evident and cannot be ignored without paying certain consequences. For example, neither the law of gravity nor the laws of thermodynamics can be ignored without penalty. The same is true for the law of sowing and reaping—in both the natural and the spiritual realms.

The farmer cannot forget to sow his seed in the spring and then suppose that in midsummer he can plant "real hard" and still have a crop when the harvest season starts in early fall. He cannot ignore the built-in timetable of the seed. Neither can he ignore the seed's requirement for moisture by giving his field one good watering at planting time and then ignoring its need for water throughout the rest of the growing season. His seed will germinate and quickly perish from drought. A farmer who ignores these laws and still expects to have a crop can only gamble that he will have a satisfactory outcome. God's laws cannot be ignored.

The book of Proverbs presents such a man—the sluggard—and even likens him to a lazy farmer. Notice the picture Solomon portrays of him in Proverbs 24:30-34. Solomon perhaps is out for an afternoon drive in his chariot inspecting the fields of his sharecropping tenants. He pauses by one man's field that is in utter disarray. I can imagine the scene as Solomon steps out of his chariot, walks over to the deteriorating stone wall, puts one foot upon the wall, bends over while leaning on his raised leg, and ponders what he sees. He later reports,

> I went by the field of the slothful, and by the vineyard of the man void of understanding; And, lo, it was all grown over with thorns, and nettles had covered the face thereof, and the stone wall thereof was broken down. Then I saw, and considered it well: [Solomon wasn't critical; he was reflective.] I looked upon it, and received instruction. [He tried to reap a lesson from this field for himself as he pondered the sluggard's excuses.] Yet a little sleep, a little slumber, a little folding of the hands to sleep: [Then he reflected on the eventual outcome of the man's laziness.] So shall thy poverty come as one that travelleth; and thy want as an armed man. [Though the consequences would come slowly as a man traveling by foot, his end would nonetheless be as if he had been robbed of everything valuable to him.]

Solomon realized that the end of this man's laziness would be total ruin. The man obviously had good intentions, for "the soul of the sluggard desireth"—he *wants* a good crop—but he "hath nothing." By contrast, "the soul of the diligent shall be made fat" (Prov. 13:4). The sluggard makes little excuses—soft choices—for himself: the job is too big and dangerous;[5] he doesn't "do" mornings;[6] and he doesn't like to be pushed—he will get to it when everyone backs off and quits hounding him.[7] If you try to hold him accountable, he can give you reason after reason to justify his inactivity.[8]

A primary characteristic of this lazy farmer is that he begs for a second chance when he begins to experience some of the fallout of his slothfulness. Solomon puts it this way: "The sluggard will not plow by reason of the cold [another one of his excuses]; therefore shall he beg in harvest, and have nothing" (Prov. 20:4).

---

[5] Proverbs 26:13.
[6] Proverbs 26:14.
[7] Proverbs 26:15.
[8] Proverbs 26:16.

This is the person who has indulged himself, ignoring the laws of life; and now, when the reaping time comes, he doesn't like the crop—or lack thereof—and begs for someone to bail him out.

This is the teen who isn't allowed to play sports because he has failed his academics and then begs his school for another chance to prove himself if he will just be allowed to play this season. This is the college student who has had his "fun and games" in school accumulating a long list of disciplinary offenses and then begs for another chance when he is placed on probation or denied further enrollment. This is the thirty-five-year-old husband and father who has ignored his family while he absorbed himself in his work or recreation and then begs his wife not to leave him when she threatens divorce. This is the family who has never really settled down in a local church. They have never joined and have attended only sporadically. They have always had some excuse for not attending regularly and for not joining. Now they are having marital problems or problems with one of the children, and they beg the pastor to help out. This is the employee who has frequently displayed an unruly temper, and though challenged by his superiors about it, he has sought no biblical help. When he is finally fired, he begs for another chance.

All of these individuals are ignoring the laws of God's world. They are not plowing, sowing, and tending their fields when the time is right. They always have some reason to explain why they can't get out into the fields. Now they look for some miraculous intervention by God and others to bail them out. They have a "lottery mentality" that ignores God's *normal* ways of provision through sowing and reaping, and then, like gamblers, they hope for a windfall from a "lucky number."

Notice some of the other observations about the sluggard in Proverbs:

> The desire of the slothful killeth him [his lusts are his ruin]; for his hands refuse to labour. [He has his own ideas about how he will make life work through pursuing his own pleasures. God's way is labor.] (Prov. 21:25)[9]

---

[9] See II Thessalonians 3:11 for a New Testament example, a Lazy Loafer, who walks "disorderly" (a military term meaning to be out of order; insubordinate; not attending to his own post) and is a "busybody" (a wanderer not attending to his own business but involved in the business of others). See also I Timothy 5:13.

The slothful man roasteth not that which he took in hunting [he doesn't even value that which he has]: but the substance of a diligent man is precious (Prov. 12:27).

The way of the slothful man is as an hedge of thorns [he is always running into difficulty]: but the way of the righteous is made plain [his way is like a level road] (Prov. 15:19).

He also that is slothful in his work is brother to him that is a great waster [and then he wonders why he got fired] (Prov. 18:9).

As vinegar to the teeth, and as smoke to the eyes [very irritating], so is the sluggard to them that send him [you cannot depend upon him to come through in his responsibilities] (Prov. 10:26).

His fleshly self-indulgence destroys every field of responsibility. This is why it is just no good to keep giving him another chance and another field no matter how hard he begs and pleads when he has been ignoring reproofs and instruction. *He will waste another chance until he has a different kind of heart.* He needs biblical change which, as we have seen, involves turning his heart toward God in repentance and dependence. He needs to develop a growing personal relationship with God by applying doctrine, reproof, correction, and instruction in righteousness. Until he has plowed, planted, and cultivated his soul *according to God's laws of growth and change*, no second chance will help him.

But What About Mercy?

Immediately some will protest, "But *God* is merciful. Why can't *you* let him have a second chance?" That question comes from a misunderstanding of what mercy is. Unfortunately, there are those who believe that no one should suffer—ever! Their main concern is that people be happy and have a sense of well-being. Consequently, when courts, parents, employers, or school officials impose some sort of penalty for unacceptable behavior, they are accused of being "unmerciful." We need to think biblically about God's mercy and compassion.

God's mercy contains two elements. The first is an inward concern for the miserable plight of someone, and the second is an outward action aimed at relieving that desperate condition even at great expense to the one relieving the suffering. We especially see this kind of compassion in our Lord in His response to the various plights of people in the Gospels. He was moved with compassion when He saw a leper who needed to be healed;[10] a widow whose son had just died, leaving her in a destitute condition;[11] a crowd who had been with him three days without food;[12] and two blind men who needed their sight restored.[13] His compassion always extended beyond their physical condition, however, to the greatest misery of all—a soul captivated by sin. His compassion led Him to challenge the disciples to pray for laborers to go into the ripe fields of the world to spread the good news of God's mercy to sinners.[14]

To represent Christ well to the world means that we too must be moved with compassion when we see the dire state of the condemned lost. We must be willing to relieve their misery at great personal cost to bring them to Christ for His mercy and forgiveness. On another level we are also to be concerned about the physical dilemma of those around us, "especially unto them who are of the household of faith" (Gal. 6:10).

But what is the biblical response to someone who is suffering the consequences of his *own* sin as the lazy farmer of Proverbs did? Should we bail him out of the consequences of his actions? To answer that question we will need to look more closely at exactly what God is trying to accomplish when He shows mercy.

We have already seen that God's mercy moves Him to rescue us from our pitiful plight. Before salvation our most urgent need was to be rescued from the penalty of our sin. After salvation our most urgent need is to be rescued from the power of sin in our life. One of the *merciful* ways God extracts us from the power of sin in our life is to allow us to experience its consequences. Notice how the writer of Hebrews records God's *loving*[15] *intervention in the lives of His sinning children*.

> For whom the Lord *loveth* he chasteneth, and scourgeth every son whom he receiveth. If ye endure chastening, God dealeth with you as with sons; for what son is he whom the father chasteneth not? . . . Now no chastening for the present seemeth to be joyous,

---

[10] Mark 1:40-42.

[11] Luke 7:11-15.

[12] Matthew 15:32-38.

[13] Matthew 20:30-34.

[14] Matthew 9:36-38.

[15] We also need to understand that God's mercy is a manifestation of His broader attribute of love.

278

but grievous: nevertheless afterward it yieldeth the peaceable fruit of righteousness unto them which are exercised thereby (Heb. 12:6-7, 11).

The most *merciful* thing God can do is to chasten us—though it is painful at the time—in order to deliver us from the miserable end of our self-indulgent living. He does this to produce the fruit of righteousness in us.

A God-loving, Word-filled, ministry-minded disciple-maker will be more concerned that his disciple be extracted from the bent of his sinful heart than from the immediate unpleasantness of his chastening. Chastening produces a test of a person's faith: Will he begin to view life from God's perspective now that God has his attention, or will he continue to go his *own* way? Can he see *God* in the picture now? And most important, will he submit to *God* now?

In every trial—and that includes the trial of chastening—James exhorts us to let it have its perfecting work in us so that we may be "perfect and entire, wanting nothing" (James 1:4). Without the consequences, both natural and imposed, the human heart will continue to gamble on the outcome—as we have seen in the case of the sluggard. He does not need to be removed from the unpleasantness of his condition. He needs to experience the unpleasantness to help him change. The writer of Hebrews agrees that it is not a "joyous" experience. Rather it is "grievous," but it will produce the righteous fruit of godliness in the believer who is "exercised thereby" (Heb. 12:11).

To cut short the trial by removing the grievous consequences is to short-circuit the merciful efforts of God to deliver us from our self-centered living—the most dangerous and miserable condition possible for a believer. The unpleasantness is part of the rebuke, correction, and instruction in righteousness that equip the man of God for usefulness in the future.[16]

Of course, that correction and penalty must be administered by an overseer with a heart that is truly concerned about the desperate spiritual condition that has been exposed by the wrong choices. If you as a

---

[16] II Timothy 3:16-17.

disciple-maker want your disciple to see the hand of God in his life through the correction you administer, you must deliver the consequences in a manner that can be readily seen as the hand of God. You cannot have a mean-spirited, "you're-going-to-pay-for-that" attitude. That will only erect an enormous stumbling block in the path of your disciple's restoration to usefulness for God. You would be fulfilling your responsibility as an *overseer,* but you would certainly not be exhibiting a *ministry-mindedness* in your actions. Thus we have the continual reminders of Scripture to examine our own lives before we deal with the faults of others.[17]

Back to the Gambling Farmer

We need to see clearly as we leave our consideration of the gambling, lazy farmer—Proverb's sluggard—that his main problem is that he is pleasing self rather than pleasing God. That condition is always destructive, and from that he needs to be rescued by the reproofs of life,[18] by the appeals of concerned brethren, and by the corrective interventions of his superiors.

THE CONTROLLING FARMER

The second kind of farmer we want to examine is the Controlling Farmer. This farmer doesn't *ignore* the laws of nature as the Gambling Farmer does. Instead, he *keeps* the laws of nature—religiously. He plants on time and studies everything he can find on seeds, soil, and weather. He diligently keeps the laws of nature to *insure* the outcome he desires. He can usually turn out a pretty good crop and can often become self-confident. He isn't totally irreligious in his self-confidence, however. He might even ask God for help to understand how to farm well and might pray that God will send the right weather conditions. Most of the time it works. He has a great crop!

He might even do so well in farming that others seek him out for advice, and he quickly gravitates to those who have the same air of seriousness about farming. He might look at the slothful farmer, however, with an air of smug contempt. When observing the sluggard's fields, he might say things to himself such as "I couldn't live with myself if I let my fields

---

[17] Matthew 7:3-5; Galatians 6:1; I Timothy 4:15-16.
[18] Proverbs 12:24; 15:19; 19:15; 20:4; 24:34.

degenerate like that" or "I don't understand what's wrong with that man! All he has to do is get out and get his hands dirty. Anybody ought to be able to figure that out!"

He works from sunup to sundown just to *make sure* that he has done everything he can. In fact, he is *so* diligent that he can become quite driven and controlling—even perfectionistic—about his labor. He might become so intense about doing right that he makes himself—and everyone close to him—miserable by continually questioning his own motives, doubting whether he has really "done his best," or wondering whether he has had "enough faith" to please God. He may become filled with self-doubt and consequently may redouble his efforts in order to *make sure* that everything is just right.

If he is in a leadership position, he can become overly critical of the work or spiritual condition of others. He can quickly demoralize his followers with his fear-driven obsession to be sure they are "doing right." Please note that the problem here is not his diligence in making his underlings accountable. That may be precisely what he should be doing in his leadership role. The problem is his confidence in *himself* to get the job done and his flesh-driven fear of failure and of loss of control that motivates his "diligence." He cannot often tolerate being vulnerable, and he doesn't like surprises. He wants to know what is going on and wants to be able to do something about it.

Early Warning Signs

A wise, "flesh-sniffing" parent can see the beginnings of Controlling Farmer tendencies in his child at an early age. We briefly touched on this approach to life in Chapter 3 when we discussed various kinds of rebels. A budding Controlling Farmer can be the "really good student" who wins the scholastic and citizenship awards in elementary school or who receives the valedictorian, Christian leadership, or sportsmanship awards in high school.

For some children and teens, the good testimony and achievement may indeed be the result of a Spirit-filled, God-dependent walk with Christ. A child or teen may have already learned how to be the Trusting Farmer we will discuss next. For others, however, the fleshly, self-pleasing motive for being good and doing well can be seen in the great depression or anger that he exhibits when he has "done his best" but didn't achieve his goal. Or it can be seen in the snobbish, exclusive, haughty, or proud spirit he displays when he wins again. He may receive many "corruptible" crowns, but his flesh-driven achievement will earn no "incorruptible" crowns from the Judge who tries the heart (I Cor. 9:24-27).

As he grows in his lust for control, you could characterize his life by one word—*intense!* That intensity can make him difficult to live with. He may even find living with himself to be a great burden at times. He may not wear well in relationships and may have a hard time getting close to people because relationships contain too many variables for him to be at ease. They are seldom risk free.

He may even begin to experience various physical problems. His body cannot sustain the intensity with which he pushes himself. He may suffer from any number of gastrointestinal disorders, stress-related illnesses, tension headaches, chronic pain or numbness, and insomnia. Because his mind is never at rest, his body is in a constant state of emergency as well. His physician may tell him to eliminate some pressures in his life, but he has difficulty understanding how he is to "try harder" not to try so hard.

Unfortunately, over time the physical effects can become chronic and the damage permanent. After all, it takes an enormous amount of physical and mental energy to be in total control! It will crush even the strongest of mortals. As you can see, the physical and relational price of being *self-insured* is high.

Don't Miss the Subtle Shift

Please realize here that the condition of the Controlling Farmer is often unwittingly the stopover point for many who have left the ways of the Gambling Farmer and are moving toward the position of the Trusting Farmer. At some point these individuals saw that their lack of discipline was dishonoring to God. They realized their self-indulgent, chaotic, unproductive lives were evidence that they were living to please themselves rather than God. Bowing in humility before God, they repented of their slothfulness and determined to abandon their self-serving ways. They knew they must bring some order back into their lives so God would use them. They sincerely at this point wanted to please God.

When they began applying some discipline to their lives, they began to see some very pleasing results. They liked the results so much, however, that they began to focus excessively on their disciplined living to produce *more* of the desired results and to *insure* that the results they had achieved would continue. Their initial focus of wanting to please God has subtly shifted to an intense desire to please themselves by achieving and maintaining the results they have grown to admire.

They are not only somewhat contemptuous of others who don't share their concerns but also increasingly intolerant of anyone—especially family members and work associates—who would stand in the way of the results they are pursuing. Like those who worked with Frank in "A Case in Point,"[19] others might think the Controlling Farmer is unnecessarily opinionated; but since he is usually right in the end, they generally follow his suggestions. After all, he usually ends up with better crops than his neighbors, who do things a different way. It isn't wrong that he is usually right. It is wrong that in his mind he always *has* to be right. He is impatient with other opinions because he cannot see how he will get the results he wants if he follows their way.

Herein is the reason we call him the Controlling Farmer and a legalist. He does what is right—at least what is right in *his* eyes—in order to *insure* and *control* the outcome that he has decided he *must* have. He is at heart a legalist—one who does the right things for self-advancing, self-preserving reasons.

Pleasing self is at the heart of legalism just as it is at the heart of slothfulness. Many today do not understand the issues of the flesh, and when they see the hard, joyless life of a Christian legalist who disciplines himself and others his own way, they abandon disciplined living altogether, supposing that the problem is his intense *discipline*. As a reaction to the fleshly rigidity of the legalist, they go to an opposite extreme of tolerant self-indulgence, often in the name of "Christian liberty."

Since the flesh can produce only destruction,[20] both the sluggard and the legalist are headed for ruin—the one through his neglectful orientation, the other through his driven intensity. The sluggard does *whatever*

---

[19] If it has been some time since you have read this extended case study in Chapter 3, I would suggest that you take some time at this point to re-read it. Frank, Craig's father, lives his Christian life with the perspective of a Controlling Farmer.

[20] Romans 8:13.

he wants to get what he wants—leisure and fun. The legalist does *right* to get what he wants—a bumper crop. Neither of them, however, experiences much peace or true rest in the soul because both are flesh driven.

In addition, neither of them will be able to give a good account at the Judgment Seat of Christ. Upon the foundation of salvation in Christ they have built only with the wood, hay, and stubble of fleshly self-indulgence or fleshly self-reliance. Their works will not stand the test of His fire, and both the Gambling Farmer and the Controlling Farmer will suffer great loss in that day.[21]

THE TRUSTING FARMER

As I have noted, many people who observe the Controlling Farmer reject his ways and adopt the ways of the Gambling Farmer. They seem to think the problem is his discipline when, as we have seen, his problem is the flesh. There is a better way—a way that truly reflects Christ. It is the way of the Trusting Farmer.

He, like the Controlling Farmer, *keeps* the laws of nature, but for an entirely different and higher motive. He keeps them, not to *insure* the results he wants but *because the Father he loves has given them*. He wishes to honor his Father by obeying them. Although he would like to see certain results, he realizes the determination of those results is entirely up to his Father—the Lord of the harvest. He is more concerned that the fruit of the Spirit be manifest in his *responses*—no matter what results the Father gives—than a certain amount of fruit come out of his fields as the result of his efforts. He is driven by a desire to please the Father in all things. He has taken the apostle Paul's admonition seriously when he said in I Corinthians 10:31, "Whether therefore ye eat, or drink, or whatsoever ye do, do all to the glory of God."

He is diligent; he is disciplined; he labors to exhaustion—but not to *gain* God's favor. He throws his life into his farm because he *has* God's favor. Every day of labor is just another page of a thank-you card to God for the riches of His grace to him in making him a child of God. He trusts God to help him do right, not to get what he wants but to faithfully give

---

[21] I Corinthians 3:10-15.

God what He deserves—unqualified trust and devotion—because He is a worthy Father. He wants to hear the law of his Father so that he can do it, and he delights in the law of his Father because he loves the *Father* and, therefore, loves His will.[22] *God-loving* people have no trouble loving God's law since His laws are reflections of His nature.

The Trusting Farmer gets his greatest delight, not in the bumper crop he reaps while keeping the laws of God but in the pleasure he brings to his Father for having done His will. When the Father chooses not to allow a bumper crop for his efforts, the Trusting Farmer is still at peace because he knows he has pleased the Father in *his part* of the enterprise—he has been faithful.[23]

The Danger of Being Good Without God

The danger, of course, is that when doing right becomes the normal way of life for him, he can gradually become somewhat dependent upon his own disciplined habits to keep up his image of godliness. He can drift into the ways of the controlling, legalistic—self-dependent and self-glorifying—farmer. For a period of time, he can appear to be good without God. His loving Father, however, will mercifully convict him or mercifully bring a trial of some sort to once again expose his self-dependent way. He can then bow with the humility of repentance and can once again please God with his dependent, trusting heart.

The Hallmark of the Trusting Farmer

The most outstanding characteristic of this man is not the bumper crop of his fields but the fruit of God's Spirit that is so evident in his life—no matter what the yield of his field. If he does have a crop that yields "a hundredfold," he will not be cocky and arrogant. He will be humbly grateful that his Father has allowed him to produce this much for His glory. If the Father has destroyed the standing grain with a hailstorm, he is humbly submissive to his Father's decision in that outcome as well. Since he delights to delight the Father, he is not moved by the calamity the Father gives. He knows he can *always* delight the Father by a trusting heart. He trusts God who promises that He is always present and always faithful to provide whatever is truly needed. He understands that the "just shall live by faith" (Heb. 10:38). He knows he cannot please the

---

[22] Romans 7:22.
[23] I Corinthians 4:2.

Father in any way without faith.[24] He wishes to be like Abraham, the father of the faithful, who "staggered not at the promise of God through unbelief; but was strong in faith, giving glory to God; And being fully persuaded that, what he had promised, he was able also to perform" (Rom. 4:20-21). He has a "spiritual eye" that "sees" God in everything.

This trust in the Father does not make him lazy. He does not think that since his Father ultimately controls the outcome, he does not need to labor so hard. He knows that response would not delight the Father. He shows as much discipline and orderliness as the Controlling Farmer, but his motive is different. He works faithfully and diligently to delight the Father and trusts the Father to control the outcome. That delight and trust in his Father is the secret of his peace, his contentment, and his joy. His *heart* bears much fruit, though his earthly fields through the providence of God may have been laid waste by his enemies or by the weather.

The Trusting Farmer heartily embraces the words of his Master, who said,

> Verily, verily, I say unto you, Except a corn of wheat [his own ambitions] fall into the ground and die, it abideth alone: but if it die, it bringeth forth much fruit. He that loveth his life shall lose it; and he that hateth his life in this world shall keep it unto life eternal. If any man serve me, let him follow me; and where I am, there shall also my servant be: if any man serve me, him will my Father honour (John 12:24-26).

His greatest delight is in pleasing the Father by being faithful as a laborer "together with God." May God help all of us to be faithful, Trusting Farmers whom the Father can honor!

TAKE TIME TO REFLECT

1. When your spiritual leaders "drive by your field," what do they see: evidence of a slothful farmer (chaos), evidence of a legalistic farmer (control, intensity), or evidence of a faithful farmer (peace, rest)?

---

[24] Hebrews 11:6.

2. Are you making small allowances and excuses for not getting the job done?

3. Are you tolerating weeds and allowing the fences or boundaries to erode?

4. What is your tolerance for chaos in someone else's life? In your life?

5. Do you see your neighbor's chaos as a threat to *his usefulness* or a threat to *your love for order*?

6. Do you panic (legalistic farmer) or trust (faithful farmer) when life goes out of control?

A WORD TO DISCIPLE-MAKERS

A Legalist with One Rule

A legalist doesn't have to be a controlling person with scores of rules he imposes upon himself and upon others to insure that life works the way he wants. He can be a controlling person with *one* rule (in this case, not one of God's rules) he imposes upon himself and others: "Thou shalt leave me alone. I will rule myself." He is an out-and-out rebel. His life is also characterized by the intensity with which he keeps his rule—even if it is only one rule. He, too, looks with contempt upon anyone else who would try to interfere with his "system" of individualism. No one has his favor unless he abides by his rule. He also delights in the company of other "single-rule legalists" who have the same rule.

In nature he is really no different from the "multiple-rule" legalist. Both kinds of legalists embrace rules for life that in their minds will give them what they want. They cannot have any peace of mind unless they are in control and everything is running according to their rule(s). This universe by God's design is a moral universe. It must operate by law. The questions to settle are these: Whose laws will you obey—your own or God's? If you choose to obey God's laws, what motive drives you to keep them—love for yourself or love for God and others?

The Dangers of Ditch Watching

When discipling others, watch out for pendulum reactions. I mentioned earlier in this chapter that when someone sees the disciplined intensity of the Controlling Farmer, he is often tempted to go to the other extreme of the Gambling Farmer. He is swinging the pendulum from one extreme to the other. This happens also when an individual has been deeply hurt and wronged by someone—particularly a parent or some other leader in his life. His response may be, "When I get a home of my own, I will *never* be like my dad! He was never there when we needed him." That mindset often sends him to the other extreme.

Help the one you are discipling to understand the dangers of "ditch watching." A person going to an opposite extreme is in some way like a person who was driving a car once when the car went into the ditch. He determined that since it was such a scary experience, he never wants to repeat it. Consequently, he now drives with both eyes fixed steadfastly on one side of the road or the other, determined to stay out of the ditch. It is obvious that this is a sure-fire way to end up in one ditch or the other.

Don't let the one you are discipling develop the habit of focusing his attention on "ditches." Help him keep his eyes straight ahead on Christ! Lasting change takes place only when we steer for the centerline of Christlikeness. When he first starts growing in his walk with Christ, he may "oversteer," but that is to be expected in beginning "drivers." Eventually, he will be able to make good progress along the road of godliness without a lot of wandering back and forth between "ditches."

EPILOGUE

*It is better to go to the house of mourning, than to go to the house of feasting:
for that is the end of all men; and the living will lay it to his heart. Sorrow is
better than laughter: for by the sadness of the countenance the heart is made
better. The heart of the wise is in the house of mourning; but the heart of fools is
in the house of mirth.*
Ecclesiastes 7:2-4

As I pondered what would be a fitting end to this book, God sent a momentous event into my life. On February 24, 1998, my father stepped into the presence of his Creator and Redeemer. Ten years earlier he had been hospitalized for quadruple bypass surgery. Five years after that he suffered a stroke that forced him into an early retirement at age sixty-three. A heart attack on February 20 put him into the hospital with pneumonia and serious damage to his heart. During his brief four-day stay in the coronary care unit, the condition of his heart continued to degenerate as the pulmonary specialists labored to clear up his lungs. He was conscious for brief moments but could not talk because of ventilator tubes. He could nod his head in answer to my questions and knew that he would not be coming out of this one. He assured me that although he was physically uncomfortable in the present, he was not fearful about the future. He knew he would soon be with his Lord. I prayed often with Dad in those brief four days. Sometimes he was awake while I prayed—often, he wasn't.

I frequently thought about the words of Solomon at the top of this page. Funerals are more instructive than parties, according to the wisest king, for a funeral will cause a man to consider his own end—the end of every man. In Dad's presence I was compelled to consider the end of all men, and my heart was "made better." Eternity was even more real to me, and I saw illustrated in his death what has been the theme of this book.

Every death for the believer—whether a death to self or, as in Dad's case, death to life itself—though it bring momentary sorrow as the believer passes through a brief veil of tears, is but the means of entrance into a fuller possession of Christ. Dad had to die to possess his inheritance in Christ. In the same way, I must die to self to possess more of Christ here. Death is at the heart of the gospel message. The death of God's dear Son paid the fearsome penalty for my sin, provided the power for godly living now, and guaranteed that I shall dwell with Him forever in the future. I was saved by His death and have been called to a paradox: a life of death.

Although I can only imagine the fullness of joy Dad experiences now in the presence of God, I can experience "a foretaste of glory divine"[1] as I repudiate any earthly source of joy and seek it only as a by-product of fellowship with Christ. The thought of heaven is sweeter, not primarily because Dad is there, but because the reality of it was impressed more deeply upon my heart as I watched him step from time to eternity. I sensed as I stood by his bed that the thin veil that separates earthly life from heaven is as temporary and as frail as the curtain that separated Dad's small room from the main floor of the coronary care unit.

I want to get better at dying. I want to struggle less when the challenge to die to something here on earth confronts me. At Dad's bedside I thought much of how exhilarating it must be to stand in the presence of God—entirely complete by the work of His own hands. Oh, how my heart yearned for that Presence! I felt again the impact of the words of Paul, who also longed for his own complete redemption.

> For I reckon that the sufferings of this present time are not worthy to be compared with the glory which shall be revealed in us. For the earnest expectation of the creature waiteth for the manifestation of the sons of God. . . . For we know that the whole creation groaneth and travaileth in pain together until now. And not only they, but ourselves also, which have the firstfruits of the Spirit, even we ourselves groan within ourselves, waiting for the adoption, to wit, the redemption of our body (Rom. 8:18-19, 22-23).

The thought of becoming entirely whole in body and fully restored in spirit to the likeness of Christ makes the thought of dying seem almost trivial. Since Dad's death I have pondered eternal things more often and more deeply, and the thought of dying to anything of earth has indeed come much easier. Truly, "our light affliction, which is but for a moment, worketh for us a far more exceeding and eternal weight of glory; While we look not at the things which are seen, but at the things which are not seen [a life of faith—*beholding* the invisible]: for the things which

---

[1] Fanny Crosby, "Blessed Assurance."

are seen are temporal; but the things which are not seen are eternal" (II Cor. 4:17-18).

While this book has been about how to die well, it has also been about how to behold well. We have all heard someone say, "He is in a better place." Heaven isn't a better place because it is a place of mansions and streets of gold. It is a better place because in it we have a better view—a view of God and of the Lamb, a view unobstructed by the soul's depravity and the body's mortality. My prayer is that God has used this book to stir within you a desire to see the unseen. Biblical change, as you have read from these pages, is the product of *beholding* the glory of God. One day that change will be complete because we will behold Him, unhindered by the limitations of this earthly existence.

John the Apostle spoke of that change when he wrote, "Beloved, now are we the sons of God, and it doth not yet appear what we shall be: but we know that, when he shall appear, *we shall be like him; for we shall see him as he is* (I John 3:2). Paul testified of that change: "Behold, I shew you a mystery; We shall not all sleep, but we shall all be *changed,* In a moment, in the twinkling of an eye, at the last trump: for the trumpet shall sound, and the dead shall be raised incorruptible, and we shall be *changed*" (I Cor. 15:51-52). Our eyes shall behold the bridegroom in all His splendor. As His bride we shall sit down at the marriage feast of the Lamb, who has loved us and bought us with His blood, and as His bride we shall "dwell in the house of the Lord for ever" (Ps. 23:6). What a blessed hope!

In Revelation 22:17 and 20, John the Beloved closes the final chapter of his revelation with the heart cry of the redeemed: "And the Spirit and the bride say, Come. And let him that heareth say, Come. And let him that is athirst come. And whosoever will, let him take the water of life freely." The bridegroom replies, "Surely I come quickly." And all the redeemed join with the apostle in exclaiming, "Amen. Even so, come, Lord Jesus." And we too, who have been beholding Him through a glass darkly, cry out with the hymn writer, "And Lord, haste the day when the faith shall be sight,"[2] when we shall be completely *changed into His image!*

---

[2] Horatio G. Spafford, "It Is Well with My Soul."

REPRODUCIBLE STUDY SHEETS

Five Significant Statements
Take Time to Reflect

Chapter _____

A. Write out five significant statements from this chapter.

1.

_____

_____

_____

_____

_____

2.

_____

_____

_____

_____

_____

3.

_____

_____

_____

_____

4.

_____

_____

_____

_____

5.

_____

_____

_____

_____

B. Write out your answers to the Take Time to Reflect questions for
   this chapter.

_____

_____

_____

_____

_____

_____

_____

_____

_____

_____

_____

_____

_____

_____

_____

Becoming God's Kind of Person

Ephesians 4:17, 22-24—"Walk not as other Gentiles walk, in the vanity of their mind," but

1. *"Put off . . . the old man, which is corrupt according to the deceit-ful lusts"*;

2. "And *be renewed in the spirit of your mind"*;

3. "And . . . *put on the new man,* which after God is created in right-eousness and true holiness."

Instructions

Use the boxes below to help you prayerfully think through a problem that keeps you from being God's kind of person. The verses quoted above outline the biblical process of change.

Step 1: Put off the old man—What thought, action, or habit do you need to eliminate from your life if you are to become like Christ? You will need to identify it and repent of it.	**Step 3: Put on the new man**—What new way of thinking or acting must you now practice with the help of the Holy Spirit if you are to be like Christ?
Step 2: Be renewed in your mind—Write out below the verses that show God's viewpoint about the issues you have identified in Step 1. You must meditate upon them in order to have a renewed mind. See the next page for help on meditating.	

How to Meditate: The MAP Method

Find a portion of Scripture relevant to your problem or find one that deals with a Bible truth you wish to master. Always meditate on Scripture that God's Spirit "highlights" as you are reading His Word.

Memorize the Passage

Memorizing often occurs automatically if the passage is studied intensely enough in the next step. During temptation you must know *exactly* what God has said *word for word*. Merely having a general idea about what is right is not enough when dealing with the deceptive nature of your own heart. A man who cannot remember God's exact words is in danger of leaning on his "own understanding" (Prov. 3:5).

Many people memorize verses by writing the first letter of each word in a verse. For example, Psalm 119:105 says, "Thy word is a lamp unto my feet, and a light unto my path." The first letters are

T w i a l u m f, a a l u m p.

The first letter of each word (include the punctuation just as it appears in the text) gives enough of a prompt so that you can recall the word, but since the whole word is not present, you do not find yourself merely *reading* the words mindlessly.

Analyze the Passage

Study the passage, asking the Holy Spirit to give you a thorough understanding of its message. You can do an *intensive* study of the passage by listing the major words of the verses and then using an English dictionary to find out the meaning for each word. If possible, look up each word in a Greek or Hebrew dictionary or check the meaning of each word in *Strong's Exhaustive Concordance*. Once you are sure of each word's meaning, put the passage in your own words (i.e., paraphrase it). A more *extensive* study would involve using a commentary or a good study Bible to help you understand more about who wrote the passage, to whom it was written, and why it was written. Most important, pray that God will illuminate your understanding. Ask Him to teach you what He wants you to know from the Scriptures.

Personalize the Passage

Plan concrete changes in your life that are consistent with your understanding of the passage. Such plans would include schedules, steps, and details. Ask yourself, "When have I failed to obey this truth in the past? When am I likely to meet a temptation again? What should be the godly response the next time I am tempted?" Think through this "game plan" _thoroughly_ and _in advance_ of the next temptation. Use the passage in a personal prayer to God. For example, a person meditating on James 4:1-11 may begin a prayer this way: "Lord, you tell me here in James 4:1 that the conflict I am having with John is the result of my own lusts—my desires to have something _my_ way. I know that isn't pleasing to You. Instead of responding in anger to John, I need Your help and grace, which You promise in James 4:6 where You say that You resist the proud but give grace to the humble. Help me to humble myself and not to insist on my own way. I want to allow You to lift me up in Your time. . . ."

How God's Attributes Affect Christian Standards[1]

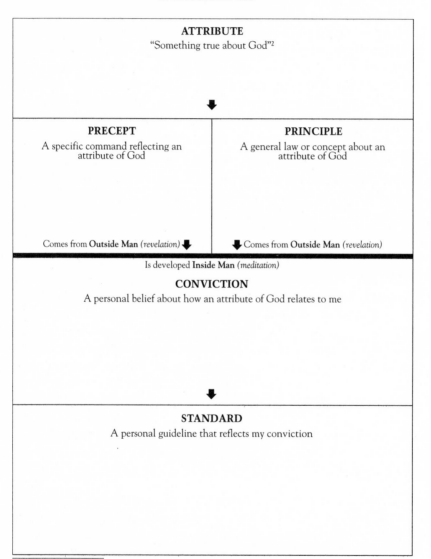

ATTRIBUTE
"Something true about God"[2]

PRECEPT	**PRINCIPLE**
A specific command reflecting an attribute of God	A general law or concept about an attribute of God
Comes from **Outside Man** (*revelation*)	Comes from **Outside Man** (*revelation*)

Is developed **Inside Man** (*meditation*)

CONVICTION
A personal belief about how an attribute of God relates to me

STANDARD
A personal guideline that reflects my conviction

[1] General concepts taken from "Standards vs. Convictions," unpublished outline by Tony Miller. Used by permission.

[2] A. W. Tozer, *The Knowledge of the Holy* (New York: Harper-Collins Publishers, 1961), 19.

Fools by Default

We need to be reminded that becoming wise is not an automatic matter. All of us are born fools (Prov. 22:15) and will continue to become "better" fools unless we submit ourselves to the disciplines of wisdom. The fact that we are *fools by default* should not surprise us if we understand the depravity of man. Neither should it surprise us that unless we take specific measures to counteract that default status, we will progress only to become increasingly useless as servants of God.

Proverbs, the parental training manual for wisdom, goes to great lengths to acquaint us with the ways of the fool so that we can avoid his path and his end. Solomon describes for us three grades of fools in Proverbs 1:22. He says, "How long, ye *simple ones*, will ye love simplicity? and the *scorners* delight in their scorning, and *fools* hate knowledge?"

The Simple Man

The simple man is the budding fool. The word "simple" means "open, wide, and spacious." The simple man is one who is open-minded and, therefore, vulnerable to all kinds of enticement. He has not developed a discriminating judgment about what is right or wrong (1:22; 9:13, 16-18; 14:15). He is gullible to temptation and is naive—not about sin, but about sin's effects on him. Because he is undiscerning, he easily drifts into moral corruption. He is aimless, but his tempters and temptresses are not (1:10 ff.; 7:6 ff.; 22:3). Apart from godly tutelage, he is on the road to death (1:32; 7:7, 27; 22:3). If he refuses to learn, he will graduate to a fool (14:18). In the end, along with the other types of fools, he will be judged because he has rejected God's wisdom and discipline (1:22-25, 32).

The Fool

The fool is the common, ordinary, generic, garden-variety fool. The word "fool" means "dullard" or "one who is obstinate." He is slow, but not in mental capacity. He is slow in his willingness to obey and has an inclination to make wrong decisions because of his stubbornness.

Proverbs describes him as self-confident (12:15; 14:3, 16; 18:2; 26:12; 28:26), unreliable (26:6), and a grief to his parents (15:20; 17:21). He is restless (17:24; 20:3), deceptive (10:18; 14:8; 17:7), resentful of correction (15:5; 17:10), and unteachable (1:7, 22; 13:19; 17:10; 18:2; 23:9;

26:11; 27:22). He does not prepare his heart for wisdom (17:16), often appears illogical (26:7, 9), and delights to speak of evil (12:23; 15:2, 14; 19:1). In addition, he makes light of sin (14:9), slanders others (10:18), is known as a mischief maker (10:23; 26:18-19), has an anger problem (12:16; 14:16; 27:3; 29:11), and will eventually fall (1:32; 3:35; 10:8, 10; 11:29).

A young person who is weak in discernment exhibits characteristics of the *simple man*. He seems easily swayed by peers and seems to end up in trouble unintentionally. These characteristics should certainly raise concerns on the part of his parents and leaders. There is much that can be done to counter his simple-mindedness, as the chart on the next page points out. The concern should escalate greatly, however, if his life is moving from this state of impressionableness to a state of stubbornness. If he now *defends* his actions and *deceives* others to cover his actions, he is fast becoming a *common fool*. If those actions and attitudes become his lifestyle, parents should have serious doubts about whether he knows Christ as his Savior. There is yet another level of fool, however.

The Scorner

The scorner is a deliberate, mean-spirited troublemaker. He is not content to be evil himself but is bent on corrupting others. He rejects rebuke (13:1), hates those who correct him (15:12), mocks justice (19:28), and enjoys despising good (1:22). He is hotheaded and arrogant (21:24) and is, therefore, odious to society (24:9; 29:8).

Satan, himself, is the master scorner—the ultimate fool. He was characterized by Jesus as destructive (i.e., a murderer) and a deceiver (John 8:44). Those two characteristics are dominant elements in this fool's life. He is becoming conformed more and more to the image of his master, Satan.

The progression of evil in these classes of men and Proverbs' instruction about how to deal with each one can be summarized in the chart on the next page.

	THE SIMPLE MAN (THE BUDDING FOOL)	THE FOOL (THE COMMON FOOL)	THE SCORNER (THE FULL-BLOWN FOOL)
CHARACTERISTICS	• Unguarded • Defenseless • Weak • Impressionable	• Unrestrained • Disobedient • Stubborn • Involved (in evil)	• Uncontrollable • Devilish • Mean • Incorrigible
METHODS OF CORRECTION	• Appeal to him about the consequences of his actions (8:5-7; 9:1, 4, 6). • Strike the scorner, and the simple will be warned (19:25; 21:11).	• Appeal to him about the consequences of his actions (8:5-7). • Rebuke him (26:5) but don't debate with him (23:9; 26:4; 29:9). • Restrain him (7:22). • Punish him (19:29; 26:3). • Don't honor him (24:7; 26:1, 8). • Avoid his companionship (13:20; 14:7)	• Punish him (19:25; 21:11). • Give him strong judgments (19:29). • Expel him/cast him out (22:10). • Expect God to mock him (3:34).

Remember, the measure of how much a fool a man remains is determined by his *response* to instruction and correction (wisdom's teaching methods). A man who has no heart for them will remain a fool (1:7; 12:15; 13:1; 14:16; 15:5; 17:10; 23:9; 28:26). We are fools by default and can be wise only on purpose.

God's Love Versus Self-Love

"Just two choices on the shelf—loving God or loving self."[3]
I Corinthians 13

GOD'S LOVE	SELF-LOVE
1. *suffereth long* (v. 4)—**sacrificing self** to wait for God's way and timing; is patient; has the divine power to wait; is long-fused; doesn't retaliate even when it has the power; gives to others not what they deserve but what God gave us!	1. desires own way and own timing; suffers if can't have its way *now!*; is impatient; resents any departure from own schedule; won't wait for God to work; snaps at people. "I want it this way, and I want it *now!*" "I will teach him a lesson he won't soon forget!"
2. *is kind* (v. 4)—**sacrificing self** to meet others' needs; has passion to be active and useful in the lives of others; is kind in words and deeds; does the unexpected, undeserved, and unrewarded.	2. is nasty and hurtful in words and deeds; acts in favor of "me" instead of others; always puts conditions on others' love. "Why should I do that for them? They didn't do it for me." "Others? It's all I can do to keep up with *my* wants and needs."
3. *envieth not* (v. 4)—**sacrificing self** to cheer for or weep with others; does not "boil, seethe, stew"; is content with God's control; doesn't compare for the purpose of looking "down on" or "up to."	3. is envious; boils, seethes; laughs when others weep; weeps when others laugh; resents and wants what others have; wants to be what others are; is displeased by prosperity of others; judges others' worthiness by comparing it with his own. "It's not fair! I should have that."
4. *vaunteth not itself, is not puffed up* (v. 4)—**sacrificing self** to remain small; doesn't "parade to gain applause"; is not proud; points to God, not self; doesn't brag or boast; doesn't inflate self.	4. is proud; a "windbag"; praises self; will become anything so others will notice; brags; attempts to impress others; tries to appear to be what he is not; never admits he is wrong; is mad when others are too selfish to notice; points to what he's accomplished. "Hey! Look at me!"
5. *doth not behave itself unseemly* (v. 5)—**sacrificing self** by being a lady or gentleman; doesn't present the love of God in an ugly, misshapen way; is proper and courteous; does the right thing at the right time.	5. is rude, crude, boorish; draws attention to self by being loud, silly, moody, harsh, or having poor manners, inappropriate actions, words, timing; giving too much attention to fashion (fads) or appearance (flashy or dowdy). "I can't help it. That's just the way I am." "I do what I want when I want to do it."

---

[3] Chart by Ken Collier, THE WILDS Christian Association. Used by permission.

6. *seeketh not her own* (v. 5)—**sacrificing self** by not demanding rights; is not selfish; is a servant; *gives*; is not grasping for "my rights, my time, my money, my comfort, my things" (Rom. 12:10; Phil. 2:3).	6. is selfish; rejects God's way for own way; seeks to please self. "I demand my rights." "I am right!" "I want my way!" "What I want is more important than what you want!" "It's my _____; I'll do what I want with it."
7. *is not easily provoked* (v. 5)— **sacrificing self** to be calm; is not soon angry for its own causes; is not oversensitive and touchy (Heb. 10:24).	7. explodes; is an earthquake in the spirit; reacts in anger instead of acting in kindness; retaliates; is given to sudden outbursts; is angry for selfish reasons. "You can't do that to me and get away with it" (Prov. 13:10).
8. *thinketh no evil* (v. 5)—**sacrificing self** by not keeping score; is not jealous; does not take permanent account of something for the purpose of bringing it back up; believes the best about a person; gives the benefit of doubt; forgives.	8. uses "indelible ink"; builds a case for evil; enters wrongs into a ledger so that they can't be forgotten; jealous; thinks evil; won't forgive and go on. "I remember when he . . ." "You always/never do that." "I haven't forgotten what you did to me!" "I know what kind of person he is." "I know what he meant when he said/did that!"
9. *rejoiceth not in iniquity, but rejoiceth in the truth* (v. 6)—**sacrificing self** to love what God loves and hate what God hates; is excited to do the biblical thing; doesn't take iniquity by the hand and escort it into some other area of life. "If God likes it, I'll like it. If God hates it, I'll hate it."	9. rejoices in iniquity; entertains sin; escorts it right into his life; gets a thrill out of sin—his own or someone else's. "It's my life; I'll do it if I want to. I'm strong enough to handle it." "It's my body; I deserve a little pleasure!" "Did you hear about what ___ did?"
10. *beareth all things* (v. 7)—**sacrificing self** to cover others' weaknesses; covers, supports, protects; covers anything it can righteously cover; bears, not bares.	10. uncovers and exposes someone's sin to others unnecessarily; bares, doesn't bear sin. "I don't mean to gossip, but . . ." "Did you hear about ___? She did a terrible thing! Don't tell anyone, but it's a fact that . . ." "Well, my wife/husband has her/his faults too!"
11. *believeth all things* (v. 7)—**sacrificing self** to believe the best about God and others; puts the best interpretation on events; believes in the best outcome; doesn't look to condemn; looks to save, not to judge.	11. wants to judge; condemns; plays up the doubts; believes the worst; is cynical, suspicious. "I told you he was no good!" "I know what he's thinking." "I know why he did that!" "So what do you want from me this time?" "He said he would change once before, but . . ."
12. *hopeth all things* (v. 7)—**sacrificing self** by not giving up; anticipates a good outcome when God's truth wins out; hopes in every situation, against all evidence; confronts people with the truth in the hope that they will obey and change. As long as God's grace operates, failure is never final.	12. acts hopeless; talks hopeless; feels hopeless; gives up; quits praying; doesn't trust God or follow His way. "He's hopeless." "Why try? He'll never change!" "That's just the way I am. I'll never change!"

305   From *Changed into His Image* by Jim Berg

13. *endureth all things* (v. 7)—**sacrificing self** by staying put when feeling like quitting; bears all things at all costs; digs a trench and stays put; stays when feels like running.	13. Quits. "I've tried, but that was the straw that broke the camel's back." "I'm not sticking my neck out there again so he can chop it off!" "I'll cut and run while I still have some dignity." "I can't handle it anymore!" "You wouldn't be able to handle it either if you were in my shoes!"
14. *Love never faileth* (v. 8)—It always accomplishes God's work on earth and in heaven. It is *supernatural* in its origin and its results.	14. *Self-love always fails!* (Gal. 6:7-9)—"He that soweth to his flesh shall of the flesh reap corruption."

RATE YOUR EXAMPLE (I Timothy 4:12)	Consistently True	Generally True	Occasionally True	Seldom True
My example in "word"				
Do I seem to know when and how to approach problems (tactful, sensitive)?				
Do I effectively challenge others to fulfill their responsibilities?				
Do I refrain from unwholesome conversation (gossip, griping, off-color remarks)?				
My example in "conversation" (lifestyle)				
Do I seem to be free from a preoccupation with material things (not greedy, not worldly)?				
Am I attentive to small, personal details (cleanliness, punctuality, manners)?				
Do I live for others instead of using my time to pursue my own interests (recreation, hobbies, television, etc.)?				
My example in "charity"				
Do I make time for others—to listen to them, to be with them?				
Do I show concern for the disappointments and needs of others (compassionate)?				
Do I genuinely serve others rather than use and manipulate them?				
My example in "spirit"				
Do I stay calm and stable under pressure and stress (not quickly angered or discouraged)?				
Do I possess a sense of humor that makes me pleasant company but does not belittle others?				
Do I patiently listen before giving advice and taking action?				
My example in "faith"				
Do I seem content with my present circumstances (not bitter, resentful, discontent)?				
Do I make my spiritual life a priority (setting aside time for personal devotions and church attendance)?				
Do I freely share with others what God is speaking to me about?				
Do I pray with them?				
My example in "purity"				
Is my speech free from sensual, crude, or vulgar words?				
Are my entertainment choices (reading, viewing, and listening) free from sensuality and worldliness?				
Do I tactfully but decidedly address the sensual and worldly elements I see in my friends?				

APPENDIX B
SUPPLEMENTAL ARTICLES

Union with Christ: The Ground of Sanctification[1]

by Michael P. V. Barrett

Natural reasoning always perverts the truth. Paul's exposition of justification by faith on the merits of Jesus Christ raised the absurd question "Shall we continue in sin, that grace may abound?" (Rom. 6:1). With forceful language, the apostle expressed his denial of that perverted reasoning. Being justified freely by grace demands purity and holiness in life. Receiving Christ's gracious deliverance from sin's penalty and guilt in order to remain in sin's power and domination is as illogical as it is perverse. Throughout his epistles, Paul exhorts converts to be holy because the gospel applied to the heart not only rescues the soul from condemnation but also inclines the soul in the direction of righteousness. Paul's argument for Christian holiness based on the application of the gospel is nowhere more compelling than in Romans 6.

Just as the atoning work of Christ is the ground of the sinner's justification, so is it the ground for the saint's sanctification. Justification has fixed the Christian's legal position and standing before God. In Christ, the believer stands before God as holy as Jesus Christ Himself. This is imputed righteousness. Sanctification is the believer's becoming in experience what the grace of the gospel has purposed him to be. Sanctifying grace enables the Christian to live piously—to live in the reality of what he is in Christ. This is imparted righteousness. Whereas justification is a single legal act or declaration of God, sanctification is a continuing work of God that progressively matures during the lifetime of every justified saint. Theologically, it is imperative to maintain the distinction between justification and sanctification. Practically, it is imperative to demonstrate the inseparable connection between the two truths. Sanctification flows necessarily from justification. Paul links these two aspects of salvation by demonstrating how the sacrifice of Christ is the ground for each.

---

[1]Stewart Custer, ed., *Biblical Viewpoint*, vol. 22, no. 1 (Greenville, S.C.: Bob Jones University, 1988), 30-36.

While most Christians agree that holiness should mark the life, there are differing views concerning how to achieve that holiness. Unfortunately, many of the suggestions for obtaining victory over sin are based on psychological tricks to increase personal resolve and determination to win over temptation. Efforts in sanctification that are founded on personal resolve and will power are doomed to failure and frustration. It is imperative to return to the biblical theology of sanctification. Romans 6 reveals this important theology. Paul essentially argues that right thinking about the gospel produces right living. His order of reasoning is clear. First, there must be a knowing of certain truths by experience (6:3, 6). Second, there must be a reckoning of those truths by faith (6:11). Third, there must be a doing of the truths by obedience (6:13). This order cannot be successfully altered. The key truth that gives motion to sanctification is the believer's union with Jesus Christ.

The Fact of the Union with Christ (6:3, 4)

There is no chance for holiness apart from spiritual union with Jesus Christ. This truth marks an essential difference between biblical Christianity and every other religion. Whereas in natural religion men try to live holy lives in order to get to God, in true Christianity men live holy lives after God has gotten to them.

Paul first expresses the believer's union with Christ in terms of baptism. He asks the Roman Christians whether they were ignorant of the nature and design of baptism. His reference must be to spiritual baptism, for no amount of water can effect the spiritual union that this passage describes. To see this as water baptism is to see baptismal regeneration, and no orthodox view of baptism tolerates the notion of saving grace in association with the act of the church ordinance. Rather, the apostle refers to that gracious act of the Holy Spirit where we are "all baptized into one body," the body of Christ (see I Cor. 12:13). The basic significance of this spiritual act is that it creates a vital, intimate union with the Savior Himself. Although the mechanics of this union remain an inexplicable mystery to the finite mind, it is nonetheless a real union. The implications of this union boggle the mind and would be unbelievable if they were not the authoritative assertions of God Himself. God's Word declares that the believer's acceptance by God is "in the beloved" (Eph. 1:6). The believer is positioned in Christ by an inseparable union. This position with Christ is so certain that the believer is blessed "with all spiritual blessings in heavenly places in Christ" (Eph. 1:3). United with Christ, the believer is where Christ is.

In this text Paul emphasizes that the believer is united to the death of Christ. When Christ died, the believer died in Him. Every believer, therefore, partakes of all the benefits that Christ accomplished by His atoning death. Christ purchased the believer's justification, adoption, assurance of divine forgiveness, peace, joy, and eternal life; and the list of benefits for both this life and the life to come goes on. This passage reveals that the Christian's holiness or sanctification was one of the benefits accomplished by Christ's death. Indeed, Christ gave Himself for the church "that he might present it to himself a glorious church . . . holy and without blemish" (Eph. 5:27).

Having stated the reality of union with Christ (verse 3), Paul reflects on the consequences of that union (verse 4). This spiritual baptism effected a burial with Christ. In the physical realm, burial is the means to dispose of the old corpse, to remove it from the presence of the living. It effects a separation. In the spiritual realm, burial with Christ involves a separation from the world, the kingdom of Satan. Although living in the world, the Christian is not of the world. Life in Christ demands and enables separation from the world (see I John 2:15-17). One aspect of sanctification is dying more and more to sin, living separate from evil. Once the Christian was dead in sin; now he must be dead to sin by virtue of his association with Christ.

The consequence of death and burial with Christ is life. Christ, having died, rose again. His resurrection was the certain and necessary consequence of His atoning death. Similarly, a new and holy life is the certain and necessary consequence of the believer's dying with Him. Newness of life is a reality in Christ. That is a fact. Sanctification is nothing more than living in the reality of what we have in Christ.

The Design of Union with Christ (6:5-7)

In verses 5-7 Paul confirms and expands his preceding thoughts by revealing the design of union with Christ. Sharing in Christ's death means sharing in Christ's victory and life. Verse 5 defines the condition of the Christian: "If we have been planted together in the likeness of his death." The apostle's language in stating the believer's condition is significant. By using the simple condition formula, Paul assumes the reality of the protasis or "if clause." By substituting the word "since" for "if," the force of this construction is more evident. It is an established fact that the believer has been planted with Christ in His death. Planting is a new image that Paul uses to describe the nature of union with Christ. The word has the idea of a common origin, things that are born or produced at the same time, things that grow together. The perfect tense of the verb used in the protasis suggests that this planting was instantaneous and final with results that continue. Being well rooted in Christ produces an inevitable experience. The apodosis or "then clause" defines what that continuing, inevitable experience is. Since the believer is planted with Christ in His death, he will be "of the resurrection." The future tense that occurs in the apodosis is a future of obligation; it refers not simply to what will happen, but what must happen. There is a certainty of sequence between the protasis and the apodosis. Because the one is true, the other is absolutely certain. Christ's death and resurrection secured for every believer a necessary and certain life. That life involves not only escape from sin's penalty but also cleansing from sin's guilt, power, and pollution.

The design of this union with Christ's resurrection relates to sanctification and is specifically stated in verse 6, where Paul remarks on the knowledge of the Christian. The word for "knowing" involves more than merely head knowledge or creedal affirmation; it refers to a personal experience of gospel truths. There must be a vital experience of the old man's crucifixion with Christ. The old man designates the old depraved nature that is thoroughly corrupted with sin. Union with Christ involved a joint crucifixion of the Savior and the believer's sin. Indeed, to pay the penalty of this sin was the reason Christ died. Having established the experiential association between "our old man" and Christ's crucifixion, Paul uses two different purpose formulas to show the design of the union. First, the union was in order to destroy the body of sin. This sinful body most likely is synonymous with the old man. The old man was crucified in order to destroy itself with all its corruption. Second, the union and destruction of the old man was in order that the believer might not be servant to sin. To live free from sin is to fulfill the purpose of salvation. This second stated purpose is the practical evidence of the theology of the first stated purpose. Because of Christ's death, the Christian is no longer in bondage to sin. Outside of Christ the sinner is in slavery to sin, a state of misery and bondage from which he cannot free himself. Sin is a terrible master that has sufficient power to coerce and control in spite of the sinner's best intentions or efforts. But in Christ are the basis and reason for and only hope of victory over sin's dominion. Because Christ destroyed sin's dominion by His death and because the believer was united to that death, it is illogical that the believer should continue under sin's control.

In verse 7 Paul summarizes the result of this union for the Christian: for the one who died has been justified from sin. Judicially, union with Christ's death frees the believer from sin's penalty. Subjectively, union with Christ's death frees the believer from sin's power. Prophetically, union with Christ's death will free the believer from sin's presence. This mystical union effects a radical change. To be in Christ is to be free, to "be free indeed" (John 8:36). Freedom in Christ is freedom to be and do what outside of Christ was impossible. To live under sin's control is to fail to use the freedom that Christ has purchased by His atoning death. Freedom from sin is not just a possibility; it is a reality in Christ. To understand this is to understand the basis of sanctification.

The Application of Union with Christ (6:8-14)

All theology has application. God never reveals truth just to satisfy man's curiosity or answer his reason. Theology must make its way from the head to the heart and then to practice, or it has been abused. Conversely, there can be no proper Christian practice unless there is a theological basis. Realizing the vital connection between doctrine and duty, Paul applies the theology of union with Christ to the experience of the everyday conflicts with sin. In theory, the Christian has victory over sin. In practice, how is that victory to be experienced?

The link between theology and practice is faith. Twice in verses 8-14 the apostle uses the vocabulary of faith to give impetus to his practical instructions. First, he uses the word "believe" (v. 8). Once again Paul uses a simple condition to assume the reality of the protasis in this conditional sentence. Since it is a fact that we died with Christ, we are constantly believing (present tense) that we will live with Him. This faith rests firmly on Christ. The value of faith is always determined by the object of faith. Just as Christ is the object of justifying faith, so must He be the object of sanctifying faith. Sanctification does not progress because of self-determination or will power; it progresses as Christ and the benefits of His sacrifice are appropriated by faith. In verses 9 and 10 Paul demonstrates the sensibility of such faith in Christ by directing attention to facts about the Savior's death and resurrection. He describes the permanent life of the risen Christ to show that the Christian's new life must be permanently free from sin's domination. Believing that there is victorious life in Christ is not just wishful thinking; it is reality.

Second, he uses the word "reckon" (v. 11). This word means to consider or regard something as being true. This word emphasizes the vital appropriation of what is believed. It is one thing to believe something to be generally true; it is another thing to regard it as personally true. What the Christian is to reckon is the same thing he is to believe: deadness to sin through union with Christ. This is the doctrine that Paul had set forth in the opening verses of the chapter. It is true; therefore, the believer must acknowledge the personal relevance of the truth. The Christian must consider himself to be in experience what he is positionally and legally in Christ. The believer must never lose sight or thought of what he is and what he has in the Lord Jesus Christ. It is noteworthy that this word "reckon" occurs also in connection with the doctrine of justification (see Rom. 4:3-4). However, in justification God is the subject of the verb. He looks at the merits of Christ's atonement and considers the sinner who believes in Christ to be legally free from sin. In sanctification, the saint looks at the same merits of Christ's atonement and considers himself to be experientially free from sin. Faith is the victory because faith lays hold of Christ.

Knowing the truth and believing the truth lead to doing the truth. In verses 12-14 Paul issues the imperatives not to let sin rule and not to yield to sin's domination. Unfortunately, many interpreters begin their explanation of sanctification with the imperatives of verses 12 and 13. To tell anyone not to sin without explaining where the ability not to sin comes from can only breed failure and discouragement in the efforts toward holiness. It must be emphasized that successful obedience to these commands is possible only because of what Christ has done and because of the inseparable union that Christ has with His people.

Although victory over sin is possible because the atonement defeated sin and Satan, the Christian nonetheless has to do his part in realizing victory. The believer is not passive in sanctification; indeed, he cooperates with God as he continually dies to sin and lives to righteousness. The Christian's responsibility in sanctification is essentially twofold. On the one hand, he is to refuse submission to sin. In verse 12 Paul gives the admonition that sin should not so reign that we would obey its lusts. The word "lust" refers to those cravings and desires generated by sin. To allow these sinful inclinations to dominate and direct the life is contrary to God's desire for our conformity to Christ. Believers must resist sin's rule. In verse 13 Paul continues this aspect by commanding Christians not to yield themselves to become agents for unrighteousness. This word "yield" simply means to put at someone's disposal. To put self at sin's disposal is nothing more than surrendering to sin's domination. To surrender to sin's persistent domination is to become a traitor. "No surrender to sin" must be the Christian's battle cry. The tense of this prohibition is significant; it is the present imperative, which in prohibition requires the ceasing of an act assumed to be in progress. "Stop surrendering to sin!" The very grammar of the text conforms to daily experience. Every Christian knows well that the conflict against sin rages constantly. One victory over sin's temptations leads only to the next temptation. In daily experience, the one united to Christ's triumphant death can never let the guard down.

On the other hand, the Christian is to submit to God. This is the positive element in sanctification: living unto righteousness. Paul uses the same word "yield" to refer to this positive aspect. Every Christian is to place himself at God's disposal, to surrender to God and the cause of righteousness. Whereas Paul used the present tense to express the prohibition against yielding to sin, he uses the aorist imperative to command allegiance to God. The use of the aorist does not preclude the idea of a continual yielding, but it emphasizes the urgency and necessity of the action. This is the proper course of action for those who are alive from the dead. Regeneration has given the Christian a new nature, a new inclination, a new power. It is by virtue of this resurrection power that willing submission to God and willing rejection of sin are possible.

Paul concludes this section with the explicit declaration that sin will "not have dominion" (v. 14). The Greek word for "have dominion" is the verb form of the root meaning "lord" or "master." Christ's people are free from sin's lordship because they are under grace and not law. Paul is not inserting here a dispensational observation about the church age; he is making an observation that is vitally necessary for victory over sin. The word law does not refer here to the Mosaic era or the Old Testament at all; it designates, rather, the principle of doing. This statement of being under grace and not law parallels Paul's question to the foolish Galatians:

"Having begun in the Spirit, are ye now made perfect by the flesh?" (Gal. 3:3). It is impossible to achieve victory over sin merely by striving to do things. All of salvation is by grace. Sanctification is God's gracious working just as justification is God's gracious act. Too often Christians today behave like the Galatians of Paul's day. They realize that they come into salvation by grace through faith in Christ. But for whatever reason, they attempt to live the Christian life by self-power without reference to the grace of the gospel. Paul reminds such as these of the grace of God, which in this entire context finds expression in the atoning sacrifice of Christ. Paul's instructions concerning sanctification can be reduced to this: "Do not go beyond the cross." When temptations come, we should consciously direct our thinking to the cross of Christ and what He accomplished for us. It is impossible to yield to sin while at the same moment placing ourselves at the disposal of God. Right thinking about the gospel will result in right behavior. To forget about the gospel in the daily battle against sin is to enter the conflict unarmed. We stand little chance against sin by ourselves. Lewis Jones, the hymn writer, reflected well Paul's theology of sanctification: "Would you o'er evil a victory win? There's wonderful pow'r in the blood."

Sanctification is not a divine "zap" that automatically makes the believer irreversibly holy. It is a lifelong battle that requires the saint to lay hold by faith of the victory that Christ has accomplished on the cross and actively enjoy that victory by living as though it is really true. The Christian's daily battle with sin is much like ancient Israel's conquest of the Promised Land. Over and again God told the people to possess the land because He had driven out the Canaanites from before them. Although God had won the victory, the Israelites had to cross the Jordan and fight the Canaanites in deadly battle. The Canaanites did not roll over and play dead or pack their bags and leave voluntarily just because Israel entered the land; they fought for their land. The Canaanites were naturally stronger than the Israelites, and the Israelites stood little chance against them in their own strength. But, believing God had given them victory, they entered and fought in the light of that certain victory. Similarly, Christ has already achieved our victory over sin. But sin does not disappear from us just because we are saved. It does not give up its territory without a fight. If we attempt to fight by ourselves, defeat is certain because sin is much stronger than we. But if we enter the conflict claiming Christ's victory and our part in it, sin and Satan must flee from us.

Basics for Angry Believers[2]

"He's So Mad He Can't See Straight!"

"Mom, I'm not sure that Jason should drive! I know he's sixteen and is legally eligible, but he'll kill someone the way he drives when he's angry. He just now squealed his tires backing out of the driveway and almost hit the mail truck."

"I know, Amy. He's mad because your father won't let him spend the weekend at the beach with the Robinsons. I'm really afraid for him. He gets so mad he can't see straight!"

How can Jason's parents help him with his anger? Jason himself has admitted that he sees a need to control his temper. Whenever he makes an effort to restrain himself, however, something else comes up, and he blows up again. It seems impossible to him, and he has quit trying.

If you are like Jason or are trying to help someone who is, you need to understand some basics about the causes of and solutions to anger.

One-Word Descriptions of Anger

Anger is by definition a strong emotion of *displeasure*. Many things happen daily that displease us—a shoelace breaks, our child loses his lunch money, the car breaks down, the boss refuses a proposal—and the list goes on.

We all experience events like these regularly. We do not necessarily respond with anger unless the event highly displeases us. We experience a high level of displeasure when we attach a high level of significance to the event. Something becomes significant when the event happens repeatedly—a child loses his lunch money *again*—or when the event involves something that is extremely important to us—like getting the boss's approval on a proposal. When we are *highly* displeased, for whatever reason, we are angry.

Second, anger is a statement of a *demand*. We feel that the event that displeases us must be corrected before we will be satisfied.

---

[2]The Basics for Believers chapters in Appendix B are available as individual pamphlets from the Bob Jones University Campus Store, Greenville, South Carolina.

Third, anger is a *destroyer* of something—the event (or person) that displeases us. It is an emotion that demands change. The angry person is declaring (often with red face, stomping foot, and slammed door), "I am highly displeased and I demand that things change!"

Except for the stomping foot and the slammed door, nothing yet mentioned has to be sinful. Jesus himself was highly *displeased* when He found the moneychangers in the temple (Mark 11:15-19). He *demanded* that His Father's house be used for worship, not for extortion. He went on to *destroy* the business of the merchants who were violating His Father's intentions.

Here then is an important principle. Anger can be righteous when the displeasure is aimed at the same things that God is displeased with, when it makes the same demands that God makes, and when it sets out to destroy (change) those things that God opposes. Most anger is sinful anger, however, because we are concerned about our own interests—not God's.

The fourth element of anger is a result of man's sinful anger only. Sinful anger causes *distortion*. Jason's mother was right when she said, "He gets so mad he can't see straight!" Sinful anger never sees the whole picture (as God sees it) and, therefore, draws the wrong conclusions and responds in the wrong way.

Three Common Causes of Anger

Numbers 20:1-13 gives a detailed account of an angry man. Moses is angry, first, because he is *frustrated*. Frustration is the result of thwarted goals. Moses has put up with this whining, complaining people for years now and, frankly, is tired of their carnal spirit.

He is also *hurt*. They accuse him of bringing them into the wilderness to kill them. The truth is that Moses has spared them from God's wrath (Exod. 32:7-14) by putting his own life on the line. If he had wanted them out of the way, he could have let God destroy them earlier. Naturally, their accusations hurt.

Third, Moses is probably *afraid*. The last time the children of Israel did not have water, they came at him with stones to murder him (Exod. 17:1-4).

All three of these elements (frustration, hurt, and fear) displease us. None of us like to have our goals thwarted. We are displeased when someone hurts us, and we tend to avoid situations where we are put into a vulnerable position (fear). When we experience strong displeasure because of any of these three elements, we become angry.

Four Common Distortions Caused by Anger

Sinful anger distorts something. In Moses' case, it distorted his *conversation* (Num. 20:10). He said in effect, "Do we have to do everything for you?" That is sarcasm. It belittles the other person. Sarcasm comes from the Greek word *sarx*, which means "flesh." Sarcasm means "to tear flesh." It would be included in the "corrupt [destructive] communication" (Eph. 4:29-30) that grieves God's Spirit. God tells us in Psalm 106:32-33 that He was not pleased with the way Moses talked to the people in his anger. As in Moses' case, our anger often shows up first in our conversation.

Anger distorts a man's *concept of himself*. He thinks his way of doing and seeing things is the only way. He has an inflated view of himself (Rom. 12:3).

His *concept of others* is also distorted. Sarcastic, cutting words are destructive. People destroy only those things that have no value to them. They throw out the trash because they have no use for it anymore. An angry man "cuts" into people because they have no value to him. His anger shows his selfish concern for himself and his contempt for others.

Finally, Moses' angry response shows how easily the *commands of God* can become distorted. Moses did not carry out God's instructions; he was so mad he could not see straight. Instead of following God's simple command to speak to the rock, he struck it in anger.

Expressions of Anger

Not everyone expresses his anger in the same way. Jason's anger was readily evident. He squealed his tires when he left the driveway. He "blew up" when he was angry. Other people keep their feelings of strong displeasure inside where they do destructive things to their bodies. We say these people "clam up."

While "clamming up" is generally less destructive to those around us, it is destructive to the angry person himself. Unless the energy of anger is aimed at the right things (those things at which God is angry) and for the right reason (God's reputation and rights), we are dealing with sinful anger. Sinful anger is wrong whether it is expressed externally or restrained internally. The energy that sinful anger produces will be destructive to something or someone.

The solution then is not to get better at controlling how and when we "blow up" or "clam up." The solution is to gain God's perspective about those things that displease us in the first place. Things that displease God should displease us. If they do not make God angry, then we need to renew our minds about them so that we do not respond in anger either. You should not merely "learn to control your anger." You should gain God's perspective about life and its events so that you can respond the way God responds. To change your perspective you must be "transformed [changed] by the renewing of your mind" (Rom. 12:2).

The Heart of the Issue
Did you notice in the account of Moses' anger in Numbers 20:1-13 that God did not reprimand Moses for his anger? When God rebuked Moses, He rebuked him for his unbelief! God said, "Ye believed me not, to sanctify me in the eyes of the children of Israel" (v. 12). To "sanctify," God means to "set Him apart as special."

Isn't that interesting? God is showing us that behind all sinful manifestations of anger are unbelief and failure to see Him as the most important element in the whole picture. He said to Moses, "Moses, you don't see the whole picture, do you? You don't really believe I'm involved in all this! You have gone ahead and handled this your way instead of using this opportunity to show My people My ways and My power. Because of your actions, these people haven't seen Me at all! All they have seen is your emotional outburst and your disobedience to Me."

You see, Moses really did know better. The last time they did not have water (Exod. 17:2), he had told the people, in effect, "Why do you come to me? Your argument is with God. And since He is the solution to your problem, why do you dishonor Him with your critical, complaining spirits?" In this earlier situation, Moses had seen the "big picture." He had used their lack of water to point out the defects in their spiritual lives and to show them that God was their only hope. He had also showed them that their murmuring was a sign of their unbelief (Exod. 17:7) and rebellion.

Please understand, then, that *the biggest obstacle to properly dealing with your anger will be your failure to believe that God's way of handling your problems is, indeed, the best way.* When we are angry, our position seems justified and our perspective seems right because carnal pride is at the heart of sinful anger.

You will probably react one of two ways to what you have just read. Either you will be relieved to know there is a way to begin dealing with your problem, and you will start working on it God's way. Or your pride will strongly react to what you have read, and you will be upset (even angry) that you are the one who has to change something. You will continue to focus on the other person or events and insist that they change. It is that stubbornness, rather than anything that has happened to you, that will keep you enslaved to your habit of anger. If you demand that something or someone else change and refuse to accept God's loving and sovereign choices for you, you will remain an angry person. There is great hope for you, however, if you are willing to face the issues from God's perspective and allow God to change you through His Word.

Where Do I Start?

First, you have to identify what things in your life are producing your displeasure. Remember the causes of anger?

You can start a systematic search by listing events, circumstances, and people in your life that fit under the main causes of anger. To begin, fill in the blanks on the next page.

323

FRUSTRATION
What things in your life (past and present) continue to frustrate you?

_____

_____

_____

_____

_____

HURT
Next, what things in your life (past and present) continue to make you hurt?

_____

_____

_____

_____

_____

FEAR
Finally, what things (past and present) continue to make you fearful because they put you into a vulnerable position?

_____

_____

_____

_____

_____

What Do I Do Next?
Dealing with anger biblically involves gaining God's perspective on each of the issues you have listed above under the three main causes of anger. "Renewing the mind" is a major part of any biblical change (see Rom. 12:2, Eph. 4:22-24, Col. 3:8-10, and James 1:21-22). Change does not come by merely seeing where we need to change and then deciding that we will "do better" in the future. No permanent change takes place

without our meditating on God's own words and then humbly depending on Him for the enablement to obey them.

For example, gaining God's perspective about those things that frustrate us means accepting God's sovereign control, learning how He says we can have contentment, and probably dealing with self-centeredness.

To address those things that hurt us includes learning God's perspective about suffering and hardship (see the Psalms, II Corinthians, I Peter, II Peter, and James). We may also need to forgive someone and learn how to overcome evil with good (Rom. 12:14-21).

Handling fear biblically means letting God have loving and sovereign control over our lives. First John 4:18 teaches that our understanding of God's perfect love for us is essential to facing our fears. Studying how Abraham, Joseph, Daniel, David, Paul, and others faced fearful events will be crucial in gaining a biblical perspective.

God reminds us in I Corinthians 10:13 that no problem is unique. Others have made it, and so can you. With God's help Jason can change his angry ways, and so can any of us who will look at life from God's perspective.

Basics for Depressed Believers

A Depression in the Making

For several weeks, Carol had noticed that Susan had been less talkative and less willing to do things they usually did together. When she asked Susan about her mood, Susan said that life did not seem worth the effort since her parents' divorce. Carol tried to encourage her friend, but she felt her words were not getting through. Then one evening Susan called and told Carol she wanted to "end it all." Alarmed, Carol begged her to get some help.

Susan's emotions are clearly toward the low end of the negative-feelings spectrum, but all of us feel "down" at times. Negative feelings may range from mild disappointment to normal discouragement to serious depression like Susan's.

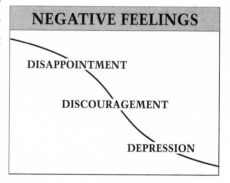

If we are to understand depression—the most extreme "down times"—we need to look at its causes. Once we see the dynamics involved, we can seek a biblical solution.

Sometimes Our Bodies Hinder Us

Depression is *occasionally* the result of a bodily malfunction: a thyroid condition, certain infections, unstable hormonal activity, reaction to a medication, and so forth. If depression persists, a physician should be consulted in order to diagnose and treat any genuine organic causes. True medical conditions of this kind, however, are seldom the cause of the depression we encounter in our lives. Too often, though, even when no organic cause is identified, some physicians still prescribe an antidepressant as the primary intervention.

In some cases the drugs do give patients a "lift," but unless there is a truly identifiable medical condition, drugs merely mask the real cause of the problem: mishandled problems of living. Unless such problems are addressed biblically, the medication has to be maintained to keep patients "emotionally stable." There is a better way, however, of dealing with the "down" feelings.

The Real Problem for Most of Us

The depression most of us experience is the result of a wrong reaction to certain *losses* in life. Here's how it works:

God designed us to experience a "down" emotion anytime we lose something that is important to us. The loss can be tangible like the loss of a loved one, a job, a pet, a friend, or money. Or it can be an intangible loss like loss of respect in someone's eyes or a loss of control in some area.

When we *think* about the loss, we experience what the Bible calls *sorrow—the God-given emotion of loss.* It is the inner ache or hurt we experience when we *think* about our loss. Jesus experienced sorrow in the Garden when He thought about the upcoming loss of fellowship with His Father when He would bear the sins of the world and experience the agonies of crucifixion (Matt. 26:38; Isa. 53). The example of Christ in the Garden is a clear testimony that sorrow, in itself, is not sinful.

Depression is the result of sorrowing without hope. We lose hope when we start thinking that things will never get better or that there is no purpose for our pain or that no one else has to go through anything similar. When we become convinced that nothing can be done because the situation is hopeless, we experience depression—sorrow without hope. Below is a summary of the dynamics of depression.

> **Step 1.** **Normal Experience When We Lose:**
> Thoughts of Loss→Sorrow (Emotion of Loss)
>
> **Step 2.** **Unbiblical Response to Loss:**
> Sorrow without Hope→Depression

Understanding and remembering the following warning can help us handle depression biblically:

Watch how you *muse*
and what you *choose*
when you *lose.*

Let's look at this warning one phrase at a time.

First, Watch How You Muse When You Lose

Muse means "to ponder or meditate; to consider or deliberate at length." Generally, emotions are the byproducts of thoughts. *We cannot sustain any emotion without thought*. We cannot sustain romance without thinking about someone a certain way. We cannot sustain anger without thinking about what the other person has done to us. To change the emotion, we must change the thoughts. We begin by asking some very hard questions and by giving some honest answers.

Ask yourself the following three questions:

Question 1

Did God arrange or allow the loss over which I am depressed because it was wrong for me to have the thing I lost in the first place?

Here are some illustrations of such losses:

- A teenage girl who lost the unsaved boy she was in love with when he began dating another girl
- A teen who lost his collection of rock CDs when his parents found them and confiscated them
- A young person who lost his chance to work at a movie theater because another applicant was chosen for the job
- An adult who experienced a serious financial loss when he impulsively purchased a time-share property, automobile, or household appliance after a high-powered sales pitch

It is important to remember that there are some things God never intended for us to have (II Cor. 6:14-17; I John 2:15-17), and He mercifully arranges for them to be removed.

Take a moment to think about your own depression. What have you lost? Was it something God never intended for you to have? If so, what was it? Write out your thoughts below.

_____

_____

_____

_____

_____

You must forsake the items that are not part of God's plan, and you must restore fellowship with God by confessing sin to Him and asking for His forgiveness (I John 1:9).

Question 2

Did God arrange or allow the loss over which I am depressed because I was becoming dependent upon the thing I lost instead of upon God for my happiness and stability? Or was I using it to make life work my way?

Again, some illustrations might help clarify this point.

- A college student who feels his happiness and stability are dependent upon getting straight A's in his classes receives a low mark on a test

- A store manager whose relational philosophy is "peace at any price" receives orders that he must lay off one-fourth of his employees due to financial cutbacks

- An industrious young man "whose life is his work" loses the use of his legs in an automobile accident and is confined to a wheelchair

- A perfectionist who has to "have everything under control" and who has to "have his act together" experiences a major setback when his son is arrested for shoplifting

Take a moment to reflect on your own situation. What have you lost that you think you must have to make life work your way? Write down your ideas below.

_____

_____

_____

_____

_____

Read Proverbs 3:5-6, Isaiah 55:1-3, and Jeremiah 2:13 for help in discerning where your trust for security, happiness, and so forth has shifted from God to something else.

Question 3

Did God arrange or allow the loss over which I am depressed because He simply wanted to show me that my Christian life was too shallow?

If you genuinely are trying to do right but lose hope and become depressed when life is hard, God may be allowing the trial to further perfect and mature you. Carefully study James 1:1-4, I Peter 1:6-7, and John 15:1-2.

Do you see that God might be trying to motivate you to further growth in your Christian life? John 15:2 says that when we begin to bear fruit, God will purge us to enable us to bear more fruit. If you think God may have allowed you to sustain your loss in order to grow, write your thoughts about it on the following lines.

_____

_____

_____

_____

_____

_____

One last thought about "thoughts": Watch out for thoughts of hopelessness and self-pity. They are as dangerous to your mind as cyanide is to your body and must be rejected whenever you are tempted to entertain them.

Psalms 42 and 73 and Lamentations 3 describe men of God who were thinking that life was too hard for them and that other people had it easier. Both of them turned their despair around, however, by thinking the right way. Notice the transition in Psalm 42:5-6, Psalm 73:16 ff., and Lamentations 3:21 ff. when these men forced themselves to think the right way. When you are feeling depressed, you must decide that you are not going to meditate upon thoughts of hopelessness or self-pity. You must allow the Scriptures to show you the right responses to losses.

For example, the apostle Paul in Romans 15:4 tells how to increase hope. He reminds us that the Scriptures are filled with examples of how God worked in the lives of His people. These examples, he says, "were written aforetime [in earlier times] . . . for our learning, that we through patience and *comfort of the scriptures* might have hope."

David says in Psalm 119:28, "My soul melteth [pours out tears] for heaviness [emotional sadness]: strengthen thou me [cause me to stand up] *according unto thy word.*" Notice how many times David in this psalm reflects upon the Word of God in his time of affliction (vv. 67, 71, 75, 92, and 107).

Increase your Bible study and meditation. Focus on His faithfulness and His promises. If you do not have a personal strategy for meditation, use the MAP Method in Appendix A of this book. God promises stability only to those who will meditate upon His Word (Josh. 1:8; Ps. 1; Matt. 7:24-28; I Tim. 4:15-16; James 1:21-25).

To honor God and to stay out of depression, you must "watch how you *muse* . . . when you lose."

Second, Watch What You Choose When You Lose

You must also decide, however, not to *do* anything sinful when you are down. Some examples of wrong choices would include the following:

- Indulging your lusts and passions in sexual fantasies or activities in order to "feel good" again

- Going on a wild spending spree in order to forget what has been troubling you or to make you feel better

- Ignoring important responsibilities at home, work, or school because you want a break from pressures

- Binging on food to experience a little bit of pleasure amidst all the disappointment

- Attempting an overdose or contemplating some other form of suicide

- Turning to alcohol or drugs for a "pick-me-up" during the down times

- Indulging in some reckless or dangerous activity because of the temporary "rush" it gives

Many people complicate their lives by making wrong *choices* like these when they are depressed. Then they also have to face the debt, addiction, work termination, shame, guilt, and other results of their sinful choices when they were down. That is the reason we must watch what we *choose* when we lose.

God's Antidepressant

God does not want His children living without hope and filling themselves with self-pity. He does have an antidote, as you have just read. Let's review it briefly.

1. When you begin to experience depression (sorrow without hope), identify what it is that you have lost.

2. Ask yourself the three questions stated earlier to determine what God might be trying to say to you through your loss.

3. Examine your thinking. Are you "leaning to your own understanding," or are you thinking about your loss from God's perspective? What *choices* have you made while you were depressed that have further complicated your situation? Does anything (thoughts or choices) need to be repented of and forsaken (Prov. 28:13)?

4. Seek the help of a parent, pastor, or other mature believer who can help you get your thinking about your loss in line with God's perspective.

5. Finally, remember: "Watch how you muse and what you choose when you lose."

Basics for Hurting Believers

"Time Doesn't Heal All Wounds!"

Brenda's tearful words penetrated Bob's soul. As a youth pastor he had dealt often with hurting teens and was grieved whenever he learned that one had been given trite, unbiblical advice for important issues. Brenda had recently joined his youth group and had just confided in him that her grandfather had sexually abused her as a young child.

"You're right, Brenda, time doesn't heal all wounds. Time can heal most physical wounds because the body goes into action repairing itself when it is damaged.

"For pain in your heart, time allows you only to temporarily forget what happened, but it doesn't really solve the problem. When you aren't thinking about your grandfather, it probably doesn't 'hurt' as much; but when something reminds you of him or of what he did, your emotions erupt in all their previous fury. And even sometimes when you aren't consciously thinking about the past, your heart probably 'aches' as if you were walking around with something important missing. Is that true, Brenda?" Brenda nodded in agreement.

"You live on a fallen planet and have been hurt by a man with a sinful heart. Furthermore, your own sinful bent further complicates the problem. You mentioned a few minutes ago that you know your hatred and bitterness for your grandfather are wrong. Time doesn't heal all wounds, but your heart can be stabilized if you will allow God to transform (change) you 'by the renewing of your mind' (Romans 12:2)."

The youth pastor continued, "The apostle Peter wrote two letters to suffering, hurting people. They had been driven from their homes in Jerusalem, ostracized, tortured, and deprived because of their Christian faith. Peter told them in I Peter 1:13 that if they were going to survive they had to exercise some clear-headed thinking.

"In the weeks ahead we'll talk in more depth about your abuse and its effects—your anger, your fears, your confusion, the shame you feel—but there are some basic principles of clear-headed thinking from I Peter you must focus on while you hurt, no matter what issue we are discussing at the moment.

"Keep in mind, Brenda, that these three principles aren't everything there is to know about suffering, but they are a starting point. They will give you something concrete to start with; we will build on them in the weeks ahead. Believers hurt just as unbelievers do. The difference is that believers can know what to do when they hurt."

Let's look at the principles Brenda's youth pastor went over in that first session.

God's Lasting Solution

You probably are reading this chapter because you or someone you know is hurting, and you are looking for some way to bring relief. That is understandable—none of us like pain. Pain in the physical world warns us of danger. When your finger senses a hot pan on the stove, you instinctively pull away—to get relief.

Likewise, whenever we are hurt by something or someone in our world, we tend to seek the quickest relief. We may find ourselves, however, drawing away from God, His people, and His Word during the times we hurt the most. To be sure, for some of us who have suffered much, even the thought of acknowledging the hurt inside our heart, let alone talking with someone about it, is a frightening prospect.

As you read this section, however, prayerfully ask God to give you the courage to begin addressing these issues in a biblical fashion. Just as the physical body "goes to work" restoring injured tissue and fighting disease, we must put our heart "to work" restoring a biblical perspective about our problems. An injured body also is more susceptible to infection, so a hurting heart is more likely to experience temptations toward bitterness, anger, and fear. Peter's instruction tells us how to overcome these temptations.

Peter says we have to have some clear-headed thinking about God, about ourselves, and about what we are going through. As we embrace God's perspective about these issues, we experience spiritual growth. It is this spiritual growth that is God's lasting solution to our hurt. It is for this reason that Peter reminds his hurting friends to put their heart to work growing through the "milk of the word" (I Pet. 2:1-2; II Pet. 3:18). If they neglect this growth, they will be unstable and will fall (II Pet. 3:17).

We Need Clear-Headed Thinking About Our Own Heart

When Peter taught hurting Christians how to respond biblically to their hurt, he said, "Sanctify the Lord God in your hearts" (I Pet. 3:15). "Sanctify" means to "set apart for something special." For example, a church "sanctuary" is a place that we "set apart" for the special purpose of worshiping God. Peter says, "When you hurt, it is especially important for God to have a 'special place' in your heart. That 'special place' is the 'throne' of our heart." Peter literally says in this verse, "set apart Christ as Lord (the Ruler) in your heart."

That means that in an act of surrender we tell God that we acknowledge His loving and wise control over the circumstances of our lives and that we are willing to handle these difficult challenges His way.

Now, why would Peter have to remind us to give special consideration to God during our times of pain?

First, our heart has a tendency to forget God. We are so prone to "lean . . . unto [our] own understanding" (Prov. 3:5). Solomon also reminds us that "he that trusteth in his own heart is a fool" (Prov. 28:26). Man's sinfulness started when Adam and Eve made decisions independently of God. Our nature today still tends to leave God out of our thinking (Isa. 55:6-11).

Second, Peter has to remind us to "set up Christ as Lord" because our heart has a tendency to fight God. We are tempted to shake a "clenched fist" at Him in rebellion and demand, "If You are so good, then why do You let bad things like this happen to me?"

We have to understand that Satan, not God, is the one trying to destroy us by sending evil our way. While God, for His own purposes, is allowing Satan to work evil in this age, God is wise enough and loving enough to have "all things work together for good to them that love God" (Rom. 8:28).

Once again, our problem is that we do not think as God thinks. We don't really know what is "good" for us. We forget that suffering isn't our greatest enemy: an evil heart is. The highest good is not "feeling good" but "being good."

When Christ suffered on the cross, He prayed, "Father, forgive them" (Luke 23:34). He was "being good" (behaving in a God-honoring way) even when He was being tortured to death by crucifixion. When we respond to pain in a similar fashion, the evil done toward us works something "good"—our Christlikeness.

Nothing will hinder growth more than a stubborn heart that refuses to recognize Christ as Lord. Whenever you seem to be at an impasse in your Christian life as you attempt to grow while you hurt, look for a "clenched fist" in your life.

Can you honestly say that you have been setting apart "Christ as Lord" in your heart? If not, take a few moments to ask yourself, "Why not?" Write down your reasons so that you don't forget your thoughts. Then ask a mature believer you can trust to show you God's answers to your struggles.

If you need more help in this area, use the MAP Method of Meditation in Appendix A of this book to work through Romans 8:18, 26-39 and II Corinthians 1:7-9; 4:7-9, 16-18; 12:7-10. Take the time to look up these verses soon.

We Need Clear-Headed Thinking About Our Hope

Peter tells us in I Peter 3:15 that we are to be "ready always to give an answer to every man that asketh you a reason of the hope that is in you." No one can long endure under a burden of suffering and pain unless he has hope—confident expectation. Biblical hope is not a mere anticipation of relief from the problem but is a confident expectation that God is accomplishing good through the trial. Hope acts as "an anchor of the soul" that allows us to remain stable during storms of sorrow (Heb. 6:19).

People who respond to sorrow with depression have lost hope. They have never learned how or have forgotten to obtain the hope they need. Paul says that we through the "comfort of the scriptures . . . have hope" (Rom.15:4). A working knowledge of the Bible is a primary source of hope for the Christian life.

When some sufferers "feel bad," they turn to food for comfort. Others turn to addictive or compulsive behaviors or become excessively dependent upon a girlfriend, boyfriend, spouse, or other friend. The danger here is that anything that replaces God as the primary source of comfort in our lives becomes an idol—a substitute for God.

In addition, these substitutes don't really work in the long run. In fact, they create more problems for us than they solve. God reminds us of this in Jeremiah 2:13, where He says, "For my people have committed two evils; they have forsaken me the fountain of living waters, and hewed them out cisterns, broken cisterns, that can hold no water."

Solutions that leave God out may give temporary relief, but they can never fully satisfy. Ultimately, they provide only a false hope because they fail us. Our Lord suffered much (Isa. 53) and offers Himself as a Comforter to anyone who comes to Him for help. The Bible says, "For in that he himself [Jesus] hath suffered being tempted, he is able to succour [help] them that are tempted" (Heb. 2:18).

When you need hope and comfort, meditate on Psalms 18, 42, 73, 77; Isaiah 55; Romans 5:2-5; 12:12; Hebrews 6:10-20; I and II Peter; and James. These passages were written either by suffering believers (e.g., David in exile) or to suffering believers (e.g., those who received the epistles of Peter and James). These passages teach the truths God wants hurting believers to know and assimilate into their thinking so that they can honor God in the midst of trouble.

STABILIZING TRUTHS FOR HANDLING TROUBLE

God's LOVE for me is unchanging.
Jeremiah 31:3; I John 4:10, 16; Romans 8:31-32, 35-39;
John 15:12-13; Deuteronomy 7:7-8

God's PURPOSE for me is Christlikeness.
Romans 8:28-29; Colossians 1:28; Ephesians 4:11-13;
II Corinthians 3:18

God's WORD to me is the final right answer.
II Timothy 3:15-17; Hebrews 4:12; I John 5:3; II Peter 1:3-4;
Deuteronomy 6:6-9; 30:11-20; John 16:13-15

God's GRACE for me is sufficient.
II Corinthians 12:9; II Timothy 2:1; Hebrews 4:15-16;
Titus 2:11-12; Psalm 116:5; Romans 5:20-21

The Stabilizing Truths for Handling Trouble[3] chart on the previous page will also give you hope in your suffering. Memorize the four truths. Use the MAP Method of Meditation to meditate on one verse for each truth, and then go back and memorize the other verses.

People are attracted to believers who exhibit hope in the midst of suffering. If you handle your suffering biblically, God can use you to help others. Second Corinthians 1:3-4 says, "Blessed be God, even the Father of our Lord Jesus Christ, the Father of mercies, and the God of all comfort; Who comforteth us in all our tribulation, that we may be able to comfort them which are in any trouble, by the comfort wherewith we ourselves are comforted of God."

Peter says, "Get your answers ready; the questions will come. People will start to ask you, 'How do you do it?' " Our stability in adversity becomes an opportunity for ministry.

We Need Clear-Headed Thinking About Our Responses

Finally, Peter instructs us that while we suffer we are to maintain a "good conscience; that, whereas they speak evil of you, as of evildoers, they may be ashamed that falsely accuse your good conversation [godly lifestyle] in Christ" (I Pet. 3:16). A godly response is always necessary for us to grow as a result of the trial and for God to be able to use our testimony during our trial.

The right response is especially critical when our suffering comes from someone who is intentionally trying to hurt us. Peter here reminds us that our abusers will be "ashamed" only as they see us react in a Christlike fashion.

Joseph was betrayed by his brothers but wasn't bitter. David had to dodge the spears of King Saul, but he didn't pick up the spears and throw them back. Job suffered much but "sinned not, nor charged God foolishly" (Job 1:22). Peter and the other apostles were flogged for preaching the gospel but "departed from the presence of the council, rejoicing that they were counted worthy to suffer shame for his name" (Acts 5:41). While being stoned to death, Stephen prayed for his executioners, "Lord, lay not this sin to their charge" (Acts 7:60).

---

[3] Stabilizing truths by Ken Collier, THE WILDS Christian Association. Used by permission.

In each of these cases, the tormentors were rebuked by the godly response of those they tormented. Even more vivid was our Lord's example of suffering. Peter recounts our Lord's Crucifixion this way in I Peter 2:20-24.

> For what glory is it, if, when ye be buffeted for your faults, ye shall take it patiently? but if, when ye do well, and suffer for it, ye take it patiently, this is acceptable with God. For even hereunto were ye called: because Christ also suffered for us, leaving us an example, that ye should follow his steps: Who did no sin, neither was guile found in his mouth: Who, when he was reviled, reviled not again; when he suffered, he threatened not; but committed himself to him that judgeth righteously: Who his own self bare our sins in his own body on the tree, that we, being dead to sins, should live unto righteousness: by whose stripes ye were healed.

Christ understands suffering and is willing to help anyone respond right who comes to Him for "mercy, and . . . grace to help in time of need" (see Heb. 2:17-18; 4:14-16).

We Need Clear-Headed Thinking While We Hurt

In summary then, when we hurt we must have a surrendered heart toward God, a steady hope (i.e., a confident expectation that God is accomplishing something good through our trial), and a good conscience arising from good responses in the midst of our trial.

Remember, these principles are just a start but will point us in the right direction while we hurt. Most people are trying to escape their problems, but God is looking for people who will go through each problem with clear-headed thinking and become examples of Christlikeness while they hurt.

Basics for Pressured Believers

Looking at Pressure Biblically

Today was a usual day in your life as pastor until your appointment with Janet, a fifth-year teacher in your Christian school. She has just left your office, and you can't believe what you have heard. Janet wants to resign and give up teaching altogether! She has always been so energetic and seems to live for her students. She runs circles around the other teachers. Her testimony has been impeccable and her desire to do right refreshing. With tears she explained how the last two months had been utterly miserable for her. She had lost all desire to get up in the mornings. Sure, there had been the usual student and parent problems, but she had always handled those so well. Now she was counting the days until May. Her doctor had told her she was "burned out" and needed a break from teaching. How can you help her? And just as important, how can you get a handle on pressure yourself? You have to admit that you have felt much the same way in the past several weeks. Let's look at this issue biblically.

Burnout is not a mysterious "illness"; it is the depression that results when we fail to handle extended pressures biblically. To understand the solution, we must know how the mind and body work together to handle pressure.

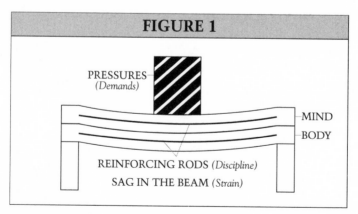

FIGURE 1

PRESSURES
(Demands)

MIND
BODY

REINFORCING RODS (*Discipline*)
SAG IN THE BEAM (*Strain*)

Figure 1 shows a pressure being supported by two beams. Pressure first "weighs" upon the mind—the top beam. When the mind is not thinking biblically about pressures, some of the following may result: depression, boredom, listlessness, dullness, lack of interest, irritability and "touch-iness," phobias (irrational fears), anxiety-related problems (panic attacks, etc.), compulsive behavior (extreme perfectionism, eating disorders, excessive exercise, etc.), and changes in personal and social habits (withdrawal, obnoxiousness, etc.).

Whatever "weight" is not handled adequately in the mind is borne by the body—the bottom beam. Most of the following effects can have other causes, but they are also common indications of bodily strain caused by wrongly handled pressures: muscular tensions and headaches, insomnia and fatigue, increased or decreased appetite, heart palpitations, tics, itching, colitis, diarrhea, ulcers, cramps, and other stomach disorders.

Many self-help books and seminars merely explain how to more effectively set goals, plan, and choose priorities. Such techniques attempt to discipline the mind. Current books and seminars also may emphasize the necessity for regular exercise and good nutrition. They correctly teach that a disciplined mind and body can withstand pressure with fewer debilitating effects.

While these disciplines act like steel reinforcing rods in the concrete beams (see Figure 1), *God never intended for man to be able to handle the pressures of life on his own* (Matt. 4:4; John 15:4-6; II Cor. 3:5; 4:7). The sagging beams in Figure 1 illustrate this truth.

Though most of us know the advantages of discipline, we do not discipline our bodies adequately. In addition, we are selective in which responsibilities we maintain disciplined mental processes. The result is a pathetic picture that might look like Figure 2.

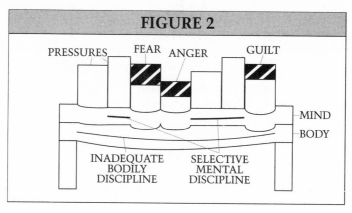

341

Each box on the beam represents the pressure that comes from a role or relationship in our lives (spouse, employee, church officer, parent, ministry, hobby, etc.). Besides the normal pressure of these roles and relationships, there may also be extra pressures from fear, anger, and unresolved guilt in some of them. To begin to unscramble this difficulty, we must examine three areas.

Overcome?

First, we must deal with any known sin. There is no greater pressure than the pressure of a guilty conscience. Hebrews 12:1 tells us to "lay aside . . . the sin which doth so easily beset us." It must be confessed to God and forsaken (I John 1:9; Prov. 28:13). Many people do not handle well the pressure that *is* God's will for them because they are already overloaded with the pressures of a burdened conscience.

What about you? Look at the pressure David felt from God while he covered his sin (Pss. 32 and 38). Our sin blocks God's ability to help us (Isa. 59:1-2). Ask God to examine your life (Ps. 139:23-24) and list below any sin you know you must confess and forsake (Prov. 28:13).

_____

_____

Overcommitted?

Second, we must remove from the beams (Figure 2) any responsibilities we have assumed outside the will of God. We may have added activities and responsibilities that are not harmful in themselves but take up too much time and energy. They may include hobbies, sports, clubs, second jobs, and additional ministries. They are usually added to meet some personal desire and may not be God's will for the present. These become "weights" that we must "lay aside" (Heb. 12:1).

What about you? List your God-given roles and responsibilities (major and minor). Can you say with confidence that *God* gave these to you, or did you add some without His permission and direction? If you did, repent of your independent spirit and then eliminate them from your schedule.

_____

_____

_____

Overdrawn?

As we have seen, pressures are first evaluated by the mind. For example, if an employer adds something to an employee's workload, the employee first evaluates whether he has enough time and energy to handle the additional demand. If so, his mind remains at peace. If his resources are deficient, his mind begins working on a solution. If he cannot find one, his mind becomes anxious. He does this in much the same way he evaluates a bill he receives in the mail. He evaluates this "demand/pressure" of the bill against his checkbook balance. If he has plenty of cash to cover the expense, he has peace. If the bill will overdraw his checking account, he feels "pressured."

A believer with a renewed mind sees every pressure and resource from God's perspective. A Christian's "spiritual checkbook" can never be overdrawn. God gives unlimited "overdraft protection" to do those things that *are* His will. He has promised to supply all that we need for godly living (II Pet. 1:3) and service (II Cor. 9:8; 12:9-10).

What about you? Is God allowing these pressures to show you that you have an inadequate view of Him? Do your pressures always seem larger to you than God seems to you? See I Chronicles 29:12, Luke 1:37, and Ephesians 3:20. Why do you suppose your view of God is so deficient? Romans 10:17 and Matthew 5:8 reveal two possible reasons for a wrong view of God. Look up these verses and write those reasons in the spaces below.

_____

_____

_____

_____

_____

A believer with a renewed mind accepts God's purposes for pressure (II Cor. 4:16-18; Heb. 12:1-3; James 1:2-3; I Pet. 1:6-7). He understands God's love, grace, and sustaining power. He knows how to pray. In short, he sees life from God's perspective. This perspective adds an extra quality of endurance to life that sustains any load *God* places upon it. Notice the extra "filling" (which represents the renewed mind) in the top beam in Figure 3 on the next page.

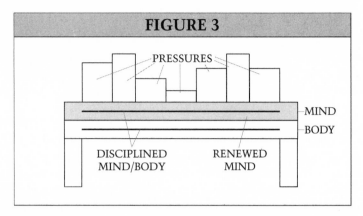

"Burnout" is God's red warning light on the dashboard that says the engine is overheating. Janet does not have to quit her job, but God is showing her that she does have to quit handling pressures her own way. She needs to be "transformed by the renewing of [her] mind" (Rom. 12:1-2). The next section shows how that is possible.

How to Develop a Renewed Mind

The Bible calls a spiritually immature mind a carnal or fleshly mind (I Cor. 3:1-2). *A carnal mind evaluates problems and pressures from a purely human perspective.* It will make evaluations like the following:

- "That's one more crummy thing I have to do this week. I'll never make it."

- "I think this requirement is stupid, but if that's the only way I can get what I want, I'll put up with it."

- "This kind of stuff always happens to me! Doesn't anybody care?"

- "I've got enough to worry about already. I don't need this!"

- "He can't get away with that. I don't have to take it!"

Can you imagine Christ handling any of His pressures with responses like that? Most Christians who realize responses like these are not right will "tell God they are sorry." Then they "try to do better" and usually do not continue very long in their new resolve. The reason that they can't continue "to do better" is clear from passages like Ephesians 4:22-24, Colossians 3:8-10, Romans 12:2, and James 1:21-22. The mind must be renewed. James 1:21-22 describes the process. The believer must

1. *Stop the old practice*—"Lay apart all filthiness and superfluity of naughtiness [remaining wickedness],"

2. *Humbly realize he cannot handle this by himself*—"with meekness,"

3. *Meditate seriously on the Word*—"receive . . . the engrafted word," and

4. *Do what the Word says*—"be ye doers of the word."

A believer must continue to meditate on the pertinent passage of Scripture until two things take place—until, first, he cannot forget what he has learned; and, second, until he is becoming a consistent "doer" of the new way of handling pressure (James 1:25). Most people do not meditate upon God's Word unless they use a structured plan. If you do not have a personal strategy for meditation, use the MAP Method in Appendix A of this book. God promises stability only to those who will meditate upon His Word (Josh. 1:8; Ps. 1; Matt. 7:24-28; I Tim. 4:15-16; James 1:21-25).

The Stabilizing Truths for Handling Trouble in the previous section, Basics for Hurting Believers, can equip a Christian to handle pressure in a God-honoring way. Memorize the four truths. Use the MAP method to meditate on one verse for each truth, and then add the other verses.

The Test of Joy

If a believer has a renewed mind about his pressures, he can consider them a source of joy (II Cor. 12:9-10; James 1:2-3; I Pet. 1:6-9). If instead they are sources of irritation, fear, and guilt, he still does not have God's perspective.

Peter tells us that a pressured believer (one who is "in heaviness through manifold temptations") can "rejoice" while he is experiencing difficult times (I Pet. 1:6). The recipients of this letter from the apostle Peter were persecuted and harassed because they were believers. He urged them to remember God's purposes for the pressure (I Pet. 1:7). He told them to "gird up the loins of [their] mind" (I Pet. 1:13). That meant they were to restrict their thinking to God's perspective only and to change their responses accordingly. The result would be *joy*. Any believer can experience that same joy if he handles his pressure God's way. The prophet Isaiah puts it this way: "Thou wilt keep him in perfect peace, whose mind is stayed on thee: because he trusteth in thee" (Isa. 26:3).

Basics for Worried Believers

Susan, the Professional Worrier

"Pastor, I'm really honored to be on the deacon board, but I didn't realize how much it would affect Susan. She was already a 'professional worrier.' The recent cutbacks at my work have her concerned about my job security in the days ahead. Besides our financial future, she worries constantly about her health. Every magazine article or news story about some new disease puts her into a tailspin. She starts worrying that she might be getting that disease. About six months ago she started having severe stomachaches, but the doctor said they were stress-related and told her to take antacids to counteract the problem. She worries now that she might have an ulcer.

"Susan is really excited about my new position as a deacon, but she now worries about whether she can be 'good enough' to be a deacon's wife. She suspects, as I do, that her worry is behind most of her physical problems. She doesn't feel she can be a credit to my ministry as a deacon when she doesn't 'have her act together,' as she puts it. She didn't even come to church last Wednesday night because she thought she might have to leave during the service because of her stomach problems. Also, about two months ago she started having trouble sleeping at nights; she is getting so discouraged and, I might say, really tired!

"You know how much she loves the Lord and wants to serve Him. She loves teaching the third-grade girls in Sunday school and is great with our own two preschoolers. She is a wonderful wife and mother! What can I do to help her, Pastor?"

Many Christians struggle with worries similar to Susan's. If you are one of them, you can begin to loosen the stranglehold of worry by learning the reasons that you worry in the first place. You can then begin practicing God's solutions to worry and become a useful servant for God and can experience peace in your own heart. Pastor Douglas told Bill that God has something to say about Susan's problems. In fact, God, through His Word, has addressed every possible problem that can interfere with a believer's ability to serve Him and accurately reflect His nature (II Pet. 1:3).

We Worry Because We Have the Wrong Concerns and Priorities

The things that worry you are the things that are most important to you. Our anxieties always reveal our priorities. We never worry about things that are unimportant to us. Make a list of your worries and ask yourself, "Are the things I worry about priorities to God?" For example, most of our worries about what we will wear result from our priority to be accepted by others. We want to have a certain kind of clothing to impress others or bolster our sagging pride. God condemns this priority (II Cor. 10:12) and says that this kind of "fear of man" will be a trap to defeat us (Prov. 29:25). He reminds us of His priorities in Matthew 6:24-34 and even teaches us in this passage how to view clothing.

In a similar manner, many of our financial worries have come because we purchased things to satisfy our lusts (strong desires). We worry about where we will get the money to pay our debts. God is concerned, however, about when we will change our value system (I Tim. 6:6-11). Before we can overcome the sinful habit of worry in cases like these, we must be ready to repent of sinful priorities that lead to trouble in the first place.

We Worry Because We Handle Our Legitimate Concerns the Wrong Way

If the concerns we have are priorities to God, He has already instructed us how to go about dealing with them. For example, a godly parent may be concerned about a wayward child. Proverbs gives abundant instruction on how to respond to someone who has chosen the ways of foolishness instead of the paths of wisdom.

Another example of a legitimate care was Paul's concern about the condition of the churches he started (II Cor. 11:28). He did something about it—God's way. He visited them, prayed for them, wrote letters to them rebuking and instructing them, and sent messengers to minister to them.

There is a Bible way to handle any concern that is a concern to God. The problem is often that we are so unfamiliar with the Scriptures that we do not know what God has said. We, therefore, "lean . . . unto [our] own understanding" (Prov. 3:5) and end up worrying and fretting about our concerns.

We Worry Because We Depend on the Wrong Person

The one we turn to when we have a problem is the one we trust most to help. If you call a friend every day to rehash your problem, you reveal that you believe your friend can help—even if all he has to offer is a listening ear. You are dependent upon your friend for relief.

If you keep your thoughts to yourself and constantly repeat them in your mind, you reveal that you believe that you have the answer to your problem. You are dependent upon yourself for the solution.

If, on the other hand, you discuss your concerns with God and seek His thoughts about your concerns, you reveal that you believe He has the solution to your problem. You are dependent upon God.

Ask yourself, "To whom do I talk most about my problem, and to whom do I listen most for advice about my problem?" The answer to these questions will reveal whom you believe has the answer.

Susan had to see that although she had a desire to please God, she was replacing God by becoming her own "problem solver." Pastor Douglas gave Bill some practical steps to help Susan think through these issues of her heart.

How Do I Start Changing?

The King James Version of the Bible translates the Greek word for anxiety and worry as "careful," "care," and "take thought." The word itself means "to divide." A sinful "care" or worry, then, is something that divides the heart (double-mindedness; serving two masters) and distracts it from God. Paul's legitimate concerns drove him *to* God in prayer, service, and dependence. Sinful worry drives us *from* God and His Word; it separates us from the most important things. See the example of Martha in Luke 10:38-42.

Think about the things that "divide" your attention and distract your heart from God. List them below:

_____

_____

_____

_____

Examine your list of worries and write out below the priorities of your life that your worries reveal. If these priorities are God's priorities, then He will have already addressed how to deal with them in His Word. Begin immediately to find the Scripture passages that tell you God's way of handling that legitimate concern. Write the references to those passages next to the concern on your list below.

If they are not His priorities, then they must be confessed and forsaken (Prov. 28:13).

_____

_____

_____

_____

_____

_____

What Do I Do Next?

Philippians 4:6-9 gives God's plan for handling worries. Paul starts this passage with a command: "Be careful for nothing." This simply means, "Don't worry about anything!" Disobedience to this command is a sin. After the command, Paul gives three steps to peace—the opposite of anxiety.

Step 1—Pray Right

Paul tells us to pray about everything that concerns us (v. 6). He intends for us to do more than simply rattle off a list of worries to God, however. He says we must begin our prayers with thanksgiving. This "gratitude test" reveals the true condition of the believer's heart. God's priority for us is our growth in Christlikeness (Rom. 8:28-29; Eph. 4:13). He intends to use every hardship and need to propel us to that end. If we do not have this growth as our priority, we will not be thankful for the struggle we are in now. A believer who is grateful for the opportunity to grow will, as he petitions God, find God's indescribable peace begin to post a sentry over his heart: "And the peace of God, which passeth all understanding, shall keep [guard] your hearts and minds through Christ Jesus" (Phil. 4:7).

Step 2—Think Right

The "thought test" (Phil. 4:8) checks your thoughts to see if they are

- True—accurate, true to fact
- Honest—honorable, worthy
- Just—right, appropriate
- Pure—uncontaminated, undefiled
- Lovely—pleasing, agreeable
- Of Good Report—gracious, fair-sounding
- Virtuous—demonstrating excellence, moral goodness
- Praiseworthy—commendable

Of course, brooding and fearful worries do not pass the "thought test." Anxious thoughts often include other unbiblical moods and attitudes—self-pity, bitterness, anger, envy, and despair.

Notice in Psalms that David meditates upon God and His promises when he is concerned about his own safety and well-being. You can read almost any psalm (try starting with Ps. 2) and see David's concern about his enemy or about his loneliness. Then notice how quickly David turns his thoughts to God's nature and His promises. It is not long before David is praising God in the middle of his trial.

Why don't we find ourselves doing this more often? The answer is simple—we don't know much about God. We have not memorized and meditated on many (if any) psalms or other passages of Scripture that teach us about God's nature and His promises. Sometimes Christians say, "But I'm not any good at meditating!" That is not true, especially for a worrier. A worrier is a master at meditating! Meditation simply means taking an idea and thinking of all its applications and implications for one's life. A worrier does that all the time—only with the wrong thoughts. He needs to first repent of sinful worry and then practice the same thing with God's thoughts.

Choose some passages to meditate upon and note them on the next page. Start meditating upon them right away. If you do not have a personal strategy for meditating on God's Word, use the MAP Method in Appendix A of this book. For more information on meditation and developing a renewed mind, see Part Two of this book.

Step 3—Do Right

Paul ends this discussion of worry by telling us, "Those things, which ye have both learned, and received, and heard, and seen in me, do: and the God of peace shall be with you" (Phil. 4:9).

He says to do the things that you have learned (you must be studying God's Word) and received (you can't be doubting that God's ways really work). You see, freedom from worry and care comes no other way. We must think as God thinks (Isa. 55:6-11) and then do right.

What does God mean when He says, "Get busy 'doing right' "? Well, you have prayed with gratitude. You have been memorizing and meditating on God's Word. Now, while you are waiting for God to answer the prayer, what is there that you ought to be doing instead of worrying? Should you be studying? taking care of the children? answering the mail on your desk? vacuuming the house? following up another sales lead? playing with your children? sleeping at night?

Susan needed to learn that when she is in bed she should be sleeping, not trying to solve problems by worrying. If she lies awake, she should pray with gratitude and review her meditations of God's nature and His promises. She may initially wake up often when she begins this new approach. But it will not be long before she is sleeping well again as she handles her worry in a biblical way.

Win the War of Worry

You probably get the idea by now. Proverbs 12:25 says, "Heaviness [anxiety] in the heart of a man maketh it stoop: but a good word [and what word can be better than God's Word?] maketh it glad." You can win the war of worry, but you must do it God's way. A fretful, anxious believer is a poor advertisement for God. His behavior shows that he believes that God is powerless or unconcerned. He thinks, therefore, that he must try to solve his problems on his own.

David shares the secret of worry-free living in Psalm 55:22: "Cast thy burden upon the Lord, and he shall sustain thee: he shall never suffer the righteous to be moved."

Peter recalls this passage and under inspiration of God rephrases parts of it: "Casting all your care upon him; for he careth for you" (I Pet. 5:7).

This is the advice Bill gave to Susan, thanks to a pastor who knew God's way of handling worry. You, too, can be free from worry if you follow God's plan for peace—pray right, think right, and do right!

Bibliography

Adams, Jay E. *How to Help People Change*. Grand Rapids: Zondervan Publishing House, 1986.

————. *A Theology of Christian Counseling*. Grand Rapids: Zondervan Publishing House, 1979.

————. *A Thirst for Wholeness*. Woodruff, S.C.: Timeless Texts, 1998.

Arndt, William, and F. Wilbur Gingrich. *A Greek-English Lexicon of the New Testament and Other Early Christian Literature*. Chicago: University of Chicago Press, 1979.

Bounds, E. M. *The Weapon of Prayer*. Grand Rapids: Baker Book House, 1975.

Bridges, Jerry. *The Pursuit of Holiness*. Colorado Springs: NavPress, 1978.

————. *Trusting God*. Colorado Springs: NavPress, 1988.

Bruce, A. B. *The Training of the Twelve*. Grand Rapids: Kregel Publications, 1971.

Chafer, Lewis Sperry. *He That Is Spiritual*. 1918. Reprint, Grand Rapids: Zondervan, 1967.

DeHaan, Dan. *The God You Can Know*. Chicago: Moody Press, 1982.

Edwards, Jonathan. *Religious Affections*. Ed. James M. Houston. Minneapolis: Bethany House Publishers, 1996.

Fugate, J. Richard. *What the Bible Says About Child Training*. Tempe, Ariz.: Aletheia Division of Alpha Omega Publications, 1980.

Gaussen, Louis. *The Inspiration of the Holy Scriptures*. Chicago: Moody, 1949.

Horton, Ronald A., ed. *Christian Education: Its Mandate and Mission*. Greenville, S.C.: Bob Jones University Press, 1992.

Hull, Bill. *Jesus Christ, Disciple-Maker*. Grand Rapids: Fleming H. Revell, 1984.

Jones, Bob, III. *Who Says So?!: A Biblical View of Authority*. Greenville, S.C.: Bob Jones University Press, 1996.

Lewis, C. S. *Mere Christianity*. New York: Macmillan Publishing Co., 1952.

————. *The Weight of Glory and Other Addresses*. Grand Rapids: Eerdmans, 1965.

Lutzer, Erwin W. *How in This World Can I Be Holy?* Chicago: Moody Press, 1974.

————. *How To Say No to a Stubborn Habit*. Wheaton, Ill.: Victor Books, 1979.

McCallum, Dennis, ed. *The Death of Truth*. Minneapolis: Bethany House Publishers, 1996.

Murray, Andrew. *Humility*. Springdale, Pa.: Whitaker House, 1982.

Orr, James, ed. *The International Standard Bible Encyclopaedia*. Vol. 3. Grand Rapids: Wm. B. Eerdmans Publishing Co., 1956.

Owen, John. *Sin and Temptation*. Ed. James M. Houston. Minneapolis: Bethany House Publishers, 1996.

Packer, J. I. *Knowing God*. Downers Grove, Ill.: InterVarsity Press, 1973.

Petersen, J. Allan. *Your Reactions Are Showing*. Lincoln, Nebr.: Back to the Bible, 1967.

Petersen, Jim. *Lifestyle Discipleship*. Colorado Springs: NavPress, 1993.

Piper, John. *Desiring God*. Portland, Oreg.: Multnomah Press, 1986.

Ray, Bruce A. *Withhold Not Correction*. Phillipsburg, N.J.: Presbyterian and Reformed, 1978.

Ryle, J. C. *Holiness*. 1879. Reprint, Darlington, England: Evangelical Press, 1997.

Ryrie, Charles C. *Balancing the Christian Life*. Chicago: Moody Press, 1969.

Sanders, J. Oswald. *Spiritual Leadership*. Chicago: Moody Press, 1994.

Sorenson, David. *Training Your Child to Turn Out Right*. Independence, Mo.: American Association of Christian Schools, 1995.

Sproul, R. C. *The Soul's Quest for God*. Wheaton, Ill.: Tyndale House Publishers, Inc., 1992.

Spurgeon, Charles Haddon. *Morning and Evening*. Peabody, Mass.: Hendrickson Publishers, 1991.

————. *The New Park Street Pulpit*. Vol. 1. 1856. Reprint, Grand Rapids: Zondervan Publishing House, 1963.

Stormer, John A. *Growing Up God's Way*. Florissant, Mo.: Liberty Bell Press, 1984.

Tozer, A. W. *The Attributes of God*. Camp Hill, Pa.: Christian Publications, 1997.

————. *The Knowledge of the Holy*. New York: Harper-Collins Publishers, 1961.

————. *The Pursuit of God*. Camp Hill, Pa.: Christian Publications, 1993.

Trench, Richard C. *Synonyms of the New Testament*. Grand Rapids: Wm. B. Eerdmans Publishing Co., 1880.

Tripp, Paul David, *Age of Opportunity: A Biblical Guide to Parenting Teens*. Phillipsburg, N.J.: Presbyterian and Reformed, 1997.

Tripp, Tedd, *Shepherding a Child's Heart*. Wapwallopen, Pa.: Shepherd Press, 1995.

BIBLIOGRAPHY

Veith, Gene Edward, Jr. *Postmodern Times*. Wheaton, Ill.: Crossway Books, 1994.

Vine, W. E. *An Expository Dictionary of New Testament Words*. Old Tappen, N.J.: Fleming H. Revell Company, 1940.

Warfield, B. B. "Imitating the Incarnation." In *The Person and Work of Christ*. Grand Rapids: Baker Book House, 1950.

Williams, Charles. *The Fundamentals*. Los Angeles: The Bible Institute of Los Angeles, 1917.

Young, Edward J. *Thy Word Is Truth*. Grand Rapids: Eerdmans, 1957.

Scriptural Index

Topical Index